Corporate Governance in Banking

Dedication

To Jean, Lincoln, Andy, Jeremy, and Carol

Corporate Governance in Banking

A Global Perspective

Edited by

Benton E. Gup

University of Alabama, USA

Edward Elgar
Cheltenham, UK • Northampton, MA, USA

Published by
Edward Elgar Publishing Limited
Glensanda House
Montpellier Parade
Cheltenham
Glos GL50 1UA
UK

Edward Elgar Publishing, Inc.
William Pratt House
9 Dewey Court
Northampton
Massachusetts 01060
USA

A catalogue record for this book
is available from the British Library

Library of Congress Cataloging in Publication Data
Gup, Benton E.
   Corporate governance in banking : a global perspective / Benton E. Gup.
      p.   cm.
   Includes bibliographical references and index.
   1. Banks and banking—Government policy. 2. Corporate governance.
   3. Banking law. I. Title.
   HG1601.G87 2007
   332.1—dc22

                                                                    2007002162

ISBN 978 1 84542 940 9

Printed and bound in Great Britain by MPG Books Ltd, Bodmin, Cornwall

Contents

Contributors

Mohamed Ariff holds a Chair in Finance at Monash University, Australia. He is a co-director of a research programme on governance at Monash. He has published in leading journals. As a recipient of fellowships, Dr Ariff has worked at Harvard, Tokyo University, in Hong Kong, Australia and Ireland. He also holds an endowed chair (Renong) professorship as a visitor at the Universiti Putra Malaysia.

James R. Barth is the Lowder Eminent Scholar in Finance at Auburn University, and a Senior Fellow at the Milken Institute. He was appointed by Presidents Ronald Reagan and George H. W. Bush as Chief Economist of the Office of Thrift Supervision and previously the Federal Home Loan Bank Board. He was Associate Director of the economics programme at the National Science Foundation. In addition, Dr Barth was the Shaw Foundation Professor of Banking and Finance at Nanyang Technological University. He is author of several books and numerous articles dealing with banking issues.

Mark J. Bertus is an Assistant Professor of Finance at Auburn University. His research focuses on the stochastic behaviour of asset prices, derivatives and information content of financial markets. He has published in the *Journal of Futures Markets* and presented papers at professional meetings.

Robert DeYoung has been named the Capitol Federal Professor in Financial Markets and Institutions at the University of Kansas, starting the 2007–8 school year. Previously he was an Associate Director at the Federal Deposit Insurance Corporation (FDIC) in the Division of Insurance and Research, and also served as programme coordinator at the FDIC's Center for Financial Research. Dr DeYoung is an associate editor of the *Journal of Money, Credit and Banking* and the *Journal of Financial Services Research*. Prior to joining the FDIC, he was an economic adviser and senior economist at the Federal Reserve Bank of Chicago, and a senior financial economist at the Office of the Comptroller of the Currency.

Horst Gischer is a Professor of Economics at the University of Magdeburg, Germany. His research interests deal with monetary theory, capital markets and political economy.

Benton E. Gup holds the Robert Hunt Cochrane-Alabama Bankers Association Chair of Banking at the University of Alabama. He also held banking chairs at the University of Tulsa and the University of Virginia. Dr Gup is the author and/or editor of 26 books and more than 90 articles about banking and financial topics. He was an economist at the Federal Reserve Bank of Cleveland, and visiting economist at the Office of the Comptroller of the Currency. Dr Gup has lectured in Australia, Latin America, South Africa and New Zealand. He serves as a consultant to government and industry.

Valentina Hartarska is an Assistant Professor in the Department of Agricultural Economics and Rural Sociology, Auburn University. Her research interests include economic development. In particular, she is interested in the governance of financial institutions serving marginalized clientele, such as Microfinance and Community Development Institutions.

Mohammad Z. Hoque teaches banking and finance courses at Monash University, Australia. Dr Hoque also taught at RMIT, Australia and Sultan Qaboos University of Oman. He is the founding president of the Bangladesh Young Economists' Association, and serves on the editorial boards of four international finance journals. He has published numerous papers and is the author or coauthor of several finance books.

Hai Jason Jiang is Professor of Finance and Deputy Department Head of Finance at Jinan University, Guangzhou, China. He has published more than 30 articles dealing with financial regulation, risk management, corporate governance and other related topics.

Júlia Király is the Chief Executive Officer of ITCB Consulting and Training (Hungary). She was Chairwoman of the Board when Postabank was privatized in 2003. Júlia has been lecturing at Budapest University of Economics since 1989. Her research interests are rational expectations and risk management in financial institutions. Her studies have been published in both Hungarian and English journals and books.

Katalin Mérő is the Managing Director of the Hungarian Financial Supervisory Authority's Economics, Risk Assessment and Regulatory Directorate. Previously she was the Deputy Head of the Financial Stability Department of the National Bank of Hungary. From 1990 to 1997, Dr Mérő was Director of Strategy and Economic Analysis at K&H, a large Hungarian commercial bank.

Doowoo Nam is an Assistant Professor of Finance in the College of Business Administration, Inha University, Korea. Dr Nam previously taught at

Mississippi State University. He has published numerous articles in academic journals.

Tareque Nasser is a student in the Finance PhD programme at The University of Alabama. He served as a Research Assistant for Dr Gup.

Triphon Phumiwasana is a Research Economist at the Milken Institute. His research focuses on banks, capital markets and economic development, with special emphasis on global issues. His articles have appeared in professional and academic journals.

Peter Reichling is a Professor of Finance at the University of Magdeburg, Germany. His research interests are risk management, credit risk and performance measurement.

Bernard Shull is Professor Emeritus, Hunter College of the City University of New York, and a Special Consultant to National Economic Research Associates, Inc. Prior to teaching at Hunter College, Dr Shull held various positions at the Board of Governors of the Federal Reserve System. He also served as a consultant to the FDIC and OCC. He is the author of three books dealing with various aspects of banking and has written numerous articles in his field of interest.

Kenneth Spong is a Senior Policy Economist in the Banking Studies and Structure Department at the Federal Reserve Bank of Kansas City. His research interests include bank ownership and management, bank performance, and related issues. He is the author of *Banking Regulation: Its Purposes, Implementation and Effects*, and numerous articles in Federal Reserve and academic publications.

Mike Stiele is a Research Assistant at the University of Magdeburg, Germany. His research interests include financial and monetary economics, banking, capital and real estate markets, competition and industrial organization.

Richard J. Sullivan is a Senior Economist in the Payments System Research at the Federal Reserve Bank of Kansas City. Dr Sullivan's research covers a wide variety of topics dealing with banks and payments systems. His articles have been published in Federal Reserve publications and in leading academic journals. Prior to joining the Federal Reserve Bank of Kansas City, he taught at Holy Cross College and the University of Colorado.

János Száz is the Head of the Finance Department at Budapest University of Economics, where he previously served as Dean of the Faculty of Economics. Dr Száz was the first Dean of the International Training Center for Bankers (Budapest, 1989–92). He was a member of the Board of

Directors of the Budapest Stock Exchange, and its President. His research interests focus on interest rate risk models.

Rowan Trayler is a Senior Lecturer in the School of Finance and Economics at the University of Sydney, Australia, where he is involved in the Master of Business Finance programme and other courses in banking and finance. Prior to his academic career, Rowan worked for 16 years in the banking industry, and helped to establish Barclays Bank Australia, Ltd. His articles have been published in both academic journals and books.

Arthur E. Wilmarth, Jr. is a Professor at The George Washington University Law School. Prior to joining the Law School, he was a partner in the Washington, DC, office of Jones, Day, Reavis & Pogue. He is the author of numerous articles in the fields of banking law and American constitutional history, and co-author of a book on corporate law. He is also a member of the international editorial board of the *Journal of Banking Regulation*.

Preface

Corporate governance became a major concern to the US government, businesses, investors and academics after Enron filed for bankruptcy in December 2001. The Enron scandal was followed by scandals at Tyco, Global Crossing, ImClone Systems, WorldCom and others. Congress reacted to the scandals by enacting the Sarbanes-Oxley Act (SOX) that was signed into law in 2002. Some say that SOX was an overreaction to the scandals; and while it has some good points, the costs of implementation are excessive.

Corporate governance also gained in importance because of globalization. For example, there is a move towards international accounting standards, and the International Accounting Standards Board (IASB), based in London, is committed to developing a single set of high quality, understandable and enforceable global accounting standards.[1] Similarly, the Basel Committee on Banking Supervision, that is part of the Bank of International Settlements (BIS), issued a guidance entitled 'Enhancing corporate governance for banking organizations'. It is based on papers published by the Committee in 1999, and the principles for corporate governance issued by the Organization for Economic Co-operation and Development (OECD) in 2004. 'This guidance is intended to help ensure the adoption and implementation of sound corporate governance practices by banking organizations worldwide, but is not intended to establish a new regulatory framework layered atop existing national legislation, regulations or codes.'[2]

Against this background, this book examines various aspects of corporate governance in banking from a global perspective. Because banking is regulated, the scandals and governance problems are less spectacular than Enron. Nevertheless, there are both international and domestic scandals and problems with bank governance. The Bank of Credit and Commerce International (1991) (BCCI), also known as the Bank of Crooks and Criminals international, is one glaring example. Penn Square Bank NA (1982) in Oklahoma City, and the First National Bank of Keystone, Keystone, West Virginia (1999) are additional examples.[3]

The contributing authors are from Asia, Australia, Europe and the United States. They include academics, consultants and regulators. Some of the chapters in this book were presented at two special sessions at the 2006 annual meeting of the Financial Management Association in Salt Lake City.

xi

NOTES

1. For additional information, see the IASB web site: http://www.iasb.org/Home.htm
2. 'Basel Committee issues guidance on corporate governance for banking organizations', Press Release, 13 February 2006, http://www.bis.org/press/p 060213.htm
3. For additional information, see: Benton E. Gup, *Bank Failures in the Major Trading Countries of the World: Causes and Remedies*, Westport, CT, Quorum Books (1998); Benton E. Gup, *Targeting Fraud: Uncovering and Deterring Fraud in Financial Institutions*, Chicago, IL, Probus Publishing Co. (1995); 'Receivership of First National Bank of Keystone', http://www.fdic.gov/news/news/press/1999/pr 9949.html

1. Corporate governance, bank regulation and activity expansion in the United States

Bernard Shull

INTRODUCTION

Characterized by principal-agent issues, the problems addressed by corporate governance have been manifest in their impact on economic efficiency and, at times, in the self-serving and/or abusive behavior by managements that jeopardizes company viability and the welfare of shareholders. Bank regulation can also be construed as deriving from agency issues, in this case, arising out of a separation between bank management and government. Problems addressed by regulation may also materialize in inefficiency and in self-serving and/or abusive managerial behavior that can jeopardize a bank's viability and the welfare of a broad group of 'stakeholders', including shareholders. Given the similarities in the nature of the problems and also in some of the solutions, an overlap in corporate governance and bank regulation is to be expected.

It is plausible that the extensive deregulation that has occurred in the United States over recent decades has affected the overlap. This could occur through new approaches to capital requirements sanctioned by international agreement, and through new approaches to supervision necessitated by the emergence of large and complex banking organizations. In particular, extension of the intersection should be manifest in the liberalization of activity restrictions that has facilitated the affiliation of banks with other financial and commercial firms. The Wal-Mart proposal to acquire a deposit-insured industrial loan corporation (ILC) presents a case-in-point.

The effects of deregulation on the corporate governance-bank regulation relationship, and particularly with respect to the developing intersection between banking and commerce, is considered below. The next section provides an historic perspective on the general relationship between governance and bank regulation in the United States. The third section reviews some relevant effects of deregulation. The fourth section focuses on the

1

impact of activity restrictions and their liberalization. The fifth section examines some issues raised by the Wal-Mart proposal to acquire an ILC.

From the earliest days of modern banking, there has been some overlap of corporate governance with bank regulation. The deregulation of recent decades has expanded the scope for corporate governance in banking. At the same time, regulation has changed to take on a corporate governance posture. The change is evident in expansion of permissible activities for banking companies in the United States and in the debate generated by the Wal-Mart proposal. Whether Wal-Mart is successful or not, it seems likely that the separation between banking and commerce in the United States will further diminish and that the governance/regulation overlap will continue to grow. The effects on economic efficiency remain uncertain, but the changes are likely to be accompanied by the continued growth of the Federal banking agencies.

HISTORICAL PERSPECTIVE

In the early days of banking, the overlap between corporate governance and bank regulation was readily observable. In eighteenth-century England, governments delegated public functions to a variety of private firms, including banks, through the issue of a corporate charter. The charter was a grant by a sovereign authority to run a specific business or to trade in a specified area for a specified number of years (Berle and Means, 1940: 128 ff.; Hurst, 1973: 152 ff.).[1]

In issuing charters, governments behaved as stakeholders and, to some degree, as protectors of shareholder interests. Capital requirements were established to protect against excessive leverage. In defining the permissible activities of the corporation, governments made certain that shareholders knew how their investment was being used. Definition 'was probably [also] designed to prevent corporations from dominating the business life of the time' (Berle and Means, 1940: 131).

In the United States, early bank charters were modeled on the charter of the Bank of England; they limited activities and provided for direct services to the chartering government. American banks were seen as 'private establishments employed as public agents' (Dunbar, 1904: 91). The issues faced by the government in aligning bank management behavior with its own interest were similar, in principle, to those faced by shareholders in any modern corporation. A major difference was governments' capacity to regulate, supervise and impose legal sanctions.

Even as states began passing general incorporation laws that produced the modern corporate charter, 'readily available and a right to conduct any lawful business', the bank charter remained a right to a defined enterprise. As one New York court put it, 'independently of the general Bank Act (1838), these banks have no corporate existence, and they are thus created with restricted and limited powers for a special purpose'. Banking, it noted, was an exercise of 'public powers', and 'public powers are never granted without some public object in view'.[2] Activity restrictions, capital requirements, reserve requirements, other restrictions and supervision were retained with the object of maintaining safety and soundness and preventing fraud. Managerial misconduct, whether the product of the owners themselves or the managers they hired were a focal point for regulatory surveillance and restraint.

In the highly regulated banking environment in the United States, where branching was limited at best, large numbers of small, closely held banks were established. In small, closely held banks, governance issues raised by the separation of management from ownership did not arise. In those urban areas where banking companies did grow to large size and have widely distributed shares, accurate financial conditions were shrouded in regulatory confidentiality; in addition, regulatory barriers to entry and regulatory agency influence and/or control over changes in ownership precluded effective external market pressures that the threat of hostile takeovers might have imposed. Regulatory monitoring for insider abuse provided a partial substitute.[3]

Regulation was augmented following the massive bank failures of the early 1930s. The Banking Act of 1933 prohibited interest payments on demand deposits and imposed maximum rates on time deposits to moderate what was seen as 'destructive competition'. Entry by new charter was severely limited through the establishment of FDIC insurance. Securities activities in which banks had engaged in the 1920s, in part through affiliates, were prohibited by the Glass-Steagall provisions of the 1933 Act.[4] Bank holding companies (BHCs) also constituted an avenue for activity expansion; the 1933 Act imposed restrictions, but these proved ineffective.[5]

By the 1950s, bank failure rates fell to minimal levels and were no longer a principal concern of Congress. Rather, Congress focused on forestalling increases in financial concentration (Shull and Hanweck, 2001: 82 ff.). To this end, the ineffectiveness of the 1933 holding company restrictions was remedied by the Bank Holding Company Act of 1956. The 1956 Act prohibited BHCs (defined as organizations that controlled two or more banks) from engaging in almost all nonbanking activities, and restricted their expansion across state lines.[6] It further insulated banks controlled by holding companies from affiliates by prohibiting almost all interaffiliate transactions (Section 6). The Act completed the wall of restrictions surrounding banking companies. Interestingly enough, as discussed below, it also initiated the era of deregulation.

The regulatory regime that existed in 1956 left little to regulatory agency discretion; entry, branching, pricing and activity restrictions were clear-cut and inflexible. Supervision was occupied with evaluating bank portfolios to assure solvency, detecting deteriorating conditions to protect the deposit insurance fund, monitoring adherence to relevant laws and regulations, and evaluating banking and vaguely defined competitive factors in mergers.

The regulatory environment had its effect on the behavior of bank management. Through the 1940s and into the 1950s, banks' portfolios held small quantities of risky loans and large quantities of safe government securities – in part the heritage of the financing of World War II. Innovation, expansion, and risk-taking in general was at a low ebb. Nevertheless, restrictions on competition helped make banks profitable. Unlike other kinds of corporate managers, bankers, both managers and owners, lived a sheltered existence, and their behavior reflected these conditions.

DEREGULATION EFFECTS

The last half-century, and particularly, the last 25 years has seen a withdrawal from both the additional regulation that had been established from 1933 to 1956 and from earlier restrictions that had characterized American banking almost from its origin. The influence of the regulatory agencies might, in these circumstances, have been expected to recede and the influence of corporate governance to advance. To some extent, this has been the case, but there have also been some counter-intuitive developments.

Deregulation

The passage of the Bank Holding Company Act in 1956 imposed, as noted, draconian restrictions on bank holding companies to prevent both their geographic and activity expansion, and to immunize banks from their affiliates. In this sense, it completed the regulatory design of the 'Great Depression'. But it also required the Federal Reserve Board (FRB) to consider the anticompetitive effects of holding company mergers and acquisitions – the first time since the 1930s that banking legislation opposed existing legal and regulatory support for tacit collusion (Shull and Hanweck, 2001, Ch. 4).

Procompetitive measures, confusing as they were at the time, heralded the unraveling of the existing regulatory arrangements. Early in the process, bank mergers, acquisitions and agreements became subject to the antitrust laws. During the course of the deregulation that followed, absolute prohibitions were liberalized or eliminated, including maximums on deposit rates of interest and on interstate branching; new activities for both holding companies and bank subsidiaries became permissible. These changes have been extensively discussed and will not be reviewed in detail here.[7] The related effects discussed below are relevant in considering the evolving intersection between regulation and corporate governance.

Large Complex Banking Organizations

Deregulation, along with global expansion, has generated a merger and acquisition movement that has produced a relatively few very 'large, complex banking organizations' (LCBOs) that control a substantial proportion of industry assets (DeFerrari and Palmer, 2001: 47–57; Shull and Hanweck, 2001, Ch. 6). The diverse activities of LCBOs through holding company affiliates and through subsidiaries, cut across many legal jurisdictions and traditional regulatory responsibilities. With widely held shares, and with the reduction in numbers and importance of small, closely held banks, these developments have increased the significance of corporate governance issues.

Capital Requirements

As regulatory concerns about disruption caused by small bank failure have diminished, concerns about failure of large banking organizations, and particularly LCBOs has grown. With their increasing economic and financial importance, the systemic threat they present is a focal point of regulatory concerns.[8] One result has been a more sophisticated approach to capital requirements.

In 1973, George Vojta of Citibank argued that the long decline in bank capital at large banks was of no relevance. 'The weight of scholarly research is overwhelmingly to the effect that the level of bank capital has not been a material factor in preventing banking insolvency, and that . . . "tests" for capital adequacy have not been useful in assessing or predicting the capability of a bank to remain solvent' (Vojta, 1973: 9, 12; Hanweck and Shull, 1996, Ch. 3, and p. 35).

While banking laws provided general authority for bank regulators to appraise the capital adequacy of banks, the Federal regulatory agency did not institute a uniform system of capital requirements until the 1980s. It was only with deregulation, the continuing decline in capital ratios and a rising failure rate that, in 1981, the Office of the Comptroller of the Currency (OCC) and the FRB announced a common set of capital standards. It was not until 1985 that the FDIC adopted the requirements of the other two agencies. Alan Greenspan, as Chairman of the FRB, later provided a rationale for regulatory requirements that would be higher than banks would establish on their own; that is, the existence of a federal 'safety net' (Greenspan, 1990).

In the course of the last 25 years, then, capital requirements have become a fundamental element in regulation. They have been 'risk-adjusted' and the subject of international agreement. As discussed below, the FRB is empowered to impose capital requirements on a consolidated basis for BHCs, including those established as financial holding companies (FHCs) under the Gramm-Leach-Bliley Act (GLB).[9]

Supervision

With restraints on activities and branching lifted, and banks no longer sheltered from competition, managers are, of necessity, concerned with new profitable opportunities, including mergers and acquisitions. In the new environment, Federal regulators have revised their supervisory approach. Banking companies have typically been examined or inspected once a year. Loans portfolios were valued, and assessments were made as to the bank's capital adequacy, assets quality, management, earnings, and liquidity (CAMEL). Composite CAMEL ratings reflected existing conditions, but not future possibilities. In recognition of the inadequacy of CAMEL ratings alone, the agencies undertook in the 1990s to develop sensitivity measures for various types of risk faced by banks. Among others, they identified, credit risk, market risk, interest rate risk, liquidity risk, compliance risk and reputation risk.

The emergence of LCBOs, in fact, required a new approach. Their size and complexity made it impossible to track their rapidly changing conditions through appraisals at a single point in time (DeFerrari and Palmer, 2001: 48). A reformulation that began in the 1990s, placed emphasis on the evaluation of internal risk-management systems installed by banks. The new approach contemplated a more or less continuous monitoring by small groups of technical experts in several different areas, and extensive interaction between supervisors and bank management (DeFerrari and Palmer, 2001: 50–1).

The new supervision is normally described as a change in technique. However, the change is substantive. It can be said that under the old regulatory regime, supervisors were 'cautious, suspicious, fearful, and alert to possible danger' (Pollack, 2006: 2–4); profits were secured through restraints on competition. The move toward the evaluation of risk-management models reflects a supervisory concern not only with safety and soundness, but with the risk-reward calculus of the banking company that aims to achieve profit targets in a deregulated environment. In its critique of Federal Reserve supervision, discussed below, the FDIC has pointed out that '[e]nterprise risk management . . . is essentially a tool to better manage private profits and safeguard the interests of holding company shareholders' (Powell, 2005: 93).

Even if size and complexity did not justify the new supervisory approach, regulatory emphasis on capital requirements would require something like it. In the current environment, bank profits are uncertain. Because capital is directly and indirectly derived from profits, they are important to regulators as well as to shareholders. In these circumstances, regulatory concerns tend to converge with the concerns of shareholders about effectiveness of bank management in balancing risk and reward.

This movement of regulation/supervision toward the aims of governance appears to have been paralleled by a movement of governance toward regulation. It has been recognized that the Sarbanes-Oxley Act derives much of its substance from well accepted banking law (Baxter, 2003: 2). Among other things, the Act expands the set of stakeholders to be protected. In doing so, it is in line with corporate governance in the Europe and elsewhere where stakeholders include creditors, employees, customers and, in some cases, the general public (Fannon, 2006).

Growth of Federal Banking Agencies

Deregulation, and the passing of the old regulatory regime, has been accompanied by the emergence of the Federal Reserve as the preeminent bank regulatory agency in the United States. Despite repeated efforts to reduce its direct participation as a regulator, or even to eliminate the System's role in regulation, its authority has expanded considerably (Shull, 2005: 146–8, 151–2). With most large banking organizations organized as bank holding companies, it attained a critical supervisory position as the sole Federal holding company regulator. Its authority and influence expanded with passage of GLB in 1999 which assigned it the role of 'umbrella regulator'.

The Federal Reserve's growth as a regulatory agency is reflected in its increased expenses for this function. System expenses for supervision/regulation were estimated at over $628 million in 2005, rising from $175.6 million in 1985 (FRB, 2006: 13, 40; 1986–7: 7).[10] Over the 20 year period, expenses increased about 258 percent, far exceeding the increase in the price level (implicit GDP deflator) which rose only about 62 percent. In 1985, System supervision/regulation expenses were about 13.6 percent of its total expenses; by 2005, they had risen to about 20 percent.

Increased Federal Reserve expenditures on supervision/regulation are to be expected given its expanding responsibilities. However, its rapid growth in expenses has been exceeded by the spending increases at the other two principal Federal banking agencies, the Federal Deposit Insurance Corporation (FDIC) and the Office of the Comptroller of the Currency (OCC). Expenses at each rose about 600 percent between 1980 and 2005.[11]

The increased spending by the Federal banking agencies over the period of deregulation may seem an anomaly. It would appear, however, that general legislatively-established standards that require regulatory agency deliberations and determinations are more expensive than absolute prohibitions; and that the new, more sophisticated approaches to regulation and supervision are costly.

REGULATED ACTIVITY EXPANSION

In the movement from absolute prohibitions in the course of deregulation to general standards and bank regulatory agency determinations, permissible banking activities have expanded substantially. There is no better example of the changes that have taken place than in this expansion.

Activity Restrictions under the Bank Holding Company Act[12]

As noted, it was not until passage of the Bank Holding Company Act in 1956 that bank holding companies were prohibited from engaging in almost all nonbanking activities. By the late 1960s, however, banks found they could affiliate with almost any kind of business without legal challenge by reorganizing as one-bank holding companies. By 1969, the largest banks in the country had done so.

Congress responded by amending the Bank Holding Company Act to include companies controlling one bank. However, it also authorized the FRB to permit new activities that were 'closely related to banking' and 'a proper incident thereto'.[13] A court decision defined 'closely related' activities as services similar to those banks generally provide.[14] The latter term established a 'net public benefits test' requiring the FRB to weigh the likely benefits against likely costs.[15]

In response to the concerns of nonbank business groups about the ability of banks to expand through the use of conditional agreements, the Amendments established restrictions to prevent coercive tie-ins and reciprocity (Section 106). Restrictions on interaffiliate transactions, for both safety and competitive purposes, were those provided by Section 23A of the Federal Reserve Act.[16]

In its concerns with bank safety, competition and overall concentration, the 1970 legislation was in line with traditional regulation that focused on the interests of a wide range of constituencies.[17] But it also was an attempt to accommodate the interests of bank shareholders. A slowly growing list of permissible activities was overseen by the FRB;[18] and by the OCC for national banks through subsidiaries.[19] Other avenues for combining banking with other financial and non-financial businesses developed over the years.[20]

The Gramm-Leach-Bliley Act: 'Paved with Good Intentions'

In passing GLB in 1999, Congress extended permissible activities for bank holding companies established as 'financial holding companies' (FHCs) and, to a more limited extent, bank subsidiaries, designated as 'financial subsidiaries'. By repealing relevant sections of the Glass-Steagall Act, it sanctioned securities dealing and specifically permitted insurance and merchant banking, among others specified as 'financial in nature or incidental to a financial activity'.[21] The law also provided for the addition of both other 'financial' activities and activities 'complementary' to a financial activity by regulatory agency determination.

GLB combined functional regulation with traditional bank regulation. It maintained the responsibilities of existing agencies such as the SEC and state insurance commissioners over the activities they normally regulate, as well as the authority of the existing Federal banking agencies for the banking companies themselves. As noted, the FRB was designated 'umbrella regulator' for bank holding companies, including the new FHCs, with authority to examine and supervise all affiliates and impose consolidated capital requirements. It also was given principal responsibility, in consultation with the Treasury, for determining new financial and complementary activities.

The new law made an effort to distinguish between the permitted combination of financial services and the non-sanctioned combination of banking and commerce. Congressman Leach repeatedly affirmed that GLB would maintain the traditional separation: 'Decision-makers came to understand the unhealthy social and competitive implications of the concentration of ownership [that would result]' (Leach, 28 March 2000). And shortly thereafter:

> the Treasury and the Fed . . . changed judgement and today adamantly stand with me against mixing commerce and banking . . . If this precept had been included . . . I would have done my best to pull the plug on financial modernization. (Leach, 12 May 2000)

Subsequently, the Treasury and the Board explicitly acknowledged a Congressional intention to maintain the separation of banking and commerce (Department of Treasury, 2000a).

Intentions notwithstanding, GLB provides a road map for integration. First, there are routes explicitly accepted in the law. 'Complementary' activities are, by definition, not financial and, therefore, 'commercial'. Merchant banking, included as a financial activity, allows, under rules established by the Board and Treasury, acquisitions by FHCs of shares in any company in any amount for indefinite periods of time. In addition, there are special provisions for securities firms, insurance companies and other nonbank affiliates permitting the acquisition of commercial companies under the rubric of 'investments', 'underwriting' or 'merchant banking'.

Second, GLB provides the FRB and the Treasury with the authority to expand permissible commercial activities through regulatory determinations. There appears to be, in fact, a potentially dynamic process of permissible activity expansion through the interaction of the old, but still relevant, 'closely related to banking' standard and the new 'financial in nature or incidental' standard. Unlike the old standard that looked to similar activities in which banks were already engaged, the new standard looks to whether an activity is 'necessary and appropriate to allow an FHC . . . to compete effectively'.[22] As a result, a determination that an activity, such as real estate brokerage, is 'closely related to banking' would seem to make other activities, such as 'ownership and development of real estate "necessary and appropriate" '. If so, and 'ownership/development' were determined to be a 'financial' activity, a wide range of other related activities might then appear to be 'complementary' if not 'closely related to banking' (Shull, 2002: 52–5).

The expansive possibilities of GLB were suggested by Lawrence Meyer, while a Governor of the FRB. '[T]he regulators and the regulated face no bright lines on the commerce and banking front' (Meyer, 2001: 3). 'The Congress . . . empowered the Federal Reserve and the Treasury to add to the permissible activities list any activity that is either "financial", without much guidance as to what that means, or is "complementary" . . . with no guidance . . . GLB grants the agencies authority to move toward mixing banking and commerce at the margin as markets and technology begin to dim the already less than bright line between them' (Meyer, 2001: 11–12).

Finally, Congress provided for at least one exception to the restrictions, such as they are, imposed by GLB; that is, the industrial loan company – a state-chartered, deposit-insured financial institution that had developed in the early twentieth century as a provider of loans to workers. This exception is discussed next.

NON-REGULATED ACTIVITY EXPANSION

Despite the expansive possibilities provided by GLB, Congress, as has been typical, also left a door open for unregulated activity expansion. The Bank Holding Company Act of 1956 exempted one-bank holding companies;

the Amendments in 1970 included one-bank companies, but redefined 'bank' so that 'non-bank banks', lacking either demand deposits or loans, could be acquired by commercial firms; the Competitive Equality Banking Act of 1987 redefined 'bank' so as to eliminate 'non-bank banks', but excluded from its definition the then obscure ILC. As experience might have suggested, ILCs soon became less conspicuous.[23]

The recent Wal-Mart proposal to acquire an ILC has raised a number of issues. In this context, the relationship between corporate governance and bank regulation is highlighted by the dispute between the FRB and the FDIC. The difference relates to whether it is necessary, in meeting regulatory objectives, that the exception be rescinded so that Wal-Mart, if it wished to acquire an ILC, would have to become a financial holding company subject to FRB authority – or whether FDIC and state regulation/supervision, as it currently exists, would be sufficient.

The FRB has argued that effective regulation and supervision, including capital requirements, must be on a consolidated basis; that is, applicable to the holding company and all its affiliates ('consolidated regulation'). In the course of its evaluations, it has indicated it assesses the holding company's risk management models, its internal controls, and its information technology; it evaluates the quality of the holding company's assets, and may obtain non-public information from the holding company and its other affiliates. Not only can it monitor interaffiliate transactions, it can interdict those that appear threatening even if they fall short of violating Sections 23A or 23B. It has authority to force holding companies transfer resources to the bank if necessary; that is, to serve as a 'source of strength' (GAO, 2005: 38 ff.).

The FDIC has argued that regulation and supervision of the bank alone is, for all practical purposes, sufficient ('bank centric regulation') (Powell, 2005). It views consolidated regulation and supervision, as implemented by the FRB, as unnecessary and potentially perverse (GAO, 2005: 28–9); that is, it could expand the bank safety net and impose bank-like regulation throughout the private sector – a long-recognized possibility (Powell, 2005: 92–3; Shull, 1983: 278–9). The FDIC has further criticized the FRB as overly dependent on the 'enterprise risk models' of companies as an unproven model for bank supervision (Powell, 2005: 93).

The FDIC, in contrast, would focus on the bank – a 'bank-centric' approach – walling it off from its affiliates *via* Sections 23A and 23B. It would insist on adequate capital requirements for the bank alone, and hold the bank's board of directors accountable. It would aim to insulate the bank from any of its affiliates' problems and from any possible abuse by the parent holding company and/or its other subsidiaries. It has contended that it has sufficient authority over affiliates if needed.

The FRB's focus on the holding company and all its affiliates is consistent with a traditional corporate governance focus with, however, a different constituency. The FRB may, in actuality, insist on more safety for the bank than would best serve the owners of the company. But by directly taking responsibility for the entire company, including the potential for insider abuse wherever it emerges, and in position to consider the potential synergies available in combining banking and other activities, it could come close to harmonizing regulation with governance.

In focusing on the bank, the FDIC's approach is reminiscent of an older kind of regulation, though clearly not as rigid. When national banks first established security affiliates in the early years of the twentieth century, the Comptroller of the Currency also focused on the banks alone. With respect to the affiliates, he took the position that they were: 'corporations . . . with which I have nothing to do . . . . They are not under my jurisdiction in any way, shape, or form' (US House, 1913: 1407). Under Section 6 of the Bank Holding Company Act of 1956, as noted, affiliated banks were almost completely insulated by prohibiting almost all transactions between the bank and its affiliates. The relationship between the FDIC's approach and corporate governance is intentionally remote.

In principle, the combination of banking and commerce should improve allocational and other types of efficiency by removing regulatory barriers that stifle competition and by permitting managers of banking companies to respond appropriately to market forces. In the long-run, these improvements will not be realized if mergers, acquisitions and increased concentration diminish competition; or if the interests of managers of large banking companies are not aligned with those of shareholders.

How effective the antitrust laws in their current state are likely to be is unclear (Shull and Hanweck, 2001, Ch. 6). If the FRB prevails, the combining of banking and commerce would be accompanied by regulation and supervision that resembles a kind of corporate governance approach to a 'social model'. The long-run effects on efficiency remain uncertain.

What seems certain is that ultimately, unless Congress changes course, the separation between banking and commerce is in the process of vanishing. The ultimate outcome of the Wal-Mart proposal is likely to determine the speed of change. If Congress eliminates the exception for ILCs, currently under consideration, separation will vanish slowly, with the FRB and Treasury extending permissible commercial activities, to the extent that Congress does not intervene, in stages. If Congress does nothing and the FDIC approves the Wal-Mart application, separation is likely to vanish abruptly. Whether the FRB's or FDIC's approach is more favorable to economic efficiency remains uncertain.

CONCLUSIONS

In banking in the United States, there has always been an overlap in corporate governance and bank regulation. However, during a period of heightened regulation beginning in the 1930s, the corporate governance element was overwhelmed by absolute regulatory restrictions; shareholders were protected from failure and bank profits were salvaged by suppressing competition.

Over recent decades an important independent role for corporate governance has emerged. Deregulation produced large, complex banking organizations with widespread ownership, and the possibility for managers to follow courses of action independent of shareholders.

At the same time, the large banking companies that now dominate the industry have raised regulatory concerns about the potential systemic impact should they flounder or fail. Old regulatory restrictions on insider behavior and interaffiliate transactions have been augmented by new regulatory approaches, including risk-adjusted capital requirements and risk-focused supervision. Regulators now evaluate bank managements' approaches to balancing risk and reward, safety and profits. In consequence, they have elaborated their corporate governance posture, albeit with the interests of a wider constituency in mind. At the same time, the Sarbanes-Oxley legislation that has established new governance standards for all private sector companies appears to draw on well-established banking law and regulation, suggesting a convergence. For a number of reasons, the impact of these changes on economic efficiency remain unclear.

The change in regulatory approach toward corporate governance is manifest in the recent dispute between the Federal Reserve and the FDIC with respect to the proposal by Wal-Mart to acquire an industrial loan company. As 'umbrella regulator' under the Gramm-Leach-Bliley Act, the Federal Reserve has taken a 'consolidated' approach to regulation that evaluates companies as a whole, parents and their affiliates. This Federal Reserve's focus is consistent with corporate governance; the FDIC's 'bank-centric' approach is not.

It is not certain, at this point, whether the Federal Reserve or the FDIC will prevail, though long experience with numerous Federal bank regulatory agency disputes suggest it will be the former. There is one thing, however, that does seem clear. Whether Congress eliminates the ILC exception or not, whether the FRB's 'consolidated' regulation or the FDIC's 'bank-centric regulation' is adopted, the Federal banking agencies will, in the process, continue to expand.

NOTES

1. Before general incorporation laws, the corporate grant typically constituted a monopoly of the activity for which it had been created.
2. The court decision, *Bank of Utica v. Smedes*, 3 Cowen 684, can be found in *Legislative History of Banking in the State of New York*, 1855, pp. 111–12.
3. The Federal Reserve Act, for example, provides for regulatory restrictions on loans to executive officers, directors and principal shareholders of member banks (Regulation O implements Sections 22(g) and 22(h)). Section 23A of the Federal Reserve Act, later bolstered by 23B, places limits on interaffiliate transactions. For a discussion of the corporate governance element in the modern regulation and supervision of banks in the United States, see Adams and Mehran (2003): 123–42.
4. The McFadden Act of 1927 gave national banks authority to buy and sell marketable debt obligations. The Comptroller ruled that national banks could underwrite all debt securities, and that their affiliates could underwrite both debt and equities. The Glass-Steagall provisions, applicable to member banks, revoked authority granted by the McFadden Act: Section 16 limited bank dealing and underwriting to specified securities; that is obligations of the US and general obligations of states and political subdivisions; Section 20 prohibited banks from having affiliates principally engaged in dealing in securities; Section 21 prohibited securities firms from accepting deposits; Section 32 prohibited interlocks of directors and officers of securities firms and banks.
5. BHCs were required to register with the Federal Reserve Board. Corporations owning more than 50 percent of the stock of one or more member bank were required to apply to the Board to secure permits to vote their stock. BHCs, however, could and did find ways to avoid the restrictions.
6. Under the 1956 Act, commercial bank activities were to be 'of a financial, fiduciary, or insurance nature' and 'so closely related to *the business of banking* or managing or controlling banks as to be a proper incident thereto' (italics added). The Board of Governors of the Federal Reserve System narrowly interpreted the term 'the business of banking' to mean a relationship between the customers of specific banks and their nonbanking affiliates.
7. Both the Bank Holding Company Act of 1956 and the Bank Merger Act of 1960 established new procompetitive conditions in banking. The principal legislation effecting deregulation has been the Amendments to Bank Holding Company Act, 1970, the Depository Institutions Deregulation and Monetary Control Act of 1980, the Riegle-Neal Interstate Banking and Branching Efficiency Act of 1994, and the Gramm-Leach-Bliley Financial Modernization Act of 1999. In addition, Amendments to the Bank Holding Company Act in 1966 repealed Section 6 of the 1956 Act, making Section 23A of the Federal Reserve Act, limiting but not prohibiting essentially all interaffiliate transactions, relevant. In 1982, Section 23B was added, requiring that all interaffiliate transactions be 'arm's-length'. Beginning in the mid-1980s, Federal Reserve interpretation of Section 20 of the Glass-Steagall Act permitted holding company affiliates to underwrite otherwise impermissible securities.
8. For an optimistic declaration about managing the problem of banks that are 'too-big-to-fail', see Stern and Feldman, 2006.
9. Consolidated requirements developed in response to several holding company failures in the 1970s that brought down seemingly well-established bank affiliates (Lawrence and Talley, 1978).
10. The period chosen, 1985 to 2005, was based on the availability of reasonably consistent functional cost data for the Federal Reserve, as reported in its *Annual Budget Report*. However, in recent years, the Board's expenses, but not the Reserve Bank's have been based on a biennial budget. The 2005 estimate was obtained by dividing Board expenses for 2004–5 by half. Because Board supervision/regulation expenses in 2005 constituted about 17 percent of total System expenses (up from a little over 13 percent in 1985), the estimate for System is unlikely to be significantly affected. Other data obtainable from

earlier FRB Annual Reports suggest that the change in supervision/regulation expenses over a longer period; for example beginning in 1970 or 1980, would show similar or even more rapid growth.

11. FDIC expenses were over $846 million in 2005; and those of OCC were about $500 million (FDIC, 1980; FDIC, 2005; OCC, 1980; OCC, 2005).
12. For a more detailed development of pre-Gramm-Leach-Bliley activity restrictions under the Bank Holding Company Act, see Shull (1999), 11 ff.
13. Removing the term 'the business of' from the expression "so closely related . . . banking', substantially liberalized the relatedness requirement. Exceptions to the general prohibitions were also established: holding companies were permitted to acquire up to 5 percent of the voting shares, and up to 25 percent of the total equity of any company without aggregate limit; and to acquire 20 percent of the voting shares and 40 percent of total equity of nonfinancial companies outside the United States; exceptions were also made for investments in small business investment companies and for low cost housing and community redevelopment.
14. In *National Courier Association v. Board of Governors of the Federal Reserve System*, 516 F.2d 1229 (1975), the Court indicated the need to show the following: '(1) banks generally have, in fact, provided the proposed services; (2) banks generally provide services that are operationally or functionally so similar to the proposed services as to equip them particularly well to provide the proposed services; and (3) banks generally provide services that are so integrally related to the proposed services as to require their provision in a specialized form' (p. 1237).
15. These costs and benefits included, but were not necessarily limited to, the likely benefits of increased competition, efficiency, and convenience and the likely costs of undue concentration of resources, decreased or unfair competition, conflicts of interest and diminished bank soundness. See Shull and White, 1998: 454–5 for additional detail on how the legislation changed the standards.
16. Section 23A imposed 10 percent maximum of capital stock and surplus on loans by a bank to any one affiliate, and a 20 percent maximum on loans to all affiliates. It aimed to safeguard banks from excessive transfers that could weaken their condition, and to protect nonbank rivals from unfair competition. Section 23B, added to the Federal Reserve Act in 1991, required that all interaffiliate transactions be on an arm's-length basis.
17. A series of consumer and community-related protection laws, from the Consumer Credit Protection and Fair Housing acts of 1968, through the Community Reinvestment Act of 1977 made clear the extended range of constituencies that would be supported by bank regulation.
18. In the mid-1980s, the FRB permitted bank holding companies to deal in and underwrite otherwise 'ineligible securities' to the extent that they were not 'principally engaged' in doing so, as defined by the FRB.
19. A series of decisions in the 1990s supported OCC determinations that permitted national banks to expand their insurance business. See *Independent Insurance Agents v. Ludwig*, 997 F.2d 958 (DC Cir 1993); *Nations Bank v. Variable Annuity Life Insurance Co.*, 115 S.Ct. 810 (1995); and *Barnett Bank of Marion County NA v. Nelson*, 517 US 25 (1996).
20. The inapplicability of the Glass-Steagall Act to state-chartered, non-member banks permitted the FDIC and a number of states to permit them to engage in securities activities. Unitary savings and loan holding companies were excepted from activity restrictions. The establishment of 'non-bank banks' permitted any business to acquire a bank as long as it did not offer both demand deposits and commercial loans.
21. GLB repealed Section 20, that prohibited banks from having affiliates principally engaged in dealing in securities, and Section 32, that prohibited interlocks of directors and officers of securities firms and banks. It did not repeal Section 16, restricting banks themselves to dealing in and underwriting obligations of the Federal government and general obligations of states and political subdivisions, nor Section 21, prohibiting firms dealing in securities from accepting deposits. The sections that remain continue to preclude the integration of securities dealing and underwriting within the bank itself.

22. 'Before passage of the GLB Act . . . the law directed the Board to consider whether banks engaged in the activity [or something similar] but did not explicitly authorize the Board to consider whether other financial service providers engaged in the activity . . . . [The] change . . . represents a significant expansion of the Board's capacity to consider the competitive realities of the US financial marketplace in determining the permissibility of activities for FHCs' (Department of Treasury, 2000b: 11–12; see also pp. 8 ff.). The Department of Treasury have also indicated that they will include 'closely related' activities among those established as "financial in nature or incidental'.

23. For a brief history of ILCs, and the conditions for exemption from the Bank Holding Company Act, see GAO (2005), pp. 16–18. At the end of 2004, the GAO reported that there were under 100 ILCs in the country, with most located in Utah and smaller numbers in California and Nevada. While their numbers have dropped in recent years, their assets have grown substantially; a few had assets of $3 billion or more. They cannot offer demand deposits, but they do make a variety of loans and offer NOW accounts. Their deposits are insured by the FDIC. Some have access to the wider capital markets. A number of ILCs are directly owned by major commercial firms or by their financial affiliates, including BMW, Volkswagen, GE Capital Financial and GMAC Commercial Mortgage Bank (GAO, 2005: 18 ff).

REFERENCES

Adams, Renee and Hamid Mehran (2003), 'Is corporate governance different for bank holding companies,' *Federal Reserve Bank of New York Economic Policy Review*, April, 123–42.

Baxter, Thomas C. (2003), 'Governing the financial or bank holding company,' *Federal Reserve Bank of New York Current Issues*, **9**(3), 1–7.

Berle, A. A. and G. C. Means (1940), *The Modern Corporation and Private Property*, New York: The Macmillan Co.

DeFerrari, Lisa M. and David E. Palmer (2001), 'Supervision of Large Complex Banking Organizations,' *Federal Reserve Bulletin*, 80, 47–57.

Department of Treasury (2000a), 'Board of Governors of the Federal Reserve System and Department of the Treasury, Interim Rules for Merchant Banking,' 12 CFR Part 225 and 12 CFR Part 1500, at 8, 9 under Joint Press Release, 17 March.

Department of Treasury (2000b), 'Board of Governors of the Federal Reserve System and Department of the Treasury, "Proposed Rule with Request for Public Comments",' 12 CFR 225 and 12 CFR 1501 under 'Joint Press Release,' 27 December.

Dunbar, C. F. (1904), *Economic Essays*, New York: The Macmillan Co.

Fannon, Irene Lynch (2006), 'The European social model of corporate governance,' in Paul U. Ali and Greg N. Gregoriou (eds), *International Corporate Governance after Sarbanes-Oxley*, Hoboken, NJ: Wiley & Sons, Inc., pp. 423–44.

Federal Deposit Insurance Corporation (FDIC) (1980), *Annual Report for 1980*, Washington, DC.

Federal Deposit Insurance Corporation (FDIC) (2005), *Annual Report for 2005*, Washington, DC.

Federal Reserve Board (FRB) (1986–7), Board of Governors of the Federal Reserve System, *Annual Report: Budget Review*, Washington, DC.

Federal Reserve Board (FRB) (2006), Board of Governors of the Federal Reserve System, *Annual Report: Budget Review*, Washington, DC.

Government Accounding Office (GAO) (2005), *Industrial Loan Corporations*, report to the Hon. James A. Leach, no. 05-621, September, 2005, Washington, DC.

Greenspan, Alan (1990), address in '*Proceedings of a conference on bank structure and competition*,' Federal Reserve Bank of Chicago, 1–8.

Hanweck, Gerald and Bernard Shull (1996), *Interest Rate Volatility*, Chicago, IL: Irwin Professional Publishing.

Hurst, James Willard (1973), *A Legal History of Money in the United States, 1774–1970*, Lincoln, NE: University of Nebraska Press.

Lawrence, Robert and Samuel Talley (1978), 'An alternative approach to regulating bank holding companies,' in *Federal Reserve Bank of Chicago Proceedings of a Conference on Bank Structure and Competition*, Chicago, IL.

Leach, James A. (2000), remarks before ABA Leadership Council, 28 March, Ritz-Carlton Hotel, Pentagon City, VA.

Leach, James A. (2000), 'Remarks prepared for delivery before the Conference of State Bank Supervisors,' 12 May, San Francisco, CA.

Legislative History of Banking in the State of New York (1855), New York: Wm. C. Bryant & Co.

Meyer, Lawrence H. (2001), 'Implementing the Gramm-Leach-Bliley Act: one year later,' remarks before the American Law Institute and American Bar Association, 15 February, Washington, DC.

Office of the Comptroller of the Currency (OCC) (1980), *Report of Operations*, Washington, DC.

Office of the Comptroller of the Currency (OCC) (2005), *Report of Operations*, Washington, DC.

Pollack Alex (2006), 'What should society want from corporate governance,' in *Financial Services Outlook*, Washington, DC: American Enterprise Institute.

Powell, Donald E. (2005), Chairman, Federal Deposit Insurance Corporation, letter to Richard Hillman, Director, US General Accounting Office, as reproduced in GAO (2005), 92–7.

Shull, Bernard (1983), 'The separation of banking and commerce,' *The Antitrust Bulletin*, 28, 255–79.

Shull, Bernard (1999), 'The separation of banking and commerce in the United States: an examination of principal issues,' *Financial Markets, Institutions & Instruments*, **8**, 1–55.

Shull, Bernard (2002), 'Banking, commerce and competition under the Gramm-Leach-Bliley Act,' *The Antitrust Bulletin*, 47, 25–61.

Shull, Bernard (2005), *The Fourth Branch: The Federal Reserve's Unlikely Rise to Power and Influence*, Westport, CT and London: Praeger.

Shull, Bernard and Gerald Hanweck (2001), *Bank Mergers in a Deregulated Economy*, Westport, CT and London: Quorum Books.

Shull, Bernard and Lawrence J. White (1998), 'The right corporate structure for expanded bank activities,' *The Banking Law Journal*, **115**, 446–76.

Stern, Gary and Ron Feldman (2006), 'Managing too big to fail by reducing systemic risk,' *Federal Reserve Bank of Minneapolis The Region*, Minneapolis, MN: 19–21.

US House of Representatives (1913), 'Hearings before a Subcommittee of the Committee on banking and currency, money trust investigation,' part 19, 62 Cong., 2d Sess.

Vojta, George (1973), *Bank Capital Adequacy*, New York: First National City Bank of NY.

2. Corporate governance in banks: does the board structure matter?

Benton E. Gup

INTRODUCTION

Globalization and the increased demand for better corporate governance are two major trends affecting banking; and the two trends are inexorably intertwined. The term globalization, as used here, refers to the cross-border operations and ownership of businesses in general and banks in particular. The growth of globalization raises issues about the corporate governance of banks. The issues are complicated by the fact that the definitions of banks, their permissible activities, and their stakeholders vary around the world.[1] Nevertheless, everyone agrees that good corporate governance is important. But what does that mean? Does it mean that organizational structure of corporate boards is important, or that good management is important, or both, or are other issues involved? The corporate governance issue is puzzling because different organizational structures exist throughout the world; and there are examples of good and bad corporate governance in every country.

DEFINITIONS OF CORPORATE GOVERNANCE

The Anglo-American Model

In an international survey of corporate governance, Shleifer and Vishny (1997) say that corporate governance 'deals with the ways in which supplier of finance to corporations assure themselves of getting a return on their investment'. They argue that corporate governance is primarily concerned with principal agency problems between ownership and control. Stated otherwise, it deals with problems that arise because of the separation between shareholders and management. This Anglo-American or 'shareholder model' of corporate governance is accepted in the United States, England and some other countries.

OECD definition of governance

The OECD is an inter-governmental body that is dedicated to sound practices for economic development. It provides an international perspective on the definition of governance. The *OECD Principles of Corporate Governance* (2004) states that 'Corporate governance involves a set of relationships between a company's management, its board, its shareholders, and other stakeholders. Corporate governance also provides the structure through which the objectives of the company are set, and the means of attaining those objectives and monitoring performance are determined.'

FDIC's definition of governance

Bank regulators play a crucial role in the corporate governance of banks. In this connection, the FDIC has a different view of corporate governance than Shleifer and Vishny (1997) and the OECD. The FDIC said

> Corporate governance generally can be defined as the process of managing an organization's affairs or ensuring accountability. It can include a range of activities, such as setting business strategies and objectives, determining risk appetite, establishing culture and values, developing internal policies, and monitoring performance. Corporate fairness, transparency, and accountability are viewed as goals of corporate governance. To some, corporate governance simply means more active and involved participation by the board of directors; others emphasize corporate 'democracy' or broader shareholder participation.[2]

Franco-German Model

The Franco-German model of corporate governance incorporates the interests of both shareholders and non-shareholders (stakeholders) such as employees.[3] For example, in France, young workers rioted in 2006 over a controversial labor bill – Beginning Workers Contract – that would make it easier to fire workers under age 26 without any reason or notice in their first two years of employment. This social issue is related to corporate governance because worker representatives serve on many European boards, and there is a conflict of interest if management wants to adjust the size of its labor force. On the other side of the world in Japan, permanent/lifetime employment plays a large role in their economy, and in corporate governance.

In the Franco-German model that is widespread in Germany and Japan, banks take large equity positions in non-bank companies, and vice versa. Craig (2004) states that virtually every country in Europe has ownership concentration higher than that in the US, and many large European firms are family owned or controlled by single stockholders. Similarly, large Japanese banks serve as the 'main banks' in keiretsus, which are corporate groups of banks, insurance companies, trading companies, and manufacturing and marketing firms. All of the firms in the keiretsus are related through cross-holdings of shares. The cross-holding of shares was established by Article 280 of the Commerce Law in order to prevent hostile takeovers by foreign firms and to keep the shares in friendly hands. In addition, Morck and Nakamura (1999) describe keiretsus as 'management entrenchment devices', that allow banks to 'prop up' weak firms in the group.

Because of these arrangements, there is greater concentration of ownership of large banks in Germany and Japan than there is in the United States. Part of the reason behind this, is the long standing separation between banking and commerce. In the US, bank holding companies are prohibited by the Bank Holding Company Act from owning more than 5 percent of the shares in non-bank related companies. In addition, the Gramm-Leach-Bliley Act restricts bank holding companies to activities that are 'closely related to banking'. However, financial holding companies can engage in activities that are incidental to banking or complementary to banking. Equally important, non-bank commercial firms are prohibited from owning banks.[4] Nevertheless, affiliations between banking and commerce do exist. Industrial loan companies (ILC) are owned by firms such as GE Capital Finance, American Express, and Volkswagen.[5] ILCs have many of the same powers as commercial banks, and they are insured by the FDIC. In December 2004, there were 57 ILCs with $140 billion in assets. Most of them were chartered in California, Nevada, and Utah.

One Model Does Not Fit All

Shleifer and Vishny (1997) find that successful corporate governance systems, such as those in the United States, Germany, and Japan, combine legal protections for some investors with an important role for large investors. They also note that most corporate governance systems around the world – including large holdings, relationship banking, and takeovers, can be viewed as examples of large investors exercising their power as a control mechanism of corporate governance.

It also is important to recognize that public sector banks have different governance systems and concerns from private sector banks. Public sector banks often provide subsidized lending to particular sectors of the economy. For example, the Banco de la Republica Oriental del Uruguay (BROU) and the Banco Hipotecario del Uruguay (BHU) provided subsidized loan rates to the agricultural and housing sectors in Uruguay during a period of economic crises. Public sector banks are found in many developing countries such as China, India, and South Africa. Such banks are likely to continue to exist for political rather than economic reasons.

Consequently, profits are not their major concern.[6] Thus, it is clear that one model of corporate governance does not fit all users.

The Organisation for Economic Co-operation and Development (OECD) holds the same view. The OECD is an inter-governmental body with 30 member countries and about 70 other countries that are committed to democracy and a market economy. The *OECD Principles of Corporate Governance* (2004) state that 'There is no single model of good corporate governance'. And the OECD does not advocate any particular board structure because of different national models. The OECD states that the 'mix between legislation, regulation, self-regulation, voluntary standards, etc. in this area will therefore vary from country to country'.

Bank regulators know this as well. The Basel Committee on Banking Supervision (2005) recognized that

> there are significant differences in legislative and regulatory frameworks across countries as regards the functions of the board of directors and senior management. In some cases the role of the board of directors is performed by an entity known as a supervisory board. This means that the board has no executive functions. In other countries, by contrast, the board has a broader competence.

Stated otherwise, in the United States, the United Kingdom, Australia, and at least 37 other countries there is a sole-board system.[7] In some other countries, there is separation between management and a supervisory board. Germany, China and Spain are examples of such countries. Finally, France, Switzerland, Finland and Bulgaria have a mixed board structure, which means that firms can choose between sole and supervisory boards.

Fanto (2006) describes bank regulators in the United States as being 'paternalistic'. He says that

> Bank regulators screen proposed executives and directors of a new bank and may even not allow the bank to begin operations if they disapprove of some or all of these individuals. They set standards of conduct for bank officers and directors and continue, through regular examinations, to monitor them and their performance. Moreover, bank regulators have considerable informal and formal enforcement powers; they can even remove executives and directors temporarily or permanently from a financial institution and from the entire banking industry.

It goes further than that on an international scale. The Basel Committee on Banking Supervisions' 'Core Principles for Effective Banking Supervision' (2006), states that bank supervisors have the power 'to review and reject any proposal to transfer significant ownership or controlling interests . . . [and] . . . review major acquisitions and investments'.

Goals of Corporate Governance

It follows from the observations that one model of corporate governance does not fit all users; that there are international differences; and that corporate governance has multiple goals. These goals include, but are not limited to:

- protecting shareholders' interests;
- protecting stakeholders' interests;
- protecting the public's interest in the banking system; and
- satisfying bank/government regulators.

Because there are different goals, investors, regulators and stakeholders have different measures of success or failure. Some of the measures may be tied to laws and regulations that affect the structure of corporate governance. The Sarbanes-Oxley Act of 2002 (SOX) is the latest example in the US. SOX was enacted to protect shareholder interests following the Enron, Tyco and WorldCom debacles. In addition to Federal laws, Self-Regulatory Organizations, such as the New York Stock Exchange, the American Stock Exchange and NASDAQ, have rules dealing with the corporate governance of listed companies.[8]

Some of the measures involve the following issues:

1. effectiveness and efficiency of operations;
2. reliability of financial reporting;
3. compliance with laws and regulations;
4. returns on investments; and
5. achieving stakeholders' goals.

The first three issues appear in the Committee on Sponsoring Organizations of the Treadway Commission (COSO) report on *Internal Control-Integrated Framework* (1992). They also serve as the basis for the Federal Deposit Insurance Corporation Improvement Act (FDICIA) enacted in 1991. Section 112 of that Act requires management to report annually concerning the quality of internal controls. FDICIA also requires outside audits of the report.[9]

In general, investors are interested in returns on their investments (No. 4 above), but the degree of interest on returns differs in various countries. For example, the '2006 ISS Global Institutional Investors Study', of 322 institutional investors in 18 countries found that in Japan, 80 percent of the 25 institutional investors surveyed cited higher returns on investments as the major advantage of corporate governance, compared with 7 percent in

China.[10] In China, 80 percent of the 30 institutional investors cited improved risk management as the major advantage. Finally, stakeholders (No. 5 above) have their interests. For example, employees are concerned about continued employment, wages, and benefits. Similarly, the communities served by banks are interested in how banks are serving their credit needs (Community Reinvestment Act).

WHAT DOES THE ACADEMIC RESEARCH SHOW?

Academic research dealing with corporate governance and shareholders' interests yields mixed results, depending on the methodology, data, definitions, time periods used, and what the researcher is trying to prove. A glimpse at recent research on selected governance topics illustrates this point. This is not intended to be an extensive review of the literature. It only provides a brief overview of two selected issues: stock returns and board composition and structure.

Stock Returns

The first topic is stock returns. Gompers *et al.* (2003) examined data for 1990–9 and found that firms with strong shareholder rights have 8.5 percent higher risk adjusted returns than firms with weak shareholder rights. Cremers and Nair (2005) find that internal and external governance mechanisms are complements and are associated with long-term abnormal returns. Aggarwal and Williamson (2006) found that the new corporate governance regulations were associated with higher stock values; but they also found that the market was already rewarding firms that had better governance. Core *et al.* (2006) did not find that support for the hypothesis that weak governance causes poor stock returns. Loosely interpreted, these studies examined whether strong corporate governance affected stock returns, and the answers are yes and no.

Board composition and structure

The second topic is the composition and structure of the boards. Fama and Jensen (1983) argued that having outside directors was a good thing. However, Klein (1998) found little association between overall board composition and firm performance, but she did find ties between committee structure and performance. Increasing the number of inside directors on finance and investment committees was associated with higher stock returns. Hermalin and Weisbach (2003) found that board composition did not predict performance, but board size was negatively related to performance.

Fich and Shivdasani (2006) find that busy boards – those with a majority of outside directors who hold multiple directorships – are associated with weak corporate governance. But, Ferris *et al.* (2003), found no correlation between multiple directorships and lower firm values. So board size, composition and structure can be good or bad depending on what you are looking for.

Management's Point of View

Murray (12 April 2006) said that 'For many executives, "corporate govern-ance" is a nuisance – or worse. It diminishes their power while increasing that of board members, shareholders and various outsiders who want a say in company affairs.'

A 2004 survey by PricewaterhouseCoopers LLP and the Economic Intelligence Unit of more than 207 executives from the financial services industry around the world found that the majority of them equated good governance with satisfying the demands of regulators and legislators.[11] It should be noted that the agencies that regulate and supervise the financial sectors and the laws that they follow also vary throughout the world.[12]

The PWC survey goes on to say that taking a view that compliance means satisfying regulators and legislators hampers the institutions from taking proactive steps to gain a strategic advantage through good governance over other institutions. Thus, there may be a significant gap between manage-ment's and investors' expectations.

Significant Breaks in Internal Controls

Federal Reserve Governor Bies (22 June 2004) observed that it is difficult for outsiders to determine the effectiveness of corporate governance. She said that it usually takes a significant break in internal control for the public to be aware of weaknesses in the process. She goes on to say that the dis-closure of deficient business and governance practices can lead to lower share prices, lawsuits, enforcement actions, loss of credibility and reputa-tion, and higher interest rates in the capital markets.

Bank regulators let management and the public know when they find significant deficiencies in corporate governance. For example, The Board of Governors of the Federal Reserve System (1 March 2005) announced in a Press Release that Huntington Bancshares Incorporated, Columbus, OH, had significant deficiencies relating to its corporate governance, internal audit, risk management, and internal controls over financial report-ing, accounting policies and procedures, and regulatory reporting. The Federal Reserve terminated the enforcement action in May 2006, meaning that the bank made the necessary changes. Another Federal Reserve Press

Release (5 January 2005) announced that Prineville Bancorporation and Community First Bank, both of Prineville, OR, had serious corporate governance problems. The point is that bank regulators react when they find problems with corporate governance. They have inside information that is not available to outside investors.

First Southern Bank[13]

In March, 2002, the FDIC and the Alabama State Banking Department issued a Cease and Desist Order to First Southern Bank, Florence, Alabama.[14] The C&D order spelled out the reasons including, but not limited to, inadequate management, a large volume of poor quality loans following hazardous lending and lax collection practices, and so on.

The story behind these losses provides important insights about the corporate governance of small thrifts that convert into banks. Some parts of this lesson may be applicable to credit unions as they attempt to act like banks.

For example, in 1935, the First Federal Savings & Loan Association was chartered in Florence, AL. It was a successful S&L. Sixty years later in 1995, management decided to convert from an S&L into a Bank Holding Company and a state chartered commercial bank – First Southern Bank. One reason for the change was because a bank could provide a wider range of loans and services to the communities served.

On the surface, First Southern Bank appeared to be a well functioning organization. However, there were significant corporate governance problems that almost resulted in the demise of the bank.

The Chief Executive Officer (CEO) of the Bank made statements to the effect that he would run the bank just like he ran the S&L. The problem is that banks are significantly different from S&Ls, and neither he nor his staff had experience in making, monitoring, or collecting commercial loans. Moreover, the CEO had an 'alpha male personality', that can be interpreted to mean 'I'm the boss, I know how to run this shop, and I don't like to be questioned'. The Board must have thought that he did an excellent job, because he was one of the highest paid CEOs in banks of equivalent size.

The CEO was not a lender. He delegated the lending to his second in command. The Loan Committee rubber stamped most of the loans that were made. The bank's outside audits were done by a local accounting firm that had little experience in banking. But they were socially close with the CEO.

The Board of Directors of the bank, like that of many small banks, consisted of successful people in the local community. The Board of Directors included the CEO, the second in command, and eight outside Directors.

However, the outside directors had little or no formal training concerning their roles as bank directors. They participated in various committees, audit, personnel, and so on. However, the outside directors passively followed the agenda set by senior management and did not fulfill their role to establish bank policies, to set strategic bank direction, and to oversee bank management. That was the CEO's job, or so he told them.

The Board members were given 'board packets' as they entered the Board of Directors' meetings. The board packets consisted of a few pages of information, simple financial statements, and other items that were on the agenda. This is the way it was always done. In hindsight, the outside Directors did not have an accurate picture of the bank's business or financial situation.

Everything appeared to be going well. The bank grew from $160 million in assets at the time of conversion to about $190 million in 2000. In management's opinion the bank was overcapitalized, and they paid large dividends.

Shortly before a senior loan officer died in 2000, Board members became suspicious that something was wrong with the loan portfolio. A number of problem loans began to appear, and provisions for loan losses were needed. Bad credit was a ticking bomb that was about to explode. The bottom line is that there was no control over the commercial loan portfolio and the bad loans almost wiped out the bank.

In order to save the bank, assets were sold, additional capital was raised, management was changed, and a qualified attorney was retained. By 2006, the bank was out from under the regulators' umbrella because of their much improved financial condition.

The outside Directors learned some important lessons about corporate governance. One of the outside Directors said that there were three things that Directors had to know – capital and management, capital and management, and capital and management. The outside Directors also learned the importance of qualified auditors, and director training and responsibilities. With such training, they might have recognized obvious red flags. For example, the dead senior loan officer never took vacation time. The outside Directors had no real oversight; they should control the Audit Committee and have meaningful contact with the outside auditing firm. Now the outside Directors are in charge of the bank. It is not likely that they will make the same mistakes again. The cultures and operations of S&Ls and banks are quite different.

Regulatory failures
While bank regulators can be thought of as the 'guardians at the gate' for protecting the public interest, their track record is far from perfect. An FDIC study of bank failures in the 1980s stated that

the record shows that 260 failed banks were not identified as requiring increased supervisory attention within 24 months of failure. Of these, 141 were not detected as troubled banks within 18 months of failure; 57 were not detected within 12 months of failure; and 9 were not detected within 6 months of failure.[15]

First National Bank of Keystone was closed in 1999 amid allegations of fraud. Bank regulators had spotted internal control problems and audit deficiencies as much as eight years before the bank failed, but they didn't act on them until it was too late.[16]

Too-Big-To-Fail

Banks and other organizations get into financial trouble periodically, and in some cases, governments consider them Too-Big-To-Fail (TBTF).[17] The term TBTF originated in 1984 when Comptroller of the Currency Todd Conover testified before Congress that Continental Illinois bank and ten others were Too Big To Fail because of the major negative impacts they would have on the economy and the payments systems. The general concept of TBTF has been applied around the world and in a variety of industries when governments want to avert major disasters. New York City in the 1960s, Lockheed Aircraft in the 1970s, the savings and loan crises in the 1980s and the airlines in the 1990s are several examples from the US. The bailout of the Japanese banks in the 1990s is another example.

One has to wonder the extent to which officers and directors of large banking organizations, such as Citigroup, take the moral hazard issue of TBTF into account when making operating decisions. I don't have an answer for the question.

Investor Activism

Institutional investors also have a say in management and governance. The California Public Employee's Retirement System (CalPERS) Board of Administration has concluded that 'good' corporate governance leads to improved long-term performance. CalPERS also strongly believes that 'good' governance requires the attention and dedication not only of a company's officers and directors, but also its owners. CalPERS is not simply a passive holder of stock. 'We are a "shareowner", and take seriously the responsibility that comes with company ownership.'[18]

Karpoff (2001), in a survey of empirical research, found that shareholder activism can lead to small changes in corporate governance, but the impact on earnings and share values was negligible. Nevertheless, institutional investor activism is on the rise. The '2006 ISS Global Institutional Investors Study' found that 71 percent of 322 institutional investors in 18 countries believe that corporate governance has become important in the past three years, primarily because of scandals and increased compliance. In the next three years, 63 percent said that corporate governance will grow in importance. The study goes on to say that hedge funds are the new activists on the block. They showed a 'willingness to take on management, focus on mergers and acquisitions, and engage in proxy fights'.

Sovereign Bank

Where does shareholder activism end and intrusion on management begin? In other words, do the shareholders know how to run the company better than management? Alternatively, to what extent should management fight dissident shareholders? Consider the case of Sovereign Bancorp Inc., a $64 billion financial institution headquartered in Philadelphia, PA. Sovereign Bancorp experienced considerable growth under the leadership of Jay S. Sidhu.[19] Sovereign Bancorp was listed as number 34 in listing of the top 100 corporate citizens in 2006.[20] The listing was compiled before the bank's encounter with Rational Investors LLC.

Rational Investors LLC, a San Diego, CA hedge fund, Sovereign's largest shareholder, holding about 7.3 percent of its shares, was a critic of Mr Sidhu. Rational Investors questioned the bank's loans to officers and directors that increased from $6.4 million to $94.1 million in a six year period. In addition, they were not satisfied with Sovereign's stock returns. Rational Investors wanted to oust the entire board of directors. Later they modified their position and wanted two seats on the board of directors. Moreover, Rational Investors disagreed with Sovereign's decision to sell 24.99 percent of its shares to Banco Santander Central Hispano SA in Spain for $2.4 billion in cash, and then use those funds and others to buy Independence Community Bank in Brooklyn, NY for $3.6 billion. One important effect of these transactions is to dilute Rational Investor's shareholdings. A federal judge in New York ruled that Sovereign Shareholders can remove directors without cause. Sovereign was expected to appeal the decision. This is consistent with the theory that shareholders have the right to elect and fire directors.

Finally, on 10 February 2006, Edward Rendell, the Governor of Pennsylvania, signed into law Senate Bill 595 'to enact the corporate governance changes that Sovereign proposed . . . for purposes of applying the definition of "controlling person or group".'[21]

Did management go too far? Is this an example of excessive shareholder activism or excessive control by top management?

Management Must have Integrity and Ethical Behavior

US Securities and Exchange Commissioner Glassman (2005) said that companies need to have an effective corporate governance process, and *corporate boards and senior management must have integrity and promote ethical behavior*. I believe that most companies do have good corporate governance processes. They follow the rules not only to avoid the reputational risk of an enforcement action, but also because it is just good business practice and the right thing to do. As regulators, while we cannot impose these values, we can encourage good behavior through well-designed rules and discourage bad behavior through civil and criminal law enforcement. In this way, we can help bridge any gaps between owners' goals and management's goals.

Integrity and ethical behavior start at the top of a bank and work their way down through the entire organization. But what happens when there is a breach at the top? First we consider the cases of Deutsche Bank and Citigroup, two of the world's largest banks. Finally, we examine Banca Popolare Italiana, Italy.

Deutsche Bank

Bank managers are accountable if and when they break the criminal laws. Consider the case of Dr Josef Ackermann, Deutsche Bank's Spokesman of the Management Board and Chairman of the Group Executive Committee. He went on trial for allegedly enriching certain corporate executives of Mannesmann AG with $74 million in bonuses and retirement packages in order to drop their opposition to being acquired by Vodafone in 2000. The deal was considered illegal because it enriched Mannesmann executives without benefiting the shareholders. Ackermann and the other defendants were acquitted of those charges, but they face a new corporate criminal trial. According to Deutsche Bank's 2005 Annual Report, 'The Düsseldorf Public Prosecutor filed notice of appeal with the Federal Supreme Court (Bundesgerichtshof). On December 21, 2005, the Federal Supreme Court ordered a retrial with the District Court in Düsseldorf. When the new criminal trial will begin is not yet known.'[22]

Citigroup Inc.

Citigroup grew to be a global giant under the leadership of Sanford Weill. But it is hard to control every aspect of a global giant bent on growth. Salaries were based on performance, and the more services you sold, the more you made. Thus, problems and scandals began to surface. For example:

Japan In 2001, Japan's Financial Services Agency (FSA) had concerns about Citibank's Japan Branch (the Marunouchi Branch of Citibank). In 2004, the FSA took administrative actions to close four offices of the Japan Branch because several of the bank officers misled customers into investing in structured bonds and complex securities in violation of Japan's security laws, as well as numerous other violations.[23]

Germany   Citigroup bond traders were accused of 'market manipulation' using the 'Dr Evil Strategy'. But that strategy did not violate Germany's laws, and the charges were dropped.[24]

Brazil   It is alleged that a Citigroup Private Equity manager tried to coerce a large investor into selling its shares in a Brazilian telecom at below market prices. The manager was fired.[25]

Australia   Citigroup faced a $715 million fine in Australia for insider trading in connection with a takeover bid of a large company.[26]

New York   Citigroup settles Enron class action law suit for $2 billion.[27]

Chicago   The headline in the Chicago Tribune Online Edition stated 'Even big boys get scammed: A tense corporate drama unfolds when one of the nation's major lenders finds its Chicago Operation enmeshed in mortgage fraud.'[28] The major lender was part of Citigroup.

When Charles Prince took over the controls as the Chief Executive Officer of Citigroup, he announced that there would be a change in the corporate culture, with increased emphasis on internal controls and ethics.[29] The organizational structure remains the same, but the corporate governance is different. In April 2006, The Federal Reserve lifted a year-long ban on Citicorp's acquisitions, citing that they now had better internal controls.[30]

Banca Popolare Italiana (BPI), Italy

Gianpiero Fiorani was the Chief Executive Officer of BPI, that acquired a much larger bank, Banca Antoniana Popolare Venta (AntonVeneta) in a hostile takeover in which they acquired almost 40 percent of the shares.[31] He was arrested on 13 December 2005, for conspiracy to embezzle in connection with a complex scheme involved in the takeover. The scandal also involved Bank of Italy Governor Antonio Fazio. It is alleged that Fiorani gave the Fazio family very expensive gifts (watches, jewelry, silverware, and so on) that he recorded as business expenses. Subsequently, Fazio blocked a bid for AntonVeneta from ABN Amro. The charges against Fiorani and others involved stock manipulation prior to the acquisition. Fazio resigned from the Bank of Italy.

The point of the examples from BPI, Citigroup, and Deutsche Bank is that integrity and ethical behavior are set at the top tiers of organizations. BCCI is the one extreme example of this point. BCCI stands for the Bank of Credit and Commerce International, but it is better known as the Bank of Crooks and Criminals International.[32] BCCI was organized in 1972 by Agha Hasan Abedi in Abu Dhabi, and it eventually operated in 73 countries. By 1990, it was the seventh largest private bank in the world, with $23 billion in assets. One of 'the stated goals of its Pakistani founder were to "fight the evil influence of the West", and finance Muslim terrorist organizations'.[33] To make a long story short, under Abedi's leadership, BCCI was involved in fraud, money laundering, illegal purchases of banks, bribery, support of terrorism, arms trafficking, tax evasion, and 'a panoply of financial crimes limited only by the imagination of its officers and customers'.[34] The scandal made news in the early 1990s in the US. The bank was closed globally in 1991. Subsequent trials went on until 2005 in England against the Bank of England that failed to adequately supervise BCCI. This also illustrates the point that although banks are regulated, bank regulators are not perfect.

Finally, the Butcher brothers who owned and ran United American Bank (Knoxville, TN) into the ground provide another example of bad top management.[35] Jake Butcher was an unsuccessful candidate for the Governor of Tennessee, and a born salesman, and crook. Jake and his brother, 'C.H.' had acquired about 14 banks with assets of over $3 billion in the early 1980s. Jake helped to put together the 1982 World's Fair in Knoxville, with the help of President Jimmy Carter, Senator Howard Baker, and other well known figures of the time. On the day after the World Fair closed, 180 bank examiners closed all of Butcher's banks. It was the third largest bank to fail in US history. Following numerous counts of fraud and other charges, Jake was sentenced to two concurrent 20-year sentences, and his brother and others were ordered to pay a $19.3 million fine.

CONCLUSIONS

Models of corporate governance are one thing, management is another. According to management expert Peter Drucker,

> Because management deals with the integration of people in a common venture, it is deeply embedded in culture. What managers do in Germany, in the United Kingdom, in the United States, in Japan or in Brazil is exactly the same. How they do it is quite different.[36]

In the US, the UK and Australia, the sole-board system of corporate governance combines management and the board of directors. Germany and China utilize a model of corporate governance that separates management from a supervisory board. And France and Switzerland have a mixed board structure, which means that firms can choose between sole and supervisory boards. Therefore one model of board structure does not fit all users. Although not discussed here, there are wide variations in the structures of board committees.

Not only do board structures differ, but Murray (2006), stated that the ISS international survey sent a clear cut signal that corporate governance means different things to different institutional investors. In China, for example, the institutional investors were concerned with achieving basic levels of board accountability and transparency. In Japan there was greater emphasis on eliminating poison pills and anti-takeover measures.

Because banks are regulated, we cannot forget the role of bank regulators in the corporate governance process. Their primary concern is whether the institutions are following the laws and regulations in order to protect the safety and soundness of the financial system. The bank examinations give regulators an informational advantage over stockholders and other investors.[37] In their role as regulators, having adequate capital and capable management are more important *per se* than structure of the board. Nevertheless, regulators still have a lot of influence over who can be a bank officer or director.

One major key to success in an organization is the internal environment. The Committee of Sponsoring Organizations of the Treadway Commission (COSO) provided a framework for Enterprise Risk Management. According to Federal Reserve Governor Bies (28 April 2006), 'The internal environment – the *tone* of an organization – is a reflection of the organization's risk-management philosophy, risk appetite, and ethical values. It determines how risk is viewed and addressed by employees throughout the organization. This tone is established at the very top of the organization.' Stated otherwise, it is the top management that sets the tone for an organization's success or failure.

Although the Fannie Mae is not a bank, it is congressional chartered, publicly traded financial institution that is listed on the New York Stock Exchange under the symbol FNM. Furthermore, it is regulated by the Office of Federal Housing and Enterprise Oversight (OFHEO). Recent revelations about Fannie Mae provide insights about corporate culture and tone at a very large financial institution.[38] It is the second largest borrower in the world, after the US Government.

In May 2006, OFHEO released a 'Report of the Special Examination of Fannie Mae' focused on the 'Corporate Culture and Tone at the Top'. The Executive Summary said that Fannie Mae CEO Franklin Raines and his inner circle of top managers created a false image that 'what was good for Fannie Mae was good for housing and the nation'. Furthermore, it was 'low risk', and 'best in class' in terms of risk management, financial reporting, internal controls, and corporate governance.

The corporate culture at Fannie

> was intensively focused on attaining EPS (i.e. earnings per share) goals . . . In 1999, Mr Raines set a goal to double Fannie Mae's EPS within five years . . . Fannie Mae's executive compensation program gave senior executives the message to focus on earnings rather than controlling risk . . . EPS mattered, not how they were achieved . . . senior management achieved those earnings targets by regularly manipulating earnings . . . In total, over $52 million of Mr Raines' compensation of $90 million during the period was directly tied to achieving EPS targets . . . The actions and inactions of the Board of Directors inappropriately reinforced rather than checked the tone and culture set by Mr Raines and other senior managers.

Fannie Mae can be considered a regulatory failure. OFHEO estimated that FNMA overstated reported income and capital by $10.6 billion. It took OFHEO too long to figure out that Fannie Mae had a problem, and then to correct it.

Does the organizational structure matter? The answer is clearly yes and no. It depends on who you ask and what they want from banks. The anecdotal evidence provided here suggests good or poor corporate governance depends more on the honesty, integrity, and goals of top management more than on the organizational structure of corporate governance. This applies whether ownership is concentrated or diffuse.

IMPLICATIONS

The implications of this chapter are that:

1. Good corporate governance matters.
2. Good corporate governance depends on the board of directors and top management setting the proper culture and tone for the organization.
3. It is not clear if one type of board structure (i.e. Anglo-American/ shareholder versus Franco-German model) is better than others, or if it matters at all.
4. The compensation/incentive structure is the core problem in many corporate governance failures.
5. Government regulators do not have a perfect track record in finding and resolving corporate governance problems and failures.
6. Corporate governance failures require prompt corrective actions with strong penalties for violators.

ACKNOWLEDGMENTS

The author is indebted to Oliver Fabel, Konstanz University, Germany; Rowan Trayler, University of Technology Sydney (UTS), Australia; J. Acker Rogers, Chairman of the Board of First Southern Bancshares, First Southern Bank, and part owner of Rogers, Carlton & Associates, Inc. Florence, AL; Robert 'Bob' Walker, Baker Donelson, Bearman, Caldwell & Berkowitz, P.C., Memphis, TN, for their helpful suggestions and comments. Any errors are mine.

NOTES

1. For further discussion of this point, see Barth *et al.* (2004); Macey and O'Hara (2003).
2. Basinger, Robert, E., Daniel F. Benton, Mary L. Garner, Lynne S. Montgomery, Nathan H. Powell, 'Implications of the Sarbanes-Oxley Act for Public Companies in the US Banking Industry,' *FDIC Outlook*, Fall 2005.
3. Macey, Jonathan R., and Maureen O'Hara, 'The Corporate Governance of Banks,' *Economic Policy Review*, Federal Reserve Bank of New York, April 2003, 91–107. For a detailed discussion of ILCs, see United States Government Accountability Office, Industrial Loan Corporations: Recent Asset Growth and Commercial Interest Highlight Differences in Regulatory Authority, GAO-05-621, September, 2005.
4. The Gramm-Leach-Bliley Act of 1999 (PL 106-102, 113 STAT 1338) prohibits affiliations and acquisitions between commercial firms and unitary thrift institutions. Existing institutions were granted exceptions.
5. Blair, Christine E., 'The Mixing of Banking and Commerce: Current Policy Issues', *FDIC Banking Review*, 16(4), 2004. The Gramm-Leach-Bliley Act placed additional restrictions on the mix of banking and commercial firms by ending the ability of commercial firms to acquire unitary thrifts. However, some firms were grandfathered (Blair, 2004).
6. Caprio *et al.* (2004).
7. Adams, Renée B. and Daniel Ferreira, 'A Theory of Friendly Boards', European Corporate Governance Institute (ECGI), Finance Working Paper no. 100/2005, October 2005.
8. For further information, see www.nyse.com; www.amex.com, and www.nasdaq.com.
9. For further discussion of FDICIA 112 and internal audits, see Bies (7 May 2003), and Board of Governors of the Federal Reserve System, Supervisory Letter, SR 93-9, 'Distribution of Reports of Examination and Other Information to Independent Auditors,' 2 March 1993; Board of Governors of the Federal Reserve System, Supervisory Letter, SR 94-3, 'Supervisory Guidance on the Implementation of Section 112 of the FDIC Improvement Act,' 13 January 1994.
10. ISS stands for Institutional Shareholder Services, a major provider of proxy voting and corporate governance services http://www.issproxy.com/index.jsp.
11. PricewaterhouseCoopers, 'Financial Institutions Fall Short of Reaping the Strategic Advantages of Corporate Governance,' Hong Kong, 6 April 2004; Pricewaterhouse-Coopers and the Economist Intelligence Unit, 'Governance: From Compliance to Strategic Advantage,' April 2004.
12. For a discussion of this issue, see Hüpkes, Eva, Marc Quintyn, and Michael W. Taylor, 'Accountability Arrangements for Financial Sector Regulators,' *Economic Issues* 39, International Monetary Fund, 2006.
13. This case study is based on publicly available information and information provided in a meeting at First Southern Bank on 20 April 2006, in Florence, AL, with several members of the current Board of Directors.

14. FDIC Enforcement Decisions and Orders, In the Matter of First Southern Bank, Florence, AL, Docket No. 02-023b, 15 March 2003.
15. 'Bank Examination and Enforcement', *History of the Eighties: Lessons for the Future*, Vol. 1, Federal Deposit Insurance Corporation, Washington, DC, 1997, p. 433.
16. For additional details, see Gup, *The New Basel Capital Accord*, 2004, p. 74.
17. For additional details, see Gup, *Too Big To Fail*, 2004.
18. Calpers Shareowner Forum, http://www.calpers-governance.org/forumhome.asp.
19. Eisinger, Jesse, 'Sovereign Bancorp's Takeover Deal Looks Like a Dis to Shareholders,' *Wall Street Journal*, 2 November 2005, C1; Enrich, David, 'Santander Enlists Giuliani Firm to Review Deal With Sovereign,' *Wall Street Journal*, 3 March 2006, C3; Pilch, Phyllis, 'NYSE Rules Divide Bank, Investors,' *Wall Street Journal*, 21 December 2005, B2A; Board of Governors of the Federal Reserve System, Federal Reserve Release, H.2A, Notice of Formations and Mergers of, and Acquisitions by, Bank Holding Companies; Change in Control, 10 February 2006.
20. 'Business Ethics 100 Best Corporate Citizens, 2006,' *Business Ethics*, Spring 2006, **20**(1), p. 22.
21. Rendell, Edward G., Governor, Commonwealth of Pennsylvania, 'Governor Rendell Sign Senate Bill 595,' News Release, 10 February 2006, http://www.state.pa.us/papower/cwp/view.asp?A=11&Q=449844.
22. Deutsche Bank, Annual Report, 2005, 7.
23. Negishi, Mayumi, 'Citibank Japan Ordered to Close Four Offices Over Legal Breaches,' *The Japan Times*, Japan Times Online, 18 September 2004; Financial Services Agency, The Government of Japan, 'The Administrative Action Against Citibank, N.A., Japan Branch,' Provisional Translation, 17 September 2004. http://www.fsa.go.jp.
24. Taylor, Edward and Oliver Biggadike, 'Germany Won't Charge Citigroup Bond Traders,' *Wall Street Journal*, 22 March 2005, C3.
25. Samor, Geraldo, 'Citigroup Parts Ways with Manager in Brazil, Dantas, Focus of Dispute, Ran Bank's Private Equity; Cleaning up Ethical Issues,' *Wall Street Journal*, 11 March 2005, C3.
26. 'Citigroup Facing $715 M Fine for Insider Trading,' CNNMoney.com, 31 March 2006.
27. 'Citigroup Settles Enron Class Action Suit for $2 Billion,' *Banking Legislation & Policy*, Federal Reserve Bank of Philadelphia, April–June, 2005.
28. Jackson, David, 'Even big boys get scammed: A tense corporate drama unfolds when one of the nation's major lenders finds its Chicago Operation enmeshed in mortgage fraud,' *Chicago Tribune Online Edition*, 8 November 2005.
29. Riley, Clint, 'Citigroup Gets Higher Grades for its Corporate Governance,' *Wall Street Journal*, 18–19 March 2006, B3; Langley, Monica, 'Course Correction – Behind Citigroup Departures: A Culture Shift by CEO Prince,' *Wall Street Journal*, 24 August 2005, A1.
30. Riley, Clint, 'Citigroup Is Cleared to Pursue Deals,' *Wall Street Journal*, 5 April 2006, C3.
31. 'Year-end Accounts: Antonio Fazio, Governor of the Bank of Italy, Resigns. About Time.' *The Economist*, 25 December 2005, 98; 'Fazio Under Renewed Pressure to Resign After Fiorani Arrest,' *Italy*, magazine, 15 December 2005. http://www.italy.mag.co.uk/2005/news-from-italy; 'Italy Bid Bank Considers Options,' BBC News, 5 August 2005.
32. For details about BCCI, see: Gup, Benton E., *Targeting Fraud: Uncovering and Deterring Fraud in Financial Institutions*, Probus Publishing Co., Chicago, IL, 1995, Chapter 3.
33. Sirota, David and Jonathan Baskin, 'Follow the Money: How John Kerr Busted the Terrorists' Favorite Bank,' *Washington Monthly*, September 2004, http://www.washingtonmonthly.com/features/2004/0409.sirota.html.
34. Kerry, John (Senator) and Senator Hank Brown, 'A Report to the Committee on Foreign Relations, United States Senate, 102d Congress, 2d Session, Senate Print 102–140, December 1992. Executive Summary.
35. For details about United American Bank, see Gup, op. cit., Chapter 10.
36. Thurm, Scott and Joann S. Lubin, 'Peter Drucker's Legacy Includes Simple Advice: It's About People,' *Wall Street Journal*, 14 November 2005, B1.

37. See: DeYoung *et al.* (2001).
38. In January 1997, the Federal National Mortgage Association changed its name to Fannie Mae. Fannie Mae is regulated by the Office of Federal Housing Enterprise Oversight (OFHEO). Office of Federal Housing Enterprise Oversight, 'OFHEO Report: Fannie Mae Façade, Fannie Criticized for Earnings Manipulation,' Press Release, 23 May 2006.

REFERENCES

Adams, Renée B. and Daniel Ferreira (2005), 'A theory of friendly boards,' European Corporate Governance Institute (ECGI), finance working paper no. 100/2005, October.

Aggarwal, Reena and Rohan G. Williamson (2006), 'Did new regulations target the relevant corporate governance attributes?' accessed 12 February at SSRN: http://ssrn.com/abstract=859264.

Barth, James R., Gerard Caprio, Jr. and Daniel E. Nolle (2004), 'Comparative international characteristics of banking,' Office of the Comptroller of the Currency economic and policy analysis working paper 2004-1, January.

Basel Committee on Banking Supervision (2005), 'Enhancing corporate governance for banking organisations,' consultative document, October.

Basel Committee on Banking Supervision (2006), 'Core principles for effective banking supervision,' consultative document, April.

Basinger, Robert, E., Daniel F. Benton, Mary L. Garner, Lynne S. Montgomery and Nathan H. Powell (2005), 'Implications of the Sarbanes-Oxley Act for public companies in the US banking industry,' *FDIC Outlook*, Fall.

BBC News (2005), 'Italy bid bank considers options,' accessed 5 August, at http://news.billinge.com/1/low/business/4748837.stm.

Bies, Susan Schmidt (2003), 'Corporate governance,' remarks by Governor Susan Schmidt Bies to the Board of Governors of the Federal Reserve System, 7 May.

Bies, Susan Schmidt (2004), 'Trends in risk management and corporate governance,' remarks by Governor Susan Schmidt Bies to the Board of Governors of the Federal Reserve System, 22 June.

Bies, Susan Schmidt (2006), 'A bank supervisor's perspective on enterprise risk management,' remarks by Governor Susan Schmidt Bies to the Board of Governors of the Federal Reserve System, 28 April.

Blair, Christine E. (2004),'The mixing of banking and commerce: current policy issues,' *FDIC Banking Review*, **16**(4).

Board of Governors of the Federal Reserve System (2005), 'Enforcement actions,' Federal Reserve press release, written agreement with Prineville Bancorporation, 5 January.

Board of Governors of the Federal Reserve System (2005), 'Enforcement actions,' Federal Reserve press release, written agreement with Huntington Bancshares Incorporated, 1 March.

Board of Governors of the Federal Reserve System (2006), 'Notice of formations and mergers of, and acquisitions by, bank holding companies: change in control,' Federal Reserve release H.2A, 10 February.

Board of Governors of the Federal Reserve System (2006), 'Enforcement actions, termination of enforcement action against Huntington Bancshares Incorporated,' Federal Reserve press release, 10 May.

Board of Governors of the Federal Reserve System (1993), 'Distribution of reports of examination and other information to independent auditors,' supervisory letter SR 93-9, 2 March.

Board of Governors of the Federal Reserve System (1994), 'Supervisory guidance on the implementation of Section 112 of the FDIC Improvement Act,' supervisory letter SR 94-3, 13 January.

Business Ethics (2006), '*Business Ethics* 100 Best Corporate Citizens,' **20**(1), 22.

Calpers Shareowner Forum, accessed 15 April 2006, at www.calpers-governance.org/forumhome.asp.

Caprio, Gerard, Jonathan Fiechter, Robert E. Litan and Michael Pomerleano (2004), 'The future of state-owned financial institutions,' Brookings Institution policy brief no. 18-2004, Washington, DC.

CNNMoney.com (2006), 'Citigroup facing $715 M fine for insider trading,' 31 March.

Committee on Sponsoring Organizations of the Treadway Commission (COSO) (1992), Report on internal control-integrated framework, the most recent version of COSO internal control-integrated framework was published in 1995, accessed at www.coso.org.

Core, John E., Wayne R. Guay and Tjomme O. Rusticus (2006), 'Does weak governance cause weak stock returns? An examination of firm operating performance and investors' expectations,' *Journal of Finance*, **61**(2), 655–87.

Craig, Valentine (2004), 'The changing corporate governance environment: implications for the banking industry,' *FDIC Banking Review*, **16**(4).

Cremers, K. J. Martijn and Vinay B. Nair (2005), 'Governance mechanisms and equity prices,' *Journal of Finance*, **60**(6), 2859–94.

Deutsche Bank (2005), *Annual Report, 2005*.

DeYoung, Robert, Mark J. Flannery, William Lang and Sorin M. Sorescu (2001), 'The informational of bank exam ratings and subordinated debt prices,' *Journal of Money, Credit, and Banking*, **33**, 900–25.

The Economist (2005), 'Year-end Accounts: Antonio Fazio, Governor of the Bank of Italy, resigns. About time,' 25 December, 98.

Eisinger, Jesse (2005), 'Sovereign Bancorp's takeover deal looks like a dis to shareholders,' *Wall Street Journal*, 2 November, C1.

Enrich, David (2006), 'Santander enlists Giuliani firm to review deal with Sovereign,' *Wall Street Journal*, 3 March, C3.

Fama, Eugene and Michael Jensen (1993), 'The separation of ownership and control,' *Journal of Law and Economics*, **26**, 301–26.

Fanto, James A. (2006), 'Paternalistic regulation of public company management: lessons from bank regulation,' Brooklyn Law School legal studies research paper series working paper no. 49, 25 January.

Federal Deposit Insurance Corporation (FDIC) (1997), 'Bank examination and enforcement,' in *History of the Eighties: Lessons for the Future*, vol. 1, Washington, DC: Federal Deposit Insurance Corporation.

Federal Deposit Insurance Corporation (FDIC) (2003), Enforcement decisions and orders, in the matter of First Southern Bank, Florence, Alabama, docket no. 02-023b, 15 March.

Federal Reserve Bank of Philadelphia (2005), 'Citigroup settles Enron class action suit for $2 billion,' *Banking Legislation & Policy*, April–June.

Ferris, Stephen, Murali Jagannathan and Adam Pritchard (2003), 'Too busy to mind the business: monitoring by directors with multiple board appointments,' *Journal of Finance*, **58**(3), 1087–111.

Fich, Eliezer M. and Anil Shivdasani (2006), 'Are busy boards effective monitors?' *Journal of Finance*, **61**(2), 689–724.

Financial Services Agency, Government of Japan (2004), 'The administrative action against Citibank, NA, Japan Branch,' provisional translation, accessed 17 September, at www.fsa.go.jp.

Glassman, Cynthia A. (2005), Remarks before the Beyond the Myth of Anglo-American Corporate Governance Roundtable speech by US Securities and Exchange Commissioner Glassman, 6 December.

Gompers, Paul A., Joy L. Ishii and Andrew Metrick (2003), 'Corporate governance and equity prices,' *Quarterly Journal of Economics*, **118**, 107–55.

Gup, Benton E. (1995), *Targeting Fraud: Uncovering and Deterring Fraud in Financial Institutions*, Chicago, IL: Probus Publishing Co.

Gup, Benton E. (2004), *The New Basel Capital Accord*, New York: Thomson/Texere.

Gup, Benton E. (2004), *Too Big To Fail, Policies and Practices in Government Bailouts*, Westport, CT: Praeger Publishers.

Hermalin, Benjamin E. and Michael S. Weisbach (2003), 'Boards of directors as an endogenously determined institution: a survey of the economic literature,' *Federal Reserve Bank of New York Economic Policy Review*, April, 7–50.

Hüpkes, Eva, Marc Quintyn and Michael W. Taylor (2006), 'Accountability arrangements for financial sector regulators,' *International Monetary Fund Economic Issues*, 39.

Institutional Shareholder Services (ISS) (2006), *2006 ISS Global Institutional Investors Study*, New York: Institutional Shareholder Services.

Italy Magazine (2005), 'Fazio under renewed pressure to resign after Fiorani arrest,' 15 December, accessed at www.italy.mag.co.uk/2005/news-from-italy.

Jackson, David (2005), 'Even big boys get scammed: a tense corporate drama unfolds when one of the nation's major lenders finds its Chicago operation enmeshed in mortgage fraud,' *Chicago Tribune Online Edition*, 8 November.

Karpoff, Jonathan M. (2001), 'The Impact of shareholder activism on target companies: a survey of empirical findings,' working paper, 18 August.

Kerry, Senator John and Senator Hank Brown (1992), 'A report to the Committee on Foreign Relations, United States Senate, 102d Congress, 2d Session,' Senate print 102-40, December.

Klein, April (1998), 'Firm performance and board committee structure,' *Journal of Law and Economics*, **41**(1), 275–303.

Langley, Monica (2005), 'Course correction – behind Citigroup departures: a culture shift by CEO Prince,' *Wall Street Journal*, 24 August, A1.

Macey, Jonathan R. and Maureen O'Hara (2003), 'The corporate governance of banks,' *Federal Reserve Bank of New York Economic Policy Review*, April, 91–107.

Morck, Randall and Masao Nakamura (1999), 'Banks and corporate control,' *Journal of Finance*, **54**(1), 319–39.

Murray, Alan (2006), 'Corporate-governance concerns are spreading, and companies should take heed,' *Wall Street Journal*, 12 April, A2.

Negishi, Mayumi (2004), 'Citibank Japan ordered to close four offices over legal breaches,' *The Japan Times* Online, 18 September.

Office of Federal Housing Enterprise Oversight (OFHEO) (2004), 'OFHEO report: Fannie Mae façade, Fannie criticized for earnings manipulation,' press release, 23 May.

Office of Federal Housing Enterprise Oversight (2006), 'Report of the special examination of Fannie Mae,' May.

Organisation for Economic Co-operation and Development (OECD) (2004), *OECD Principles of Corporate Governance*, Paris: OECD.

Pilch, Phyllis (2005), 'NYSE rules divide bank investors,' *Wall Street Journal*, 21 December, B2A.

PricewaterhouseCoopers LLP (2004), 'Financial institutions fall short of reaping the strategic advantages of corporate governance,' Hong Kong, accessed 6 April, at www.pwchk.com/home/eng/pr_060404.html.

PricewaterhouseCoopers LLP and *The Economist* Intelligence Unit (2004), 'Governance: from compliance to strategic advantage,' April.

Rendell, Governor Edward G. (2006), 'Governor Rendell signs Senate Bill 595,' Commonwealth of Pennsylvania news release, accessed 10 February, at www.state.pa.us/papower/cwp/view.asp?A=11&Q=449844.

Riley, Clint (2006a), 'Citigroup gets higher grades for its corporate governance,' *Wall Street Journal*, 18–19 March, B3.

Riley, Clint (2006b), 'Citigroup is cleared to pursue deals,' *Wall Street Journal*, 5 April, C3.

Samor, Geraldo (2005), 'Citigroup parts ways with manager in Brazil, Dantas, focus of dispute, ran bank's private equity; cleaning up ethical issues,' *Wall Street Journal*, 11 March, C3.

Shleifer, Andrei and Robert W. Vishny (1997), 'A survey of corporate governance,' *Journal of Finance*, **52**(2), 737–83.

Sirota, David and Jonathan Baskin (2004), 'Follow the money: how John Kerr busted the terrorists' favorite bank,' *Washington Monthly*, September, accessed at www.washingtonmonthly.com/features/2004/0409.sirota.html.

Taylor, Edward and Oliver Biggadike (2005), 'Germany won't charge Citigroup bond traders,' *Wall Street Journal*, 22 March, C3.

Thurm, Scott and Joann S. Lubin (2005), 'Peter Drucker's legacy includes simple advice: it's about people,' *Wall Street Journal*, 14 November, B1.

United States Government Accountability Office (2005), 'Industrial loan corporations: recent asset growth and commercial interest highlight differences in regulatory authority,' GAO-05-621, September.

3. Corporate governance and bank performance

Kenneth Spong and Richard J. Sullivan

The bank corporate governance process is a complex framework. This governance framework encompasses a bank's stockholders, its managers and other employees, and the board of directors. Banks further operate under a unique system of public oversight in the form of bank supervisors and a comprehensive body of banking laws and regulations. The interaction between all of these elements determines how well the performance of a bank will satisfy the desires of its stockholders, while also complying with public objectives. For investors and regulators, this bank corporate governance framework is thus of critical importance in a bank's success and its daily operations.

While governance by bank stockholders and directors has always been viewed as important, this topic has drawn increased attention in recent years. Among the reasons for this interest are banking deregulation and a rising role for market discipline and governance; substantial banking consolidation and resulting changes in the management, board, and ownership structure of many banking organizations; and a movement in many countries from state-owned banking systems to greater private ownership and control. Another factor is recent corporate scandals, such as Enron, Tyco and WorldCom, and the ensuing passage of the Sarbanes-Oxley Act of 2002, with its provisions aimed at improving corporate disclosures, increasing managerial responsibility and involvement, and tightening board oversight.

However, in spite of all this recent attention and the many pronouncements that have been made by so-called corporate governance experts, a range of opinions exists on what would constitute a good governance system in a bank or any other corporation. In addition, much of the bank corporate governance research narrowly focuses on a single aspect of governance, such as the role of directors or that of stockholders, while omitting other factors and interactions that may be important within this governance framework. One other weakness is that such research is often limited to the largest, actively traded organizations – many of which show little variation in their ownership, management and board structures.

In this bank governance framework, much of the driving force behind how a bank performs is based on the monitoring and financial incentive structures that are in place for managers, stockholders and directors. Ownership and wealth, in fact, provide many of the financial incentives that direct the actions of key players in a firm. It is well understood that stock ownership, by establishing which parties are entitled to the benefits from a bank's operations, will determine who has the most to gain and the greatest incentive to lead a bank to peak performance. A concept that is less understood, perhaps because of data constraints and limited research work, is how key players may act differently based on the amount of their own wealth that they have tied up in a bank's stock. Individuals with much of their wealth concentrated in a bank are likely to have a strong incentive to put forth greater effort and also to be more careful in the risks they choose to take.

This chapter provides an overview of some research we have done on how different aspects of corporate governance influence bank performance. To provide a more complete look at these governance issues, we use a sample of community banks where a wide range of management, ownership and board structures are present. We also collect much of our data from bank examination reports to gain a detailed look at various parts of the bank governance framework and the financial incentives that influence key players in this governance process, such as their bank stock ownership and the importance of this ownership to their overall financial wealth.

The first section of this chapter discusses how different elements of the bank corporate governance framework might affect the subsequent performance of banks, with previous research on this topic providing a context to the discussion. A second section describes the banks and data used in our research and also looks at how the amount of stock held by bank owners, managers, and directors influences their actions and the performance of their banks. A third section examines the extent to which ownership and the amount of personal wealth that bank managers and key directors have concentrated in their banks influence risk taking within an institution. The final section offers a summary and conclusion.

POSSIBLE RELATIONSHIPS BETWEEN BANK CORPORATE GOVERNANCE AND PERFORMANCE

Bank governance must address a range of issues within a bank, including who will run the bank, what will be the makeup of the board of directors, how will the board carry out its oversight of management officials, and what financial incentives and other factors will be used to align the actions of all these key players with that of stockholders. With regard to who will run a bank, the management or top officers might be composed of the principal owners or be hired from outside this ownership group. While many banks begin operations with major stockholders serving in management positions, a manager might be hired from outside if the owners don't have the background or the experience to run the daily operations of a bank or have other business interests occupying much of their time. Hiring a manager might also be the best option when the principal owners retire from management positions and no other insiders or family members are in a position to manage the bank. Professional or hired managers may further provide a means for stockholders to bring in someone with the needed expertise, experience and outside perspective to run the bank well.

From a governance perspective, managers with significant stockholdings may differ notably from hired managers in their motivations and financial incentives. Owner managers will not only benefit financially from their salaries in running a bank, but, as stockholders, will also be rewarded for good performance through their claim to bank earnings and capital appreciation. Hired managers with little or no stockholdings, on the other hand, will have their principal compensation coming through their salary. Consequently, hired managers will not have the same incentive to maximize the value of the stockholder's investment, and a hired manager's behavior may therefore fail to serve the interests of the bank's owners. This separation between management and ownership is commonly referred to in financial theory as the principal-agent problem, which may lead hired managers to maximize their own utility rather than that of the firm. Jensen and Meckling (1976) used the term agency costs to describe the reduction in a firm's value that arises when hired managers fail to serve stockholder interests.[1]

In banking and other businesses, these agency costs may manifest themselves in several ways. Since hired managers won't receive the same equity returns that owner managers would, a hired manager may not be motivated to put forth as much effort (shirking) as an owner manager. A hired manager might also attempt to maximize his or her utility by seeking to expand the firm beyond a profitable level (empire building), playing it safe and avoiding projects that stockholders and owner managers would be willing to pursue (risk aversion), and taking advantage of his or her position by consuming excessive perquisites (expense preference). All of these behaviors would benefit the hired manager at the expense of stockholders, and this inherent divergence in interests is the source of principal-agent problems.

Agency costs can be reduced through several market and governance mechanisms. Labor markets, for example, provide some incentives for hired managers to serve stockholder interests, since better-performing managers will be regarded and rewarded more highly and have greater marketability (Fama, 1980; Cannella *et al.*, 1995). Capital markets can also encourage better performance on the part of hired managers, since any performance issues could put pressure on stock prices and increase the potential for takeover and new management. These market mechanisms, though, may only partially substitute for the more direct incentives that owner managers have.

From a governance perspective, shareholders may be able to align the interests of hired managers more closely with their own through two other mechanisms – effective board oversight of management and an ownership stake in the bank for the hired managers. For instance, the board of directors in their oversight function would have the responsibility of monitoring hired managers and encouraging them to operate their banks in a manner compatible with stockholder desires.[2] For hired managers, a bank ownership stake or stock options would give them an added return from improving a bank's performance, thus aligning their interests more closely to those of stockholders and to the objectives set by the board of directors.

One other factor that may influence the preferences of the key players in a bank, as well as the governance process, is how much of their own wealth managers, directors or major stockholders have concentrated in their bank investments. This wealth concentration factor has not received much attention in banking and corporate governance research, but it could lead to a different outcome than would otherwise be expected under principal-agent theory. For example, managers with nearly all they own tied up in a bank's stock are likely to focus more attention and effort toward their bank and be more selective in the risks they take compared to managers with more diversified investments.

The governance process in banks is further complicated by deposit insurance and supervisory oversight. With bank deposit insurance, managers may have an incentive to take more risks (moral hazard), because insured depositors have no need to extract a price for this higher risk exposure (Merton, 1977). The ability of bankers to exploit this incentive will depend on such factors as bank regulatory and supervisory discipline and how much bank owners and managers have to lose from taking excessive risk. These potential losses from risk taking are likely to be related to such parameters as the franchise value of a bank (market-to-book value), a bank's capital level and the degree to which key players have their wealth concentrated in the bank.[3]

All these elements – managers and their ownership incentives, directors and their monitoring role, all the key policymakers/owners and the amount of wealth they have concentrated in the bank, and deposit insurance incentives and regulatory discipline – have a key influence on the governance framework at banks. Each of these elements may serve to reinforce other elements, be a substitute for other pieces of the governance framework, or interact in other ways in the governance process. As a result, getting a true picture of how bank governance operates may require that these elements be examined together.

From the discussion above, several effects can be hypothesized. Greater stock ownership by managers and directors should, by itself, encourage increased effort from these individuals, as well as better bank performance and less reluctance to take risk. In the case of directors, stock ownership should provide an incentive to monitor hired managers and bring their performance closer to stockholder expectations. The more a manager's, director's, or large shareholder's wealth is concentrated in a bank, the greater one's commitment to the bank and the more careful one will be about taking risks and trying to exploit moral hazard incentives from deposit insurance. Thus, while greater stock ownership might be expected to make managers and directors less averse to taking risk, having more of one's wealth tied up in a bank's stock could lead to the opposite result – a negative relationship with risk taking.

Several of these hypotheses have been tested in previous banking research. For instance, Glassman and Rhoades (1980) compared financial institutions controlled by their owners with those controlled by managers and found that the owner-controlled institutions had higher earnings. Allen and Cebenoyan (1991) found that bank holding companies were more likely to make acquisitions that added to firm value when they had high inside stock ownership and more concentrated ownership. Cole and Mehran (1996) discovered higher stock returns at thrifts that had either had a large inside shareholder or a large outside shareholder. These studies thus offer some support for the hypothesis that stock holdings provide an incentive to run a bank better and achieve higher earnings for its stockholders.[4]

A number of studies have also examined possible relationships between ownership and risk taking. Saunders *et al.* (1990) looked at a group of large, publicly traded banking organizations and found a higher level of risk in organizations where the managers and directors had higher ownership stakes, much as might be expected under principal-agent theory. Other studies have also looked at risk measures derived from stock prices (Anderson and Fraser, 2000; Brewer and Saidenberg, 1996; Chen *et al.*, 1998; Demsetz *et al.*, 1996; Demsetz and Strahan, 1997; Knopf and Teall, 1996) or from balance sheet indicators (Cebenoyan *et al.*, 1996; Gorton and

Rosen, 1995; Knopf and Teall, 1996), but have not come to consistent conclusions on the effect of inside ownership on bank risk taking. Several of these studies also explored the influence of outside shareholders on bank risk. For instance, Cebenoyan *et al.* (1999) found reduced risk levels at thrifts with large outside investors, and Knopf and Teall (1996) found the same type of relationship in thrifts with institutional investors, thus indicating that such shareholders may be protecting their investments by monitoring bank management.

Most of these studies thus focus on only one or two parts of the corporate governance framework. None, in fact, have looked at the wealth that managers or other policymakers have concentrated in their own bank and how this wealth effect might influence the governance process. This exclusion could be important because wealth concentration is likely to have a notable influence on risk-taking behavior, as well as on the level of commitment to one's bank. Parrino *et al.* (2005), in fact, develop a model of a firm that indicates outside wealth will have a substantial influence on a manager's decision to adopt risky projects.

DIRECTORS, MANAGERS, AND STOCKHOLDERS AND THEIR EFFECT ON BANK EFFICIENCY

To analyze the corporate governance framework in banks, we use a sample of state-chartered banks in the Kansas City Federal Reserve District. Each bank in this sample has total assets of under $1 billion. These community banks operate with a wide diversity of management, ownership and board structures, which range from hired managers with little or no stock ownership to owner managers controlling virtually all of their bank's stock.[5] Because our sample only contains community banks, various elements of the corporate governance framework that we examine may not be directly applicable to larger banks that are more widely held and face the discipline imposed in actively traded markets. However, many of the financial incentives facing managers, owners and directors at community banks also have their counterparts in larger institutions.

Bank examination reports provide much of the corporate governance information on the sample banks, including a detailed look at the specific responsibilities of the bank managers and other key policymakers, the amount of stock held by individual investors, family relationships among all the participants, and personal wealth and other characteristics of bank directors. We also use the quarterly Reports of Condition and Income that banks file with their federal supervisor to derive performance data on each bank.

Boards of Directors and Bank Efficiency

In the corporate governance framework, bank directors have a number of important responsibilities, including hiring and overseeing the management team, setting major policies and objectives, monitoring compliance with these policies, and participating in the significant decisions within the bank. Thus, directors play a key role in setting the parameters under which management is to operate, and board decisions should have a significant influence on a bank's performance.

The contribution that directors make in the governance of a bank will depend on a number of factors. First and foremost will be the ability of the bank to attract knowledgeable and thoughtful individuals to the board. In addition, many of the consultants giving advice on corporate governance contend that having more outside or independent directors is better since such directors will not be tied too closely with bank management and will be more likely to take a critical look at management proposals and decisions. On the other hand, much of the economics and finance literature points out that the monitoring role boards play is a costly activity in terms of time and effort. Consequently, directors with significant stock holdings or other ties to their bank might be expected to have a greater financial incentive to put in the time and perform their role well compared to independent directors.[6]

Table 3.1 explores the governance role that directors play by comparing the boards of directors at two categories of banks in our sample – banks that do well on the basis of a combined cost efficiency and revenue test and banks that rate lower on this combined test.[7] As shown in this table, the makeup of the board does not differ in any significant way between the most efficient and the least efficient banks with regard to the number of directors on the board, their average age, or length of tenure. However, directors at the most efficient banks have a higher median net worth, a greater ownership share in their banks, and are less likely to be outside directors.[8] Other significant characteristics of the boards at the most efficient banks include more frequent meetings, better attendance rates, and higher director fees.

These results thus suggest that banks are likely to perform better when the directors have a greater financial stake in their bank's success and, accordingly, more reason to be actively involved and to monitor the performance of management. Efficient banks also appear to be more willing to pay higher directors' fees and, on the basis of net worth figures, seem to have succeeded in attracting a more successful group of people to their boards. Consequently, while independent directors have a role to play on bank boards, our analysis implies that community bank boards will do better in monitoring management and setting policies when the directors have a greater ownership interest in their banks.

Table 3.1   Characteristics of the board of directors and bank efficiency*

	Most efficient banks	Least efficient banks
Number of directors	6.6	6.7
Average age	57.1	56.9
Average tenure with bank (years)	16.3	14.4
Net worth per director (Median value in thousands of dollars)	**$1317**	**$835**
Share of bank owned by the entire board	**66.3%**	**55.9%**
Percent outside directors	**25.9%**	**34.3%**
Meetings per year	**11.6**	**10.6**
Attendance rate	**94.2%**	92.1%
Annual fees per director	**$3326**	**$2257**

Notes: * Figures in this table are group averages for the most or least efficient banks, except for the net worth of directors, which are group medians. There are 73 banks in the most efficient group and 70 banks in the least efficient group.
Bold Face indicates a statistically significant difference.

Source: adapted from Spong *et al.* (1995), p. 9.

Bank Management, Ownership and Profit Efficiency

A bank's performance can be expected to reflect the motivation and goals of officers and stockholders. The incentives driving managers in community banks may vary, depending on whether major stockholders form much of the management team or the managers are hired from outside.

As financial theory suggests, officers that are also major stockholders will directly benefit through improved stock returns for any steps they take to control costs and improve bank performance. Hired managers with little ownership interest, on the other hand, would not be rewarded in the same manner as owner managers or other stockholders when a bank does well. To deal with the agency problems associated with hired managers, stockholders and directors may have to be more careful in conveying their objectives to these managers, monitoring their performance and finding more effective ways to reward the managers for superior performance. In terms of rewarding managers, many banks have attempted to use performance bonuses, stock options, and other means. While these and other steps may help elicit better performance, they are hard to design and may fail to provide the same incentives as significant stock ownership.

To investigate the effects of ownership and management structure on bank performance, we look at how managers and their ownership positions in our sample banks are linked to bank profit efficiency (that is, a bank's ability to generate profits compared to other banks). This analysis focuses on the daily managing officer of a bank and his or her stockholdings. In community bank examination reports, examiners characteristically identify one individual as the daily managing officer of a bank. This officer is the one who is responsible for the bank's daily operations and must make and oversee many of the decisions that come up within the normal course of business. The daily managing officer is thus in a position to have the most impact on bank profitability, and his or her ability to serve the interests of stockholders will be a major factor in a bank's performance. This person is usually the bank's CEO or President, but occasionally the CEO or President may be a figurehead and examiners will identify someone else as being in charge of daily operations.

Because agency problems will be more prominent in banks with hired managers, we separate our sample banks into two groups. In one group, the daily managing officer is either a bank's largest stockholder or is part of a family or other close-knit group controlling the largest block of bank stock (an owner manager). In the other group, the daily managing officer is hired from outside of the control group (a hired manager).

To measure the performance of each sample bank, we estimated its profit efficiency relative to other banks in the Tenth Federal Reserve District. These performance measures were based on an econometric model that estimated an efficient profit frontier for Tenth District banks. The financial performance of the sample banks was then compared to this 'best practices' benchmark.[9] Because the profit efficiency estimates capture a bank's performance after adjusting for differences in what banks produce, the input prices they face, their locations and other factors, these estimates should provide a more refined metric for bank and managerial performance than standard accounting measures such as ROA or ROE.[10]

Multivariate regression analysis was then used to relate these profit efficiency measures to such explanatory variables as the shareholdings of the daily managing officers and their families, additional variables designed to capture other elements of corporate governance (such as director and large shareholder monitoring) and a set of control variables.[11] Figure 3.1 depicts the estimated relationship between bank profit efficiency and stock ownership by hired and owner managers and their families.[12]

The estimated relationship between bank profit efficiency and the manager's family ownership of the bank is distinctly different for hired managers compared to owner managers. For instance, there is a marked change in profit efficiency for small changes in ownership of hired managers. In

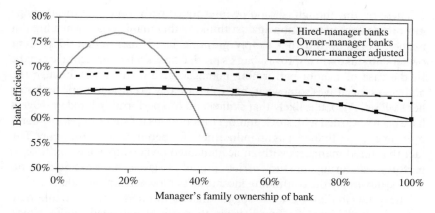

*Figure 3.1   Estimated relationship between a bank's efficiency and a
manager's family ownership*

owner-manager banks, by contrast, profit efficiency changes little in response
to changes in manager ownership. This reflects the fact that owner managers
already have substantial control over their organizations so that added
ownership provides little incentive to alter behavior.

For hired managers, profit efficiency reaches a peak when these managers
have a 17 percent ownership stake in their banks. Before this ownership
level is reached, additional stock holdings are associated with improved
efficiency, but afterwards profit efficiency declines. This effect of managerial ownership, moreover, is economically meaningful. Banks whose hired
managers had no ownership operated with an average profit efficiency ratio
of 68 percent. In contrast, banks where hired managers had a 17 percent
ownership stake achieved average profit efficiency ratios of 77 percent.
Thus, the optimum use of ownership holdings for hired managers would
allow banks to close 28 percent of the gap in performance with the most
efficient bank.[13]

These results imply that the incentive of ownership can help to mitigate
principal-agent conflicts and corporate governance issues by spurring hired
managers to improve the performance of their banks. Given these benefits,
it is surprising that only one-third of hired managers have more than a
trivial ownership stake in their banks. This outcome suggests that ownership is a greatly underutilized tool in combating agency costs and governance problems. At the same time, only a small number of banks operated
with hired managers that had over a 17 percent ownership stake, which is
the point at which entrenchment and conflicts with principal owners began
to have an adverse effect on performance in our sample banks.[14]

These results, though, should be interpreted with some caution. Perhaps most important, we caution against thinking that managerial ownership is a magical solution and that simply granting hired managers a 17 percent ownership stake will improve a bank's profit efficiency by 9 percentage points. In the case of a poor-performing manager, giving stock may change the manager's incentives somewhat, but will probably do little to improve his or her skill set. Also, it is likely that skilled and top performing hired managers have been rewarded with stock and/or stock options for superior performance over time rather than just as an inducement for better performance now. The fact that hired managers with an accumulated ownership stake continue to perform well during our study period, though, suggests that we should, by no means, downplay the continuing incentives that ownership provides.

The results in Figure 3.1 also suggest that many hired-manager banks may have achieved higher profit efficiency than owner-managed banks, which seems to dispel part of the principal-agent hypothesis. However, the solid lines in Figure 3.1 are constructed by setting the control variables at the mean values for each particular group: hired-manager banks and owner-manager banks. When we control for differences between these groups in such factors as the size of banks, their location and organizational form, much of this per-formance difference disappears, as shown by the dotted adjusted line for owner-manager banks.

A number of other factors further suggest that the overall performance of many owner-managed banks may meet or exceed that of hired-manager banks. First, owner managers in community banks have incentives to shift part of the remuneration they would otherwise receive in the form of bank earnings and dividends into additional salary and other benefits for them-selves, thus reducing the double taxation they would face on bank earnings. This tax avoidance strategy would thus serve to understate a bank's actual earnings and reduce the bank's 'estimated' profit efficiency.[15] Second, as we will see next, many owner managers may perform well, but, due to their per-sonal financial situation, are willing to trade off better returns for a lower risk exposure and more secure financial position. A third factor is that some bank owners in small towns might elect to place a higher priority on activities benefiting the local community and its long-run development compared to steps most likely to maximize current bank profitability.

HOW MANAGERIAL OWNERSHIP AND WEALTH CONCENTRATIONS AFFECT BANK RISK

Managing risk is a complicated task in any firm. Assessing whether a firm is taking an appropriate amount of risk is especially difficult because preferences for risk are an individual matter. Thus, it may not be easy for outsiders to determine if a particular firm is doing well in managing its risk exposure. This becomes even more challenging in banks where a public safety net exists to ensure financial stability and where banks are subject to close oversight by banking agencies. Compared to many other industries, banks therefore face an additional layer of supervisory constraints on the options they consider in managing risk.

We use our sample of banks to assess whether incentives to take risk, as reflected in ownership stakes in the bank, are related to risk in the manner we hypothesized above. In particular, ownership should motivate hired managers to take on more risk and bring a bank's risk level more closely to that desired by the principal owners. Also, according to financial theory, as a bank owner's wealth becomes more concentrated in his or her bank investment, a more cautious approach to risk taking would be expected. We explore whether this wealth concentration relationship holds for a bank's manager and for a director with the greatest financial incentive to monitor a hired manager.

Measuring Risk in the Sample Banks

To measure bank risk we employ a comprehensive measure of risk called the 'distance to default'. It is based on the probability distribution of the income earned by the bank and is derived by asking the question: How far would income have to fall before the bank would be forced to default on its debt? Specifically, the distance to default is defined as:[16]

$$\frac{\text{capital-to-asset ratio} + \text{average value of return on assets}}{\text{standard deviation of return on assets.}}$$

This number represents the number of standard deviations below the mean that return on assets would have to fall in order to eliminate capital and force the bank to default.[17] The higher the value of this distance to default, the lower a bank's risk. An increase in the capital-to-asset ratio would raise the index, as would an increase in the mean value of operating return on assets, both of which imply less risk. A decrease in the standard deviation of operating return on assets would also raise the index and lower a bank's risk exposure.

As a summary measure of risk, the distance to default encompasses decisions made across the entire banking organization concerning liquidity, credit, interest rates, operations and other matters.[18] The distance to default is of particular importance to stockholders and regulators since bank failure can eliminate a stockholder's investment and expose the bank insurance fund

Corporate governance in banking

to loss. An advantage of this risk measure is that it incorporates three elements of bank risk: fluctuations in income; the overall level of profitability; and capitalization. For example, a bank may have a highly variable income stream, but it could offset some of this risk with higher capital protection or a higher level of average profitability.

Manager Characteristics and Bank Risk

Much of the net worth of owner managers is often tied up in their bank investment. In our sample, the average ratio of the daily managing officer's bank investment to personal net worth is 86 percent in owner-managed banks, and the corresponding value for managers in hired-manager banks is only 21 percent (Table 3.2).[19] If other factors affecting risk were the same, this would suggest that the typical owner manager has much more of his or her livelihood at stake and should be more careful in running the bank than a diversified hired manager would be. And in fact the distance to default for owner-managed banks averages 20.58, somewhat higher than the 18.96 average for hired-manager banks, although this difference is not statistically significant.

To gain a clearer understanding of the numerous factors that affect risk taking, we employ multiple regression analysis. The model equation makes risk a function of several explanatory variables: the manager's ratio of bank investment to personal net worth, the ownership share of the hired manager (when the bank has a hired manager), the ownership share of the owner manager (when the bank has an owner manager), a 'monitor's' ratio of bank investment to personal net worth (for hired-manager banks only),

Table 3.2   Sample averages for the daily managing officer's bank investment/personal net worth and the bank's distance to default*

	Owner-managed banks	Hired-manager banks
Personal net worth (millions)	**$1.719**	**$0.472**
Value of bank investment/ personal net worth	**0.86**	**0.21**
Distance to default	20.58	18.96

Notes: * There are 100 owner-managed banks and 160 hired-manager banks in the sample.
Bold Face indicates a statistically significant difference.

Source: adapted from Sullivan and Spong (1998), Tables 1 and 5.

and some control variables. In this analysis, a 'monitor' is the director who holds the most shares of any board member and is also part of the largest ownership group. This monitor-director thus has the greatest financial incentive of anyone to monitor management and to play a role in deciding appropriate bank risk exposures. The equation also includes variables to account for a bank's location (metropolitan or rural) and its asset size.

This multivariate approach especially helps to distinguish between the effects of ownership and wealth concentration on risk-taking behavior. Although a person's bank stockholdings would enter into both of these variables, the financial implications can be quite different. Increased stock ownership, all else equal, is likely to encourage greater risk taking, given one's increased claim on the returns from successful ventures. However, the more that a person's wealth is concentrated in the bank, the less willing they will be to put this investment at a greater risk.[20]

Estimates suggests that bank stock ownership by hired managers can help to overcome a tendency by them to take on less risk at their banks than would be desired by stockholders. The estimated relation between a hired manager's ownership in his or her bank is plotted by the solid line in Figure 3.2 and shows that distance to default falls considerably (bank risk increases) as hired-manager ownership increases.[21] Figure 3.2 also shows that, for a given change in ownership, the predicted change in the distance to default is larger for hired managers compared to that for owner-manager banks.[22] This result is expected because owner managers already have a significant ownership position in their banks and additional ownership would not provide much incentive to alter bank risk.

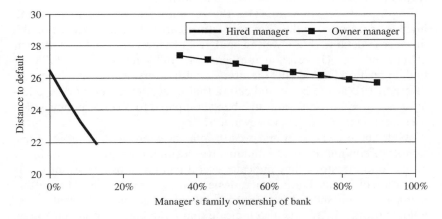

Figure 3.2   Estimated relationship between a bank's distance to default and a manager's family ownership

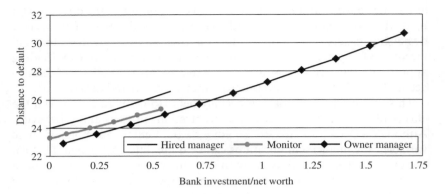

*Figure 3.3   Estimated relationship between a bank's distance to default
             and concentration of wealth in a bank investment*

Estimates also suggest that manager wealth concentration is negatively
related to bank risk. Figure 3.3 plots the estimated relationship and shows
that as a manager's portfolio becomes more highly concentrated in his or
her bank investment, the distance to default rises, meaning a lower level of
bank risk.[23] The effect that wealth concentration has on bank risk, moreover, is economically important and of a similar magnitude to the impact
of changes in managerial ownership (Sullivan and Spong, 2005: 29–31). To
the extent that stockholders and corporate governance researchers regard
ownership structure as a key determinant of firm risk, they should also
regard portfolio effects of comparable importance.

Finally, our research indicates that monitors who have their wealth
highly concentrated in their bank investment are able to increase the bank's
distance to default, thus lowering bank risk to a level more in line with their
own preferences. However, in another work (Sullivan and Spong, 1998) we
find no relation between the monitor's wealth diversification and measures
of credit risk at the bank, indicating that major investors may have less
influence over daily decisions in a bank compared to broader policy issues,
such as capital and aggregate revenue.

While these ownership and wealth influences on risk taking are for a
sample of community banks and involve wealth information not normally
available to investors, they indicate several relationships important to the
operation of banks. For instance, ownership can provide a tool for getting
managers to pursue risk-return trade-offs more in line with what stockholders want. The results also indicate that a manager's approach to risk
taking may be greatly influenced by his or her financial position. Managers
with much of their wealth tied up in their own firms certainly have a strong

incentive to put forth their best effort in running the firm, and this wealth concentration may also manifest itself in a more conservative approach to risk taking.

THE ROLE OF CORPORATE GOVERNANCE IN BANK PERFORMANCE

Banks operate under a wide variety of management and ownership structures, particularly in the case of community banks. Some banks have hired managers and others are managed by individuals with a controlling interest in the bank. Ownership structures can also vary from having just a few owners to having a widely dispersed group of shareholders or being an actively traded company. Other differences range from bank boards with few outside directors to many outsiders and from key stockholders with diversified portfolios to those that have all their financial resources tied up in a bank. The fact that banks continue to operate with such substantial differences and are still competitive indicates that no single 'optimal' governance framework is the answer for all banks. Instead, banks – both small and large – must base their operating structure on the type of investors they are able to attract, the quality of management that is available, and the individuals that are willing to serve as directors.

Within each bank's governance framework, a variety of inherent weaknesses, potential problems and conflicts of interest can exist among the key participants. Financial theory and the results of our research, though, demonstrate a number of steps that stockholders and directors can take to address shortcomings in their ownership and management structure and bring bank performance closer to stockholder and regulatory preferences. These corrective steps largely reflect the critical role that ownership and wealth play in business ventures. One of our key findings is that an ownership stake for hired managers can help improve bank performance and align the interests of managers more closely with that of stockholders, thus reducing the principal-agent problems posited by financial theory.

In a similar manner, we find that boards of directors are likely to have a more positive effect on community bank performance when directors have a significant financial interest in the bank. This financial stake provides a means for directors to benefit directly from their own actions and thereby encourages directors to play a more active role in monitoring management.

We also find that managerial ownership, along with wealth and the financial positions of managers and directors, significantly influences a bank's risk decisions and risk-return trade-offs. While no single risk position is appropriate for all banks and all investors, it is important for shareholders to ensure that their own preferences are reflected in their company's operations. Our results suggest that hired managers with no stock ownership may be reluctant to take on as much risk as other managers, since non-stockholding managers will not directly receive the returns from successful ventures and may be putting their jobs at risk in the event of adverse outcomes. An ownership stake for these managers, though, can help to overcome this risk aversion. Wealth concentration or the portion of assets managers have tied up in their own bank can play a separate and equally significant role in a bank's risk taking and its default risk. Banks in which managers or principal owners and directors have invested much of their own wealth in the business operate with lower risk exposures and have much less chance of default.

Our research indicates that each of these ownership and wealth relationships can have a significant effect on a bank's overall performance, and that banks with management and ownership weaknesses have the potential to improve their operations substantially by addressing these shortcomings. Although some of these ownership and management adjustments may take time, it is important for banks and bank regulators to identify corporate governance problems and decide what corrective steps are needed.

ACKNOWLEDGMENTS

The views expressed in this article are those of the authors and do not necessarily reflect the views of the Federal Reserve Bank of Kansas City or the Federal Reserve System.

NOTES

1. The effect of separating control from corporate ownership and the resulting governance problems have long been recognized in financial theory, with an early recognition of this problem provided in Berle and Means (1932).
2. Alchian and Demsetz (1972) suggest that minority shareholders will rely on major shareholders to perform monitoring functions, particularly since the added returns minority shareholders might receive from monitoring activities may not be spread over enough shares to cover their cost of monitoring. This reasoning suggests that boards of directors may fulfill more of a monitoring role when they have substantial stock ownership in their bank.
3. For studies that look at bank franchise values and their effect on moral hazard and bank risk taking, see Marcus (1984), Keeley (1990), and Demsetz *et al.* (1997).
4. Several studies (Stulz, 1988; Morck *et al.*, 1988; Gorton and Rosen, 1995), though, suggest that there may be a point at which further increases in a hired manager's stock ownership could lead to entrenchment, more severe conflicts with majority owners, and less threat of takeover, thereby contributing to a reduction in firm value.
5. For a more detailed description of these banks, see DeYoung *et al.* (2001). Our bank sample consisted of nearly 270 state-chartered banks after we removed a handful of

banks because of missing data or significant changes in management or ownership during the time of the study.

6. See Alchian and Demsetz (1972) for a discussion of the monitoring role in a firm and the incentives for better monitoring provided by ownership.

7. Under this combined test, banks in the 'most efficient' group had to be in the upper quartile of Tenth Federal Reserve District banks on a cost efficiency test and in the upper half on their adjusted return on assets. The 'least efficient' banks ranked in the bottom quartile on cost efficiency and the lower half on adjusted return on assets. The cost efficiency model used in this analysis relates a bank's costs (interest plus noninterest expenses) to the major outputs it produces, the prices it faces for various inputs, bank risk factors, market conditions and a cost residual to capture bank cost inefficiences. The adjusted return on assets test was added to measure whether the expenditures in a bank lead to profitable results. For more on this, see Spong *et al.* (1995).

8. Outside directors are defined here as directors that have less than a 5 percent ownership stake in the bank, are not current or former employees of the bank, and are not related to anyone that either is in a management position in the bank or has at least a 5 percent ownership position in the institution.

9. For more on this model, see DeYoung *et al.* (2001).

10. Market-based performance measures, such as stock returns, could not be used in this analysis because only a few of the sample banks were in organizations that had actively traded stock.

11. The estimated equation is presented in Appendix Table 3.A1.

12. Figure 3.1 is based on the estimated equation presented in Appendix Table 3.A1, with continuous independent variables set to the means of hired-manager banks for hired managers and to the means of owner-manager banks for owner-managers.

13. This result is based on the calculation $28\% = (77 - 68)/(100 - 68)$.

14. In our sample, only ten of 55 hired managers with nonzero family ownership had a stake greater than 17 percent.

15. In DeYoung *et al.* (2001), we find that salaries and bonuses are significantly higher for owner managers in our sample banks, thus lending support to this idea of tax avoidance behavior on their part.

16. The distance to default is derived from the probability of bankruptcy $P\{\pi < -K\}$, where $\pi =$ earnings and $K =$ equity capital. Let $A =$ total assets, $\mu = E(\pi/A) =$ mean return on assets, and $\sigma =$ standard deviation of return on assets. Then, assuming earnings has a normal distribution, $P\{\pi < -K\} = P\{\pi/A < -K/A\} = P\{Z < [(-K/A) - \mu]/\sigma\}$, where Z has the standard normal distribution. The distance to default is defined as $[(K/A) + \mu]/\sigma$.

17. Our research uses operating income (income before taxes and extraordinary items) to calculate return on assets in order to focus more closely on risk in bank operations.

18. See Sullivan and Spong (1998) for analysis of risk measures that address credit risk (the loan-to-asset ratio, loan losses, and past due loans), financial risk (the equity-to-asset ratio, the fixed-to-total asset ratio, non-core funding), and interest rate risk. Previous results are consistent with what we report here and can provide some insight into the mechanisms with which management and ownership control the distance to default.

19. Table 3.2 may overstate the extent of concentration of financial wealth in the manager's bank investment because our measure of bank investment does not adjust for any underlying debt the manager or the holding company may have used to purchase the bank.

20. The estimated equation is presented in Appendix Table 3.A2.

21. Figure 3.2 is adapted from Sullivan and Spong (2005, Fig. 3). Regression estimates, shown in Appendix Table 3.A1, are used in these calculations. To illustrate common experience, the range of a manager's family ownership of a bank is limited to the mean plus and minus one standard deviation. Other continuous independent variables are set to the means of hired-manager banks for hired managers and to the means of owner-manager banks for owner managers.

22. In fact, we do not find a statistically significant relation between an owner manager's stockholdings and bank risk.

23. Figure 3.3 is adapted from Sullivan and Spong (2005, Fig. 2). Regression estimates, shown in Appendix Table 3.A2, are used in these calculations. To illustrate common experience, the range of a manager's bank investment/net worth is limited to the mean plus and minus one standard deviation. Other continuous independent variables are set to the means of hired-manager banks for hired managers and to the means of owner-manager banks for owner managers.

The estimation technique assumes that bank risk for both hired managers and owner managers responds similarly for given changes in the portion of a manager's wealth that is concentrated in his or her bank investment. In Figure 3.3 this causes the slope of the estimated relation for each of these types of managers to be the same. However, the level of risk between hired-manager and owner-manager banks in Figure 3.3 is different as shown by the fact that the hired-manager relationship begins slightly above that for owner managers. This gap in Figure 3.3 arises because the mean values for other variables in the regression equation differ for hired-manager and owner-manager banks. If these variables are set to the same level for both hired- and owner-manager banks, the gap depicted in Figure 3.3 would close.

REFERENCES

Alchian, A. and H. Demsetz (1972), 'Production, information costs, and economic organization,' *American Economic Review*, **62**, 777–95.

Allen, L. and A. S. Cebenoyan (1991), 'Bank acquisitions and ownership structure: theory and evidence,' *Journal of Banking and Finance*, **15**, 425–48.

Anderson, R. C. and D. R. Fraser (2000), 'Corporate control, bank risk taking, and the health of the banking industry,' *Journal of Banking and Finance*, **24**, 1383–98.

Berle, A. and G. Means (1932), *The Modern Corporation and Private Property*, New York: Macmillan.

Brewer, E. III and M. R. Saidenberg (1996), 'Franchise value, ownership structure, and risk at savings institutions,' Federal Reserve Bank of New York research paper 9632.

Cannela, A., D. Fraser and D. Lee (1995), 'Firm failure and managerial labor markets: evidence from Texas banking,' *Journal of Financial Economics*, **38**, 185–210.

Cebenoyan, A. S., E. S. Cooperman and C. A. Register (1999), 'Ownership structure, charter value and risk-taking behavior for thrifts,' *Financial Management*, **28**, 43–60.

Chen, C. R., T. L. Steiner and A. M. Whyte (1998), 'Risk-taking behavior and management ownership in depository institutions,' *The Journal of Financial Research*, **21**, 1–16.

Cole, R. A. and H. Mehran (1996), 'The effect of changes in ownership structure on performance: evidence from the thrift industry,' Board of Governors of the Federal Reserve System finance and economics discussion series 96-6.

Demsetz, R. S. and P. E. Strahan (1997), 'Diversification, size, and risk at bank holding companies,' *Journal of Money, Credit and Banking*, **29**, 300–13.

Demsetz, R. S., M. R. Saidenberg and P. E. Strahan (1996), 'Banks with something to lose: the disciplinary role of franchise value,' *Federal Reserve Bank of New York Economic Policy Review* (October), pp. 1–14.

Demsetz, R. S., M. R. Saidenberg and P. E. Strahan (1997), 'Agency problems and risk taking at banks,' Federal Reserve Bank of New York staff report no. 29.

DeYoung, R., K. Spong and R. J. Sullivan (2001), 'Who's minding the store? Motivating and monitoring hired managers at small, closely held commercial banks,' *Journal of Banking and Finance*, **25**(7), 1209–43.

Fama, E. (1980), 'Agency problems and the theory of the firm,' *Journal of Political Economy*, **88**, 288–307.

Glassman, C. A. and S. A. Rhoades (1980), 'Owner vs manager control effects on bank performance,' *The Review of Economics and Statistics*, **62**, 263–70.

Gorton, G. and R. Rosen (1995), 'Corporate control, portfolio choice, and the decline of banking,' *The Journal of Finance*, **50**, 1377–420.

Jensen, M. and W. Meckling (1976), 'Theory of the firm: managerial behavior, agency costs, and ownership structure,' *Journal of Financial Economics*, **3**, 305–60.

Keeley, M. C. (1990), 'Deposit insurance, risk and market power in banking,' *American Economic Review*, **80**, 1183–200.

Knopf, J. D. and J. L. Teall (1996), 'Risk-taking behavior in the US thrift industry: ownership structure and regulatory changes,' *Journal of Banking and Finance*, **20**, 1329–50.

Marcus, A. J. (1984), 'Deregulation and bank financial policy,' *Journal of Banking and Finance*, **8**, 557–65.

Merton, R. (1977), 'An analytical derivation of the cost of deposit insurance loan guarantees,' *Journal of Banking and Finance*, **1**, 3–11.

Morck, R., A. Schleifer and R. W. Vishny (1988), 'Management ownership and market valuation: an empirical analysis,' *Journal of Financial Economics*, **20**, 293–315.

Parrino, R., A. M. Poteshman and M. S. Weisbach (2002), 'Measuring investment distortions when risk-averse managers decide whether to undertake risky projects,' *Financial Management*, **34**, 21–60.

Saunders, A., E. Strock and N. Travlos (1990), 'Ownership structure, deregulation, and bank risk taking,' *Journal of Finance*, **45**, 643–54.

Spong, K., R. J. Sullivan and R. DeYoung (1995), 'What makes a bank efficient? – a look at financial characteristics and management and ownership structure,' *Federal Reserve Bank of Kansas City Financial Industry Perspectives*, (December), pp. 1–19.

Stulz, R. M. (1988), 'On takeover resistance, managerial discretion, and shareholder wealth,' *Journal of Financial Economics*, **20**, 25–54.

Sullivan, R. J. and K. R. Spong (1998), 'How does ownership structure and manager wealth influence risk? A look at ownership structure, manager wealth, and risk in commercial banks,' *Federal Reserve Bank of Kansas City Financial Industry Perspectives*, (December), pp. 15–40.

Sullivan, R. J. and K. R. Spong (2005), 'Managerial wealth, ownership structure, and risk in commercial banks,' Federal Reserve Bank of Kansas City working paper, accessed at http://ssrn.com/ abstract=558684.

APPENDIX

Table 3.A1   Regression analysis of profit efficiency on ownership and management variables

Independent variable	Dependent variable: Profit efficiency index
Manager's personal plus family ownership share	0.0766
	(0.2402)
Manager's personal plus family ownership share^2	−0.1235
	(0.1959)
Hired-manager indicator variable	−0.0046
	(0.0670)
Hired-manager indicator variable* Manager's personal plus family ownership share	1.0159**
	(0.4647)
Hired-manager indicator variable* Manager's personal plus family ownership share^2	−3.0975***
	(1.124)
Metropolitan indicator variable	−0.0311
	(0.0216)
Log (total assets)	0.1827***
	(0.0111)
Multi-bank holding company indicator variable	−0.0269
	(0.0251)
Lead bank of a multi-bank holding company indicator variable	−0.0368*
	(0.0202)
Constant term	−1.283***
	(0.143)
R^2	0.5582
n	266

Note: Standard errors are displayed below coefficient estimates in parentheses. ***, **, and * indicate a significant difference from zero at the 1, 5, and 10 percent levels. Not shown are estimated coefficients for indicator variables for membership in holding companies that had more than one subsidiary bank in the sample.

Source: DeYoung *et al.* (2001), Table 5, regression (7).

Table 3.A2   *Regression analysis of distance to default on wealth and ownership variables*

Independent variable	Dependent variable: Log [distance to default]
Manager's bank investment/net worth	0.1820***
	(0.0600)
Monitor's bank investment/net worth	0.1657***
	(0.0629)
Personal plus family ownership share of hired manager	−1.5121***
	(0.4802)
Personal plus family ownership share of owner manager	−0.1248
	(0.1450)
Fixed assets/total assets	−9.2680***
	(3.593)
Metropolitan indicator variable	−0.2156**
	(0.1021)
Log (total assets)	0.2217***
	(0.0504)
Constant term	2.4340***
	(0.1840)
R^2	0.1530
n	267

Note: Standard errors are displayed below coefficient estimates in parentheses. ***, **, and * indicate a significant difference from zero at the 1, 5, and 10 percent levels.

Source: Sullivan and Spong (2005), Table 4, regression (5).

4. Corporate governance at community banks: one size does not fit all

Robert DeYoung

The corporate form of organization is one of the cornerstones of market capitalism. Business firms with good investment opportunities can access the necessary growth capital from household savers, and household savers can own (portions of) these business firms with the protection of limited liability. While this set-up yields tremendous economic efficiencies, it contains a seed of inefficiency as well. The shareholders obviously want the highest possible return on their investment, but as absentee owners they are in a poor position to observe how well the business is being run. To achieve some amount of control over the business, the owners select from among themselves a corporate board of directors to represent shareholder interests. The most important task for the directors is to hire professional managers to run the firm in a manner that maximizes the shareholders' investment. While this framework solves the owners' most immediate problem, it also gives rise to two fundamental 'corporate governance' problems: what is the best way for directors to motivate managers to maximize the value of the business, and what is the best way to motivate the directors to see that this is done?

Unfortunately, there is no generally agreed-upon set of 'best practices' for good corporate governance. The optimal combination of base salary, stock grants, stock options, and other forms of executive compensation is a greatly debated issue. Less debated, but perhaps no less important, are the incentives facing the board of directors – for example, what is the best size and composition for the board, the amount and form of director pay, limits on the number of boards on which directors can serve, or the degree to which directors are protected from law suits? To make the situation even more complicated, best practice corporate governance solutions are likely to differ for different types of business, depending on the organizational, ownership, legal, and informational environment surrounding the firm. Another way of saying this is that one size does not fit all firms when it comes to corporate governance.

This chapter explores whether standard corporate governance practices affect the financial performance of some community banks differently from others. Corporate organizational structures vary greater within the community banking industry. Some community banks are independent, while some are affiliates in multi-bank holding companies. Most community banks are privately held, although an increasing number are publicly traded. Some community banks are family-owned and family-managed, others are closely held but have hired professional 'outside' managers, while some are widely held with truly absentee ownership. A substantial minority of community banks are organized as Subchapter S corporations and pay no corporate taxes. Because of these and other differences, it is likely that some corporate governance practices will be relatively effective at some community banks, but relatively ineffective at others.

The emphasis here is on 115 community banks in the Midwest United States. A database of corporate governance practices and financial performance was originally constructed for these banks and analyzed in a staff study performed at the Federal Reserve Bank of Chicago (Robert DeYoung *et al.*, 2005). That study found that financial performance was somewhat better at community banks that stressed: (a) bonus pay for their top manager; (b) pay-per-meeting contracts for their directors; and (c) management succession planning, and was somewhat worse at community banks where (d) a large share of the top manager's wealth was invested in bank stock. I review the results of the original study below, and report those findings in greater statistical detail. I then extend the results of the original study by testing whether the impact of these four corporate governance practices on bank performance was different depending on the organizational structure of the banks. In particular, I compare these financial performance effects at small, closely held community banks organized as Subchapter S corporations versus these financial performance effects at larger, publicly traded community banks.

A VARIETY OF GOVERNANCE ENVIRONMENTS AT COMMUNITY BANKS

Over 90 percent of the commercial banks in the US can be described as 'community banks'. There is no strict definition for a community bank: typically, analysts simply define community banks as commercial banks with assets less than $1 billion or $2 billion.[1] Community banking companies almost always have a local geographic focus, and make 'relationship loans' to small businesses based on their superior knowledge of local business conditions. The corporate governance environment can vary tremendously across community banks. For example, the prototypical community bank is closely held and owner-operated – that is, the top managers and their families hold the controlling interest in the bank – and in these banks there is less scope for conflicts of interest between management and stockholders because these two sets of people largely overlap.[2] In other words, the owners need not rely on a board of directors to monitor the managers. At the other extreme, some community banks are affiliates in publicly traded, multi-bank holding companies. These banks are larger and can be quite widely held, and are run by professional managers with a relatively low ownership stake. At these companies, shareholders rely heavily on a board of directors to monitor the managers.

In addition to relying on bank directors to act as their 'agent' in overseeing the performance of bank management, shareholders often receive a stream of information from other sources that helps them learn how well the bank is being run. For publicly traded community banks, variations in the price of the bank's stock inform the owners about the performance of the bank. For smaller, closely held community banks, shareholders often receive information about the performance of the bank through changes in their dividend checks – and this is especially the case at banks organized as Subchapter S corporations. A bank organized as an 'S Corp' pays no taxes at the corporate level, so long as it has no more than 100 shareholders and it pays out a large portion of its earnings to shareholders as dividends. In both cases, the challenge facing directors is to design a set of managerial incentives that encourages managers to run the bank in a manner that maximizes the value of the shareholders' investment in the bank, and that disciplines managers when they act otherwise.

Figure 4.1 offers a stylized depiction of these differences in corporate governance environments. Moving from left-to-right, the number of shareholders increases, and hence the typical shareholder – who owns an

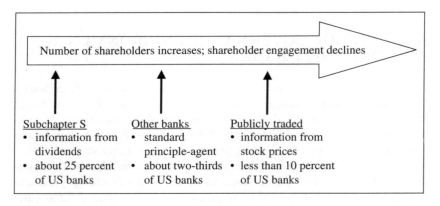

Figure 4.1   Governance environments in banks

increasingly smaller portion of the bank – has less incentive to be actively engaged in monitoring the performance of bank managers. Approximately one quarter of commercial banks in the US are organized as Subchapter S corporations: these firms have only a few shareholders, many of which hold non-trivial stakes in the bank and, thus, are likely to be engaged owners rather than disinterested owners. Less than 10 percent of US commercial banks are publicly traded or affiliates in publicly traded companies: these firms have many shareholders, most (or all) of which hold only trivial stakes in the bank and, thus, are likely to be disinterested owners rather than engaged owners.

To be sure, directors face different incentive problems in these two extreme cases. At the extremes, shareholders receive more frequent and reliable information flows – periodic dividend checks for S Corps, and daily stock prices for traded banks – and these information flows arguably reduce the principle-agent problem and may help bank directors do their job. This is in contrast to the 'normal' community banks located at the center of Figure 4.1, for which agency problems may be more difficult: these banks have a larger number of (presumably disengaged) shareholders, and these shareholders observe less information about bank/manager performance. Thus, best corporate governance practices for disciplining managers at these banks are likely to be different from those for S Corps and traded banks. The purpose of the analysis performed in this chapter is to reveal some of those differences.

THE ORIGINAL STUDY

One key objective of the original Chicago Fed study was to construct a database to describe the corporate governance environment at community banks. The data analyzed here were constructed from previous bank examination records, internal supervisory databases, interviews with bank managers, and internal bank documents. Because the survey was taken during late 2003 and early 2004, the database provides a good representation of the corporate governance environment present at each bank prior to 2004. Banks were included in the database only if they were headquartered in the Seventh Federal Reserve District,[3] were state chartered, were members of the Federal Reserve System, and could arguably be considered to be community banks based on their size and product mix.[4] Any bank that sustained a material change in control or top management between 2001 and 2004, as well as any bank for which information was substantially incomplete, was excluded from the data. This left 115 banks in the database, out of a possible 185 community banks in the Seventh District in 2004. These data were then combined with financial statement information from standing regulatory databases, such as the Federal Deposit Insurance Corporation's *Reports of Income and Condition*, also known as the 'call reports'.

The top panels in Table 4.1 describe the size, financial performance and organizational details of the sample banks based on financial data from 2004. The average bank had about $250 million in assets, but size ranged widely from about $10 million to as much as $3 billion. Bank profits also varied substantially: return on assets (ROA) averaged 1.06 percent and ranged from −0.26 percent to 2.55 percent, while return on equity (ROE) averaged 10.89 percent and ranged from −2.69 percent to 25.68 percent. A substantial minority of banks were located in urban markets (39.3 percent), and/or were organized as Subchapter S corporations (31.3 percent). Smaller percentages were affiliated with multi-bank holding companies (MBHCs), were newly chartered 'de novo' banks less than ten years old, and/or were publicly traded corporations.

Table 4.1 also displays information on the corporate governance environment for average community bank in the sample. The daily managing officer (DMO) is responsible for making the day-to-day operating decisions; this person is usually the president or chief executive officer (CEO) of the bank.[5] The typical DMO owned 10.7 percent of the bank's stock, and this ownership stake accounted for 39.6 percent of the DMO's personal wealth. An additional 13.9 percent of the average bank was owned by the DMO's immediate family members – a clear illustration of the closely held, owner-operator environment at most community banks – while large shareholders (holdings greater than 5 percent) who were unrelated to the DMO's family held a 14 percent stake. Overall, members of the board of directors (including the DMO and his or her family) held a 40.4 percent stake at the average bank. In addition, 14.8 percent of the banks had employee stock ownership plans (ESOPs).

The typical DMO had been at the job for over 11 years and received a $146 000 base salary with a $39 000 cash bonus. About 43 percent of the DMOs had contractual incentives linking their pay to the financial performance of the bank, while 22.1 percent and 11.3 percent had received stock options and stock grants, respectively, during the past four years. The DMO was a 'hired manager' at 41.2 percent of the banks, which we define as a DMO with less than a 1 percent ownership stake in the bank.

Outside directors (that is, non-managers) made up about 63 percent of the board of directors. The typical director was about 59 years old and sat on the board for over 14 years. On average, directors received $2724 in lump sum pay (as opposed to per-meeting pay) each year, $418 per board meeting attended, and attended 92.7 percent of the scheduled meetings. Only about one-quarter of these boards ever met without the DMO being present.

Table 4.1   *Mean values for 115 state-chartered, Federal Reserve-member community banks in the Seventh Federal Reserve District*

Profitability (2004)	
ROA	1.06%
ROE	10.89%
Other bank characteristics (2003)	
Assets	$251.4 million
Less than 10 years old	12.0%
Subchapter S corporation	31.3%
Non-lead affiliate in MBHC	12.8%
Urban market	39.3%
Publicly traded	10.4%
Corporation governance characteristics (2003)	
Bank Ownership	
DMO ownership stake	10.7%
DMO ownership as % of personal wealth	39.6%
DMO family ownership stake	24.6%
Board of directors ownership stake	40.4%
Large block (>5%) non-DMO family stake	14.0%
Banks with employee stock ownership plans	14.8%
DMO status and pay	
Hired DMO (<1% ownership stake)	41.2%
DMO tenure	11.4 years
Formal succession plan in place	54.0%
DMO base pay	$146 340
DMO bonus pay	$39 110
DMO contract contains incentives	43.2%
DMO received stock options	22.1%
DMO received stock grants	11.3%
Director status and pay	
Outside directors (%)	62.6%
Director age	59.1 years
Director tenure	14.5 years
Director pay (lump sum)	$2724
Director pay (per meeting)	$418
Director attendance	92.7%
Board sometimes meets without DMO	25.4%
Mandatory director training	21.4%
Limits on number of other boards	2.9%

Source: DeYoung *et al.* (2005).

Finally, only about 21 percent of the banks required mandatory training for their directors, and only about 3 percent of the banks limited the number of other boards upon which their directors could sit.

A second key objective of the original study was to determine whether and how corporate governance practices influence the financial performance of community banks – and from those findings begin to identify a set of corporate governance 'best-practices' for community banks. The study used a series of multiple regression analyses to test whether any of the corporate governance characteristics observed at community banks in 2003 were statistically related to the ROA or ROE earned by community banks in 2004.

The first regression tests build a 'baseline' model to explain the general variation in ROA and ROE across the 115 banks in the data sample, using variables that are well-known to impact bank profitability:

$$\text{ROA or ROE} = \alpha + \beta_1 * \ln ASSETS + \beta_2 * AFFILIATE + \beta_3 * DENOVO$$
$$+ \beta_4 * URBAN + \beta_5 * SCORP + \beta_1 * PUBLIC + \varepsilon \qquad (4.1)$$

where $\ln ASSETS$ is the natural log of bank asset size, $AFFILIATE$ is a dummy variable equal to one for banks that were non-lead affiliates in multi-bank holding companies, $DENOVO$ is a dummy variable equal to one for banks that were less than five years old, $URBAN$ is a dummy variable equal to 1 for banks located in Metropolitan Statistical Areas (MSAs), $SCORP$ is a dummy variable equal to 1 for banks organized as Sub-chapter S corporations, and $PUBLIC$ is a dummy variable equal to 1 for banks with stock that is publicly traded. All of these right-hand side variables were observed at year-end 2003, while ROA and ROE were observed at year-end 2004.[6] The average values for all of these regression variables can be found in Table 4.1. Since ordinary least squares (OLS) techniques were used to estimate the regressions, the disturbance term ε is assumed to be normally distributed with an expected value of zero.

The first two columns in Table 4.2 display the results of the baseline regressions. The six bank characteristics on the right-hand side of the model explain about 32 percent of the variation in ROA across banks and about 40 percent of the variation in ROE. Bank profitability was positively and statistically significantly related to bank size, Subchapter S status, and MBHC affiliation, and negatively and statistically significantly related to de novo status, urban location, and publicly traded status. The positive effect of bank size ($\ln ASSETS$) on profitability reflects the presence of scale economies for community banks. The positive effect of Subchapter S status ($SCORP$) on profitability is merely an artifact of tax law, and reflects the fact that net income at S Corporations is higher because these firms do not pay taxes at the corporate level. The positive effect of non-lead affiliate

Table 4.2   *Detailed results from the baseline regressions (Equation 4.1)*
and the governance regressions (Equation 4.2) originally
performed for, but not reported in, DeYoung et al. (2005)

Equation: Dependent variable:	4.1 ROA	4.1 ROE	4.2 ROA	4.2 ROE
Intercept	−0.0052	−0.1197*	−0.0037	−0.1003*
	(0.0039)	(0.0424)	(0.0039)	(0.0413)
ln*ASSETS*	0.0014*	0.0189*	0.0012*	0.0171*
	(0.0003)	(0.0037)	(0.0003)	(0.0035)
SCORP	0.0021*	0.0398*	0.0017*	0.0353*
	(0.0006)	(0.0069)	(0.0006)	(0.0068)
DENOVO	−0.0037*	−0.0359*	−0.0036*	−0.0325*
	(0.0009)	(0.0098)	(0.0009)	(0.0094)
PUBLIC	−0.0031*	−0.0327*	−0.0031*	−0.0322*
	(0.0011)	(0.0122)	(0.0011)	(0.0117)
AFFILIATE	0.0012	0.0193*	0.0009	0.0127
	(0.0009)	(0.0097)	(0.0009)	(0.0095)
URBAN	−0.0011*	−0.0030	−0.0008	−0.0003
	(0.0006)	(0.0070)	(0.0006)	(0.0068)
WEALTH_IN_BANK			−0.0003	−0.0167*
			(0.0010)	(0.0102)
DIR_LUMPSUM			−0.0226*	−0.2177*
			(0.0110)	(0.1171)
SUCCESSION_PLAN			0.0014*	0.0123*
			(0.0006)	(0.0061)
DMO_BONUS			0.0021*	0.0276*
			(0.0012)	(0.0123)
Adjusted *R*-square	0.2943	0.3887	0.3791	0.4574

Note: The superscript * indicates that the coefficient estimate is statistically different from
zero at the 10 percent level of significance or better. Coefficient estimates appear above
parenthetical standard errors.

status (*AFFILIATE*) on profitability likely occurs because the lead bank
in the holding company absorbs a disproportionate share of the cost of
providing administrative services. The negative effect of de novo status
(*DENOVO*) indicates that banks earn lower profits during their formative
years. The negative effect of urban location (*URBAN*) reflects the higher
degree of competition faced by banks that operate in cities (as opposed to
banks that operate in rural towns, which often face only a few competitors).
The negative effect of publicly traded status (*PUBLIC*) is somewhat surprising given that publicly traded firms arguably face greater pressure to

perform well – this may reflect idiosyncrasies among the small number (12) of publicly traded banks in our sample, or may indicate that publicly traded firms concentrate on maximizing stock returns rather than accounting performance.

Once the baseline regression models were established, the original study tested whether the corporate governance characteristics observed in 2003 helped further explain the differences in ROA and ROE across community banks in 2004. As reported in the original study, only six of the 23 corporate governance characteristics displayed in Table 4.1 were statistically related to ROA or ROE when added one-at-a-time to the baseline regression equations. Moreover, when these six characteristics were added simultaneously to the baseline regression equations, only four – DMO bonus pay, DMO ownership as a share of personal wealth, director lump sum pay, and formal succession plan – retained their statistical significance. This method resulted in the following 'governance' regression model:

$$\text{ROA or ROE} = \alpha + \beta_1 * \ln ASSETS + \beta_2 * AFFILIATE$$
$$+ \beta_3 * DENOVO + \beta_4 * URBAN + \beta_5 * SCORP$$
$$+ \beta_1 * PUBLIC + \gamma_1 * DMO\_BONUS$$
$$+ \gamma_2 * DIR\_LUMPSUM$$
$$+ \gamma_3 * SUCCESSION\_PLAN$$
$$+ \gamma_4 * WEALTH\_IN\_BANK + \varepsilon \qquad (4.2)$$

where *DMO_BONUS* is the daily managing officer's annual cash bonus as a percentage of his total annual pay (salary plus bonus), *DIR_LUMPSUM* is the percentage of directors' annual pay that is fixed (rather than per-meeting fees), *SUCCESSION_PLAN* is a dummy variable equal to 1 if a formal succession plan is in place, and *WEALTH_IN_BANK* is the percentage of the DMO's personal wealth that is invested in bank stock.

The results of these governance regressions are displayed in the last two columns of Table 4.2. Together, the four corporate governance measures explained an additional 11 percent of the variation in ROA across banks and an additional 10 percent of the variation in ROE. Moreover, all four measures are related to community bank profits in the manner predicted by various theories of corporate governance or best supervisory practices.

Based on calculations using the information reported in Tables 4.1 and 4.2, profitability was about 13 percent higher in terms of ROA (that is, 1.20 percent instead of 1.06 percent) at community banks with formal management succession plans in place, and about 11 percent higher in terms of ROE (that is, 12.09 percent instead of 10.89 percent).[7] Succession planning is recognized as a good corporate governance practice in all industries, and bank supervisors strongly advocate that banks have such plans in place. While the mere existence of such a plan is unlikely to enhance profits, this result likely indicates that forward-looking banks that are attentive to this managerial best practice are likely to be attentive to other profit-enhancing controls and managerial best practices as well.

The results also suggested that banks perform better when their managers and directors face the proper monetary incentives. Paying managers bonuses (as opposed to straight salary) is associated with higher profitability. According to the regression estimates, a 10 percent increase in DMO bonus pay is associated with about a 0.4 percent improvement in bank ROA and a 0.5 percent improvement in bank ROE.[8] The results also suggested that bank directors respond to monetary incentives, albeit unfavorably in this case: a 10 percent increase in lump sum director compensation is associated with about a 0.5 percent reduction in both ROA and ROE, an indication that rewarding directors regardless of their efforts may result in less active monitoring of bank management. Finally, a 10 percent increase in the share of the DMO's personal wealth that is invested in the bank is associated with a 0.7 percent decrease in a bank's ROE, but is unrelated to a bank's ROA. The most likely explanation for these results is managerial risk aversion, that is, DMOs invested heavily in bank stock operate their banks with larger-than-optimal equity capital cushions in order to hedge their own personal (non-diversified) financial position. Although this leaves ROA unchanged, it not only reduces the return on investment earned by the other stockholders, but it also constrains the bank's growth opportunities.

Although some of these ROA and ROE effects are relatively small, note that these effects are not mutually exclusive. Making several of these corporate governance adjustments simultaneously would, arguably, result in larger improvements in profitability. For example, increasing the DMO's cash bonus by 10 percent and decreasing the lump sum portion of directors' fees by 10 percent could generate as much as a 1.0 percent improvement in ROE (0.5 percent plus 0.5 percent).

EXTENDING THE ORIGINAL STUDY

The original study generated some interesting results about the financial impact of governance conditions and practices at community banks – results that agree with existing theories and anecdotes about incentive structures facing bank managers and bank directors. In addition, the original study showed that these governance practices had an economically meaningful relationship with bank financial performance – that is, the incentive structures placed in front of bank managers and directors appeared to make a substantial financial difference, on average.

Although the original study did control for the performance effects of (a) Subchapter S organizational form and (b) publicly traded corporate status, the study did not test whether corporate governance worked differently at banks with these two organizational features. That is, the study did not consider whether CEO bonus pay, per-meeting director fees, formal management succession planning, and CEO wealth exposure affected financial performance at S Corps and publicly traded banks differently than at other banks; as discussed above, the informational environments and levels of stockholder engagement at these banks can be quite different from at a typical community bank.

To test for these possibilities, I created a third regression specification that included two interactive dummy variables:

$$\begin{aligned} ROA \text{ or } ROE = \alpha &+ \beta_1 * \ln ASSETS + \beta_2 * AFFILIATE \\ &+ \beta_3 * DENOVO + \beta_4 * URBAN + \beta_5 * SCORP \\ &+ \beta_1 * PUBLIC + \lambda_1 * GOVERNANCE \\ &+ \lambda_2 * GOVERNANCE * ORGANIZATION + \varepsilon \quad (4.3) \end{aligned}$$

where, in alternative regressions, *ORGANIZATION* takes the value of either *SCORP* or *PUBLIC*, and *GOVERNANCE* takes the value of either *DMO_BONUS*, *DIR_LUMPSUM*, *SUCCESSION_PLAN*, and *WEALTH_IN_BANK*. For example, the estimated result reported in the first (upper right-hand) cell in Table 4.3 comes from a regression in which *ORGANIZATION* takes the value of *SCORP*, and *GOVERNANCE* takes the value of *WEALTH_IN_BANK*. For that regression, the sum of the coefficients $\lambda_1 + \lambda_2$ (which equals -0.0018) is the estimated marginal effect of *WEALTH_IN_BANK* on ROA for banks organized as Subchapter S corporations. (Note: The coefficient λ_1 alone would represent the estimated marginal effect of *WEALTH_IN_BANK* on ROA for banks that are *not* organized as Subchapter S corporations.) The various cells in Table 4.3 report the estimated marginal effects of the four governance conditions on ROA and ROE for both S Corp banks (in the first column) and publicly traded banks (in the second column), and compares them to the marginal effects from the 'average' bank from the full sample (in the third column, repeated from Table 4.2).

The results of these regressions suggest that corporate governance practices work differently at different types of community banks. For the full sample of banks, the original study suggested that managers with large

Table 4.3 *Estimated marginal relationships between corporate governance practices and financial performance*

Regression specification: Estimated marginal effect for:	Equation 4.3 Subchapter S banks	Equation 4.3 Publicly traded banks	Equation 4.2 'average' bank (repeated from Table 4.2 above)
Dependent variable is ROA			
DMO wealth in bank stock (%)	−0.0018	−0.0032	−0.0003
Director fees lump sum (%)	0.0000	−0.0000003*	−0.0266*
Management succession plan?	0.0018*	0.0015	0.0014*
DMO pay as cash bonus (%)	0.0044*	−0.0108	0.0021*
Dependent variable is ROE			
DMO wealth in bank stock (%)	−0.0263	−0.0403	−0.0167*
Director fees lump sum (%)	0.0000	−0.000004*	−0.2177*
Management succession plan?	0.0149*	0.0091	0.0123*
DMO pay as cash bonus (%)	0.0448*	0.0776	0.0276*

Note: The superscript * indicates that the coefficient estimate is statistically different from zero at the 10 percent level of significance or better.

amounts of their wealth invested in the bank ran the bank in a relatively more risk-averse fashion, chiefly by holding high levels of capital. The Equation 4.3 regressions reveal no systematic evidence of risk-averse managerial behavior for either subchapter S banks or for publicly traded banks. This suggests that these alternative organizational forms provided shareholders additional information about firm performance (for example, dividend streams at S Corp banks, stock price movements at traded banks) and/or the level of shareholder engagement (for example, high level of engagement at S Corps which relies less on directors to serve as agents for shareholders, low level of engagement at traded banks which relies heavily on directors to serve as agents for shareholders) combine to discipline heavily invested managers.

In the original study, banks that paid high lump sum directors' fees (as opposed to per-meeting fees) performed poorly, which implies that these bank directors were not given efficient incentives. Equation 4.3 regressions reveal no relationship between director fees and performance at S Corp banks. Because S Corp banks are closely held, directors tend to have substantial ownership stakes, and the returns to these shareholdings will overwhelm income from their director fees. While director pay does seem to matter for publicly traded community banks, the magnitude of the marginal effect is tiny. Evidently, incentivizing bank directors with per-meeting fees may be a useful corporate governance tool at the typical community bank, but director effort is not very responsive to this practice at larger, publicly traded community banks.

Having a formal management succession plan in place was a significant indicator of strong financial performance in the original study, and this is also a significant indicator of strong financial performance for S Corp banks. However, management succession plans are statistically unimportant at publicly traded community banks. This is not surprising: at small, closely held community banks, the successor to the DMO is likely to be chosen from within one or several families, and not having a management succession plan in place could indicate discord within or across ownership families that is hurting the financial performance of the bank. At a publicly traded bank, the successor to the DMO is more likely to be chosen externally from the labor pool of experienced, professional financial managers.

Finally, paying the DMO with large bonuses (as opposed to large fixed salary) was a significant indicator of strong financial performance for the typical bank in the original study, and this appears to be an even stronger performance indicator for S Corp banks, where the marginal impact is about twice as large (for example, 0.0044 versus 0.0021 in the ROA regressions). In contrast, there is no statistical relationship between managerial bonuses and bank performance for the publicly traded banks. Again, this is no surprise: cash bonuses are relatively more valuable to S Corp managers because the market for selling stock is very illiquid, while cash bonuses are relatively less valuable to managers of publicly traded banks because their stock can be sold into liquid markets.

CONCLUSIONS

The findings presented here provide a useful extension to previous work performed at the Chicago Fed (DeYoung *et al.*, 2005). The findings conform with the sensible conjecture that best practices corporate governance programs should vary in design from bank-to-bank, depending on the organization, informational environment, tax status, ownership structure, and other characteristics of banking companies. Of course, these findings are suggestive and not definitive, because they are derived from a small set of community banking companies using a single year of data. Also note that all of the corporate governance results presented here – from the original study and from the extension performed here – are derived from firms that have an additional outside monitor not present at most other corporations: federal and state bank supervisors. Bank supervisors regularly review banks for financial safety and soundness, internal controls, auditing policies, and compliance with numerous financial regulations. In their role as outside monitors, state and federal bank supervisors have long sought to foster strong corporate governance practice at community banks, with the recognition that best practices at these small privately held organizations may differ from best practices at large publicly traded banking companies.

ACKNOWLEDGMENTS

The opinions expressed in this chapter are those of the author, and are not necessarily those of the Federal Deposit Insurance Corporation or the Federal Reserve Bank of Chicago. Portions of this chapter are derived from an earlier Federal Reserve Bank of Chicago study by Robert DeYoung, Patrick Driscoll and Colette Fried, 'Corporate governance at community banks: a Seventh District analysis,' *Chicago Federal Letter*, Number 219, October 2005.

NOTES

1. For an in-depth discussion of community banking, see Robert DeYoung, 'Community banks at their best: Serving local financial needs,' Federal Reserve Bank of Chicago, *2004 Annual Report*, available at http://www.chicagofed.org/about_the_fed/annual_report_new.cfm.
2. For evidence of this phenomenon, see Robert DeYoung, Kenneth Spong and Richard Sullivan, 2001, 'Who's minding the store? Motivating and monitoring hired managers at small closely held commercial banks,' *Journal of Banking and Finance*, **25**(7), 1209–43.
3. The Seventh Federal Reserve District comprises all of Iowa and most of Illinois, Indiana, Michigan and Wisconsin.
4. The banks included in the database all have less than $5 billion of assets, participated in at least two different kinds of lending (business loans, consumer loans, real estate loans, or agricultural loans), and issued insured deposits.
5. The DMO designation was assigned by examiners, following the convention used in DeYoung *et al.* (2001).
6. To remove the influence of outlying values, the values of ROA, ROE, and the corporate governance characteristics were truncated (not dropped) at the 5th and 95th percentiles of their sample distributions.
7. For example, for ROA the calculation is $0.0014/0.0106 = 0.1321$ or about 13 percent.
8. For example, for ROA the calculation is $0.0021*(0.10*0.2109)/0.0106 = 0.0040$ or about 4/10ths of one percent, where 0.2109 is the mean value of *DMO_BONUS*.

REFERENCES

DeYoung, Robert (2004), 'Community banks at their best: serving local financial needs,' in *2004 Annual Report*, Federal Reserve Bank of Chicago, accessed at www.chicagofed.org/about_the_fed/annual_report_new.cfm.

DeYoung, Robert, Kenneth Spong and Richard Sullivan (2001), 'Who's minding the store? Motivating and monitoring hired managers at small closely held commercial banks,' *Journal of Banking and Finance*, **25**(7), 1209–43.

DeYoung, Robert, Patrick Driscoll and Colette Fried (2005), 'Corporate governance at community banks: a Seventh District analysis,' *Chicago Fed Letter*, 219, October.

5. Bank mergers and insider trading

Tareque Nasser and Benton E. Gup

INTRODUCTION

Recently, the Australian Securities and Investment Commission (ASIC) accused Citigroup of trading on its knowledge of a client's takeover bid. If found guilty, Citigroup will be subject to fines approaching $715 million.[1] This example demonstrates how regulators around the world are enforcing securities and investment laws in the wake of the notorious Enron and WorldCom debacles in the US. Ensuring that financial institutions and their managers comply with securities and investment laws is crucial for maintaining a sound financial system. Furthermore, violations of investor protection laws indicate bad corporate governance, which can increase an institution's cost of capital.

This chapter examines whether insiders at target banks use private information to trade their firms' shares before merger announcements. Informed trading around merger and acquisitions events has received much attention in the finance literature because a target firm's abnormal return is almost always significantly positive following a merger announcement. (See Schwert, 1996; Andrade *et al.*, 2001.) Madison *et al.* (2004) examined insider trading of target banks prior to their merger announcements during the period 1991–7. However, our sample, methodology, and time period differ from Madison *et al.* (2004).

We examined insider trading data prior to bank merger announcements from 1 January 1995 to 31 December 2005. We exclude unsuccessful mergers and mergers with target price below $100 million. Our study is important for two reasons. First, our sample period is marked by several regulatory changes that increased the merger activity in the banking sector. In 1994, Congress passed the Riegle-Neal Interstate Banking and Branching Efficiency Act (IBBEA) to deregulate bank mergers. This legislation induced a spate of interstate bank acquisitions. The Financial Service Modernization Act (FSMA), also known as the Gramm-Leach-Bliley Act of 1999, is another catalyst for merger activity in the banking industry. The Gramm-Leach-Bliley Act ended the Glass-Steagall Act of 1933, which prohibited banks from offering investment banking services. In addition to these two acts, numerous acquisitions have resulted from foreign financial institutions trying to establish a strong foothold in the US by acquiring US banks.

Second, recent incidences of fraud, insider trading, and earnings manipulation have forced regulators, investors, and academics to scrutinize corporate governance in the US. Hence, measuring insider trading prior to bank mergers using recent data will provide evidence concerning the effectiveness of corporate governance in the US.

We use three measures of insider trading: trading volume, number of insiders trading, and number of insider trades. We emphasize the last two measures to assess the informed trading for reasons explained later in the article. Based on these measures, we find a significant decrease in selling, but not a significant decrease in purchasing by target bank insiders in the months preceding merger announcements. This finding is different from Madison *et al.* (2004) who found that insiders reduce both their purchases and sales before the merger announcement. In addition, we find that few insiders at target banks are buying. Less than 20 percent of the banks in our sample have insider buying shares; and less than 3 percent have more than one insider buying shares in two months preceding merger announcements.

The remainder of the chapter is organized as follows. The next section discusses the literature and bank regulations relevant to this study. The third section describes data sources and the data collection process. The fourth section presents our methodology and empirical results. Our conclusions are presented in the final section.

MERGERS AND INSIDER TRADING LITERATURE AND LAWS

This section reviews literature and laws pertinent to our study. First, we consider how bank mergers affect the insiders at target banks. Second, we discuss the literature on insider trading prior to merger activity. Third, we examine the applicable insider trading laws. Finally, to determine the effectiveness of current regulations, we review recent studies on insider trading.

Mergers and Bank Mergers

Morck, Shliefer, and Vishny (1987) categorize mergers as either disciplinary or synergistic. They find that, in most cases, disciplinary mergers are hostile and synergistic mergers are friendly. Morck *et al.* (1987) assert that 'the gains in the synergistic takeovers could well be gains for the managers as well as for the shareholders' (p. 1). Cheng *et al.* (1989) argue that bank regulations cause bank takeovers to differ from non-bank takeovers. Hostile takeovers in the banking industry are rare. When mergers are friendly, target managements have more opportunity during the negotiation process to extract private rents that reduce target shareholder wealth.

When merged banks consolidate their operations, the number of employees required to run the merged company is smaller than pre-merger combined workforces. Top management and the directors of target banks are, in general, not retained in their original capacity by the surviving entity. In many cases the target CEO negotiates a generous severance package rather than become an officer of the merged company. Hartzell *et al.* (2004) find that the acquiring firms reward target CEOs with special bonuses, job offers, or board seats in exchange for lower acquisition premiums. Wulf (2004) examines 'mergers of equals' and finds that target returns are negatively correlated with target CEO representation on the combined companies' board. Hartzell *et al.* (2004) and Wulf's (2004) findings suggest that the top officers and directors of target banks make deals prior to friendly mergers. Thus, some target insiders have ways to benefit themselves without resorting to informed insider trading. For other insiders, however, the only way to extract benefits may be through informed trading.

Insider Trading Laws

Prior to the 1960s, the primary insider-trading law was Section 16(b) of the Securities Exchange Act of 1934 (hereafter, the 1934 Act), which deterred insider trading with its 'short-swing rule'. Under Section 16(b), insiders are obligated to disgorge any profits from buying and subsequently selling their firms' share within a six month period.

According to Section 16(a), insiders – directors, officers, and beneficial owners as defined by Section 12 of the 1934 Act – are required to report their ownership and trading. The insider trading reporting requirements are intended to make all insider trading activity transparent.

Rule 10(b)-5 of the 1934 Act, prohibits using any nonpublic information to obtain profit through trading. ITSA of 1984 and the Insider Trading and Securities Fraud Enforcement Act of 1988 (the 1988 Act) have increased the civil and criminal penalties for insider trading. For instance, ITSA stipulates that the severity of penalties imposed on a person found guilty of violating insider trading laws is determined by the court in light of the facts and circumstances of the case. However, ITSA limit penalties to three times the profit gained or the loss avoided from unlawful insider purchases, sales, or communications. For individuals, the 1988 Act allows criminal fines up to $1 000 000 and prison terms up to ten years.

Prior Studies on Mergers and Insider Trading

The run-up of target firms' stock price before merger announcements is a well-documented phenomenon in the finance literature. Andrade *et al.* (2001) report that the average three-day abnormal return prior to merger announcements during the period 1973–98 is 16 percent; the average abnormal return is 24 percent over a 20-day window. Earlier studies of insider trading before merger announcements use abnormal returns and pre-bid price run-ups, rather than insider trading data, as evidence of informed trading.

Keown and Pinkerton (1981) find target firm share price appreciation prior to merger announcements. They attribute the price run-ups and abnormal returns of target firms' shares before merger announcements to informed trading. However, Jarrell and Poulsen (1989) assert that the presence of rumors in the news media is the strongest determinant of unanticipated premiums and pre-bid run-ups for tender offer targets.

Meulbroek (1992) shows that daily stock returns are correlated with the pre-takeover trading activities of insiders when the SEC successfully prosecuted insider trading. For the average target firm, she estimates that almost half the share price run-up in the month before an announced tender offer occurs on days when insiders traded. The average target firms' insiders traded on a small subset of the days during the month preceding the announcement.

Arshadi and Eyssell (1991) use insiders' cumulative net purchase transactions preceding tender-offer announcements to assess insider trading. They find that insiders do not trade based on private information following the Insider Trading Sanction Act (ITSA) of 1984. However, Arshadi and Eyssell (1991) find that during the pre-ITSA period insiders timed their trades based on price movement. Eyssell and Arshadi (1993) attribute the share price appreciation before tender offer announcements during the period 1982–85 to trading by registered insiders.

Agrawal and Jaffe (1995) examine the deterrence effect of the 'short-swing rule' (Section 16(b) of 1934 Act) prior to mergers during the period 1941–61, when no other insider trading laws were enforced. They find that insider purchases were significantly less than those of the time series control and the matched sample control. Agrawal and Jaffe (1995) find that insiders do not decrease their sales prior to merger. This second result is surprising, since deferring sales is economically advantageous and does not violate insider trading laws.

Madison *et al.* (2004) measure the insider trading by target firms management insiders prior to announced bank merger. They find that target bank insiders significantly decrease both share purchases and sales prior to the announcements.

The empirical evidence cited above indicates informed insider trading in the US has decreased significantly since the 1980s, arguably because of stricter regulations and enforcement. Using acquisition data from 52 countries, Bris (2005) examines whether insider trading laws are effective deterrents. He finds that the combination of strict laws and their enforcement reduce incidences of insider trading. Bris (2005) concludes that the US has the toughest insider trading regulations.

Agrawal and Cooper (2006) examine insider trading activity of firms that announced their financial statements restatement to correct GAAP violations during the period 1 January 1997–30 June 2002.[2] Agrawal and Cooper do not find any abnormal insider trading during periods when financial statements are misstated. Similarly, Nasser and Gup (2006) analyze insider trading at large firms (with total assets exceeding $1 billion) that filed for bankruptcy during the period 1995–2005. They do not find abnormal insider selling activity prior to bankruptcy filings.

Announced restatement and bankruptcies produce significant, negative abnormal returns. Insiders possessing private information about these events could avoid significant loss by selling their shareholdings before the announcements. We find insiders refraining from informed trading despite the benefits. Based on the studies by Agrawal and Cooper (2006) and Nasser and Gup (2006), can we expect insiders to not trade on their private information prior to merger announcements?

After the Enron, WorldCom and similar scandals, regulators, media and other interested parties have closely monitored US corporations to uncover or prevent the unscrupulous behavior by corporate executives that siphon shareholder wealth. The Sarbanes-Oxley Act of 2002 strengthened insider trading laws and their enforcement. Previously insiders were to report any changes in their holdings by the tenth day of the following month. However, since the Sarbanes-Oxley Act insiders have been required to report their trade within two business days after the trade has occurred. In this post-Enron environment, we do not expect the blatant use of private information by insiders for private gain, when information of insider trading is almost immediately accessible to anyone.

DATA

In this section, we describe the sample of target banks, the matched control sample, and the insider trading data for both samples.

Target Sample

Our sample of bank merger targets was obtained from the Securities Data Corporation Platinum (SDC) Merger and Acquisitions database. We examined merger and acquisitions announcements for deals $100 million or more during the period 1995–2005. The firms in our sample are commercial banks and bank holding companies incorporated in the US. These criteria yield 609 announced acquisitions and repurchases. Only 333 announcements resulted in acquisitions. Some of the 333 acquisitions are purchases of certain branch operations of the target banks rather than complete mergers. We exclude target banks whose data are not available in CRSP, Compustat or the Thomson Financial Insider Filing Data (hereafter, TF). Our final sample consists of 217 merger announcements.

The Matched Control Sample

Firms are matched according to size and industry. We define industry using the first two digits of firms' SIC codes. We measure size using total assets from Compustat. The two-digit SIC codes of the target banks are either 60 (depository institutions) or 67 (bank holding companies and other investment offices). Total assets are observed at the end of year, one year prior to the merger announcements.

Table 5.1 shows the summary statistics of the asset size of the target banks and the matched sample. We report mean and median values and their differences for all banks and three asset size sub-groups: large (more than $10 billion), medium (between $1 billion and $10 billion), and small (less than $1 billion). None of the mean differences between the target and control banks are significantly different from zero. Similarly, the Wilcoxon sign rank test confirms that the median sizes of target banks and their matched sample are not significantly different from each other.

Seyhun and Bradley (1997) criticize matching by industry because firms in the same industry are likely to have similar problems (for example financial distress or likely candidate for merger). However, Agrawal and Jaffe (1995) contend that matching based on two-digit SIC codes is broad enough that the events being studied will have little if any effect on control firms. To confirm that Seyhun and Bradley's criticism is not valid in our case, we compare the average abnormal return (AAR) and cumulative average abnormal return (CAAR) target banks and the matched control sample in Figure 5.1.

Panel A of Figure 5.1 shows the AAR and CAAR of the target banks. We observe that the AAR over the six calendar days before the merger announcement becomes significantly different from zero. The target bank

Table 5.1 Summary statistics of the asset size

This table provides the summary statistics of the asset size of the merger target banks, their matched control firms, and the absolute difference between the two. The summary statistics are provided for all firms as well as for three different categories based on size. The table also provides the *t*-test and Wilcoxon signed rank test statistics.

Bank category	N	Target	Matched	Difference	*t*-test
Panel A: Mean					
All	217	11 288.17	11 625.44	613.57	−1.124
Large (>$10 billion)	39	53 504.96	55 397.66	3337.57	−1.137
Medium					
(>$1 billion)	102	3088.53	3082.67	27.26	1.268
Small (<$1 billion)	76	629.07	628.68	2.63	0.727
	N	Target	Matched	Difference	Wilcoxon Z
Panel B: Median					
All	217	11 288.17	11 625.44	613.57	0.018
Large (>$10 billion)	39	32 398.60	32 114.00	744.20	−1.061
Medium					
(>$1 billion)	102	2176.86	2168.66	11.93	0.628
Small (<$1 billion)	76	616.25	614.54	1.24	1.701
	N	Target	Matched	Difference	
Panel C: Standard deviation					
All	217	34 576.46	37 448.66	4391.03	
Large (>$10 billion)	39	67 423.21	74 528.91	10 015.45	
Medium					
(>$1 billion)	102	2197.04	2189.50	38.30	
Small (<$1 billion)	76	188.78	189.15	3.95	

AAR lasts until two days after the announcement date, when the CAAR peaks at around 20 percent and stays approximately the same thereafter. In Panel B, we observe that for any particular day, the matched control firms' AAR is not significantly different from zero. Table 5.2 shows the significance of CAARs for different periods.

The evidence presented in Figure 5.1 and Table 5.2 shows that target banks' shares produced a 20 percent CAAR around merger announcements. The target bank CAAR indicates that insiders may be tempted to purchase their firms' shares, given their prior knowledge of the merger announcement. As expected, the matched control firms are not significantly affected by the target banks' merger announcements. Seyhun and Bradley's (1997)

Panel A:

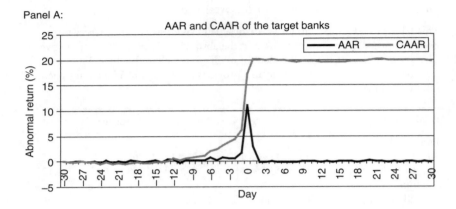

Panel B:

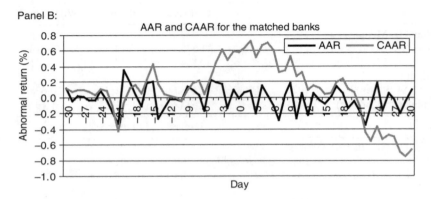

Figure 5.1　Average abnormal return and cumulative average abnormal
return

concern about matching by industry does not appear to be an issue in our
sample.

Insider Trading Data

We obtained insider trading data from TF for the years prior to merger
announcements. TF includes insider trades and changes in ownership
reported to the SEC are on Forms 3, 4, and 5. Form 3 is the initial statement of beneficial ownership for all officers. Form 4 reports changes in an
insider's ownership position. Form 5 is the annual statement of change in
beneficial ownership.

Table 5.2   Average cumulative abnormal return

The Patell z-test examines whether abnormal stock return equals zero assuming cross-sectional independence. This test uses a 1-tail test.

Days	N	Mean CAR	Patell Z
Panel A: Average CAR of the target firms			
$(-30, -2)$	215	4.45%	5.458***
-1	215	1.67%	10.728***
0	215	11.03%	83.644***
$+1$	215	3.04%	24.190***
$(+2, +30)$	215	-0.42%	-0.857
Panel B: Average CAR of the matched sample firms			
$(-30, -2)$	198	0.51%	0.643
-1	198	0.10%	0.483
0	198	-0.01%	0.740
$+1$	198	0.06%	1.147
$(+2, +30)$	198	-1.29%	$-1.914*$

Note: The symbols *, **, and *** denote statistical significance at the 0.05, 0.01 and 0.001 levels, respectively, using a 1-tail test.

We only use the open market purchases or sales data in TF and exclude purchases related to options exercises. Insider trading activity equals zero for any firm that has a registered insider documented by TF but has no open market trades reported by TF during the sample period. We exclude trades that buy or sell fewer than 100 shares. Trades lacking transaction prices in TF are excluded from our sample.

RESULTS AND ANALYSIS

We use simple methodology to systematically analyze the presence of informed insider trading. Insider trading tends to be infrequent. We find that, on average, there is less than a 25 percent chance that insiders of a particular bank either buy or sell their bank's shares during a given month. Hence, the insider trading data is highly non-normal and not suitable for regression analysis as a dependent variable.[3] Therefore, our analysis relies principally on univariate tests such as matched pair t-test and Wilcoxon signed rank tests.

Insider trading is measured using trading volume, number of insiders trading (hereafter, number of insiders), and number of insider trades (hereafter, number of trades). Purchases and sales are reported separately.

Trading volume equals transaction price multiplied by the number of shares traded. Trading volume measures the magnitude of trading. We also quantify insider trading activity using the number of insiders because if more insiders are either buying or selling during the same period, their trades are likely based on their private information. Finally, insider trading activity is measured by using the number of trades because, as noted by Kyle (1985), informed traders tend to use numerous small trades to camouflage their trading activities.

Basic Evidence

Panel A of Table 5.3 shows that the percentage of target banks with no insiders trading ranges from 70.5 percent to 84.8 percent; the average is 78.8 percent. On average only 21.2 percent of target firms have at least one insider purchasing during the same period. For the matched sample, 24.9 percent of the firms have at least one insider purchasing shares. For the one (two) month(s) prior to the merger announcement only 15.2 percent (16.6 percent) of target banks have insiders purchasing their shares; the same figure for matched banks is 21.7 percent (20.7 percent). Panel B of Table 5.3 shows insiders selling activity. One (two) month(s) prior to the merger announcement, 11.6 percent (17.6 percent) of target banks have insiders selling compared to 24.0 percent (27.7 percent) of matched firms.

Panel A of Figure 5.2 shows each month's percentage of target and matched banks with more than one insider purchasing. Panel A of Figure 5.2 shows that insider purchasing activity is low during the 12-month period preceding announced merger.[4] Panel B of Figure 5.2 shows the percentage of target and matched banks with insider using more than one purchasing trade. From both Panels A and B of Figure 5.2, it is apparent that a very small number of target firms' insiders may trade based on inside information. In fact, in the month before the merger announcement, only 4 (3) of the 217 target banks in our sample have more than one insider purchasing (selling). Figure 5.3 shows similar results for insider sales.

Statistical Evidence

We next used univariate tests to determine if insider trading at target banks is abnormal or indicates that insiders are taking advantage of private information. Table 5.3 reports summary statistics for the trading volume of purchases (Panel A) and sales (Panel B) of target banks and their matched sample. Test statistics from matched pair t-tests for differences in means and Wilcoxon signed rank tests for differences in medians are reported in Table 5.3. All median values equal zero and are, therefore, not reported.

Table 5.3 Purchase volume

This table presents the summary statistics of the trading volume along with *t*-test for mean equality and Wilcoxon signed rank test for the equality of the median. The last two columns present the percentage of banks that have zero insiders trading (in Panel A only purchase, and in Panel B only sales). Note that since the median data is always zero, it is not presented here.

Month	Target firms		Matched samples		Statistics		Zeros (%)	
	Mean	S.D.	Mean	S.D.	*t*-test	Wilcoxon Z	Target	Matched
Panel A: Purchase volume								
−1	25 793	18 483	1 052 267	13 700 000	−1.105	−1.912*	84.80	78.34
−2	79 568	56 176	19 715	91 360	1.057	−0.83	83.41	79.26
−3	303 484	244 499	53 023	398 395	1.017	0.657	76.50	79.26
−4	286 958	259 668	44 817	516 009	0.923	−0.524	81.57	77.88
−5	110 864	95 857	10 758	42 001	1.043	−0.502	80.18	77.88
−6	31 288	12 668	103 705	794 516	−1.301	−1.323	79.72	75.58
−7	88 772	52 834	41 137	176 872	0.875	−1.741*	76.50	69.12
−8	21 702	9 702	51 072	303 715	−1.313	−1.515	80.65	74.19
−9	52 139	20 804	40 455	325 076	0.384	0.077	77.88	78.80
−10	22 648	6 438	37 504	217 128	−0.917	0.823	70.51	77.42
−11	24 044	6 570	22 604	94 090	0.155	−0.966	80.18	76.04
−12	88 575	32 211	18 543	67 493	2.143*	0.786	73.27	75.12
Panel B: Sales volume								
−1	48 898	396 357	6 157 644	82 800 000	−1.087	−3.360***	89.40	76.96
−2	82 951	435 136	5 446 741	76 400 000	−1.034	−2.436**	82.45	72.35
−3	122 179	745 144	6 377 919	82 700 000	−1.114	−2.450**	82.45	74.65
−4	188 111	1 200 117	470 152	2 303 681	−1.675*	−1.796*	76.96	73.27
−5	175 967	1 548 974	738 560	4 149 069	−2.049*	−0.716	76.04	74.65
−6	702 565	5 543 678	530 550	4 543 305	0.352	−0.948	77.88	75.58
−7	239 531	1 239 823	3 516 402	31 900 000	−1.513	0.248	76.04	75.58
−8	173 121	1 345 455	1 473 715	18 300 000	−1.045	−2.168*	81.57	72.81
−9	223 227	1 143 635	2 412 487	28 300 000	−1.139	−0.724	78.34	77.42
−10	391 282	1 902 504	1 426 409	18 300 000	−0.830	−0.225	77.42	76.04
−11	218 518	1 070 403	647 133	6 131 559	−1.016	0.194	79.72	76.50
−12	156 183	1 032 445	375 881	3 102 752	−0.992	−0.532	81.11	76.96

Note: The symbols *, **, and *** denote statistical significance at the 0.05, 0.01 and 0.001 levels, respectively, using a 1-tail test.

Panel A of Table 5.3 shows that in the month prior to the merger announcement, the purchasing volume of target firm insiders is much less dispersed than that of insiders at matched firms. The differences between the two samples' means and medians for each of the six months prior to the merger announcements are not significantly different from zero. One exception is the difference in median purchasing volume one month prior to merger announcements.

Panel A:

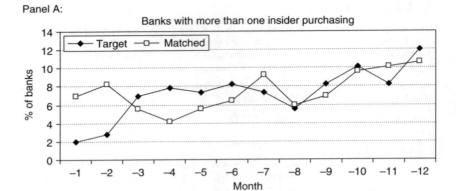

Panel B:

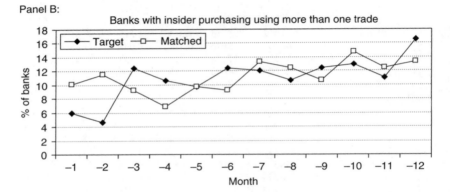

Figure 5.2   Banks insider purchasing pattern

Panel B of Table 5.3 reports mean and median sales volume and the corresponding test statistics. Here we find that for each of the four months preceding merger announcements, the median sales volume of target bank insiders is significantly lower than that of the matched firm insiders. The mean differences between the two samples, however, are not significantly different from zero. If acquiring firms first communicate to target firms their interests in merging much earlier than one month prior to the merger announcement, then the statistical significant differences in median sales volume is expected. It is in the best interest of target insiders to defer sales until after the merger announcement.

Table 5.4 analyzes the number of buying (Panel A) or selling (Panel B) insiders. The results in Table 5.4 are similar to those in Table 5.3. Panel A

Panel A:

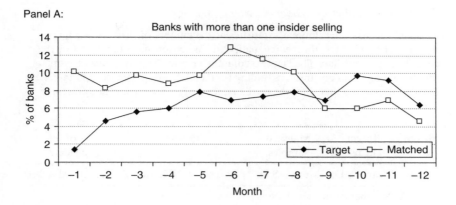

Panel B:

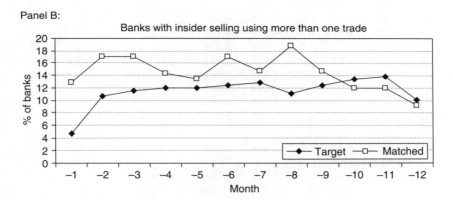

Figure 5.3   Banks insider selling pattern

of Table 5.4 shows that the mean and the median numbers of buying insiders for the first few months prior to merger announcements are not
significantly different for the two samples. Panel B shows that the median
number of insiders selling is lower for target firms compared to that of the
matched firms.

Table 5.5 presents statistics for the number of insider purchases (Panel A)
or sales (Panel B) during the 12-month period before merger announcements. The results in Table 5.5 are similar to those in Tables 5.3 and 5.4.

Overall, we observe no abnormal buying behavior by the insiders of
target banks using all three measures of buying activity. When median
selling activity is compared, we find significantly lower sales by target bank
insiders for all three measures.

Table 5.4   Number of insiders buying or selling

This table presents the summary statistics of the number of insiders buying or selling along with *t*-test for mean equality and Wilcoxon signed rank test of the equality for the median. The last two columns present the percentage of banks that have more than one insiders trading (in Panel A only purchase, and in Panel B only sales). Note that since the median data is always zero, it is not presented here.

Month	Target firms		Matched samples		Statistics		% of >1 insiders	
	Mean	S.D.	Mean	S.D.	*t*-test	Wilcoxon Z	Target	Matched
Panel A: Number of insiders buying								
−1	0.258	0.881	0.309	0.681	−0.651	−1.589	2.30	6.91
−2	0.272	1.047	0.392	1.150	−1.107	−1.468	2.76	8.29
−3	0.327	0.693	0.309	0.812	0.249	0.635	6.91	5.53
−4	0.341	0.940	0.327	0.957	0.153	−0.276	7.83	4.15
−5	0.438	1.373	0.336	0.996	0.929	−0.157	7.37	5.53
−6	0.396	1.138	0.359	0.811	0.395	−0.787	8.29	6.45
−7	0.392	0.902	0.447	0.838	−0.701	−1.525	7.37	9.22
−8	0.373	1.386	0.382	0.869	−0.084	−1.385	5.53	5.99
−9	0.433	1.137	0.433	1.666	0.000	0.642	8.29	6.91
−10	0.507	1.102	0.410	1.073	0.929	1.464	10.14	9.68
−11	0.475	1.647	0.359	0.733	0.956	−1.096	8.29	10.14
−12	0.521	1.175	0.493	1.273	0.258	0.417	11.98	10.60
Panel B: Number of insiders selling								
−1	0.120	0.366	0.424	1.128	−3.740***	−3.524***	1.38	10.14
−2	0.267	0.722	0.406	0.812	−2.047*	−2.212*	4.61	8.29
−3	0.263	0.660	0.433	0.951	−2.094*	−1.901*	5.66	9.68
−4	0.355	0.976	0.456	1.182	−1.079	−1.116	5.99	8.76
−5	0.364	0.764	0.512	1.561	−1.265	−0.015	7.83	9.68
−6	0.382	1.048	0.525	1.244	−1.299	−0.877	6.91	12.90
−7	0.392	0.942	0.484	1.171	−1.018	−0.463	7.37	11.52
−8	0.309	0.777	0.442	0.927	−1.673*	−1.921*	7.83	10.14
−9	0.373	1.016	0.350	0.864	0.258	−0.054	6.91	5.99
−10	0.429	1.100	0.350	0.798	0.873	0.132	9.68	5.99
−11	0.350	0.854	0.341	0.735	0.130	−0.370	9.22	6.91
−12	0.313	0.830	0.327	0.799	−0.186	−0.456	6.45	4.61

Notes: The symbols *, **, and *** denote statistical significance at the 0.05, 0.01 and 0.001 levels, respectively, using a 1-tail test.

Table 5.5   Number of insider purchase or sales trades

This table presents the summary statistics of the number of insiders purchase or sales along with a *t*-test for mean equality and Wilcoxon signed rank test of the equality for the median. The last two columns present the percentage of banks that have more than one purchasing or selling trades by any insider (in Panel A only purchase, and in Panel B only sales). Note that since the median data is always zero, it is not presented here.

Month	Target firms		Matched samples		Statistics		% of >1 trades	
	Mean	S.D.	Mean	S.D.	*t*-test	Wilcoxon Z	Target	Matched
Panel A: Number of insider purchase trades								
−1	0.341	1.132	0.415	1.060	−0.678	−1.630	5.99	10.14
−2	0.359	1.475	0.498	1.358	−0.985	−1.513	4.61	11.52
−3	0.594	1.743	0.433	1.189	1.086	0.846	12.44	9.22
−4	0.618	2.242	0.424	1.553	1.041	0.121	10.60	6.91
−5	0.668	2.217	0.424	1.161	1.483	−0.462	9.68	9.68
−6	0.765	2.806	0.585	1.809	0.789	−0.520	12.44	9.22
−7	1.032	6.862	0.664	1.876	0.761	−1.120	11.98	13.36
−8	0.562	2.147	0.604	1.530	−0.236	−1.276	10.60	12.44
−9	0.705	2.227	0.585	1.916	0.615	0.697	12.44	10.60
−10	0.733	1.772	0.705	2.020	0.154	1.246	12.90	14.75
−11	0.705	2.624	0.502	1.202	1.058	−0.703	11.06	12.44
−12	0.862	2.117	0.664	1.656	1.162	0.569	16.59	13.36
Panel B: Number of insider sales trades								
−1	0.207	0.947	0.806	3.043	−2.737**	−3.309***	4.61	12.90
−2	0.613	2.401	0.774	1.853	−0.823	−2.099*	10.60	17.05
−3	0.576	1.933	1.783	9.569	−1.808*	−1.753*	11.52	17.05
−4	0.645	1.910	0.908	2.691	−1.289	−1.155	11.98	14.29
−5	0.714	2.048	1.009	3.235	−1.186	−0.002	11.98	13.36
−6	0.806	3.003	0.908	2.911	−0.350	−0.695	12.44	17.05
−7	0.825	2.896	0.779	2.399	0.199	−0.092	12.90	14.75
−8	0.562	2.045	1.005	2.603	−1.939	−2.283	11.06	18.89
−9	0.779	3.089	1.355	8.646	−0.922	0.013	12.44	14.75
−10	0.788	2.517	0.687	2.131	0.477	0.003	13.36	11.98
−11	0.770	2.420	0.645	2.428	0.541	0.238	13.82	11.98
−12	0.899	5.168	1.018	7.572	−0.199	−0.239	10.14	9.22

Notes: The symbols *, **, and *** denote statistical significance at the 0.05, 0.01 and 0.001 levels, respectively, using a 1-tail test.

Insider Trading and Non-trading

The statistical evidence presented indicates no abnormal buying and some abnormal deferral of sales prior to merger. Our results can be interpreted in a variety of ways. One argument is that the result is consistent with the other studies that suggest successful use of current regulations prohibiting private information based trading.[5] In effect, insiders are not trading more, but in some cases are deferring trades to their advantage.

However, based on current insider trading regulation philosophy, it can be argued that insiders should refrain from trading prior to any potential 'price-moving' private news. We observed significant decreases in selling, but not a significant decrease in buying. Although the buying activity is not abnormally high, the 'disclosure or refrain' philosophy stipulates that there should be no insider buying activity before merger announcements. One could argue that less than 20 percent of target banks' insiders are buying, and less than 3 percent banks have more than one insider that is buying stocks. However, it should be noted that the usual liquidity argument for trading does not hold in this case because the trade involves buying.

Hence, our result is different from that of Madison *et al.* (2004) who found that target bank insiders' purchases and sales two months prior to the merger announcement are both significantly less compared to the (time series) control's insiders. We, on the other hand, find that the insiders at target banks indeed significantly reduce their selling, but do not significantly reduce their purchasing.

As a robustness check, we use Poisson regression analysis where the dependent variable is either the number of insiders buying (or selling) or the number of buying (or selling) trades. The independent variables in the regression are merger dummy (equal to 1 when the bank is the merger target and otherwise equal to 0) and asset size[6] (in thousands of dollars). Here, merger dummy is the choice variable, and asset size is a control variable. The results are presented in Table 5.6. We are primarily interested in insider trading during the month prior to the merger announcement. For insider buying activity, the merger dummy is not significant for both of the insider trading measures. For insider selling activity, the merger dummy is significant for both insider trading measures. This finding is consistent with our findings in Tables 5.4 and 5.5.

CONCLUSIONS

In this study we examined insider trading data of US commercial banks and bank holding companies prior to the announcement that they are

Table 5.6 Poisson regression

This table presents the Poisson regression results where the dependent variable is the number of buying/selling insider/trades by insider and the independent variables are merger dummy and asset size. Our variable of interest is the merger dummy where it assumes the value 1 when the bank is a merger target, otherwise it is 0. Asset size is the actual asset size, in thousand dollars, of the bank or its corresponding matched sample one year prior to the merger announcement. We present the regression results for the preceding three months of the merger announcement.

Month	Dependent variable	Number of buying insiders		Number of buying trades		Number of selling insiders		Number of selling trades	
		Coefficient	$P>|z|$	Coefficient	$P>|z|$	Coefficient	$P>|z|$	Coefficient	$P>|z|$
−1	Merger	−0.179742	0.321	−0.196122	0.211	−1.254775	0.000	−1.352022	0.000
	Asset size	−0.000006	0.197	−0.000007	0.109	0.000005	0.000	0.000004	0.000
	Constant	−1.122897	0.000	−0.821276	0.000	−0.949488	0.000	−0.288176	0.000
	p>chi-square	0.177		0.062		0.000		0.000	
	Pseudo R^2	0.005		0.007		0.079		0.077	
−2	Merger	−0.364267	0.032	−0.323898	0.029	−0.414220	0.014	−0.232560	0.045
	Asset size	0.000002	0.413	0.000002	0.141	0.000003	0.048	0.000002	0.160
	Constant	−0.957212	0.000	−0.728163	0.000	−0.946619	0.000	−0.279396	0.000
	p>chi-square	0.070		0.036		0.010		0.055	
	Pseudo R^2	0.007		0.007		0.013		0.004	
−3	Merger	0.057566	0.735	0.316112	0.020	−0.487796	0.004	−1.114112	0.000
	Asset size	−0.000005	0.216	−0.000003	0.310	0.000006	0.000	0.000006	0.000
	Constant	−1.130097	0.000	−0.810998	0.000	−0.947659	0.000	0.449884	0.000
	p>chi-square	0.322		0.034		0.000		0.000	
	Pseudo R^2	0.003		0.006		0.040		0.081	

merger targets during the period 1995–2005. We compared the target banks' insiders trading with that of asset size and industry matched control firms' insider trading. We use three different constructs to measure insider trading, namely trading volume, number of insiders trading and number of trades of an insider. We emphasize the last two measures to assess the informed trading for our analysis; and based on these measures, we find a significant decrease in selling, but not a significant decrease in purchases by insiders at the target bank.

Our finding is not very different from other high-CAAR producing events like restatement (Agrawal and Cooper, 2006) or bankruptcy (Nasser and Gup, 2006), as the insiders are not actively taking advantage of the private information with abnormal trading. However, our results are different from Madison *et al.*'s (2004) findings that insiders at target banks reduce their purchase and selling significantly prior to merger announcement.

It is possible to argue that current insider trading regulation philosophy, 'disclosure or refrain', mandates that there should be a significant decrease in purchasing, if not complete absence of purchasing, prior to a merger announcement. This is not what we find in our results. Based on extant literature, Bris (2004) asserts that '[in the US] even though strict IT [insider trading] laws are in place, there is plenty of evidence that corporate insiders still profit from private information, especially preceding takeover announcements' (p. 280). So, how one explains the incidence of insider trading depends on what method one uses and how one interprets the results.

We, however, should be mindful of few caveats in this study. First, it is possible that there could be trading by insiders that was not reported, and thereby not included in our study. Second, insiders could use some cleverly devised methods of self-dealing that go undetected. Given these, we can conclude that the absence of abnormal purchase prior to bank mergers implies insider trading laws are effective in deterring informed trading.

ACKNOWLEDGMENTS

The authors thank Tommy Cooper for his helpful comments and discussion.

NOTES

1. CNNMoney.com, 31 March 2006.
2. Note that this period is pre-Sarbanes-Oxley.

3. Using a Poisson regression or Negative Binomial regression where the number of insiders or number of trade per insider is the dependent variable does not violate the assumptions of the regression, and can be used without a problem.
4. Lorie and Niederhoffer (1968) and Jaffe (1974), both in their unique ways defined information event where more than two net buyers or net sellers are trading in a firm. In that regard, our measure is more conservative. Also, we do not use net buyer or seller; rather, we use buyer and seller separately for reasons similar to that of Agrawal and Jaffe (1995).
5. 'Discloser or refrain' is the current insider trading regulation philosophy. Bettis *et al.* (1998) provide a critique of this philosophy. However, Fried (2003) argues that insiders by abstaining from trading based on private information cannot systematically earn abnormal returns.
6. Using asset size in log value do not change the results.

REFERENCES

Agrawal, Anup and R. Thomas Cooper (2006), 'Do insiders trade on accounting fraud?' University of Alabama working paper.

Agrawal, Anup and Jeffery F. Jaffe (1995), 'Does Section 16b deter insider trading by target managers?' *Journal of Financial Economics*, **39**, 295–319.

Andrade, Gregor, Mark Mitchell and Erik Stafford (2001), 'New evidence and perspective on mergers,' *Journal of Economic Perspective*, **15**, 103–20.

Arshadi, Nasser and Thomas H. Eyssell (1991), 'Regulatory deterrence and registered insider trading: the case of tender offer,' *Financial Management*, **20**, 30–9.

Bettis, J. C., W. A. Duncan and W. K. Harmon (1998), 'The effectiveness of insider trading regulations,' *Journal of Applied Business Research*, **14**, 53–70.

Bris, Arturo (2005), 'Do insider trading laws work?' *European Financial Management*, **11**, 267–312.

Cheng, David C., Benton E. Gup and Larry D. Wall (1989), 'Financial determinants of bank takeovers: note,' *Journal of Money, Credit and Banking*, **21**, 524–36.

CNNMoney.com (2006), 'Citigroup facing $715M fine for insider trading,' 31 March.

Eyssell, Thomas H. and Nasser Arshadi (1993), 'Insiders, outsiders, or trend chasers? An investigation of pre-takeover transactions in the share of target firms,' *Journal of Financial Research*, **16**, 49–59.

Fried, Jesse M. (2003), 'Insider abstention,' *Yale Law Journal*, **113**, 455–92.

Jaffe, Jeffery F. (1974), 'Special information and insider trading,' *Journal of Business*, **47**, 410–28.

Jarrell, Gregg A. and Annette B. Poulsen (1989), 'Stock trading before the announcement of tender offers: insider trading or market anticipation?' *Journal of Law, Economics and Organization*, **5**, 225–48.

Hartzell, Jay C., Eli Ofek and David Yermack (2004), 'What's in it for me? CEOs whose firms are acquired,' *Review of Financial Studies*, **17**, 37–61.

Keown, Arthur J. and John M. Pinkerton (1981), 'Merger announcements and insider trading activity: an empirical investigation,' *Journal of Finance*, **36**, 855–69.

Kyle, Albert S. (1985), 'Continuous auctions and insider trading', *Econometrica*, **53**, 1315–35.

Lorie, James H. and Victor Niederhoffer (1968), 'Predictive and statistical properties of insider trading', *Journal of Law and Economics*, **11**, 35–51.

Madison, Tom, Greg Roth and Andy Saporoschenko (2004), 'Bank mergers and insider nontrading,' *Financial Review*, **39**, 203–29.

Meulbroek, Lisa K. (1992), 'An empirical analysis of illegal insider trading,' *Journal of Finance*, **47**, 1661–99.

Morck, Randall, Andrei Shleifer and Robert W. Vishny (1987), 'Characteristics of hostile and friendly takeover targets', NBER working paper.

Nasser, Tareque and Benton E. Gup (2006), 'Insider trading and large Chapter 11 bankruptcies: 1995–2005,' University of Alabama working paper.

Schwert, G. William (1996), 'Markup pricing in mergers and acquisitions,' *Journal of Financial Economics*, **41**, 153–92.

Seyhun, N. and M. Bradley (1997), 'Corporate bankruptcy and insider trading,' *Journal of Business*, **70**, 189–216.

Wulf, Julie (2004), 'Do CEOs in mergers trade power for premium? Evidence from "Mergers of Equals",' *Journal of Law, Economics and Organization*, **20**, 60–101.

6. Conflicts of interest and corporate governance failures at universal banks during the stock market boom of the 1990s: the cases of Enron and WorldCom

Arthur E. Wilmarth, Jr.

INTRODUCTION

The re-entry of commercial banks into the securities business transformed US financial markets during the 1990s. Beginning in the 1980s, federal regulators and courts began to open loopholes in the Glass-Steagall Act of 1933 (Glass-Steagall), which had effectively banished commercial banks from the securities industry. In 1989, the Federal Reserve Board permitted bank holding companies to establish 'Section 20 subsidiaries' that could underwrite debt and equity securities to a limited extent. By 1996, Section 20 subsidiaries were able to compete effectively with securities firms as a result of the Federal Reserve's liberalization of the rules governing those subsidiaries. In 1998, the Federal Reserve took a more dramatic step by allowing Citicorp, the largest US bank holding company, to merge with Travelers, a financial conglomerate that owned a major securities firm, Salomon Smith Barney (SSB). That merger produced Citigroup, the first US universal bank since 1933, and it placed great pressure on Congress to repeal Glass-Steagall. In November 1999, Congress enacted the Gramm-Leach-Bliley Act (GLBA), which removed the most important Glass-Steagall barriers and allowed commercial banks to affiliate with securities firms and insurance companies by forming financial holding companies.[1]

In adopting GLBA, Congress determined that the potential benefits of combining commercial and investment banking outweighed concerns about promotional pressures and conflicts of interest that were reflected in Glass-Steagall. Congress concluded in 1999 that Glass-Steagall was obsolete and counterproductive. Congress therefore dismissed the relevance of

Glass-Steagall's findings that the combination of commercial and investment banking during the 1920s had produced a wave of speculative financings, an unsustainable economic boom, and the distribution of high-risk securities that inflicted massive losses on unsophisticated investors.[2]

GLBA essentially ratified the securities powers that bank holding companies had already obtained through the Federal Reserve's Section 20 orders. By 1999, 45 banking organizations (including all of the 25 largest banks) had established Section 20 subsidiaries. Three of those banks – Citigroup, J. P. Morgan Chase (Chase) and Bank of America – ranked among the top ten underwriters for US securities in 1999.[3] During 1999–2000, Citigroup's investment banking fees exceeded $6.6 billion and accounted for more than one-fifth of Citigroup's total revenues.[4] In 2000, Citigroup, Chase and Bank of America ranked among the top ten underwriters of global securities, along with three major foreign banks (Credit Suisse, Deutsche and UBS) and four US securities firms (Goldman Sachs, Merrill Lynch, Morgan Stanley and Lehman Brothers). That group of top global underwriters remained essentially the same during 2001–5.[5]

The six domestic and foreign banks included within that group achieved their status in large part by acquiring securities firms in the United States and the United Kingdom.[6] Leading securities firms responded to the banks' competitive challenge by acquiring FDIC-insured depository institutions. Securities firms were able to acquire these bank-like institutions by taking advantage of loopholes in the statutes governing bank and thrift holding companies. For example, Merrill Lynch acquired a thrift institution and an industrial loan company (ILC) during the 1990s. Those institutions currently hold $80 billion of deposits, and Merrill Lynch uses their deposits as the primary funding source for its commercial lending, consumer lending and bond trading activities.[7] Morgan Stanley, Lehman Brothers and Goldman Sachs also own ILCs, although each of those ILCs currently holds less than $8 billion of deposits.[8] Thus, Merrill Lynch certainly qualifies as a universal bank in terms of offering a full range of banking and securities services, and the other three major securities firms arguably fall within that category as well.

Competition between commercial banks and securities firms helped to stimulate a spectacular growth in the issuance of corporate securities during the late 1990s. Total underwritings and private placements of corporate securities in US financial markets more than tripled, from $860 billion to $3.12 trillion, during 1994–2001.[9] This rapid expansion in corporate issues contributed to the stock market boom of 1994–2000, which was comparable to the great bull market of 1923–9. Unfortunately, as in the 1920s, the stock market boom of the 1990s was followed by a sharp decline during 2000–2. During that decline, the total value of all publicly traded

US stocks fell by 40 percent, from $17 trillion to $10 trillion, representing the worst long-term decline in stock values since 1929–32.[10]

The drop in stock prices accelerated between December 2001 and October 2002, as investors reacted to reports of accounting fraud and self-dealing at many 'new economy' firms that had been viewed as 'stars' during the stock market boom of the 1990s.[11] The sudden collapses of Enron and WorldCom were especially shocking to investors. With assets of $63 billion and $104 billion, Enron and WorldCom represented the largest corporate bankruptcies in US history.[12] Investigations and lawsuits revealed that universal banks played central roles in financing the rapid growth of Enron and WorldCom, and in promoting the sale of their securities. Government officials penalized universal banks for their involvement with Enron and WorldCom, and officials also brought enforcement actions against universal banks for a wide range of other misconduct related to their securities activities, including (a) conflicts of interest among research analysts, resulting in the issuance of biased and misleading reports to investors, (b) manipulative and abusive practices connected with initial public offerings (IPOs), and (c) late trading, market timing and other abuses involving mutual funds.[13]

This chapter is part of a larger project that will examine the role of universal banks during the US economy's boom-and-bust cycle of 1994–2002. In particular, I intend to consider whether the combination of commercial and investment banking activities during the 1990s created promotional pressures and conflicts of interest that (a) caused universal banks to underwrite risky securities and extend speculative loans, (b) led universal banks to issue offering prospectuses and research reports that promoted the sale of those risky securities without proper disclosure of the investment risks, and (c) induced universal banks to disregard legal prohibitions on deceptive practices and their own policies against abusive transactions. This chapter focuses on the involvement of universal banks with Enron and WorldCom. While many scholars have analyzed the Enron and WorldCom scandals, to my knowledge only two legal academics – James Fanto and Hillary Sale – have given substantial attention to the role of universal banks in those scandals.[14] The analysis in this chapter builds upon their important work.

The evidence presented below supports several conclusions. First, the desire for investment banking fees caused universal banks to enter into structured-finance transactions with Enron, even though bank officials recognized that that the transactions (a) were inherently deceptive, (b) were contrary to their banks' risk management policies and (c) exposed their banks to serious reputational risk and legal liability. Second, universal banks competed for investment banking mandates by providing extraordinary financial favors to senior corporate executives of Enron and WorldCom, notwithstanding the obvious corruption inherent in those favors. Third, universal banks distributed offering prospectuses and research reports that encouraged investors to buy Enron's and WorldCom's securities, even though bank officials knew or should have known that the promotional documents were materially misleading and failed to disclose significant investment risks. Indeed, some banks quietly arranged hedging transactions to reduce their credit exposures to Enron and WorldCom concurrently with their publication of materials encouraging investors to buy the companies' securities. Other banks fired analysts who published critical reports about Enron. Finally, universal banks repeatedly extended credit to Enron and WorldCom in order to attract investment banking business, even though bank officers had serious concerns about the financial viability of both companies.

Thus, the Enron and WorldCom episodes demonstrated an appalling failure of corporate governance safeguards at universal banks as well as their clients. The actions of universal banks with respect to Enron and WorldCom also revealed the existence of promotional pressures, conflicts of interest, speculative financing and exploitation of investors, which were similar to the perceived abuses that caused Congress to separate commercial and investment banking in 1933. Beyond the injuries suffered by investors and the broader economy, the universal banks' misconduct related to Enron and WorldCom raises troubling questions about the risks to the financial system created by the commingling of commercial and investment banking. By September 2006, universal banks had paid almost $15 billion, and had surrendered creditor claims of about $3 billion, in order to settle enforcement actions, civil lawsuits and bankruptcy proceedings related to Enron and WorldCom. Hence, the losses suffered by universal banks, which have not yet been fully determined, far exceed the fees they received from Enron and WorldCom. For example, Enron and WorldCom paid Citigroup about $330 million, but Citigroup has already paid nearly $5 billion to settle claims related to its work for those companies.[15] The magnitude of the foregoing losses indicates that GLBA's regulatory scheme is not adequate to control the risks posed by universal banking powers to our largest banks – the same banks that are most likely to receive 'too big to fail' treatment from financial regulators.[16]

UNIVERSAL BANKS AND ENRON

The Rise and Fall of Enron

Enron was one of the most glamorous and admired companies during the stock market boom of the late 1990s. Enron's reported revenues increased from less than $10 billion in 1995 to $20 billion in 1997, $30 billion in 1998, $40 billion in 1999 and $100 billion in 2000. Enron's market capitalization reached $70 billion at its peak in August 2000. Measured by reported revenues and market capitalization, Enron was the seventh largest corporation in the United States. For five consecutive years, from 1997 through 2001, *Fortune* magazine ranked Enron as the 'Most Innovative Company in America'.[17]

Enron's management, led by Kenneth Lay and Jeffrey Skilling, transformed Enron from an operator of natural gas pipelines in the 1980s to a highly diversified company with four primary business segments at the end of the 1990s. Enron's major segments were: (a) Transportation Services, which operated Enron's traditional natural gas pipelines and an electric utility; (b) Wholesale Services, which operated trading markets for futures contracts and other derivative instruments based on a wide range of commodities; (c) Energy Services, which sold energy products to commercial and retail customers; and (d) Broadband Services, which sought to be 'the world's largest marketer of bandwidth and network services [and] . . . the world's largest provider of premium content delivery services'. Enron also made extensive 'merchant investments' in a wide array of ventures, including foreign power plants, foreign water systems, and many speculative, high-technology companies.[18] By 2000, Enron's highly-publicized business units for trading in bandwidth and the provision of broadband services to households persuaded Wall Street that Enron deserved an 'Internet-style valuation' that was far higher than Enron could have achieved as an energy company.[19]

Enron became a de facto financial institution by the late 1990s, due to its heavy involvement in trading commodities and financial instruments. Skilling was the architect of Enron's financial services strategy, which grew out of his success in establishing a 'gas bank' at Enron in the early 1990s. The 'gas bank' was very profitable, and Enron became the leading supplier of futures and other derivative contracts for delivery of natural gas. Enron sought to extend Skilling's 'gas bank' concept by creating trading markets and risk management products for a wide variety of commodities, including electricity, water, pulp and paper, coal, steel and broadband. Skilling believed that Enron should buy 'hard assets' in targeted industries solely for the purpose of establishing a base for trading operations, and should then sell off the assets after it developed a trading capability.[20]

Skilling's based his 'asset light' strategy on the assumption that Enron could use its trading expertise and Internet technology to 'monetize' all types of assets. Skilling was convinced that Enron could become the dominant trader for every conceivable type of commodity or contract.[21] In Enron's 2000 annual report, the company proclaimed its 'unrivaled access to markets and liquidity' and also declared that '[w]hen customers do business with Enron, they get our commitment to reliably deliver their product at a predictable price, regardless of market conditions'.[22]

Enron pursued three additional strategies, which contained the seeds of its destruction. First, Enron obtained permission from the Securities and Exchange Commission (SEC) to adopt the mark-to-market (MTM) accounting method for certain of Enron's trading activities. Without seeking the SEC's approval, Enron extended MTM accounting to many of its other businesses. By 2000, Enron accounted for more than a third of its assets under the MTM method. MTM accounting allowed Enron to carry those assets at 'fair value' based upon publicly quoted prices or (in most cases) its own estimates of fair value. Additionally, MTM accounting enabled Enron to record in a single year all the profits that it expected to accrue over the life of a financial contract, power plant or other newly-acquired asset. Second, Enron's compensation system rewarded employees for increasing the company's quarterly earnings, thereby encouraging Enron's officers to make deals with the maximum short-term impact on profits. In combination, MTM accounting and Enron's compensation system produced an aggressive, deal-oriented corporate culture in which managers approved contracts and authorized new projects to achieve short-term earnings goals, with little or no regard for a venture's long-term viability.[23]

Third, as stated in its 2000 annual report, Enron pledged that it would be 'laser-focused on earnings per share', and that it would maintain 'investment grade status', which was 'critical to the success of [Enron's] wholesale [trading] business as well as its ability to maintain adequate liquidity'.[24] Enron's commitment to produce steady growth in earnings per share (EPS) and to maintain an investment-grade credit rating made the company a favorite of institutional investors. By late 2000, mutual funds, pension funds and other institutional investors held 60 percent of Enron's stock, and those investors did not begin to abandon Enron until October 2001, after the company disclosed that accounting violations would force it to write down its assets by more than $2 billion.[25]

Enron's promises ultimately created a financial trap from which it could not escape without fraud. Analysts and credit ratings agencies expected Enron to produce consistent growth in cash flow revenues and EPS. However, Enron's MTM accounting produced a mismatch between cash flow and earnings, because Enron reported MTM earnings well in advance of its receipt of actual revenues. Many of Enron's speculative ventures proved to be disappointments or outright disasters and did not produce the expected revenues. Enron therefore needed external funding sources to provide the cash flow that its internal operations failed to generate. Enron's management was unwilling to obtain the needed funds by issuing new stock, because that would dilute the company's EPS. Management was also unwilling to issue new debt, because that would undermine Enron's investment-grade credit rating.[26]

Because of its unwillingness to issue equity or debt, Enron entered into a bewildering array of structured-finance transactions. Enron's structured-finance deals were designed to achieve the following objectives: (a) to generate fictitious revenues and earnings; (b) to obtain de facto loans while disguising Enron's obligations to repay those loans; (c) to move poorly-performing assets off Enron's balance sheet into special-purpose entities (SPEs) controlled by Enron or its officers; and (d) to create accounting hedges against declines in the MTM values of Enron's more volatile assets.[27] By November 2001, Enron had accumulated actual debt obligations of $38 billion, but only $13 billion appeared on its balance sheet.[28]

Enron's officers believed that the company's SPE transactions would provide 'bridge' financing and would 'maintain the impression that Enron was humming until . . . [the company] started raking in *real* profits' from the 'big enchilada' projects conceived by Skilling.[29] Unfortunately, Skilling's projects failed, and the hoped-for profits did not materialize.[30] When Enron finally began to disclose the magnitude of its accounting manipulations in October 2001, the company quickly lost the confidence of its investors, creditors and trading counterparties. Enron filed for Chapter 11 bankruptcy reorganization on 2 December 2001, shortly after last-ditch merger negotiations with Dynegy failed.[31]

Universal Banks as 'Enablers' of Enron's Fraud

Neal Batson, Enron's bankruptcy examiner, determined that '[t]here is sufficient evidence from which a fact-finder could conclude' that nine universal banks 'had *actual knowledge* of the wrongful conduct of [Enron's] officers' and 'gave *substantial assistance* to the officers by participating in the structuring and closing of the SPE transactions'.[32] Similarly, Bethany McLean and Peter Elkind concluded that banks were 'Enron's enablers . . . the best supporting actors of the Enron scandal – without whose zealous participation Enron's financial shenanigans would simply not have been possible'.[33] Hillary Sale also agreed that '[b]anks were a significant part of what "went wrong" at Enron . . . Without the banks, the [SPE] transactions would not have occurred'.[34]

Enron's deal-focused culture and its constant need for new sources of financing made it a favorite client of universal and investment banks. 'By the late 1990s, Enron had become one of the largest payers of investment banking fees in the world' and obtained services from more than 70 banks.[35]

Andrew Fastow, Enron's chief financial officer, created a tournament that forced banks to compete against each other for Enron's favor. Fastow divided Enron's banks into 'Tier 1, Tier 2, and Tier 3', and a bank could earn 'Tier 1' status only if it was prepared 'to lead/structure complex, mission-critical deals', to '[u]nderwrite $1 billion in [a] short period of time', and to provide an '[a]ccount officer capable of delivering [the] institution' so that it would do Enron's bidding.[36] Many banks readily accepted Fastow's terms, even though Enron was a notoriously difficult client. As one banker said: 'It was hell doing business with them, but you had to because they were so big.'[37]

The Enron bankruptcy examiner's reports provide detailed descriptions of the involvement of universal banks in Enron's structured-finance deals.[38] This chapter focuses on four types of transactions, which banks arranged for Enron despite their clear awareness of the deception and corruption inherent in those transactions.

First, Enron used prepaid commodity swaps ('prepays') to obtain disguised loans. In the typical prepay, the lending bank transferred funds to a bank-controlled SPE, and the SPE then 'paid' those funds to Enron in exchange for Enron's 'agreement' to deliver specified commodities. A series of offsetting swap agreements among the bank, the SPE and Enron effectively eliminated Enron's agreement to deliver the commodities and instead obligated Enron to pay a fixed sum of money plus interest to the lending bank. Although the transaction was functionally equivalent to a loan, Enron reported the proceeds as cash flow from operating activities and recorded its payment obligation as a liability from 'price risk management activities'. Thus, prepays enabled Enron to inflate its reported cash flow and to disguise its actual debt obligations.[39] Citigroup and Chase arranged more than $8.3 billion of prepay transactions for Enron between 1992 and 2001. Barclays, Credit Suisse, Royal Bank of Scotland (RBS) and Toronto Dominion Bank also participated in prepay transactions.[40] According to one Enron risk manager, '[t]he banks liked [prepays] because Enron got addicted . . . Enron had to repay the loan[s], but the cash flow didn't materialize. So [the prepays] snowballed.'[41]

'Minority interest transactions' were a second type of structured-finance device that provided disguised loans to Enron. Citigroup provided $1.75 billion of de facto loans to Enron through three 'minority interest transactions' that were completed at the end of 1997, 1998 and 1999. Citigroup developed the concept for these transactions and marketed the concept as a proprietary product. In the 1999 transaction (known as Project Nahanni), Citigroup provided a $485 million loan to Nahanni, an SPE established and controlled by Citigroup. Citigroup also arranged for a group of investors to buy $15 million of equity in Nahanni in order to meet the SEC's 3 percent outside equity ownership requirement for avoiding consolidation of Nahanni with either Enron or Citigroup. Nahanni used the funds it received from Citigroup and the investors to purchase $500 million of Treasury securities, which it then contributed as a 'minority investment' in Marengo, an Enron-controlled entity. At Enron's direction, Marengo sold the Treasury bills on 29 December 1999, and Marengo sent the $500 million sale proceeds to Enron.

In January 2000, Enron caused Marengo to 'repurchase' Nahanni's minority interest for $487.1 million. Nahanni used those funds to repay Citigroup's $485 million loan together with $2.1 million in imputed interest. Thus, in practical effect, Citigroup used Project Nahanni to provide a $485 million loan to Enron for a one-month period. However, Enron did not report Project Nahanni as a loan. Instead, Enron reported the $500 million of Treasury bills contributed by Nahanni as a 'minority interest' on its 1999 balance sheet, which it then 'repurchased' in 2000. In addition, Enron reported the sale of the Treasury bills on its 1999 income statement as $500 million of cash flow from 'merchant investment' activities. Like the commodity 'prepays', Project Nahanni and the other 'minority interest' transactions inflated Enron's reported cash flow while disguising its actual debt.[42]

A third series of structured transactions enabled Enron to record fictitious 'sales' of assets to Enron-controlled SPEs. During 2000 alone, Enron relied on asset sales to SPEs to increase its reported operating cash flow and its reported earnings by more than 35 percent.[43] For example, in Project Bacchus, Enron contributed its pulp and paper trading business to an off-balance-sheet SPE named Fishtail, in exchange for 80 percent of Fishtail's equity. Enron asserted that it did not have to consolidate Fishtail on its balance sheet, because 3 percent of Fishtail's equity was held by LJM2, a purportedly independent partnership that was actually controlled by Fastow. On 20 December 2000, Enron sold its 80 percent interest in Fishtail for $200 million to Sonoma, another SPE. Citigroup provided Sonoma with a $194 million loan and a $6 million equity infusion, thereby enabling Sonoma to 'buy' Enron's interest in Fishtail and to avoid any consolidation with Enron. Using a total return swap, Enron guaranteed repayment of Citigroup's $194 million loan, and Fastow orally committed to repurchase Citigroup's $6 million equity investment. Enron's bankruptcy examiner concluded that: (a) Project Bacchus did not represent a 'true sale' of Enron's pulp and paper trading business, because both Fishtail and Sonoma should have been consolidated with Enron; and (b) Project Bacchus effectively represented a $200 million loan from Citigroup to Enron. Nevertheless, Enron reported Project Bacchus on its 2000 income statement as generating $200 million in cash flow from operations and \$112 million in MTM earnings resulting from the 'sale' of its pulp and paper trading business. In addition, Enron did not report its swap obligation to repay Citigroup's loan as debt on its balance sheet.[44]

Barclays, Canadian Imperial Bank of Commerce (CIBC), Credit Suisse and RBS helped Enron to make similar fictitious 'sales' of assets to off-balance-sheet SPEs. CIBC's role was particularly significant, as it participated in 11 SPE transactions that enabled Enron to inflate its reported MTM earnings by nearly \$600 million and its reported cash flow by more than \$1.7 billion, while understating its reported debt by more than \$1 billion.[45]

The most notorious of these asset 'sales' was Enron's sale of Nigerian barges to an SPE established by Merrill Lynch at the end of 1999. Enron needed to sell the barges to generate earnings but could not find an arms' length buyer at the desired price. At Enron's request, Merrill Lynch established an SPE to purchase the barges and invested \$7 million to capitalize the SPE. Fastow gave his oral assurance that Enron would repurchase Merrill Lynch's equity interest within six months and would also give Merrill Lynch a 15 percent return on its investment. Merrill Lynch's \$7 million investment (together with a \$21 million loan from Enron) provided the SPE with funds that were used to buy the Nigerian barges for \$28 million. Enron reported the transaction on its 1999 income statement as producing \$12 million in MTM earnings from the 'sale' of the barges, even though the transaction did not meet the requirements for a 'true sale' to an unaffiliated party. Merrill Lynch also participated in another sham transaction requested by Enron at the end of 1999 – a pair of offsetting electricity swaps that were effectively 'mirror images' in their essential terms. The matched swaps had no substance, but Enron used them to report \$50 million of additional earnings on its 1999 income statement.[46]

A fourth series of SPE transactions provided accounting hedges for Enron's merchant investments in speculative, high-technology companies. These hedging transactions had two primary purposes: (a) to lock in gains in the MTM values of some of Enron's merchant investments; and (b) to protect Enron's balance sheet against future declines in the values of such investments. To create each of the desired hedges, Enron established an SPE in which either LJM1 or LJM2 – purportedly independent partnerships that were controlled by Fastow – held the required 3 percent equity interest. Enron then entered into a total return swap with the SPE. Under the swap, Enron agreed to pay an amount equal to any increase in the MTM value of the underlying investment and the SPE agreed to pay an amount equal to any decline in the MTM value of that investment. Thus, the SPE's payment obligation under the swap offset any MTM loss that Enron might suffer on the underlying investment. However, the hedges were illusory, because Enron capitalized the SPEs with contributions of its own stock.

When Enron's stock price plummeted in 2001, the SPEs could no longer perform their payment obligations and the hedges collapsed.[47]

Credit Suisse and RBS provided the outside capital for LJM1 and received handsome returns on their investments. They also participated in transactions involving LJM1 that enabled Fastow and his associates to reap personal benefits of more than $40 million, even though officials at both banks recognized the impropriety of Fastow's self-dealing.[48] Based on LJM1's success, Fastow persuaded Enron's board to authorize LJM2 – 'a big, all-purpose private equity fund' that would enable Enron to 'manage its investment portfolio risk, funds flow, and financial flexibility'.[49] Fastow chose Merrill Lynch to serve as the financial advisor and private placement agent for LJM2. Fastow insisted that Enron's banks must make substantial equity investments in LJM2 if they wanted to maintain 'Tier 1' status for Enron's banking business. Merrill Lynch and its partners invested more than $20 million in LJM2, and Enron's other banks contributed an additional $80 million. The banks' up-front investments enabled Fastow and Merrill Lynch to recruit other institutional investors, including insurance companies and pension funds. Fastow and Merrill Lynch ultimately raised $400 million of equity capital for LJM2, which enabled LJM2 to become 'the single most powerful tool for managing Enron's earnings'.[50]

In addition to the foregoing SPE deals, Deutsche engineered a set of tax-related SPE transactions for Enron. Deutsche's structured transactions produced tax benefits that increased Enron's reported income by more than $400 million during 1997–2001. Enron's bankruptcy examiner concluded that these transactions 'were, for the most part, artificial transactions lacking a bona fide business purpose other than the creation of accounting income for Enron'.[51]

The Banks' Awareness of Enron's Fraud

Enron's bankruptcy examiner determined that the SPE transactions disguised $14 billion of debt obligations by moving those obligations off Enron's balance sheet.[52] The banks were well aware that Enron was using SPE transactions to mislead investors, analysts and credit ratings agencies by inflating its reported cash flows and earnings and by hiding debt. Credit Suisse and RBS also recognized that their involvement in LJM1 enabled Fastow and his associates to receive improper self-dealing benefits. Despite this knowledge, the banks viewed Enron as a highly desirable customer, and they disregarded the financial and reputational risks created by Enron's manipulative transactions.

Bank officials plainly recognized the deceptive nature of the structured-finance deals that their banks arranged for Enron. A Chase officer remarked that 'Enron loves [prepay] deals as they are able to *hide funded debt from their equity analysts*'.[53] Similarly, Citibank's Capital Markets Approval Committee noted that a prepay swap requested by Enron was 'effectively a loan, [but] the form of the transaction would allow [Enron] to reflect it as "liabilities from price risk management activity" on their [*sic*] balance sheet and also provide a favourable [*sic*] impact on reported cash flow from operations'.[54] Officials at Credit Suisse acknowledged that a prepay transaction the bank was structuring for Enron had 'accounting driven' elements, and one officer asked, 'Is it OK for us to be entering into such an "obvious" loan transaction?'[55]

Bank officials also knew about the deceptive impact of Enron's other SPE transactions. A Merrill Lynch officer noted that his firm's 'mirror image' electricity swap with Enron at the end of 1999 'clearly help[ed] them make earnings for the quarter and year (which had a great value in their stock price, not to mention personal compensation)'.[56] Several banks understood that Enron was probably violating accounting rules when it excluded the assets and liabilities of various SPEs from Enron's balance sheet. As a condition of investing in those SPEs, the banks required Enron's officers to give oral assurances that Enron would repurchase the banks' 3 percent equity interests. Given Enron's assurances, the banks understood that their equity investments were not truly 'at risk', a situation that required consolidation of the SPEs onto Enron's financial statements.[57] For example, CIBC officers described their bank's equity investments in SPEs as 'trust me' transactions, because: (a) '[u]nfortunately there can be no documented means of guaranteeing the equity [investment] . . . or the sale accounting treatment is affected'; and (b) CIBC obtained 'the strongest assurance (but not guarantee) from Enron senior management that we would not incur losses. They have lived up to their word so far.'[58] A Barclays official similarly reported that he had received 'explicit verbal support' from Ben Glisan, Enron's treasurer, who stated that 'under all circumstances' Enron would 'repay in full' Barclays' equity investment in the SPE.[59]

The banks also recognized that Enron was structuring deals with SPEs to inflate earnings and hide debt. A Credit Suisse officer described the Osprey Trust SPE transaction as 'a vehicle enabling Enron to raise disguised debt which appears as equity on Enron's balance sheet' while 'serv[ing] the added purpose for Enron of being an off balance sheet parking lot for certain assets'.[60] RBS officials described Enron's SPE transactions as '21st Century Alchemy'.[61] Citigroup's managers referred to Project Nahanni as 'year-end window dressing' and 'essentially, an insurance policy for [year-end] balancing'.[62] In describing Project Bacchus, a Citigroup officer explained that 'Enron's motivation in the deal now appears to be writing up the asset in question from a basis of about

$100MM to as high as $250MM, thereby creating earnings.'[63] Another Citigroup officer confirmed that 'Bacchus is part of a program designed to ensure that Enron will meet its debt/cap targets'.[64]

Several bank officials objected to Enron's SPE deals because of the transactions' deceptive nature and the potential risks they created for the banks. One Merrill Lynch officer opposed the Nigerian barge transaction because it would 'aid/abet Enron income statement manipulation', and he warned that his firm would face serious 'reputational risk' if a 'credit meltdown' occurred at Enron.[65] Similarly, a Citigroup officer questioned the 'appropriateness' of Project Bacchus in view of the 'earnings dimension to this deal'.[66] Citigroup's head of global risk management objected to the Sundance Industrial transaction, whose purpose was to refinance Project Nahanni, because '[t]he GAAP accounting is aggressive and a franchise risk to us if there is publicity'.[67] Similarly, two Credit Suisse officers expressed serious concerns about the 'significant reputational risk' created by their bank's involvement in LJM1, given Fastow's clear conflicts of interest and the personal benefits Fastow expected to receive from LJM1's dealings with Enron.[68]

In each case, however, the banks went forward with the deals because they wanted to maintain their lucrative relationships with Enron. A Merrill Lynch officer defended the Nigerian barge deal by arguing that the deal would 'differentiate [Merrill Lynch] from the pack and add significant value'.[69] A Citigroup officer highlighted the importance of Project Bacchus by explaining that '[f]or Enron, this transaction is "mission critical" (their label not mine) for [year-end 2000] and a "must" for us'.[70] After Project Bacchus was approved, a Citigroup officer remarked, 'Sounds like we made a lot of exceptions to our standard policies. I am sure we have gone out of our way to let them know that we are bending over backwards for them . . . let's remember to collect this iou when it really counts.'[71] Credit Suisse decided to invest in LJM1 because Skilling told a Credit Suisse officer that the LJM1/Rhythms transaction was very important to Enron, and because Credit Suisse wanted to strengthen its relationship with Enron and Fastow. After completing a refinancing of LJM1 that resulted in significantly higher payments to Credit Suisse, RBS and Fastow, a Credit Suisse banker explained that the refinancing 'has provided a significant return to [Credit Suisse] and has further enhanced our relationship with Andrew Fastow'. The banker's supervisor praised her for doing 'an excellent job'.[72]

In fact, Enron's banks had powerful financial incentives to satisfy Enron's demands. During 1997–2001, Enron's top banks received the following fees from Enron: Citigroup – $188 million; Credit Suisse – $94 million; Chase – $86 million; Deutsche – $72 million; Merrill Lynch – $63 million; RBS – $60 million; and CIBC – $30 million.[73] Not surprisingly, the banks prized their relationships with Enron. Citigroup ranked Enron as 'one of the highest revenue clients within Citigroup', Chase described Enron as 'our single largest client', RBS lauded Enron as one of its 'most remunerative clients' and Credit Suisse viewed Enron as 'a Firm wide . . . priority'.[74] Perhaps the most revealing comment appeared in a CIBC internal memorandum, which explained that Enron's SPE transactions were '[n]ot terribly popular with [CIBC's] risk management [group], but the returns changed their minds!'[75]

The Banks' Failure to Protect Enron Investors

In addition to their roles in Enron's SPE transactions, universal banks served as underwriters or private placement agents for many public offerings and private placements of debt and equity securities by Enron and its affiliates. Citigroup, Merrill Lynch and Credit Suisse each participated in more than 20 public and private offerings of Enron-related securities.[76] During 1998–2001, those three banks, along with Chase, CIBC, Barclays, Lehman Brothers and Bank of America, underwrote offerings for several billion dollars of Enron-related securities.[77] A class action lawsuit alleged that the banks failed to satisfy their duties as underwriters under Section 11 of the Securities Act of 1933 (1933 Act). The lawsuit alleged that the banks did not exercise due diligence and, as a consequence, the offering materials failed to disclose Enron's business and financial problems and its deceptive accounting.[78] In addition, the lawsuit claimed that the banks were liable for securities fraud under Section 10(b) of the Securities Exchange Act of 1934 (1934 Act), because they knowingly or recklessly distributed misleading offering materials and participated in other fraudulent practices (including the SPE transactions).[79]

The class action plaintiffs further alleged that the banks committed securities fraud by causing their investment analysts to issue highly favorable research reports about Enron despite the banks' knowledge of Enron's growing problems.[80] By 1999, Enron's banks were aware of Enron's difficulties in generating operating revenues to match its reported MTM earnings, and the banks also knew that Enron was executing dozens of accounting-driven SPE transactions that generated large off-balance-sheet liabilities. By 2001, Enron's banks recognized that the company was heavily leveraged, had significant liquidity problems and depended on a continuous stream of new financings. During this period, several of the banks quietly reduced their credit exposures to Enron by entering into credit default swaps, surety agreements and other hedging transactions.[81]

Despite the banks' awareness of Enron's increasingly severe problems, their investment analysts continued to publish favorable reports about Enron until shortly before Enron's collapse. In October 2001, 'all sixteen investment analysts tracked by Thomson Financial/First Call rated Enron a "buy", and thirteen called it a "strong buy"', notwithstanding a 50 percent decline in Enron's stock price and the publication of articles in the financial press that questioned the validity of Enron's financial statements.[82] In November 2001, 'eleven of the thirteen analysts following Enron still recommended that the public purchase the stock, and only one recommended selling it', even though Enron had disclosed a $1.2 billion writedown in its assets as well as an SEC investigation into its accounting practices.[83] The only analyst with a 'sell' recommendation in November 2001 was employed by Prudential Securities, which did not engage in investment banking activities.[84]

Indeed, universal banks placed great pressure on their investment analysts to issue only favorable comments about Enron. Merrill Lynch and Citigroup fired analysts who published critical reports about Enron during the late 1990s. Enron's senior management complained about those reports and warned Merrill Lynch and Citigroup that their analysts were undermining the banks' relationships with Enron.[85] BNP Paribas allegedly forced an analyst to resign after he (a) published a research report downgrading Enron to 'neutral' in August 2001, and (b) told his clients that Enron's securities 'should be sold at all costs and sold now'.[86] Also in August 2001, UBS fired a broker, Chung Wu, after he advised a number of clients – who were also Enron employees – that Enron's financial situation was 'deteriorating' and they should 'take some money off the table'. After receiving a strongly-worded complaint from Enron, UBS terminated Wu and apologized to Enron. UBS also sent a message to Wu's clients to assure them that Enron was 'likely heading higher than lower from here on out'. UBS's message included a copy of UBS's most recent research report on Enron, which included a 'strong buy' rating and said that '[w]e would be aggressive buyers of Enron at current levels'. Like Merrill Lynch and Citigroup, UBS wanted to preserve its relationship with Enron, which included investment banking work and a lucrative appointment as administrator of Enron's employee stock option plan.[87]

Credit Suisse's research analysts faced similar conflicts of interest with respect to Enron. Two Credit Suisse analysts warned a Chase analyst to stay away from Enron's stock in October 2001, at a time when Credit Suisse's research department maintained a 'strong buy' rating on Enron. In response, Chase questioned why 'you're telling me one thing but [your] clients a different story??? A little shady if you ask me . . . [A]fraid to lose the banking business??? [A]re you an investment banker or equity research analyst???'[88] In a subsequent email message to his colleague, one of the Credit Suisse analysts admitted that '[w]e were [Enron's] number 1 supporter so the threat of a damaging research note was zero. [T]hey needed us to publicly sell the stock almost as much as we needed them for the fees.'[89]

Credit Suisse's senior managers and investment bankers pressured another analyst, Jill Sakol, not to publish critical reports about Enron in 2001.[90] At the same time, the head of Credit Suisse's research department praised Sakol for communicating her negative assessment of Enron to Credit Suisse's bond traders, who quickly sold off the bank's position in debt securities issued by an Enron SPE.[91] Thus, Credit Suisse, like other universal banks, evidently saw no problem in subordinating the interests of retail investors to the bank's interests in generating trading profits and earning fees from Enron.

The Banks' Losses from the Enron Debacle

Enron proved to be a very costly client for its banks. By September 2006, universal banks had paid more than $8 billion, and had surrendered about $3 billion of their creditor claims against Enron, in order to settle various claims asserted by the SEC, Enron's investors, and Enron itself. Those amounts will almost certainly increase as Enron's investors and Enron itself continue to pursue their claims against non-settling banks.

Citigroup, Chase, CIBC and Merrill Lynch paid nearly $400 million to settle Enron-related charges filed against them by the SEC.[92] Citigroup, Chase, CIBC, Lehman Brothers and Bank of America paid $6.9 billion to settle claims filed against them in a class action lawsuit by Enron investors.[93] In September 2006, Fastow stated at his sentencing hearing that he would provide evidence to help Enron's investors litigate their class action claims against non-settling banks, including Credit Suisse, Deutsche, Merrill Lynch, Royal Bank of Canada ('RBC'), RBS and Toronto Dominion.[94] In order to settle claims filed by Enron itself, Chase, CIBC, Merrill Lynch, RBC, RBS and Toronto Dominion paid Enron almost $800 million and surrendered creditor claims worth about $3 billion. As of September 2006, Enron was still pursuing more than $10 billion of claims against Citigroup, Credit Suisse, Barclays, Bank of America, Deutsche and Merrill Lynch.[95]

UNIVERSAL BANKS AND WORLDCOM

The Rise and Fall of WorldCom

The chronicle of WorldCom's rapid ascent and sudden collapse resembles Enron's story in a number of respects. Like Enron, WorldCom grew from humble beginnings to become a leading 'New Economy' firm and a favorite of institutional investors during the late 1990s. Like Enron's officials, WorldCom's managers sought to pump up their company's stock price by promising to meet aggressive earnings targets set by Wall Street analysts. Like Enron, WorldCom depended on universal banks to provide the financing the company needed for its rapid expansion. Like Enron, WorldCom resorted to accounting fraud when it could not produce the revenues and earnings it promised to Wall Street.[96] Finally, the top managers of WorldCom – like those of Enron – were unrelenting in their drive to achieve dominance in their industry. For a time, Wall Street analysts and institutional investors had complete confidence in the ability of WorldCom's managers to achieve their ambitious goals. Bernie Ebbers and Scott Sullivan (WorldCom's CEO and CFO) 'were considered one of the best pairings in American business in the late 1990s as WorldCom's stock soared, often finishing each other's sentences when talking to adoring Wall Street analysts'.[97] At the end of 2001, institutional investors owned 56.5 percent of WorldCom's stock (just as institutional investors had owned about 60 percent of Enron's stock at the end of 2000).[98]

WorldCom and its predecessor, Long Distance Discount Services, Inc. ('LDDS'), sought to take advantage of opportunities created by the deregulation of the telecommunications (telecom) industry following the breakup of AT&T's telephone monopoly in 1984. LDDS began operating in 1983 as a small provider of discount long-distance telephone services to Mississippi customers. In 1985, LDDS hired Bernie Ebbers as its CEO. Ebbers was a former high school basketball coach who owned a chain of motels. He had no prior experience in the telecom business, but he had unlimited ambition and 'unshakeable optimism'.[99]

Between 1985 and 2001, LDDS (renamed WorldCom in 1995) acquired more than 70 companies for total consideration valued at more than $100 billion. By 2001, WorldCom was the second largest long-distance telephone company and the largest provider of Internet-based communications services in the United States.[100] The rapid growth of LDDS and WorldCom occurred in several stages. First, LDDS and WorldCom acquired a series of domestic and international providers of long-distance telephone services to exploit the deregulation of the long-distance market that began in 1984. Second, WorldCom entered the local telephone business shortly after the Telecommunications Act of 1996 removed legal barriers that had previously barred long-distance carriers from offering local calling services. In December 1996, WorldCom acquired MFS Communications, thereby securing access to local telephone networks in a number of major US and European metropolitan markets. In addition, by acquiring UUNet, a subsidiary of MFS, WorldCom gained the ability to offer Internet communications services. Third, WorldCom cemented its status as a leading competitor in markets for local, long-distance and international communications when it acquired MCI Communications in 1998. Fourth, WorldCom significantly expanded its wireless communications business by purchasing Skytel Communications and two other wireless providers in 1999. WorldCom then agreed to a merger with Sprint, which would have created the largest telecom firm in the United States. However, WorldCom was forced to abandon the Sprint transaction in July 2000, after the US Justice Department and the European Union opposed the deal on antitrust grounds. WorldCom's last major acquisition occurred in September 2000, when it agreed to purchase Intermedia, primarily for the purpose of acquiring the web hosting business operated by Digex (a subsidiary of Intermedia).[101]

WorldCom invested massive amounts in an effort to create a global network of fiber-optic cables, telephone lines and wireless facilities that could offer a full range of telecom, video and Internet services to commercial and residential customers. In addition to installing its own network of lines, WorldCom entered into long-term leases to use the lines of other telecom firms. Many leases required WorldCom to make fixed monthly payments regardless of whether WorldCom or its customers actually used the leased lines. By 2000, line costs were WorldCom's largest expense item and represented about half of its operating costs.[102]

At its peak in mid-1999, WorldCom had a market capitalization of $180 billion. For the year 2000, WorldCom reported revenues of $39 billion from operations in 65 nations.[103] WorldCom's growth strategy depended on continuous increases in its stock price, which it used as currency to pay for acquiring other companies. Wall Street analysts and institutional investors supported a high stock price for WorldCom as long as its reported revenues grew at an annual rate of 12–15 percent. Through the first quarter of 2000, WorldCom met Wall Street's expectations. However, WorldCom improperly boosted its reported revenues and earnings by drawing down accounting reserves, including reserves for estimated merger-related expenses that WorldCom had established when it acquired other companies. Analysts and investors had not questioned WorldCom's establishment of large reserves to cover merger-related costs, and WorldCom drew upon those reserves to inflate its revenues and profits.[104]

The collapse of the Sprint merger in 2000 deprived WorldCom of a major source of additional revenues and also prevented it from creating new reserves for merger costs. Moreover, conditions in the telecom business became intensely competitive and WorldCom's profits fell sharply after 1999. Like WorldCom, thousands of firms had entered domestic and foreign markets for local, long-distance, Internet and wireless communications services during the 1990s. By 2000, the telecom industry was plagued by overinvestment, heavy debt burdens and excess capacity. Compounding these problems, the collapse of many 'dot com' firms in 2000 caused a sharp decline in the demand for communications services.[105] Because of these adverse developments, WorldCom's operating revenues declined after the fourth quarter of 1999. Beginning in late 1999 and continuing through early 2001, Sullivan (with Ebbers' knowledge) instructed WorldCom's accounting staff to use at least $3.3 billion in reserves to absorb line costs and increase WorldCom's reported earnings, in violation of generally accepted accounting principles (GAAP). After WorldCom exhausted its available reserves in early 2001, Sullivan (again with Ebbers' knowledge) directed WorldCom's accounting staff to capitalize $3.8 billion of WorldCom's line costs during 2001 and the first quarter of 2002. Sullivan's capitalization of line costs reduced WorldCom's reported expenses and boosted its reported profits, once again in clear violation of GAAP.[106]

According to Sullivan's testimony during Ebbers' criminal trial, Ebbers repeatedly told Sullivan that '[w]e have to hit our numbers' during 2000–2. At the same time, Ebbers assured the public that WorldCom was achieving 'very solid growth' and 'there were no storms on the horizon'. In February 2002, Ebbers declared during a conference call with investors and analysts that '[w]e stand by our accounting' and '[t]o question WorldCom's viability is utter nonsense'.[107] Ebbers resigned as CEO at the end of April 2002. Less than two months later, WorldCom's internal auditors discovered Sullivan's illegal capitalization of line costs. On 25 June 2002, WorldCom's board of directors fired Sullivan and publicly announced a restatement that reduced its previously reported earnings by $3.8 billion. As was true at Enron, WorldCom's disclosure of its accounting violations triggered a rapid collapse of confidence among its investors and creditors. On 21 July 2002, WorldCom filed for Chapter 11 bankruptcy reorganization.[108]

At the time of its bankruptcy filing, WorldCom reported assets of $107 billion and debts of $41 billion. However, about half of WorldCom's reported assets consisted of goodwill, representing the premium above fair market value that WorldCom had paid in acquiring other companies.[109] In 2004, WorldCom (renamed MCI) issued a final restatement that reduced its previously-reported pretax earnings by $74.4 billion. Of that amount, MCI allocated $10.6 billion to accounting fraud and attributed most of the remainder to the decline in value of MCI's goodwill.[110] Less than two years later, Verizon acquired MCI's remaining assets for only $8.5 billion.[111]

The Banks' Involvement in the WorldCom Debacle

As described in the previous section, WorldCom's managers accomplished their fraud primarily by manipulating accounting entries. James Fanto has pointed out that WorldCom's fraud was different from Enron's deceptions, because WorldCom's managers did not use 'SPEs and structured finance, which demand intensive investment banking involvement'.[112] As a consequence, universal banks did not have the same degree of direct involvement in WorldCom's fraud as they did with Enron's abuses. Nevertheless, in at least two ways, banks played a 'significant' role in the WorldCom disaster.[113] First, they actively supported WorldCom's aggressive and ultimately fatal growth strategy by persuading investors to purchase WorldCom's securities, by providing large loans to WorldCom, and by issuing analysts' reports with glowing evaluations of WorldCom's future prospects. Second, at least three banks – Citigroup, Bank of America and Chase – participated in the corruption of WorldCom's management by providing Ebbers with extraordinary financial benefits in order to win WorldCom's business.

Universal banks underwrote huge public and private offerings of debt and equity securities by WorldCom. Citigroup and its predecessors were sole lead managers for public offerings of more than $8 billion of WorldCom debt securities in 1997 and 1998. Citigroup and Chase jointly led two public offerings of WorldCom bonds – the first for $5 billion in 2000, and the second for $11.9 billion in 2001. Chase acted as sole lead manager for a $2 billion private offering of WorldCom notes in 2000.[114] Both Citigroup and Chase were also directly involved in offerings of WorldCom stock. Citigroup was the principal financial advisor for WorldCom's acquisitions of MFS and MCI, resulting in the issuance of more than $50 billion of WorldCom stock to the shareholders of MFS and MCI. Chase was the principal financial advisor for WorldCom's acquisition of Intermedia, resulting in the issuance of $5.8 billion of WorldCom stock to Intermedia's shareholders.[115] Bank of America acted as lead arranger for a $10.75 billion syndicated loan in 2000, and it was also one of five arrangers for a $2 billion trade receivable securitization program. Bank of America also participated in WorldCom's public bond offerings in 1998, 2000 and 2001.[116]

Events in 2001 revealed the close connection between the underwriting and lending activities of WorldCom's banks. In March 2001, WorldCom asked its banks for a syndicated loan for up to $10 billion in order to refinance its existing bank debt. WorldCom told its leading banks – including Citigroup, Chase and Bank of America – that they must each provide at least $800 million of the new syndicated loan in order to secure roles as lead underwriters for WorldCom's planned $11.9 billion bond offering in May 2001. The banks agreed to provide the requested loan, even though they had increasing doubts about WorldCom's financial position.[117] As discussed below, some of the banks quietly reduced their lending exposures to WorldCom but none of them disclosed their doubts to public investors.

Bank of America, Chase and Citigroup also provided extensive personal benefits to Ebbers to solidify their positions as WorldCom's leading bankers. Bank of America provided Ebbers with $200 million of personal loans that were secured by his WorldCom stock. Ebbers used those loans (together with more than $100 million of loans from other banks and securities brokers) to purchase a large Canadian ranch, a shipyard and yacht building business in Georgia, a trucking company, and 600 000 acres of timberland in Alabama and Mississippi. The relationship between Bank of America and Ebbers became problematic, however, when WorldCom's stock price declined sharply during 2000 and 2001. The fall in WorldCom's stock price triggered repeated margin calls on Ebbers by Bank of America. WorldCom ultimately agreed to repay all of Ebbers' loans from Bank of America in order to avoid a massive sale of WorldCom stock by the bank.[118]

In April 2001, Chase gave Ebbers a $20 million line of credit even though Chase knew that Ebbers already had more than $300 million in outstanding personal loans secured by his WorldCom stock. Investment bankers at Chase urged their personal banking colleagues to approve the loan in order to strengthen Chase's relationship with Ebbers and WorldCom.[119]

Citigroup and its predecessors, Salomon Brothers and SSB, provided the most extraordinary favors to Ebbers. In June 1996, at a time when Salomon was seeking to establish an investment banking relationship with WorldCom, Salomon allocated to Ebbers 200 000 shares of an IPO made by McLeod Inc., a Salomon underwriting client. Salomon's allocation of McLeod stock to Ebbers was more than four times larger than any other allocation made to a retail customer. Two months after the McLeod IPO, WorldCom retained Salomon as its financial advisor for the acquisition of MFS. From 1996 through 2002, WorldCom paid Salomon/SSB and Citigroup more than $140 million of fees, including $107 million of fees for nine major transactions. During the same period, Salomon and Citigroup allocated stock to Ebbers in 22 IPOs or secondary offerings made by underwriting clients. Ebbers earned trading profits of $12.8 million from those allocations (including $2.16 million from the McLeod IPO). WorldCom's bankruptcy examiner concluded that these allocations 'were intended to and did influence Mr Ebbers to award WorldCom investment banking business to Salomon/SSB . . . Salomon/SSB came to be WorldCom's preferred investment banker on both acquisition and financings.'[120]

Significantly, SSB continued to provide IPO allocations to Ebbers after Travelers acquired Salomon in 1997, even though SSB had adopted a policy prohibiting 'spinning' – the allocation of IPO shares to corporate executives with the expectation of securing investment banking mandates from their companies. SSB's policy specifically declared that 'shares may not be allocated to an executive of a corporate client or prospect as a *quid pro quo* for receiving investment banking or other business from his or her corporate employer'. SSB apparently disregarded its policy because WorldCom was such an important client. In April 2003, Citigroup consented to the entry of an SEC order declaring that Salomon/SSB's allocations of IPO shares to Ebbers constituted unlawful 'spinning' in violation of rules of the National Association of Securities Dealers and the New York Stock Exchange.[121]

Citigroup also provided huge loans to Ebbers. In 1999, Citigroup lent $63 million to Ebbers to refinance the loan on his Canadian ranch.[122] In February 2000, Travelers syndicated a $499 million loan to Joshua Timberland, a company controlled by Ebbers.[123] In October 2000, Ebbers asked Citigroup for additional credit. After an extensive review, Citigroup's senior management approved an additional personal loan in light of the 'high profile/quality of Ebbers as a Citigroup client, both individually and as CEO of WorldCom'. Citigroup lent Ebbers $53 million, including a refinancing of his existing loan balance of $41.7 million.[124] Citigroup had good reasons to accommodate Ebbers because: (a) Citigroup knew that Ebbers resented Bank of America's margin calls, and Citigroup hoped to replace Bank of America as WorldCom's primary provider of corporate banking services; and (b) Citigroup was concerned that WorldCom was developing a strong investment banking relationship with Chase. In November 2000, Citigroup decided not to make a margin call on Ebbers because of 'the strength of the corporate finance relationship between SSB and WorldCom'. Citigroup did not make any margin calls on Ebbers until 3 May 2002, four days after he resigned as WorldCom's CEO.[125] WorldCom's bankruptcy examiner concluded that Citigroup's loans to Ebbers 'constituted another form of "spinning", a means of obtaining and/or keeping corporate business as a result of personal financial favors provided to corporate executives'.[126]

The Bank Underwriters' Failure to Protect WorldCom's Investors

In February 2001, Bank of America, Chase and Deutsche each downgraded WorldCom in their confidential internal credit ratings. The banks reduced their internal credit ratings for WorldCom due to concerns about the company's rapidly increasing debt, its lack of revenue growth, competitive pressures on its long-distance business, and its lack of a strategic plan after abandoning the proposed merger with Sprint.[127] In addition, Bank of America and Chase reduced their lending exposures to WorldCom by entering into credit default swaps and other hedging transactions, but both banks did so quietly in order to avoid offending WorldCom.[128] Notwithstanding their growing concerns about WorldCom, all three banks acted as underwriters for WorldCom's $11.9 billion public offering of bonds in May 2001. Chase acted as a joint lead manager for the bond offering along with

Citigroup, and both banks participated in a 'road show' in America and Europe to promote the sale of the bonds. The road show script stated that '[w]e are excited about the WorldCom credit story and this debt offering . . . WorldCom's financial position gives it the strongest credit profile of any of the largest broadband providers.'[129]

The offering prospectus and road show script for the 2001 bond offering did not disclose that any of the bank underwriters had previously downgraded WorldCom in their internal credit ratings or had reduced their credit exposure to WorldCom through hedging transactions. The prospectuses for the 2000 and 2001 bond offerings also did not contain a 'risk factors' section describing the specific investment risks associated with the bonds. In August 2002, bond purchasers filed a class action lawsuit against the 17 bank underwriters, alleging that the underwriters failed to exercise due diligence to ensure that the prospectus for each offering disclosed all material facts concerning the bonds' investment risks. The purchasers alleged that the underwriters knew sufficient facts to put them on notice that WorldCom's financial statements for 1999 and 2000 were materially misleading, particularly with respect to the treatment of line costs as capital expenditures rather than operating expenses. The purchasers also charged that the underwriters should have known that the bond offering prospectuses omitted many other material facts, including: (a) the lack of specific disclosure of the 'risk factors' associated with the bonds, including the deterioration of WorldCom's long-distance business; (b) the omission of information concerning the loans and IPO allocations Ebbers received from bank underwriters; and (c) the absence of any information about the underwriters' actions in reducing their internal credit ratings and hedging their credit exposures during early 2001.[130] The federal district court ruled in 2004 that federal law did not explicitly require the underwriters to disclose their internal credit ratings or hedging activities with regard to WorldCom. However, the court held that the underwriters' actions (which indicated their concerns about WorldCom) and the other omissions cited above raised legitimate issues to be resolved at trial as to whether the underwriters failed to satisfy their duties of due diligence and reasonable care under Sections 11 and 12(a)(2) of the 1933 Act.[131]

The conflicts of interest faced by the bank underwriters were further reflected in Deutsche's conduct shortly before WorldCom collapsed. On 12 April 2002, John Tierney, Deutsche's head of credit derivatives strategy, published a note stating that WorldCom was headed for bankruptcy or an involuntary merger. Tierney also warned that 'recovery values for a WorldCom bankruptcy could be quite low, less than 30 percent'. Five days later, Deutsche retracted Tierney's note and claimed that it had been issued by mistake.[132] As discussed in the next section, the bank underwriters settled the claims filed against them by the bond purchasers, and Chase, Bank of America and Deutsche paid the largest amounts with the exception of Citigroup.

Citigroup's Disregard for Investors' Interests

Citigroup undoubtedly played the most significant role in encouraging investors to buy WorldCom's securities. The class action filed by purchasers of WorldCom's bonds and stock alleged that Citigroup violated its duty as an underwriter under the 1933 Act and also committed securities fraud under Section 10(b) of the 1934 Act. The purchasers' allegation of securities fraud presented two major claims. First, the purchasers maintained that Citigroup and Jack Grubman (its leading telecom analyst) established 'an illicit *quid pro quo* arrangement' with WorldCom's senior management and had actual knowledge about material misstatements and omissions contained in the bond offering prospectuses. Second, the purchasers charged that Grubman and Citigroup's research department knowingly issued misleading reports to investors 'that touted WorldCom's value and vigorously encouraged investors' to buy WorldCom's securities despite Citigroup's knowledge that 'the integrity and objectivity of its research department was compromised by the department's decision to serve the needs of the firm's investment bankers at the expense of providing investors with independent analysis'.[133] As discussed below, Citigroup was the first bank underwriter to settle the purchasers' claims, and it paid the largest amount of any settling bank.

Grubman developed a close personal relationship with WorldCom's senior management and became a principal advisor to Ebbers and WorldCom's board. After he joined Salomon in 1994, Grubman coordinated Salomon's efforts to attract WorldCom as a client. As noted above, Salomon became WorldCom's primary investment bank after it provided an exceptionally generous allocation to Ebbers in the McLeod IPO and also helped to arrange WorldCom's acquisition of MFS (a Salomon client).[134] Grubman attended at least four WorldCom board meetings and advised WorldCom's directors on major transactions, including the merger with MCI in late 1997 and the attempted merger with Sprint in late 1999. Grubman also gave advice to WorldCom's managers as to how they should respond to press reports about WorldCom and how they should answer anticipated questions during conference calls with investors and analysts. WorldCom's board minutes described Grubman as a 'financial advisor' to the company, notwithstanding his official position as an investment analyst.[135]

Grubman saw no conflict between his status as an investment analyst and his role as a key business advisor to Ebbers and other CEOs of telecom firms. Nor did Grubman see any problem with his active role in helping Citigroup to arrange investment banking transactions for his clients. Grubman claimed credit for helping to generate over $600 million in investment banking revenues for Citigroup in 2000, and he charged Citigroup's investment banking department for his expenses in attending Ebbers' wedding.[136] In a May 2000 interview, Grubman proclaimed, 'I'm sculpting the industry . . . I get feedback from institutions and CEOs. It feeds on itself. It's a virtuous circle.' Grubman dismissed critics who claimed that his close ties with telecom executives compromised his objectivity. Grubman declared, 'What used to be a conflict is now a synergy . . . [Institutional investors] know that I'm in the flow of what's going on . . . Objective? The other word for that is uninformed.'[137]

WorldCom's growth strategy dovetailed perfectly with Grubman's vision of the telecom industry's future. Grubman maintained that telecom firms must build broadband networks that would transmit a full range of voice, video and Internet services. He argued that 'the demand for bandwidth is basically insatiable' because telecom services were becoming 'part of the Web-centric society'. Thus, in Grubman's view, the long-term survivors in the telecom industry would be firms that pursued an aggressive strategy 'to marry [bandwidth] networks and customers'.[138] His prediction of an inexhaustible demand for bandwidth was consistent with WorldCom's repeated claims that Internet traffic was doubling every 100 days.[139] His clients and other telecom firms rushed to build national and global fiber-optic networks, and the amount of installed fiber increased fivefold between 1998 and 2001.[140]

Grubman's status as the 'king of telecom' helped Citigroup to become the top underwriter for telecom firms. During 1996–2002, Citigroup earned $1.2 billion in fees from telecom firms and underwrote $190 billion of their debt and equity securities, representing a quarter of all issuances of telecom stocks and bonds during that period.[141] Citigroup rewarded Grubman by paying him $67.5 million between 1999 and 2002.[142] In May 2000, Eduardo Mestre, Citigroup's co-head of investment banking, commented that Grubman 'has had a thesis for creating value in the telecom sector that's been dead right: Build it and they will come . . . It wasn't a foregone conclusion that the thesis would be correct.'[143]

Mestre's comment soon proved to be cruelly ironic. By 2002, analysts denounced Grubman's vision of telecom's future as 'wildly hyped'.[144] Instead of doubling every 100 days, Internet traffic doubled only every year. Meanwhile, technological advances increased the data transmission capacity of fiber-optic lines by up to 1000 times between 1995 and 2002. Consequently, the frenzied installation of broadband networks by Grubman's clients and their rivals produced a massive glut of transmission capacity. By September 2002, only about 3 percent of installed bandwidth capacity was being used, and many of Grubman's leading clients – including WorldCom, Global Crossing, McLeodUSA, Metromedia Fiber Networks, Rhythms Netconnections, Winstar and XO Communications – had filed for bankruptcy.[145]

Grubman's research reports promoted WorldCom more than any other firm. His reports described WorldCom as 'our favorite stock' in August 1997 and as a 'must-own' stock in November 1998. He urged investors to 'load up the truck' with WorldCom stock in August 1999.[146] In response to the severe decline in WorldCom's stock price during 2000–1, Grubman argued that WorldCom's critics were mistaken, and he encouraged investors to take advantage of the company's 'dirt cheap' stock price.[147] He maintained the highest 'buy' rating on WorldCom's stock from January 1997 through April 2002. On 4 February 2002, Grubman published a research note in which he contended that WorldCom's stock price 'has been unduly punished by a multitude of factors . . . [and] has more than corrected for any actual impacts from those issues. Therefore, we believe that [WorldCom] at this point represents a very compelling value proposition for a telecom company.'[148] Also in February 2002, Grubman supported WorldCom's projection that it would generate positive free cash flow during the second quarter of 2002.[149]

Grubman did not reduce his rating on WorldCom to 'neutral' until 21 April 2002, eight days before Ebbers resigned as CEO. He did not downgrade WorldCom to 'underperform' (sell) until 21 June 2002, a month before WorldCom filed for bankruptcy.[150] Of course, Grubman was hardly alone in giving WorldCom strong 'buy' ratings during 2000–2. Many analysts (including those employed by three major Wall Street brokerage firms) maintained such ratings on WorldCom at the end of 2001. However, other analysts disagreed with Grubman Analysts at Wachovia Securities and BlueStone Capital (an independent research firm) posted neutral ratings on WorldCom beginning in March 2001. Analysts at Credit Suisse and Morgan Stanley also issued neutral ratings before the end of 2001.[151]

Grubman's consistently bullish investment ratings were matched by his unusually aggressive target prices for WorldCom's stock. From February 1997 through January 2002, Grubman established target prices for WorldCom's stock that were (with few exceptions) the highest quoted by any analyst. During that period, virtually all of Grubman's target prices were at least 50 percent above WorldCom's actual stock price, and many of his target prices were 100 percent or more above the actual stock price.[152]

During an appearance before a congressional committee on 8 July 2002, Grubman testified that he did not know about any fraudulent accounting at WorldCom until it was disclosed by the company two weeks earlier. Grubman declared that 'WorldCom is a company I believed in wholeheartedly for a long time' and '[a]ll my beliefs have been honestly held'.[153] He also stated that he was 'sorry to see investors suffer losses' based on his faulty analysis of the telecom industry, and he denied that his analysis was motivated by conflicts of interest.[154] Similarly, in his letter of resignation to Citigroup in August 2002, Grubman apologized for 'failing to predict' the telecom industry's collapse, but he again insisted, 'I always wrote what I believed and based my opinions on a long and sincerely held investment thesis.'[155]

Despite his protestations of honesty and good faith, Grubman consented to the SEC's entry of an order on 28 April 2003, finding that (a) Grubman published fraudulent research reports in 2001 on two telecom firms (Focal Communications and Metromedia Fiber), and (b) Grubman wanted to downgrade Focal and five other telecom providers in April 2001, but he refrained from doing so because of pressure applied by Citigroup's investment bankers. In addition, the SEC charged that Grubman raised his rating on AT&T's stock from neutral to strong buy in November 1999, at the urging of Citigroup's co-CEO, Sanford (Sandy) Weill. Weill asked Grubman take a 'fresh look' at AT&T in order to help Citigroup win an underwriting mandate for AT&T's planned offering of a wireless tracking stock. In return, Grubman asked Weill to help persuade the 92nd Street Y's highly selective preschool to admit Grubman's children. Grubman's upgrade of AT&T's stock was a crucial factor in persuading AT&T to appoint Citigroup as lead underwriter for its $10.6 billion offering of wireless tracking stock. Grubman's children were admitted to the Y's preschool after Weill spoke to a member of the Y's board and arranged for the Citigroup Foundation to make a $1 million donation to the Y.[156]

The SEC quoted internal emails sent by Grubman to colleagues in which: (a) he called Focal a 'pig'; (b) he acknowledged that 'most of our banking clients are going to zero and you know I wanted to downgrade them months ago but got huge pushback from banking'; and (c) he admitted that he 'upgraded [AT&T] to get . . . Sandy to get my kids into 92nd St Y pre-school (which is harder than Harvard)', and he subsequently 'went back to my normal negative self on [AT&T]'.[157] While Grubman did not admit or deny the SEC's allegations, he paid a $15 million penalty and consented to a lifetime ban from the securities industry.[158]

On the same date that Grubman settled with the SEC, Citigroup paid a $400 million penalty and consented to the entry of an SEC enforcement order. The SEC charged that: (a) Citigroup encouraged Grubman and other investment analysts to support Citigroup's investment banking activities and allowed Grubman and other analysts to issue false and misleading reports to investors about several telecom firms; and (b) Citigroup approved unlawful 'spinning' of IPO allocations to Ebbers and other executives of existing or potential clients for the purpose of attracting additional investment banking business.[159] In May 2004, Citigroup agreed to pay $2.6 billion to settle the WorldCom investors' class action soon after the investors' counsel filed a court brief, which cited evidence indicating that 'the "most senior officers of Salomon" acknowledged privately that its investment bankers had pressured its analysts to avoid negative ratings and that "providing accurate stock ratings conflicted with Salomon's paramount goals of securing investment banking business"'.[160]

The SEC's complaints against Grubman and Citigroup did not allege that Grubman issued false research reports with respect to WorldCom. However, the SEC's charges seriously undermined Grubman's claims of objectivity and honesty. Moreover, the WorldCom investors' class action alleged that, in early 2000, Grubman began to use a 'cash earnings' model for WorldCom's operating results that departed from his previous 'discounted cash flow' model. The investors charged that Grubman's new model – which he did not use for any other telecom firm – omitted capital expenditures, a central component of WorldCom's fraud. A federal district court denied motions by Citigroup and Grubman to dismiss the investors' complaint, finding that the complaint 'describes strong circumstantial evidence that Grubman learned of at least the capital expenditure fraud'.[161]

The Banks' Losses from the WorldCom Disaster

Like Enron, WorldCom proved to be an extremely costly client. Seventeen banks that served as underwriters for WorldCom paid more than $6 billion to settle the WorldCom investors' class action, with the largest amounts being paid by Citigroup ($2.6 billion), Chase ($2 billion), Bank of America ($460 million), and Deutsche ($325 million).[162] The same group of banks paid over $600 million to settle additional lawsuits filed by institutional investors who did not participate in the class action.[163] In announcing Citigroup's decision to settle the class action, chairman Charles Prince denied that his bank had violated any laws and said that it had chosen to buy an 'insurance policy . . . against a roll of a dice in front of a jury . . . [on] a $54 billion claim'.[164] However, a prominent bank analyst concluded that Citigroup had effectively 'admitted guilt' in view of the extraordinary size of its settlement payment.[165]

CONCLUSIONS

The evidence presented above shows that universal banks aided and abetted violations of corporate governance rules and federal securities laws by officers of Enron and WorldCom. Bank officials also repeatedly disregarded risk management policies established by their own banks. In my view, the Enron and WorldCom episodes indicate that GLBA's current regulatory framework is not adequate to control the promotional pressures, conflicts of interest and risk-taking incentives that are generated by the commingling of commercial and investment banking. A comprehensive reform of the supervisory system for universal banks is urgently needed and must become a top priority for Congress and financial regulators.

NOTES

1. Melanie L. Fein, *Securities Activities of Banks* §§ 1.02–1.06 and 4.03 (New York: Aspen Publishers, 3d ed. 2005); Patricia A. McCoy, *Banking Law Manual* §§ 7.01–7.03 and 7.04[1] (Newark, NJ: LexisNexis Group, 2d ed. 2004); Arthur E. Wilmarth, Jr., 'The Transformation of the US financial services industry, 1975–2000: competition, consolidation, and increased risks,' 2002 *University of Illinois Law Review* 215 [hereinafter Wilmarth, 'Transformation'], at 219–22, 306–7, 318–21.
2. Arthur E. Wilmarth, Jr., 'Did Universal Banks play a significant role in the US economy's boom-and-bust cycle of 1921–33? A preliminary assessment,' 4 *Current Developments in Monetary and Financial Law* 559 (International Monetary Fund, 2005) [hereinafter Wilmarth, 'Universal Banks'], at 560–8.
3. Timothy J. Yeager, F. C. Yeager and E. F. Harshman, 'The Financial Modernization Act: evolution or revolution?', Federal Reserve Bank of St Louis Supervisory Policy Working Paper 2004–05, December 2004 (available at http://ssrn.com/abstract=646261); Wilmarth, 'Transformation,' supra note 1, at 319–20.
4. Complaint in *SEC v. Citigroup Global Markets Inc.* (SDNY, 28 April 2003) (available at www.sec.gov/litigation/complaints/comp18111.htm) [hereinafter SEC Citigroup Complaint], ¶ 142.
5. Roy C. Smith, 'Strategic directions in investment banking – a retrospective analysis,' 14 *Journal of Applied Corporate Finance* 1, Spring 2001, at 111, 116–21; Wilmarth, 'Transformation,' supra note 1, at 319–23; 'Year-end review of underwriting: 2001 underwriting rankings: global stocks and bonds,' *Wall Street Journal*, 2 January 2002, at R19 (showing that 'top ten' list of global underwriters remained the same during 2000 and 2001); 'Year-end review of markets & finance: 2003 underwriting rankings: global stocks and bonds,' *Wall Street Journal*, 2 January 2004, at R17 (same with regard to 2002 and 2003); 'Year-end review of markets & finance: 2005 underwriting rankings: global stocks and bonds,' *Wall Street Journal*, 3 January 2006, at R10 (same with regard to 2004 and 2005, except that Barclays Capital replaced Bank of America as the tenth-rated underwriter in 2005).
6. Jean Dermine, 'European banking integration: don't put the cart before the horse,' 15 *Financial Markets, Institutions & Instruments* 2, May 2006, at 57, 69 tbl. 4.b.; Smith, supra note 5, at 116–20; Wilmarth, 'Transformation,' supra note 1, at 323–4.
7. Wilmarth, 'Transformation,' supra note 1, at 423–4, 448–9; Statement by Douglas H. Jones, FDIC Acting General Counsel, before the House Committee on Financial Services, 12 July 2006 (available at www.fdic.gov/news/news/speeches/chairman/spjul1107.html); at 3–5, 11 (attach. 1); Matt Ackerman, 'Merrill eyes organic growth but may do a banking deal,' *American Banker*, 19 April 2006, at 9; Landon Thomas Jr., 'Bond trader at Merrill taps the firm's bank to spin gold,' *New York Times*, 8 August 2003, at C1; Matthias Rieker, 'Merrill's retail banking strategy seen paying off,' *American Banker*, 12 June 2003, at 20 (reporting that bank deposits provided 51 percent of Merrill Lynch's funding in 2003, compared with 14 percent in 1998); Katherine

Fraser, 'Merrill Lynch using thrift charter to build its personal trust business,' *American Banker*, 10 August 1998, at 1.

8. Statement by Douglas H. Jones, supra note 7, at 4–5, 11, 14 (attach. 1).
9. Securities Industry Association, *Securities Industry Fact Book 2002*, at 12.
10. Robert J. Gordon, 'The 1920s and the 1990s in mutual reflection,' National Bureau of Economic Research Working Paper 11778, November 2005, at 5–10, 28–9; Eugene H. White, 'Bubbles and busts: the 1990s in the mirror of the 1920s,' National Bureau of Economic Research Working Paper 12138, March 2006, at 2–13; Wilmarth, 'Universal banks,' supra note 2, at 559.
11. E. S. Browning and Ianthe J. Dugan, 'Stocks unwound: aftermath of a market mania,' *Wall Street Journal*, 16 December 2002, at C1; Anthony Bianco, 'The angry market,' *Business Week*, 29 July, 2002, at 32; Marcia Vickers et al., 'The betrayed investor,' *Business Week*, 25 February 2002, at 104.
12. Aigbe Akhigbe, Anna D. Martin and Anne Marie White, 'Contagion effects of the world's largest bankruptcy: the case of WorldCom,' 45 *Quarterly Review of Economics and Finance* 48, 49 (2005).
13. Wilmarth, 'Universal Banks,' supra note 2, at 562–3.
14. James A. Fanto, 'Subtle hazards revisited: the corruption of a financial holding company by a corporate client's inner circle,' 70 *Brooklyn Law Review* 7, 18–28 (2004) (discussing Enron and WorldCom); Hillary A. Sale, 'Banks: the forgotten(?) partners in fraud,' 73 *University of Cincinnati Law Review* 139, 143–54, 163–9 (2004) (discussing Enron).
15. See infra notes 92–5, 162–5 and accompanying text; see also supra note 4 and accompanying text (reporting that Citigroup earned $6.6 billion of investment banking fees from all of its clients during 1999–2000).
16. For a general analysis concluding that current federal regulations are inadequate to control the risks posed by universal banks, see Wilmarth, 'Transformation,' supra note 1, at 223–5, 300–12, 437–76.
17. William W. Bratton, 'Enron and the dark side of shareholder value,' 76 *Tulane Law Review* 1275, 1276, 1299–300 (2002); Paul M. Healy and Krishna G. Palepu, 'The Fall of Enron,' 17 *Journal of Economic Perspectives* 2, Spring 2003, at 3, 6 (exh. 2); Second Interim Report of Neal Batson, Court-Appointed Examiner, *In re Enron Corp.*, Case No. 01-16034 (AJG) (Bankr. SDNY, 21 January 2003) [hereinafter Enron Examiner's Second Report], at 5 and nn. 8–9; Robin Sidel and Mitchell Pacelle, 'J. P. Morgan settles Enron lawsuit,' *Wall Street Journal*, 15 June 2005, at A3.
18. Bratton, supra note 17, at 1300–2; Healy and Palepu, supra note 17, at 5–9; Third Interim Report of Neal Batson, Court-Appointed Examiner, *In re Enron Corp.*, Case No. 01-16034 (AJG) (Bankr. SDNY, 30 June 2003) [hereinafter Enron Examiner's Third Report], at 14–18; Final Report of Neal Batson, Court-Appointed Examiner, *In re Enron Corp.*, Case No. 01–16034 (AJG) (Bankr. SDNY, 4 November 2003) [hereinafter Enron Examiner's Final Report], at 84–6.
19. Bethany McLean and Peter Elkind, *The Smartest Guys in the Room* 184–8, 242–5 (2003); see also Enron Examiner's Second Report, supra note 17, App. D, at 98.
20. Bratton, supra note 17, at 1288–92, 1320–3; Healy and Palepu, supra note 17, at 6–9; McLean and Elkind, supra note 19, at 34–9, 101–12, 212–28, 286–90; Milton C. Regan, Jr., 'Teaching Enron,' 74 *Fordham Law Review* 1139, 1144–6 (2005).
21. Bratton, supra note 17, at 1288–94; Enron Examiner's Second Report, supra note 17, App. D, at 86–98.
22. Quoted in Bratton, supra note 17, at 1290.
23. Healy and Palepu, supra note 17, at 9–14; McLean and Elkind, supra note 19, at 39–42, 92–4, 121–7; Regan, supra note 20, at 1146–54; Bennett Stewart, 'The *real* reasons Enron failed,' 18 *Journal of Applied Corporate Finance* 2, Spring 2006, at 116, 116–17; Enron Examiner's Second Report, supra note 17, at 22–6; Enron Examiner's Final Report, supra note 18, at 85–6, 89–93.
24. Quoted in Enron Examiner's Final Report, supra note 18, at 84.
25. Healy and Palepu, supra note 17, at 11–12, 16–17.

26. McLean and Elkind, supra note 19, at 125–31, 150–1, 154; Enron Examiner's Second Report, supra note 17, at 25–6; Enron Examiner's Third Report, supra note 18, at 14–19; Enron Examiner's Final Report, supra note 18, at 83–7.
27. McLean and Elkind, supra note 19, at 125–31, 151–70, 286–312; Enron Examiner's Second Report, supra note 17, at 15–49; Enron Examiner's Third Report 18, supra note 18, at 14–19, 25–30; Enron Examiner's Final Report, supra note 18, at 83–9.
28. Enron Examiner's Final Report, supra note 18, at 16–17.
29. McLean and Elkind, supra note 19, at 171.
30. *Id.* at 284–312, 331–2, 339–41, 345–6, 362–4.
31. *Id.* at 367–405.
32. Enron Examiner's Third Report, supra note 18, at 4–5 (summarizing roles of Citigroup, Chase, Barclays, Deutsche, Canadian Imperial Bank of Commerce and Merrill Lynch); see also Enron Examiner's Final Report, supra note 18, at 12–13 (providing similar summary for roles of Royal Bank of Scotland, Credit Suisse and Toronto Dominion).
33. McLean and Elkind, supra note 19, at 162, 407.
34. Sale, supra note 14, at 139, 144.
35. McLean and Elkind, supra note 19, at 162 (quote), 164.
36. *Id.* at 163–5; Enron Examiner's Third Report, supra note 18, at 46 n. 121 (quoting Enron Relationship Review, Mid-Year 1999, July 1999).
37. Quoted in McLean and Elkind, supra note 19, at 165.
38. Enron Examiner's Third Report, supra note 18, at 34–85 and App. D–I; Enron Examiner's Final Report, supra note 18, at 63–81 and App. E–G.
39. McLean and Elkind, supra note 19, at 159–61; Enron Examiner's Second Report, supra note 17, at 58–66; *id.*, App. D (Enron's Disclosure of SPEs), at 11–19; *id.*, App. E (Prepays), at 1–45.
40. Enron Examiner's Third Report, supra note 18, App. D (Citigroup), at 45–83; *id.*, App. E (Chase), at 18–49; *id.*, App. F (Barclays), at 48–52; Enron Examiner's Final Report, supra note 18, at 72–4, 77–80.
41. Quoted in McLean and Elkind, supra note 19, at 160–1.
42. For discussions of Project Nahanni, see McLean and Elkind, supra note 19, at 157; Regan, supra note 20, at 1180–6; Enron Examiner's Second Report, supra note 17, App. D (Enron's Disclosure of SPEs), at 44–5, 48–9; Enron Examiner's Third Report, supra note 18, App. D (Citigroup), at 107–15.
43. Enron Examiner's Second Report, supra note 17, at 36–9, 95–112.
44. Sale, supra note 14, at 145–6; Enron Examiner's Second Report, supra note 17, at 95–9; Enron Examiner's Third Report, supra note 18, App. D (Citigroup), at 115–25.
45. Enron Examiner's Third Report, supra note 18, App. F (Barclays), at 20–48; *id.* App. H (CIBC), at 2–9, 25–60; Enron Examiner's Final Report, supra note 18, App. F (Credit Suisse), at 1–4, 8–9, 73–8.
46. Complaint in *SEC v. Merrill Lynch & Co.*, attached to SEC Litigation Release No. 18038, 17 March 2003 (available at www.sec.gov/litigation/litreleases/lr18038.htm) (hereinafter SEC Merrill Lynch Release); Enron Examiner's Third Report, supra note 18, App. I (Merrill Lynch), at 4–7, 23–42.
47. Bratton, supra note 17, at 1307–10, 1316–27; McLean and Elkind, supra note 19, at 191–206, 362–4; Regan, supra note 20, at 1202–20.
48. McLean and Elkind, supra note 19, at 191–206; Enron Examiner's Final Report, supra note 18, at 68–71, 75–6; *id.*, App. F (Credit Suisse), at 2–4, 6–7, 36–62; *id.*, App. E (RBS), at 3–4, 6–7, 29–62.
49. McLean and Elkind, supra note 19, at 197.
50. *Id.* at 197–206 (quote at 202); Bratton, supra note 17, at 1309–10; Enron Examiner's Third Report, supra note 18, App. I (Merrill Lynch), at 44–6.
51. Enron Examiner's Third Report, supra note 18, at 72–6 (quote at 74); *id.*, App. G (Deutsche), at 1–4, 27–57, 71–80.
52. Enron Examiner's Second Report, supra note 17, at 16–17.

53. Enron Examiner's Third Report, supra note 18, App. E (Chase), at 19 (quoting memorandum from Rick Walker of 15 December 1994); *id.* at 22–3 (quoting email from George Serice to Karen Simon on 25 November 1998) (emphasis in original).
54. Enron Examiner's Third Report, supra note 18, App. D (Citigroup), at 70 (quoting the Committee's minutes of 22 June 1999).
55. Enron Examiner's Final Report, supra note 18, App. F (Credit Suisse) at 69 (quoting sworn statement by James Moran); *id.* at 68 (quoting email from Ian Emmett to Steve Wootton on 12 December 2000).
56. Enron Examiner's Third Report, supra note 18, App. I (Merrill Lynch), at 42–3 (quoting email from Schuyler Tilney to Dan Gordon of 30 May 2000).
57. Enron Examiner's Third Report, supra note 18, at 27–9, 41–5, 57–8, 60–1, 68–71, 80–1 (quote at 80); Enron Examiner's Final Report, supra note 18, at 71–2, 77.
58. Enron Examiner's Third Report, supra note 18, App. H (CIBC), at 55, 56 (quoting emails, each dated 21 June 2001, from Mercedes Arrango to Gerry Beauclair and from Ian Schottlaender to Arrango).
59. Enron Examiner's Third Report, supra note 18, App. F (Barclays), at 23 (quoting Richard Williams' Transaction Comment of 14 November 2000).
60. Enron Examiner's Final Report, supra note 18, App. F (Credit Suisse), at 22 n. 81 (quoting email from Wesley Jones to Jonathan Yellen of 16 September 1999).
61. Enron Examiner's Final Report, supra note 18, at 72 (quoting Group Credit Committee minutes of September 2000).
62. Enron Examiner's Third Report, supra note 18, App. D (Citigroup), at 113 (quoting undated 'Citigroup exposure spreadsheet' and email from James Reilly to Michael Nepveux on 24 July 2001).
63. *Id.*, App. I (Merrill Lynch), at 120 (quoting email from Steve Baillie to William Fox on 24 November 2000).
64. *Id.* at 122, 121 (quoting emails from James Reilly to Maureen Hendricks on 28 November 2000, and from James Reilly to Steven Becton on 6 December 2000).
65. Enron Examiner's Third Report, supra note 18, App. I (Merrill Lynch), at 26–7 (quoting sworn statement by James Brown).
66. Enron Examiner's Third Report, supra note 18, App. D (Citigroup) at 120 (quoting email from Steve Baillie to William Fox of 24 November 2000).
67. *Id.* at 131 (quoting internal memorandum prepared by David Bushnell).
68. Enron Examiner's Final Report, supra note 18, App. F (Credit Suisse), at 40, 46 and n. 171 (quote) (summarizing testimony by Mary Beth Mandanas and Robert Jeffe).
69. Enron Examiner's Third Report, supra note 18, App. I (Merrill Lynch), at 25 (quoting memorandum from Robert Furst to Dan Bayly and Schuyler Tilney of 21 December 1999).
70. Enron Examiner's Third Report, supra note 18, App. D (Citigroup), at 122 (quoting email from Steve Baillie to William Fox of 24 November 2000).
71. *Id.* at 124 (quoting email from Steve Wagman to Amanda Angelini of 27 December 2000).
72. Enron Examiner's Final Report, supra note 18, App. F (Credit Suisse), at 45–6 (summarizing testimony of Adebayo Ogunlesi and Robert Jeffe); *id.* at 56 (quoting two memoranda, each dated 9 December 1999, prepared by Mary Beth Mandanas and Richard Ivers).
73. Enron Examiner's Third Report, supra note 18, App. D (Citigroup), at 19–20; *id.*, App. E (Chase), at 10; *id.*, App. H (CIBC), at 17; *id.*, App. I (Merrill Lynch), at 16; Enron Examiner's Final Report, supra note 18, App. F (Credit Suisse), at 17.
74. Enron Examiner's Third Report, supra note 18, App. D (Citigroup), at 20 (quoting Citigroup interoffice memorandum of 24 September 2001); *id.*, App. E (Chase), at 12 (quoting email from Todd Maclin to Richard Walker of 30 September 1999); Enron Examiner's Final Report, supra note 18, App. F (Credit Suisse), at 49 (quoting email from David Koczan to Osmar Abib of 17 June 2001).
75. Enron Examiner's Third Report, supra note 18, App. H (CIBC), at 18 n. 51 (quoting memorandum). A CIBC officer similarly explained that the returns from one SPE

transaction were 'so outrageous that [CIBC's] Risk Management [group was] softened into agreeing' to the bank's involvement in the transaction. *Id.* at 18 (quoting credit application submitted by Shannon Ernst on 15 December 1998).

76. Enron Examiner's Third Report, supra note 18, App. D (Citigroup), at 16–17; *id.*, App. I (Merrill Lynch), at 15–16; Enron Examiner's Final Report, supra note 18, App. F (Credit Suisse), at 16–17.

77. *In re Enron Corp. Securities, Derivative and ERISA Litigation*, 235 F. Supp. 2d 549, 640, 643–56 (SD Tex. 2002).

78. *Id.* at 596–7, 612–13, 637–56, 707–8 (discussing legal standards and factual allegations related to plaintiffs' claims under § 11 of the 1933 Act).

79. *Id.* at 570–94, 637–56, 692–704 (discussing legal standards and factual allegations related to plaintiffs' claims under § 10(b) of the 1934 Act).

80. *Id.* at 640–1, 644–5, 648, 651, 653–6.

81. *Id.* at 638–53; Enron Examiner's Third Report, supra note 18, App. D (Citigroup), at 21–6, 32–44; *id.*, App. E (Chase), at 12–17, 29–30; *id.*, App. F (Barclays), at 9–19; *id.*, App. H (CIBC), at 19–24, 43–4, 53–4; Enron Examiner's Final Report, supra note 18, App. E (RBS), at 20–7; *id.*, App. F (Credit Suisse), at 20–9; *id.*, App. G (Toronto Dominion), at 20–2.

82. Jonathan Macey, 'Efficient capital markets, corporate disclosure, and Enron,' 89 *Cornell Law Review* 394, 403–4 (2004).

83. *Id.* at 404; *see also id.* at n. 55 (quoting Charles Hill's testimony).

84. John C. Coffee, 'What caused Enron? A capsule social and economic history of the 1990s,' 89 *Cornell Law Review*, 269, 286 (2004).

85. For discussions of Merrill Lynch's decision to fire John Olson in 1998, and Citigroup's decision to terminate Don Dufresne in 1999, following complaints by Enron, see Kurt Eichenwald, *Conspiracy of Fools* 181–4, 186, 220 (2005); McLean and Elkind, supra note 19, at 230–5.

86. Rebecca Smith, 'The analyst who warned about Enron,' *Wall Street Journal*, 29 January 2002, at C1 (reporting on allegations made by Daniel Scotto).

87. Richard J. Oppel, Jr., 'The man who paid the price for sizing up Enron,' *New York Times*, 27 March 2002, at C1 (cited in Macey, supra note 82, at 404 n. 56); Frank Ahrens, 'Broker's tale probed for link to Enron,' *Washington Post*, 16 March 2002, at E01 (reporting on Wu's firing and stating that UBS acted as an underwriter for initial public offerings made by two Enron affiliates).

88. Enron Examiner's Final Report, supra note 18, App. F (Credit Suisse), at 34 n. 123 (quoting emails exchanged between Andy DeVries of Credit Suisse and Wade Suki of Chase on 25 October 2001).

89. *Id.* at 35 n. 123 (quoting email from Brian Gibbons to Andy DeVries on 29 November 2001).

90. *Id.* at 30–3.

91. William Battey, the head of Credit Suisse's research department, 'praised [Sakol] for getting timely information to [Credit Suisse's] bond traders,' but he also 'reminded her of the importance of the Enron relationship for [Credit Suisse].' *Id.* at 32–3.

92. SEC Administrative Proceedings Release No. 34-48230, 28 July 2003 (consent order requiring Citigroup to pay $101.25 million to settle Enron-related charges) (available at www.sec.gov/litigation/admin/34-48230.htm); SEC Litigation Release No. 18252, 28 July 2003 (announcing consent judgment requiring Chase to pay $135 million) (available at www.sec.gov/litigation/litreleases/lr18252.htm); SEC Litigation Release No. 18517, 22 December 2003 (announcing consent judgment requiring CIBC to pay $80 million) (available at www.sec.gov/litigation/litreleases/lr18517.htm); SEC Merrill Lynch Release, supra note 46 (announcing consent judgment requiring Merrill Lynch to pay $80 million).

93. 'Class Actions: CIBC to Pay $2.4 Billion To Settle Enron Stockholder Suit,' 37 *Securities Regulation and Law Report* (BNA) 1324 (8 August 2005) (reporting the following settlement payments: CIBC – $2.4 billion; Chase – $2.2 billion; Citigroup – $2 billion; Lehman – $222.5 million; Bank of America – $69 million).

94. Carrie Johnson, 'Fastow Takes Aim at Banks He Says Helped Enron,' *Washington Post*, 26 September 2006, at D01; Sheila McNulty and Ben White, 'Fastow accuses Enron bankers,' *Financial Times* (US ed.), 27 September 2006, at 17.

95. 'Moving the Market: Merrill Settles Enron Claims,' *Wall Street Journal*, 7 July 2006, at C3; David Enrich, 'Moving the Market: Two Banks Settle Enron Lawsuit,' *Wall Street Journal*, 17 August 2005, at C3; Rebecca Smith, 'Executives on Trial: Trial Begins With a Tale of Two Enrons,' *Wall Street Journal*, 1 February 2006, at C1.

96. For an insightful discussion of similarities among Enron, WorldCom and other well-known corporate scandals during the past three decades, see Geoffrey P. Miller, 'Catastrophic financial failures: Enron and more,' 89 *Cornell Law Review* 423 (2004).

97. Almar Latour *et al.*, 'Held accountable: Ebbers is convicted in massive fraud,' *Wall Street Journal*, 16 March 2005, at A1.

98. Akhigbe *et al.*, supra note 12, at 51.

99. Miller, supra note 96, at 436; First Interim Report of Dick Thorburgh, Bankruptcy Court Examiner, *In re WorldCom, Inc.*, Case No. 02-13533 (AJG) (Bankr. SDNY, 4 November 2002) [hereinafter WorldCom Examiner's First Report], at 12–13.

100. Akhigbe *et al.*, supra note 12, at 49; Miller, supra note 96, at 425; Latour *et al.*, supra note 97.

101. WorldCom Examiner's First Report, supra note 99, at 11–20, 58–60; Fotios Harmantzis, 'Inside the telecom crash: bankruptcies, fallacies and scandals – a closer look at the WorldCom case,' 30 March 2004 (available at http://ssrn.com/abstract= 575881), at 5–8; *In re WorldCom, Inc. Securities Litigation*, 346 F. Supp. 2d 628, 637–38 (SDNY 2004).

102. *United States v. Ebbers*, 458 F.3d 110, 113 (2d Cir. 2006); *In re WorldCom, Inc. Securities Litigation*, 346 F. Supp. 2d 628, 640 (SDNY 2004); *In re WorldCom, Inc. Securities Litigation*, 294 F. Supp. 2d 392, 401 (SDNY 2003).

103. WorldCom Examiner's First Report, supra note 99, at 20–1; Latour *et al.*, supra note 97; *United States v. Ebbers*, 458 F.3d 110, 113 (2d Cir. 2006).

104. WorldCom Examiner's First Report, supra note 99, at 11–12, 99–108; Third and Final Report of Dick Thornburgh, Bankruptcy Court Examiner, *In re WorldCom, Inc.*, Case No. 02-13533 (AJG) (Bankr. SDNY, 26 January 2004) [hereinafter WorldCom Examiner's Final Report], at 271–7; *In re WorldCom, Inc. Securities Litigation*, 294 F. Supp. 2d 392, 400–1 (SDNY 2003).

105. Elise A Couper, John P. Hejkal and Alexander L. Wolman, 'Boom and bust in telecommunications,' 89 *Economic Quarterly* No. 4, Federal Reserve Bank of Richmond, VA, Fall 2003, at 1; Harmantzis, supra note 101, at 3–7; Jonathan McCarthy, 'What investment patterns across equipment and industries tell us about the recent investment boom and bust,' 10 *Current Issues in Economics and Finance* No. 6, Federal Reserve Bank of NY, May 2004, at 1; Dennis K. Berman, 'Behind the fiber glut: innovation outpaced the marketplace,' *Wall Street Journal*, 26 September 2002, at B1; Steven Rosenbush *et al.*, 'Inside the telecom game,' *Business Week*, 5 August 2002, at 34, 37–40; 'Special report: The telecoms crisis: Too many debts; too few calls,' *Economist*, 20 July 2002, at 59 [hereinafter *Economist* report on telecoms crisis]; WorldCom Examiner's First Report, supra note 99, at 20–1.

106. WorldCom Examiner's First Report, supra note 99, at 102–9; WorldCom Examiner's Final Report, supra note 104, at 273–91;*United States v. Ebbers*, 458 F.3d 110, 114–16 (2d Cir. 2006); *In re WorldCom, Inc. Securities Litigation*, 346 F. Supp. 2d 628, 640–1 (SDNY 2004).

107. *United States v. Ebbers*, 458 F.3d 110, 114–16 (2d Cir. 2006); *In re WorldCom, Inc. Securities Litigation*, 294 F. Supp. 2d 392, 402 (SDNY 2003); Ken Belson, 'Witness says Ebbers urged manipulations at WorldCom,' *New York Times*, 9 February 2005, at C1 (summarizing Sullivan's testimony at Ebbers' criminal trial); Floyd Norris, 'MCI Chief says he repaid debt, borrowing from his company,' *New York Times*, 8 February 2002, at C2 (quoting 'utter nonsense' statement made by Ebbers during a conference call with investors).

108. WorldCom Examiner's First Report, supra note 99, at 23–30.

109. *Id.* at 112–14; Deborah Solomon, 'Leading the news: WorldCom's creditors seek to broaden review prior to 1999,' *Wall Street Journal*, 12 August 2002, at A3; Shawn Young *et al.*, 'Leading the news: WorldCom plans bankruptcy filing,' *Wall Street Journal*, 22 July 2002, at A3.
110. Jonathan Weil, 'WorldCom suit elicits unusual legal strategy,' *Wall Street Journal*, 25 August 2004, at C1; Shawn Young, 'MCI to state fraud was $11 billion,' *Wall Street Journal*, 12 March 2004, at A3.
111. 'Virginia: Verizon has completed its purchase of MCI,' *Richmond (VA) Times Dispatch*, 7 January 2006, at C-2.
112. Fanto, supra note 14, at 26.
113. *Id.*
114. WorldCom Examiner's Final Report, supra note 104, at 140.
115. *Id.* at 137–9; WorldCom Examiner's First Report, supra note 99, at 16–17, 20.
116. *In re WorldCom, Inc. Securities Litigation*, 346 F. Supp. 2d 628, 645–7 (quote at 647), 651–2 (SDNY 2004).
117. *Id.* at 651 and n. 27; Gretchen Morgenson, '3 banks had early concern on WorldCom,' *New York Times*, 17 March 2004, at A1 [hereinafter Morgenson, '3 Banks'].
118. WorldCom Examiner's Final Report, supra note 104, at 183–6, 220–30, 238–44.
119. *In re WorldCom, Inc. Securities Litigation*, 346 F. Supp. 2d 628, 639 (SDNY 2004).
120. WorldCom Examiner's Final Report, supra note 104, at 115–16 (quote), 118–22, 135–41, 151–77; Rosenbush *et al.*, supra note 105, at 36 ('Jack's Inner Circle' box, stating that Citigroup earned $140.7 million of fees from WorldCom).
121. WorldCom Examiner's Final Report, supra note 104, at 119–21, 143–4 (quote), 173–6, 182; SEC Citigroup Complaint, supra note 4, ¶¶ 150, 158, 189–95.
122. WorldCom Examiner's Final Report, supra note 104, at 184 n. 166.
123. Gretchen Morgenson, 'When Citigroup met WorldCom,' *New York Times*, 16 May 2004, § 3, at 1; Jonathan Weil, 'Citigroup calls Ebbers loans proper,' *Wall Street Journal*, 15 October 2002, at A6.
124. WorldCom Examiner's Final Report, supra note 104, at 183–94 (quote at 188).
125. *Id.* at 194–202 (quote at 198).
126. *Id.* at 183.
127. *In re WorldCom, Inc. Securities Litigation*, 346 F. Supp. 2d 628, 650 (SDNY 2004).
128. *Id.* at 651–2. An internal Chase email cautioned that 'if [WorldCom] gets any sense that we're laying off [credit] exposure DURING the syndication process (and wouldn't [Citigroup] love to pass that along), it would not be good news.' *Id.* at 651. Similarly, a Bank of America internal memorandum warned that WorldCom would 'go nuts' if it learned that the bank was reducing its credit exposure through credit default swaps or loan sales in the secondary market. *Id.* at 652 n. 30.
129. *Id.* at 654.
130. *Id.* at 641–55, 678–87, 690–7.
131. *Id.* at 635–7, 649–55, 662–4, 683, 695–6; see also *id.* at 656–78 (discussing legal standards governing claims under §§ 11 and 12(a)(2) of the 1933 Act); Morgenson, '3 Banks,' supra note 117; Gretchen Morgenson, 'Judge in WorldCom action sides with plaintiffs on issue of due diligence by banks,' *New York Times*, 16 December 2004, at C4.
132. Gretchen Morgenson, 'Despite access, star analyst missed WorldCom trouble signs,' *New York Times*, 9 July 2002, at C1 [hereinafter Morgenson, 'Star analyst'] (quoting Tierney's note).
133. *In re WorldCom, Inc. Securities Litigation*, 294 F. Supp. 2d 392, 404–5 (SDNY 2003).
134. WorldCom Examiner's Final Report, supra note 104, at 116–19, 134–41, 203–4 and App. 1.
135. WorldCom Examiner's First Report, supra note 99, at 98; Gretchen Morgenson, 'Analyst coached WorldCom chief on his script,' *New York Times*, 27 February 2003, at A1.
136. SEC Citigroup Complaint, supra note 4, ¶¶ 19, 28; *In re WorldCom, Inc. Securities Litigation*, 294 F. Supp. 2d 392, 405 (SDNY 2003).
137. Quoted in Peter Elstrom, 'The Power Broker,' *Business Week*, 15 May 2000, at 70.

138. Quoted in *id.*
139. Yochi Dreazen, 'Behind the fiber glut: telecom carriers were driven by wildly optimistic data on internet's growth,' *Wall Street Journal*, 26 September 2002, at B1 (describing claims made by WorldCom executives, and quoting Grubman's prediction in 1998 that 'no matter how much bandwidth is available, it will get used').
140. Rosenbush *et al.*, supra note 105, at 38–40; *Economist* report on telecoms crisis, supra note 105, at 59–60.
141. Rosenbush *et al.*, supra note 105, at 34, 36 ('Jack's inner circle' box); Berman, supra note 105 (reporting that investors bought $757 billion of telecom stocks and bonds during 1996–2002); see also Gretchen Morgenson, 'Bullish analyst of tech stocks quits Salomon,' *New York Times*, 16 August 2002, at A1 [hereinafter Morgenson, 'Bullish analyst'] (reporting that Grubman helped Citigroup earn $1 billion of underwriting and merger advisory fees paid by telecom clients during 1997–2001, a figure that was 43 percent higher than the fees earned by Merrill Lynch, the second-ranked underwriter and merger advisor for the telecom industry); Elstrom, supra note 137 (quoting telecom executive Robert Knowling's comment that Grubman was 'almost a demigod . . . the king of telecom').
142. SEC Citigroup Complaint, supra note 4, ¶¶ 4, 41, 51.
143. Quoted in Elston, supra note 137.
144. Rosenbush *et al.*, supra note 105, at 37; see also Dreazen, supra note 139; Harmantzis, supra note 101.
145. Berman, supra note 105; Dreazen, supra note 139; Harmantzis, supra note 101, at 5–7; Morgenson, 'Bullish analyst,' supra note 141; *Economist* report on telecoms crisis, supra note 105, at 59–60.
146. WorldCom Examiner's First Report, supra note 99, at 90, 91.
147. *Id.* at 92–4.
148. 'A lot was riding on these words,' *Washington Post*, 14 July 2002, at B04.
149. Morgenson, 'Star analyst,' supra note 132.
150. WorldCom Examiner's First Report, supra note 99, at 92–7; WorldCom Examiner's Final Report, supra note 104, App. 7.
151. *Id.*; Morgenson, 'Star analyst,' supra note 132.
152. WorldCom Examiner's First Report, supra note 99, at 91–5; WorldCom Examiner's Final Report, supra note 104, App. 9.
153. Quoted in Morgenson, 'Star analyst,' supra note 132.
154. Quoted in Rosenbush *et al.*, supra note 105, at 37.
155. Quoted in Charles Gasparino, 'Salomon's Grubman resigns: NASD finds "Spinning" at firm,' *Wall Street Journal*, 16 August 2002, at A1.
156. SEC Litigation Release No. 18111, 28 April 2003 (available at www.sec.gov/litigation/litreleases/lr18111.htm) [hereinafter SEC Citigroup/Grubman Release], at 2–4; Complaint in *SEC v. Grubman* (SDNY, 28 April 2003) [hereinafter SEC Grubman Complaint] (available at www.sec.gov/litigation/complaints/comp18111b.htm); Elstrom supra note 137.
157. SEC Grubman Complaint, supra note 156, ¶¶ 46–7, 39, 99. In his email of 13 January 2001, Grubman said that Weill also wanted him to upgrade AT&T's stock so that Weill could win the support of AT&T's CEO (a member of Citigroup's board) for Weill's plan to become sole CEO of Citigroup and to remove co-CEO John Reed. *Id.*, ¶ 99.
158. SEC Citigroup/Grubman Release, supra note 156, at 1, 5 (stating that Grubman agreed to pay $15 million as disgorgement and penalties and consented to the entry of an SEC order that 'permanently bars him from associating with any broker, dealer, or investment adviser').
159. *Id.* at 1–4; SEC Citigroup Complaint, supra note 4.
160. Gretchen Morgenson, 'Citigroup agrees to a settlement over WorldCom,' *New York Times*, 11 May 2004, at A1 [hereinafter Morgenson, 'Citigroup settlement'] (quoting brief).
161. *In re WorldCom, Inc. Securities Litigation*, 294 F. Supp. 2d 392, 405, 425 (quote) (SDNY 2003).

162. *In re WorldCom, Inc. Securities Litigation*, 388 F. Supp. 2d 319, 324, 327–9 (SDNY 2005) (discussing amounts paid by underwriters to settle class action lawsuit); Robin Sidel, 'J. P. Morgan to pay $2 billion as Street's bill for bubble soars,' *Wall Street Journal*, 17 March 2005, at A1.
163. Jonathan Weil and Robin Sidel, 'WorldCom investors settle lawsuits,' *Wall Street Journal*, 27 October 2005, at A3.
164. Robert Julavits, 'For Citi, $5B is price of "moving on",' *American Banker*, 11 May 2004, at 1; Morgenson, 'Citigroup settlement,' supra note 160.
165. Timothy L. O'Brien, 'Citigroup assesses a risk and decides to settle,' *New York Times*, 11 May 2004, at C1 (quoting analyst Richard Bove).

7. Basel II: operational risk and corporate culture

Benton E. Gup

BASEL II

The New Basel Capital Accord (hereafter called Basel II) replaces the 1988 Capital Accord (Basel I). Whereas Basel I has a simple one size fits all 8 percent capital standard for banks, Basel II is very complex; and is targeted primarily at large complex financial organizations (LCFOs). By definition, LCFOs are internationally active. ABN-Amro, Citigroup, and HSBC are examples of LCFOs.

The major difference between the two capital accords is that Basel II provides for more flexibility and risk sensitivity than Basel I 'to promote adequate capitalization of banks and to encourage improvements in risk management'.

Basel II[1] consists of three mutually reinforcing pillars: Pillar 1– minimum capital requirements, Pillar 2 – supervisory review process, and Pillar 3 – market discipline. As shown in Equation 7.1, Pillar 1 retains the current definition of capital and the minimum 8 percent requirement in the numerator. In the denominator, the measures for credit risk are more complex than Basel I, market risk is the same, and operational risk is new. This chapter focuses on operational risk.

$$\frac{\text{Total Capital (definition unchanged)}}{\text{Credit risk + Market risk + Operational risk}} \geq 8\% \text{ maximum capital ratio} \qquad (7.1)$$

The United States, will have a 'bifurcated regulatory capital framework', where the rules involving advanced measures of credit risk and operational risk will only apply to about ten LCFOs. Other banking organizations can 'opt in' to applying the new rules, while the remaining banks will continue to apply the existing capital rules.[2] The affected LCFO banks have assets greater than \$250 billion or foreign exposures greater than \$10 billion.

Although operational risk capital requirements of Basel II will only affect LCFOs, operational risk is of concern to all banks and financial institutions.

This chapter shows that corporate culture has had a major impact on operational risk losses. Therefore, bankers, regulators, and investors must place increased emphasis on selected aspects of corporate governance. The remainder of the chapter is divided into three parts. The next part deals with operational risk and corporate culture. The following part examines the Routine Activities Theory. The final part is the conclusion.

OPERATIONAL RISK

Basel II defines operational risk as the risk of direct or indirect loss resulting from inadequate or failed internal processes, people and systems or from external events.[3] Operational risk includes, but is not limited to fraud, accounting issues, legal issues, damage to physical assets, business practices/judgment, and so on. Table 7.1 lists the 11 largest losses at banking

Table 7.1   Large losses from operational risk 1992–2002

No.	Amount US$ millions	Firms	Description
1	2390	Australia National Bank Group – National Australia Bank (NAB)	HomeSide Lending, Inc., $2.2 billion; Currency options fraud, $191 million
2	1330	Barings PLC	Unauthorized trading
3	1110	Daiwa Bank Ltd.	Unauthorized trading
4	900	J.P. Morgan Chase	Enron related litigation
5	770	First National Bank of Keystone	Internal fraud
6	691	Allied Irish Banks	Unauthorized trading
7	636	Morgan Grenfell Asset Management (Deutsche Bank)	Mutual fund/ securities related
8	611	Republic Bank of New York	Securities related
9	490	Bank of America	Law suit
10	440	Standard Chartered Bank PLC	Securities related
11	440	Superior Bank	Accounting issues
Total	9808		

Source: Firms 2–11 are from Roger W. Ferguson (2003).

organizations from operational risk during the period from 1992–2002. The total losses amounted to $9.8 billion dollars!

Corporate Culture

In dealing with operational risk, Pillar 2 – the Supervisory Process – states that a bank's framework for managing operational risk 'should cover the bank's appetite and tolerance for operational risk'.[4] The extent to which this is done depends largely on a bank's corporate culture. Every organization has a corporate culture. The Basel Committee on Banking Supervision (February 2003, p. 1) defines operational risk culture as 'the combined set of individual and corporate value, attitudes, competencies and behaviour that determine a firm's commitment to and style of operational risk management'.

Marvin Bowers, former managing director of McKinsey & Company, has a simple definition of corporate culture. It is 'the way we do things around here'.[5] It is not what the companies say – it is what they do that counts. Corporate culture is set by the top executives in a firm. If they don't insist on doing things right, they will send the wrong message to employees. The employees will pick up on the top managements' values and that is what they will subscribe to in their operations.[6]

Corporate culture played a significant role in the operational losses shown in Table 7.1. By way of illustration, consider the losses at the National Australia Bank (NAB), Australia's largest bank. A report by PricewaterhouseCoopers *Investigation into Foreign Exchange Losses at the National Bank of Australia* (2004, p. 32) in connection with the US$ 191 (A$ 360) million foreign exchange loss at NAB said 'Meetings with staff and external third parties more directly connected with the Traders reveal that the culture surrounding currency options provided the opportunity for the Trader to trade, incur losses, and for them not to be detected despite warning signs. Some of the Traders treated aggressively anyone who questioned their activities . . . It appears that CIB (Corporate and Institutional Banking) and Markets Division management either allowed this culture to exist or took no action to prevent it insofar as it related to the currency options desk. Essentially this allowed the Traders to operate unchecked and flout the rules and standards of the bank.'

David Bullen, one of the suspended Traders said 'We were already over the limits for a number of months and the bank knew about it . . . It was signed off every day by the risk-management people.'[7]

But the culture of arrogance went beyond the Traders. The Australian Prudential Regulatory Authority (APRA) *Report into Irregular Currency Trading at National Australia Bank* (2004, p. 6) found that:

Line Management turned a blind eye to known risk management concerns.

Operations (the back office) verification procedures contained significant gaps.

Market Risk (the middle office), while noting a number of irregularities, failed to engage the trading desk effectively to resolve them and failed to attract the attention of higher management.

Executive Risk Committees were particularly ineffective, missing or dismissing risk information pertinent to the problems that emerged and failing to escalate warnings.

The Principal Board (the Board) was not sufficiently proactive on risk issues . . . The Board paid insufficient attention to risk issues.

Their most telling statement was: '*Cultural issues are at the heart of these failings.*'[8]

The $191 million FX trading losses seem small in comparison to NAB's $2.2 billion loss in connection with HomeSide Lending. Headquartered in Jacksonville Florida, HomeSide was the sixth largest servicer of mortgage loans in the US when NAB purchased it for $1.2 billion in 1998. In 2001, it was servicing more than $180 billion in mortgages. On 5 July and 3 September 2001, HomeSide recognized large losses of $450 million and $1.75 billion on HomeSide. Part of the loss was due to the fact that mortgage service companies, such as HomeSide, pay a front-end fee (for example 0.025 percent of the value of the mortgage) for the right to service mortgages (Mortgage Service Rights, MSR) over the life of the loans. Many mortgages have original maturities up to 30 years. However, because of declining mortgage rates, there was unprecedented refinancing of mortgage loans. The consequence of the large-scale refinancing was that HomeSide was unable to recapture the front-end fees that it paid.

In addition, the volatile interest rate environment and incorrect interest rate assumptions in their financial model caused HomeSide to overvalue their MSRs and not have the correct hedging strategies. Part of their loss is associated with Financial Accounting Standards No. 133, Accounting for Certain Derivative Instruments and Certain Hedging Activities. FAS 133 was issued in 1998, but it did not have to be implemented until 2001. It required that MSRs be valued at their market value rather than their theoretical value. This means that the balance may have to reflect some MSRs at a loss even though the contracts have years to run. In the remaining years of the contracts, the market values could be positive.

Some might argue that the refinancing that adversely affected the MSRs was market risk rather than operational risk. There can be some overlap between market risk and operational risk. Moreover, operational risk losses that are related to market risk losses are treated as operational risk for purposes of calculating capital requirements.[9] Because internal data were not available to distinguish between the two, the entire loss is considered operational risk in the context of this article. In either case, it was a loss that could have been hedged more effectively.

A National Australia Bank Group press release giving the results of an investigation into the losses found 'no evidence of unlawful or improper conduct by Group personnel, . . . no basis for . . . any disciplinary action against any of the Group's executives, directors, or auditors'.[10]

Nevertheless, one wonders about the influence of NAB's corporate culture on the interest rate assumptions and why they waited until 2001 to implement FAS 133. Their profits probably would not have been so high if it had been implemented earlier. And bonuses are tied to profits. More than 47 percent of NABs revenues were from outside of Australia in 2000.

On the other side of the coin, Freddie Mac, a stockholder owned corporation that was chartered by the US Congress, and it is one of the US's largest financial institutions with total assets of $752 billion in 2002. Freddie Mac got into trouble for smoothing its earnings in connection with FAS 133. The report by the Baker Botts law firm (2003) on the Freddie Mac accounting scandal revealed that 'It was understood throughout the organization that the tone of "steady Freddie" came from the its Chief Executive Officer: Employees in F&I, Corporate Accounting and other business units were expected to take actions that would help achieve the goal of steady, non-volatile earnings growth. The Board was aware of this strategy.'

The CEO and other executives were fired, and the company paid a $125 million civil fine in December in a settlement with its federal regulator – the Office of Federal Housing Enterprise Oversight (OFHEO) who charged Freddie Mac with faulty accounting and disseminating materially false and misleading statements. The Freddie Mac press release (10 December 2003) said 'the company is undertaking remedial actions relating to *governance, corporate culture, internal controls*, accounting practices, disclosure and oversight'.[11]

The bottom line is that NAB can be faulted for overstating earnings. And Freddie Mac was faulted for smoothing earnings. 'Managing' earnings *per se* is not illegal and many firms, including General Electric, have done so to their advantage.[12] Maybe the solution is that companies should reveal not only what they are doing but also why they are doing it.

Finally, Riggs Bank NA was assessed a $25 million civil money penalty for various violations of the Bank Secrecy Act (BSA) in connection with the anti-money laundering (AML) program.[13] A US Senate Report said that

The *corporate culture* at Riggs failed to communicate the importance of the bank's anti-money laundering program . . . Even more telling is the fact that Riggs Board failed over a five year period to ensure that regulators' directives to improve the bank's AML program were implemented . . . Riggs 'willfully violated' the requirements of the US anti-money laundering laws.[14]

One of the key findings of the report was that Riggs management '*turned a blind eye* to evidence suggesting the bank was handling the proceeds of foreign corruption'. 'Turned a blind eye' is exactly the same term used to describe NAB's management.

In review, corporate culture played key roles in the operational risk problems and losses associated with NAB, Freddie Mac, Riggs, and at other banks that are discussed below. However, it should be noted issues such as smoothing earnings and failing to prevent transactions that allowed money laundering are not unique to the previously mentioned institutions. Fannie Mae was criticized for its accounting practices and Citibank's branch in Tokyo in connection with money laundering and other charges.[15] The Office of Federal Housing Enterprise Oversight (OFHEO) *Report of Findings* (2004, i) about Fannie Mae stated that their accounting problems

> have emerged from an environment that made these problems possible. Characteristics of this culture include:
>
> - management's desire to portray Fannie Mae as a consistent generator of stable growing earnings;
> - a dysfunctional and ineffective process for developing accounting policies;
> - an operating environment that tolerated weak or non-existent internal controls;
> - key person dependencies and poor segregation of duties;
> - incomplete and ineffective reviews by the Office of Auditing;
> - an inordinate concentration of responsibility vested with the Chief Financial Officer; and
> - an executive compensation structure that rewarded management for meeting goals tied to earnings per share, a metric subject to manipulation by management.

These characteristics also could be listed below as red flags.

Red Flags

Red flags represent warning signs. In this section, we present six indicators that may give clues about potential operational risk problems.

Ineffective internal controls

As previously noted, corporate culture 'is the way we do things around here'. That definition also applies to internal controls – 'the checks and balances against undesired actions and are essential for banks to operate in a safe and sound manner'.[16] To some extent this is accomplished by having rules that must be followed and documentation to show that they were followed. However, having rules and documentation is necessary, but not sufficient to provide internal controls. The Executive Summary of the Pricewater-houseCoopers *Investigation into Foreign Exchange Losses at the National Bank of Australia* (2004, p. 4) said:

> *The National's culture* – there was excessive focus on process, documentation and procedure manuals rather than on understanding the substance of issues, taking responsibility and resolving matters. In addition, there was arrogance in dealing with warning signs (i.e. APRA letters, market comments, etc.). Our investigation revealed that management had a tendency to 'pass on', rather than assume responsibility. Similarly, issues were not escalated to the Board and its committees and bad news was suppressed.

The point here is that effective internal controls go beyond having rules and documentation.

Lax internal controls are a major problem. A US General Accounting Office (1991) study of 39 failed banks found that 'internal control weaknesses continue to be a significant cause of bank failures and that the regulatory early warning system to identify troubled banks is seriously flawed'. Section 112 of the Federal Deposit Insurance Corporation Improvement Act (FDICIA) of 1991 required management to have annual reports on the quality of their internal controls, and for outside auditors to attest to that quality. Federal Reserve Governor Susan Bies (22 June 2004) said that Section 112 of FDICIA 'became routine, delegated to lower levels of management, and no longer relevant to the way businesses were run. That is when the breakdown in internal controls began to occur'. Riggs Bank is an example of such a breakdown in controls. A US Senate report said that Riggs was 'employing a dysfunctional system that failed to safeguard the bank against money laundering and foreign corruption'.[17]

Section 404 of the Sarbanes-Oxley Act of 2002 requires publicly traded companies to adopt and evaluate their internal controls. The internal controls must provide reasonable assurance regarding the achievement of their objectives in operations, financial reporting, and compliance with laws and regulations.[18]

The most cost-effective way to deal with operational risk is to prevent it from happening. Effective internal controls are a step in that direction. The Basel Committee on Banking Supervision (1998) provided a 'Framework for internal control systems in banking organizations'. However, the success or failure of the internal controls depends on corporate culture. Jensen (1993, p. 852) said that 'By nature, organizations abhor control systems, and ineffective governance is a major part of the problem with internal control mechanisms. They seldom respond in the absence of a crisis.'

Size and complexity

Large size organizations in general and highly complex ones in particular offer more opportunities for the types of operational risks and losses described in this article. This is best described in Warren Buffett's (2003) letter to the shareholders of Berkshire Hathaway Inc., explaining the losses associated with General Re, a property/casualty insurance company. Buffet said that their insurance operations must: (a) underwrite with unwavering discipline; (b) reserve conservatively; and (c) avoid exposures that would allow a supposedly 'impossible' incident to threaten the company's solvency.

> When I agreed in 1998 to merge Berkshire with General Re, I thought that company stuck to the three rules I've enumerated . . . I was dead wrong. General Re's *culture and practices* had changed and unbeknownst to management – and to me – the company was grossly mispricing its current business. In addition, General Re had accumulated an aggregation of risks that would have been fatal had, say, terrorists detonated several large-scale nuclear bombs in an attack on the US.[19]

General Re lost $173 million, and part of that loss was due to derivatives that came from General Re Securities. Buffett goes on to say that 'the re-insurance business and derivatives business are similar: Like Hell, both are easy to enter and almost impossible to exit . . . Once you write a contract – which may require large payments decades later – you are usually stuck with it . . . Another commonality of reinsurance and derivatives is that both generate reported earnings that are often wildly overstated. That's true because today's earnings are in a significant way based on estimates whose inaccuracy may not be exposed for many years.' Finally he said that 'derivatives are financial weapons of mass destruction, carrying the dangers that while now latent, are potentially lethal'. When Buffett/Berkshire Hathaway bought General Re, he did not understand the complexity of derivatives or that their valuation involves a lot of judgment that may be flawed.

Similarly, many of the other examples cited in this chapter involve complex transactions or processes that were not understood or properly controlled by top management.

Although this chapter focuses primarily on operational risk at LCFOs, it should be noted that operational risk is also present in small banks. *Oakwood Deposit Bank Company* is a case in point. Oakwood had $72.3 million in assets when it failed in February 2002. Barry Snyder (2002), Inspector General of the Federal Reserve System, said 'The Oakwood Deposit Bank Company (Oakwood) failed because a massive and pervasive fraud was perpetrated by a trusted senior executive who exploited a weak corporate governance environment and inadequate control structure.' The Report on the Failure of Oakwood (2002) reported the following lessons from that failure, which also may apply to some LCFOs.

- A weak board of directors,
- Dominant senior executive,
- Inadequate separation of duties,
- A weak or non-existent internal and external audit program, and
- A history of internal control deficiencies.

Risk tolerance

Banking is the management of risk. The risks include, but are not limited to credit risk, interest rate risk, foreign exchange and country risks, and operational risk. Each bank has its own tolerance for risk. Objective measures of risk that can be found in bank financial statements and reports include, but are not limited to provisions for loan losses, net charge-offs to loans, and Value at Risk (VaR). Both objective and subjective measures of risk can be considered collectively to determine a bank's tolerance for risk.

Figure 7.1 shows the relationship between various degrees of risk tolerance and how strictly internal controls are followed. A low tolerance for risk and strict adherence to internal controls result in relatively low operational and other risk. As the tolerance for risk increases, and the enforcement of internal controls lessens, the opportunities for operational risk and other risks increase. High risk tolerance and lax internal controls are the danger zone. The figure can be used as an early warning indicator to help prevent future losses due to operational risk.

Arrogant culture

Conversations with bank regulators and accountants about several banks that sustained large losses due to frauds used the term 'arrogance' to describe the failed corporate cultures. The dictionary defines arrogance as being overly convinced of one's self importance or superiority. Such an attitude allows the offenders to cut corners in order to enhance their wealth in the form of bonuses and or higher stock values.

Financial incentives

Financial incentives are the principal reason behind the large financial losses shown in Table 7.1 at NAB, Daiwa Bank, Barings, Keystone, Allied Irish Bank, and perhaps the remaining banks. For example, currency, bond and derivatives traders receive their salary plus a bonus. The more they trade at a profit, the more they make. Toshihide Iguchi at Daiwa Bank, Nicholas Leeson at Barings Bank, and David Rusnak at Allfirst, all mid-level employees, were

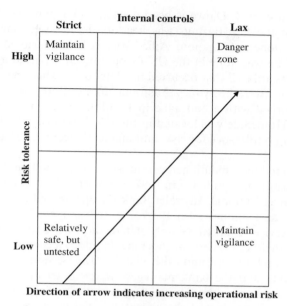

Figure 7.1   Internal controls and risk tolerance

successful at trading for awhile, and then the markets turned. Not wanting to lose their bonuses, they committed trades and frauds that resulted in large losses.

Financial incentives are not limited to mid-level traders. Consider the case of the First National Bank of Keystone, West Virginia. Keystone West Virginia was a coal mining town with a population of 600 and a high unemployment rate when J. Knox McConnell bought the First National Bank of Keystone in 1977. It had assets of about $20 million. But when the Office of the Comptroller of the Currency closed the bank in 1999, it had $1.1 billion in assets recorded on its books, but investigators were unable to account for $515 million of them. The bank sold the assets, but didn't take them off of the books. The bank 'Regulators later wondered whether the complex risky loan investment program had been set up primarily as a "front" so that certain bank executives could disguise irregular payments to themselves and businesses that they owned.'[20] McConnell died a rich man in 1997 before the scandal was made public.

Geographic distance
The final aspect of operational risk at the banks listed in Table 7.1, is the geographic distance between the headquarters of the banks, and where

their losses occurred. Daiwa is headquartered in Japan, but the trading was done in the US. Barings was headquartered in England, but the trading was done in Singapore. Allied Irish is headquartered in Ireland, but the trading was done in the US. Geography also played a role in the trading losses at NAB that occurred in Melbourne, when the other treasury operations were in Sydney Australia. In addition, the NAB traders allegedly worked with a colleague in London to hide their positions.[21] Recall that HomeSide was located in the US. Obviously, the lax internal controls, a high tolerance for risk, and financial incentives all contributed to the losses.

All of the red flags mentioned previously can also be found in losses in National Irish Bank Limited.[22] In 1987, a subsidiary of National Australia Bank known as National Australia Bank Europe limited acquired what is now known as National Irish Bank Limited and National Irish Bank Financial Services Limited. Simply stated, the Irish bank facilitated tax evasion by their customers by opening fictitious accounts, improperly charged fees and interest, and other charges. Tax evasion was the 'culture of the period', and the bank managers were 'target driven . . . for fee income and deposits . . . but limited support by way of systems or training to enable the achievement of these targets'.[23] The estimated cost of funds returned to customers and the tax authority is €30 million or more.

Culture of Corruption

Corruption and bribery are the norm in many countries. Transparency International is a global anti-corruption organization that publishes a Corruptions Perceptions Index (CPI), a Bribe Payers Index (BPI) as well as other indexes and surveys.[24] The maximum index score is 10 indicating the least corruption or bribery. The low scores indicate greater corruption and bribery. The CPI score for 91 countries in 2001 ranged from a high of 9.9 to a low of 0.4. Table 7.2 lists the countries with the five lowest scores of 2 or less suggesting that they have the most corruption. At the other end of the spectrum, Finland had the highest score (9.9). The scores for Australia and the US were 7.8 and 7.6 respectively.

The BPI was for 15 countries in 2002. The data in Table 7.2 lists the countries with the five lowest scores. Russia had the lowest score, indicating the most bribery. At the other end of the spectrum, Australia had the highest score (8.5), indicating that it was the least susceptible to bribery. The United States had a score of 5.3.

Consider the following incident from Russia. The July 2004 banking crisis in Russia began with Sodbiznesbank having its license revoked in connection with money laundering connected to a murder investigation.

Table 7.2   Countries with the lowest corruption and bribery indexes (CPI, BPI) (Low indexes suggest high corruption and bribery)

Country	CPI
Azerbaijan	2.0
Bolivia	2.0
Cameroon	2.0
Kenya	2.0
Indonesia	1.9
Uganda	1.9
Nigeria	1.0
Bangladesh	0.4

Country	BPI
Italy	4.1
South Korea	3.9
Taiwan	3.8
People's Republic of China	3.5
Russia	3.2

Source: Transparency International (2001, 2002), www.transparency.org

Accepting money from who-knows-where and from who-knows-whom was Sodbiznesbank's core business . . . Moreover, the bank, which more than anything resembled a launderette, had succeeded in attracting depositors. Just as terrorists need hostages, so the bank needed depositors to serve as human shields. When the bank's license was revoked, its unfortunate depositors began to panic.[25]

The panic spread to other banks.

The operational risk problem here is how do internationally active banks, in say the US, deal with foreign customers in countries that have a culture of corruption? How do they deal with banks they acquire or with correspondent banks in such countries? Do they follow US laws and rules, or local customs? Riggs Bank provides one answer to those questions. Riggs Bank lacked 'oversight, *internal controls*[26] and procedures to ensure compliance with the Bank Secrecy Act'. It 'allowed or, at times, actively facilitated suspicious financial activity' in connection with money laundering involving Equatorial Guinea, Saudi Arabia, and Augusto Pinochet, former president of Chile.[27] As previously noted, Riggs was fined $25 million.

Two Senate hearings, one on correspondent banking and the other on private banking shed additional light on these issues.[28] The findings in these hearings are that drug traffickers and other criminals using foreign banks' correspondent accounts with US banks to have access to US bank accounts. In addition, private banking has also served as a conduit for dirty money. Once again corporate culture and internal controls played a role in these issues.

Finally, some banks are inherently corrupt. The Bank of Commerce and Credit International (BCCI) is a prime example. It is also known as the Bank of Crooks and Criminals International. It was described by Senator Hank Brown as 'one of the smartest, deadliest, criminal organizations yet assembled. From the outside, it appeared to be full of successful bankers with impressive ties to some of the nation's most powerful leaders.'[29] BCCI was organized in Abu Dhabi in the early 1970s. It had global operations in more than 30 countries, and more than 1 million depositors. In the United States, BCCI had equity interests directly or through others in National Bank of Georgia, Independence Bank in California, Central Trust in Florida, First America Bankshares, and a commodities futures firm, Capcom Financial Services. BCCI was one of the principal banks used by General Manuel Noriega to launder drug money in the US. BCCI was also involved in a wide range of other crimes. The corruption was facilitated by its organizational structure of multiple layers of entities that were tied together through holding companies, affiliate firms, subsidiaries, and nominee relationships. In other words, it was an LCFO. BCCI was closed on 5 July 1991, but the legal proceedings on this case continued through to 2003.

THE ROUTINE ACTIVITIES THEORY

Cohen and Felson (1979) developed the 'Routine Activities Theory', that is widely used in criminology to explain certain types of crimes, such as theft. The theory has three main elements: a motivated offender, a suitable target, and absence of a suitable guardian. In other words, the theory deals with the means, motive, and opportunity to commit crimes.

This theory can be used to explain some of the operational risk losses listed in Table 7.1. For example, Nicholas Leeson, at Barings Bank, had the means to commit fraud because he was a director and chief trader of Barings Futures Singapore. He understood trading and the back office processes surrounding the trades. Leeson was a motivated offender because he saw the opportunity for personal financial gain. And the lack of effective internal controls (one of the guardian's tools), and the fact that he had some control over Barings' back office in Singapore, gave him the opportunity to speculate on the direction of Japanese stock prices and try to hide his losses. As a result of his fraudulent trading, Barings lost $1.3 billion, and it failed. Leeson went to jail.[30]

Similarly, the losses at NAB, Daiwa, Keystone, Allied Irish and maybe several of the others listed in Table 7.1 can be viewed in the context of means, motive, and opportunity. The losses were attributable to insiders (means) who had strong financial incentives (motive), and the lack of a 'guardian' provided the opportunity. The guardian is a strong board of directors that makes effective use of internal controls and other means to deter corporate wrongdoing.

CONCLUSIONS

Basel II is a complex set of rules and guidelines that places increased emphasis on the risk management of LCFOs. It is a step in the right direction. However, Basel II rules and processes can be effective only if they are implemented in the proper corporate culture. This chapter demonstrated that corporate culture has a major effect on operational risk. Corporate culture is a top-down concept. It starts at the top of the organization and it flows down to the employees. Two studies, one by Committee on Sponsoring Organizations (COSO, 1999) and the other by Uzun *et al.* (2004), showed that the composition of the board of directors and the oversight committee are correlated with corporate fraud. A higher proportion of outside independent directors was associated with less likelihood of corporate wrongdoing.

Some of the operational risk losses listed in Table 7.1 involving frauds and other crimes might have been prevented if 'the guardian' – a strong board of directors and effective internal controls – were present. Effective internal controls are part of a strong corporate culture. Stated otherwise, poor corporate governance facilitated the losses. Therefore corporate governance must place increased emphasis on corporate culture to reduce such losses in the future. The composition of the board of directors is another factor that influences corporate culture, internal controls, and fraud. Finally, Federal Reserve Governor Susan Bies (22 June 2004) said that 'Those institutions leading the way recognize that the culture of governance, ethics, and controls cannot be switched on and off. They build a culture of accountability and ethics to make governance a part of every strategic plan and daily operation. These organizations are also beginning to focus more attention on operational risk issues.'

NOTES

1. Bank for International Settlements, Press Release, 26 June 2004.
2. FDIC, PR 70–2004, 26 June 2004. For additional details on Basel II, see Gup (2004).

3. For detailed information on operational risk, see Basel Committee on Banking Supervision, January 2001. Also see, Basel Committee on Banking Supervision, February 2003.
4. Basel Committee on Banking Supervision, June 2004, paragraph 737.
5. Deal and Kennedy (1982), page 4.
6. An extensive examination of corporate culture is beyond the scope of this article. For additional information about corporate culture, see Ashkanasy *et al.* (2000) and Want (2003).
7. Oldfield, 2004, p. 1.
8. Emphasis added.
9. Basel Committee on Banking Supervision (June 2004), paragraph 673.
10. 'National Board Releases HomeSide Review Outcomes', 21 January 2002.
11. Emphasis added.
12. For a discussion of GE's earnings, see Birger (2000).
13. Comptroller of the Currency, New Release 2004-34 (2004).
14. US Senate (15 July 2004), pp. 71 and 7. Emphasis added.
15. Morse and Pacelle (20 September 2004).
16. US General Accounting Office (1991), 5. For additional discussion of internal controls, see Gup (1995).
17. US Senate, 'Money laundering . . .' (15 July 2004), p. 66.
18. For additional information on internal controls, see The Institute of Internal Auditors (http://www.theiia.org/iia/index.cfm) and various position papers by the Committee on Sponsoring Organizations (COSO) on that subject.
19. Emphasis added.
20. 'First National Bank of Keystone,' ERisk.com Case Study, June 2002, 1.
21. Crow (2004).
22. For complete details, see *Report on Investigations into the Affairs of National Irish Bank and National Irish Bank Financial Services Limited*, 2004.
23. Ibid., Summary and Inspectors' Observations, p. ii.
24. For further information, see www.transparency.org
25. Latynina (7 July 2004).
26. Federal Reserve Press Release, 14 May 2004. Emphasis added.
27. US Senate, 'Money Laundering . . .,' (15 July 2004), p. 2.
28. US Senate, 'Private Banking . . .' (9, 10 November 1999); US Senate, 'Role of US correspondent banking . . .' (1, 2, 6, March 2001).
29. Gup (1995), 31.
30. For additional information on Barings failure, see Gup (1998), 50–1.

REFERENCES

Ashkanasy, Neal M., Celeste P. M. Wilderom and Mark F. Peterson (eds) (2000), *Handbook of Organizational Culture & Climate*, Thousand Oaks, CA: Sage Publications, Inc.

Australian Prudential Regulatory Authority (APRA) (2004), *Report into Irregular Currency Trading at National Australia Bank*, Sydney, Australia, 23 March.

Baker Botts L. L. P. (2003), 'Internal investigation on certain accounting matters December 10, 2002–July 21, 2003, executive summary,' see Freddie Mac press release, 23 July 2003: 'Freddie Mac releases board counsel's report' accessed at www.freddiemac.com.

Bank for International Settlements (2004), 'G10 Central Bank governors and heads of supervision endorse the publication of the revised capital framework,' press release, 26 June, accessed at www.bis.org.

Basel Committee on Banking Supervision (1998), 'Framework for internal control systems in banking organizations,' September, accessed at www.bis.org.

Basel Committee on Banking Supervision (2001), 'Operational risk: supporting document to the New Basel Capital Accord,' consultative document, January, accessed at www.bis.org.

Basel Committee on Banking Supervision (2003), 'Sound practices for the management and supervision of operational risk,' no. 96, February, accessed at www.bis.org.

Basel Committee on Banking Supervision (2004), 'International convergence of capital measurement and capital standards: a revised framework,' no. 107, June, accessed at www.bis.org.

Bies, Susan Schmidt (2004), 'Trends in risk management and corporate governance,' remarks by Governor Susan Schmidt Bies at the Financial Managers Society Finance and Accounting Forum for Financial Institutions, Washington, DC, 22 June.

Birger, Jon (2000), 'Glowing numbers,' *Money Magazine*, November, 112–22.

Buffett, Warren E. (2003), 'To the shareholders of Berkshire Hathaway Inc.,' *Berkshire Hathaway Inc., 2002 Annual Report*, 21 February.

Cohen, Larry and Marcus Felson (1979), 'Social change and crime trends: a routine activities approach,' *American Sociological Review*, 44, 588–608.

Committee on Sponsoring Organizations (COSO) of the Treadway Commission (1999), 'Fraudulent financial reporting, 1987–1997: an analysis of US public companies,' accessed at www.coso.org/publications.htm.

Comptroller of the Currency (2004), 'OCC assesses $25 million penalty against Riggs Bank NA,' press release NR 2004-34, 13 May.

Crow, Robert (2004), 'Playing with financial fire,' *The Australian Financial Review*, 2 February, 61.

Deal, Terrence E. and Allan A. Kennedy (1982), *Corporate Cultures: The Rites and Rituals of Corporate Life*, Reading, MA: Addison-Wesley Publishing Co.

ERisk.com (2002), 'First National Bank of Keystone,' case study, June.

Federal Reserve (2004), 'Consent order to cease and desist against Riggs National Corp and Riggs International Banking Corporation,' press release, 14 May.

Ferguson, Roger W. (2003), testimony of the Vice Chairman Federal Reserve before the Subcommittee on Financial Institutions and Consumer and Credit, Committee on Financial Services, US House of Representatives, 19 June.

Federal Deposit Insurance Corporation (FDIC) (2004), 'Banking agencies announce publication of revised capital framework and describe US implementation efforts,' press release PR-70-2004, 6 June.

Freddie Mac (2003), 'Freddie Mac announces settlement with Office of Federal Housing Enterprise Oversight,' press release, 10 December.

Gup, Benton E. (2004), *The New Basel Capital Accord*, Mason, OH: Thomson-Texere.

Gup, Benton E. (1995), *Targeting Fraud: Uncovering and Deterring Fraud in Financial Institutions*, Chicago, IL: Probus Publishing.

Gup, Benton E. (1998), *Bank Failures in the Major Trading Countries of the World: Causes and Remedies*, Westport, CT: Quorum Books.

Jensen, Michael, C. (1993), 'The modern industrial revolution, exit, and the failure of internal control systems,' *Journal of Finance*, July, 831–80.

Latynina, Yulia (2004), 'Banking crisis Russian style,' *The MoscowTimes.com*, 7 July, page 7, accessed at www.themoscowtimes.com/stories/2004/07/07/008.html.

Morse, Andrew and Mitchell Pacelle (2004), 'Japan orders Citibank to halt private banking,' *The Wall Street Journal*, 20 September, A3.

National Australia Bank Group (2002), 'National Board releases HomeSide review outcomes – Wachetell, Lipton, Rosen & Katz Report', Melbourne, Australia, 21 January.

Office of the Director of Corporate Enforcement (ODCE) (2004), 'Report On Investigations into the Affairs of National Irish Bank Limited and National Irish Bank Financial Services Limited, by High Court Inspectors Mr Justice Blayney and Tom Grace FCA, appointed 30 March 1998 and 15 June 1998,' published by the High Court, 30 July, accessed at www.odce.ie.

Office of Federal Housing Enterprise Oversight (2004), 'Report of findings to date special examination of Fannie Mae,' Washington, DC, 17 September.

Office of the Inspector General of the Board of Governors of the Federal Reserve System (2002), 'Report on the failure of the Oakwood Deposit Bank Company', October.

Oldfield, Stewart (2004), 'NAB scandal: trader hits back,' *The Australian Financial Review*, **1**, 16 January, 63.

PricewaterhouseCoopers (2004), *Investigation into Foreign Exchange Losses at the National Bank of Australia*, Sydney, Australia: PricewaterhouseCoopers, 12 March.

Snyder, Barry R. (2002), letter to The Honorable Susan S. Bies, 25 October, in connection with the Board of Governors of the Federal Reserve System, Office of Inspector General, 'Report on the failure of the Oakwood Deposit Bank Company.'

Transparency International (2001), 'New index highlights worldwide corruption crisis, says Transparency International,' press release, Paris, 27 June.

Transparency International (2002), 'Russian, Chinese, Taiwanese and S. Korean companies widely seen using bribes in developing countries,' press release, Berlin, 14 May.

United States General Accounting Office (1991), *Failed Banks: Accounting and Auditing Reforms Urgently Needed*, GAO/AFMD-91-43, April, Washington, DC.

United States Senate (1999), 'Private banking and money laundering: a case study of opportunities and vulnerabilities,' Permanent Subcommittee on Investigations, Committee on Governmental Affairs, 9, 10 November.

United States Senate (2001), 'Role of US correspondent banking in international money laundering,' Permanent Subcommittee on Investigations, Committee on Governmental Affairs, 1, 2, 6 March.

United States Senate (2004), 'Money laundering and foreign corruption: enforcement and effectiveness of the Patriot Act: case study involving Riggs Bank,' Permanent Subcommittee on Investigations, Committee on Governmental Affairs, report prepared by the Minority Staff of the Permanent Subcommittee, 15 July.

Uzun, Hatice, Samuel H. Szewczyk and Raj Varma (2004), 'Board composition and corporate fraud,' *Financial Analysts Journal*, May/June, 33–43.

Want, Jerry (2003), 'Corporate culture – illuminating the black hole,' *Journal of Business Strategy*, **24**(4), 14–21.

8. A cross-country analysis of bank performance: the role of external governance

James R. Barth, Mark J. Bertus, Valentina Hartarska, Hai Jason Jiang and Triphon Phumiwasana

INTRODUCTION

Perhaps the most striking feature of the financial landscape of the past two decades is the number and severity of banking crises across the globe. While many of these crises occurred in association with currency crises, many did not, being rather the result of, for example, excessive growth in bank credit. Regardless of the causes, over the past decade or so – and particularly in the wake of the East Asian and Russian banking crises of the late 1990s – a strong consensus has emerged among policymakers and industry observers that, fundamentally, both the existing management practices of bankers and bank regulatory and supervisory practices were insufficient to promote well-functioning banking systems.

It is by now commonly understood that healthy banking systems require a more insightful approach to regulation and supervision, and that information and discipline from market participants can complement and support sound regulatory and supervisory practices. Such an approach is in the process of being implemented under the New Basel Capital Accord ('Basel II'). In addition, supervisors around the world are switching from traditional financial ratio analysis and 'counting the cash' to 'risk-based' supervision, a process that requires supervisory authorities to develop both tools and insights that allow them to more accurately assess banks' risk profiles and risk management measures. Beyond this, it is widely recognized that government ownership of banks is generally at odds with efficient, as well as safe and sound, banking.

A major change in focus that has emerged over the recent past is a new emphasis on market discipline. Some policy prescriptions emphasize the importance of augmenting and complementing improved regulation and supervision with greater reliance on market forces. The Basel II process has brought considerable attention to bear on the issue of market discipline in banking; indeed, 'Pillar 3' of Basel II is devoted to this dimension of safety and soundness.

A rapidly growing body of research has focused on both measures internal to the firm (or, in the case of banking, 'the bank') – 'corporate governance' – and other measures likely to enhance the ability of the market to work in a manner that promotes safe and sound banking practices. The current chapter examines the issue of 'external governance' – that is, measures that complement good internal corporate governance by improving the information available to external market participants – features that improve bank information accuracy, transparency and accountability. In particular, using a large and new cross-country database, we develop measures of the efficacy of accounting standards, the strength of external auditing, financial statement transparency, and the efficacy of external ratings and credit monitoring activities. These measures address the issue of the quality of the information available to allow market forces to work, such as the extent to which those parties disclosing information to the public are held accountable for its accuracy. We add these country-specific variables to bank-specific data, and use them to augment standard explanatory variables in extant empirical models of bank performance. In general, we find that, looking across several thousand banks in dozens of countries, these measures of external governance matter across several dimensions of bank performance.

The chapter is organized as follows. The next section undertakes a review of representative studies of external governance in banking. The third section describes our large unique cross-country database in detail, noting both that few before us have modeled all four of our dimensions of external governance, and that a large segment of our country-specific data is new. The fourth section explains our model, while the fifth section discusses the empirical results. The final section concludes.

REVIEW OF SELECTED LITERATURE ON EXTERNAL GOVERNANCE IN BANKING

Overview

A widely accepted definition of corporate governance is provided by Shleifer and Vishny (1997), who define corporate governance as the ways in which investors ensure themselves that they will receive maximum return on their investments.[1] Key mechanisms of an effective governance framework include ownership (including institutional and managerial ownership), structure of the board of directors (size and composition), CEO and directors' remuneration, auditing, information disclosure, and the market for corporate control (Keasey and Wright, 1997).

These governance mechanisms are sometimes grouped into 'internal' and 'external' mechanisms.[2] There are different perspectives in the literature regarding 'internal' and 'external' governance. Some researchers refer to 'internal' governance in the context of the owners or the board of directors and their ability to control managers, while others define it as the collection of incentives designed to improve decision making and monitoring. 'External governance' is referred to as the control exercised by stakeholders and markets, or as the accountability mechanisms that operate to enforce internal governance (Halme, 2000). We define the external governance framework as the collection of rules, external to the banking firm, which complement good internal corporate governance because they expose management to disciplining forces external to the bank and regulatory authorities. In particular, the focus of this chapter is on the disciplining impact of accounting standards, the strength of external auditing, financial statement transparency, and the efficacy of external ratings and credit monitoring activities, all of which improve the quality or quantity of information available to the market.[3]

The issue of good governance for banks is particularly important, as Caprio and Levine (2002) and Macey and O'Hara (2003) argue. Banks and other financial intermediaries themselves exert governance impacts on other firms, both as creditors of those firms and, in many countries, as shareholders. Indeed, as Caprio and Levine (2002) point out, in many countries, especially developing ones, where banks dominate as financial intermediaries, banks are among the most important sources of external governance for firms. To the extent banks are well-managed, the allocation of capital will be more efficient than otherwise. Indeed, Bushman and Smith (2003) make an explicit connection between corporate governance of financial intermediaries and the finance-and-economic-growth literature. Furthermore, Beck *et al.* (2003) find that bank supervisory policies that force banks to disclose accurate information and enhance private monitoring tend to ease the financing obstacles faced by firms.

Despite the importance of this issue, 'very little attention has been paid to the corporate governance of banks'.[4] However, in the wake of recent well-publicized governance scandals at multinational firms headquartered in the United States and elsewhere, there has been a renewed interest in research on corporate governance, and this interest seems in part to have stimulated new interest in research on corporate governance for banking.[5] Conceptually, Macey and O'Hara (2003) argue that given the special nature of banking, it is worthwhile to consider as 'stakeholders' constituents beyond shareholders.

Because banks' liabilities, especially to depositors, play such a crucial role in the economy, Macey and O'Hara argue that 'bank directors should owe fiduciary duties to fixed claimants as well as to equity claimants'.[6] In a complementary vein, Caprio and Levine (2002) explain that there are four sources of governance for banks: shareholders, debtholders, the competitive discipline of output markets, and governments.[7]

One purpose of both market discipline mechanisms and government regulation is to ameliorate information asymmetries between various stakeholders and improve bank performance. Yet, government involvement in the form of deposit insurance and lender of last resort support may interact negatively with the disciplining role of the external governance framework. For instance, deposit insurance serves to protect depositors, but it also decreases their motivation to monitor banks. In such a situation, shareholders and managers may attempt to undertake excessively risky activities. As another example, whether private investors in uninsured bank debt impose market discipline on bank managers may depend on whether they consider their investments at risk. In the presence of a 'too big to fail' policy, they may not consider their investment at risk and thus inadequately monitor banks (Morgan and Stiroh, 2000). It is for these reasons that whether market discipline actually improves bank performance or not is ultimately an empirical question.

Sub-components of External Governance

Accounting standards
An important dimension of external governance is the degree of transparency that exists for the operations of a firm. One key to the provision of accurate information is the use of accurate accounting standards. In this respect, it is worthwhile noting that when examining the impact of accounting standards at the firm level, Leutz and Verrecchia (2000) find that German firms voluntarily adopting either International Accounting Standards (IAS) or US Generally Accepted Accounting Practices (GAAP) have lower information asymmetry as reflected by bid-ask spreads and higher stock liquidity than those that employ the German reporting standard.

Currently, a major obstacle to the application of a single, well-recognized set of accounting standards is that there are several major alternatives employed across the globe (as well as a number of local, country-specific accounting standards that are difficult or impossible for stakeholders and potential investors to 'translate' into terms similar to one of the major global standards). Table 8.1 shows that there is variation in standards, with the majority of countries having adopted IAS. There are 20 countries that employ neither IAS nor GAAP.

Table 8.1   Bank Accounting Standards: An International Comparison

Countries Applying International Accounting Standards (IAS)	Countries Applying US Generally Accepted Accounting Standards (GAAP)	Countries Applying Both	Countries Applying Neither
Austria	United States	Australia	Argentina
Azerbaijan		Bosnia and	Belgium
Benin		Herzegovina	Chile
Burkina Faso		Brazil	Denmark
Bulgaria		Costa Rica	Germany
Bahrain		El Salvador	Finland
Bolivia		Japan	Greece
Botswana		Korea	India
Canada		Nigeria	Israel
Côte d'Ivoire		Panama	Italy
Croatia		Philippines	Luxembourg
Cyprus		Thailand	Morocco
Czech Republic		Ukraine	Macedonia
Egypt			Netherlands
Estonia			Portugal
Hong Kong, China			Russia
Hungary			Slovenia
Jordan			Spain
Kuwait			United Kingdom
Lebanon			Venezuela
Lithuania			
Latvia			
Macau, China			
Mali			
Malta			
Mauritius			
Pakistan			
Peru			
Romania			
Saudi Arabia			
Senegal			
Slovakia			
South Africa			
Sri Lanka			
Trinidad and Tobago			
Tunisia			
Turkey			
Uruguay			
Zimbabwe			

Source: World Bank Regulation and Supervision Survey (2004).

Strength of external audits

The objective of external financial reporting is to reduce information asymmetries between the different stakeholders of a company (Healy and Palepu, 2001). Audited financial statements are important for countries where firms rely more on equity finance than on debt for funding. The corporate governance role of audits in markets or industries where firms rely more on debt may be less important, as debtholders generally have greater access to financial information than individual shareholders. Similarly, when firm ownership is concentrated, shareholders with substantial stakes could provide sufficient monitoring so that the benefits of external audits may be less pronounced. Yet, high concentration may be a reason for mandatory audits because large owners may collude with management and engage in excessively risky activities rather than provide effective monitoring. Perhaps because most countries have mandatory audits this issue does not appear to have received much attention. Nonetheless it is an issue worth pursuing, particularly since Izan (1980) finds that many banks were not pleased when mandatory audits were imposed on them.

Financial statement transparency

The ability of shareholders to effectively monitor managers depends crucially on the completeness and accuracy of the information they receive. Accurate accounting standards and the degree of transparency help determine the extent to which securities markets are able to monitor and influence bank performance. Llewellyn and Mayes (2003) argue that relevant and accurate information about the status of banks is a necessary condition for an efficient operation of market discipline as reflected in Pillar 3 of Basel II.[8]

A few empirical studies have examined the impact of bank disclosure and transparency on bank performance. For example, Barth *et al.* (2004a, 2006) find that policies that require accurate information disclosure, empower private sector control of banks, and foster incentives for private agents to assert corporate control, work best to promote bank development, performance and stability. Jordan *et al.* (1999) find that improving bank disclosure during a banking crisis is not destabilizing, but instead provides conditions for market discipline to work more effectively. In addition, Tadesse (2003) finds cross-country evidence that more comprehensive, informative and timely bank disclosure can mitigate the likelihood of a systematic banking crisis. Further, Baumann and Nier (2003) find that banks that disclose more information tend to have higher capital ratios, and hence more protection against unexpected loss.

Some authors focus on the effect that the availability and type of deposit insurance scheme in place has on disclosure policies' impact on bank performance. Cordella and Yeyati (1998), for example, note that the ability of investors to control banks' risk-taking depends on a portion of deposits not being insured so that depositors are motivated to monitor bank risk. They show that the disciplining effect of disclosure would be limited only to risk which the bank is able to control. When risk is exogenous to the bank, disclosure of bank portfolio information increases the probability of bank failure. These authors conclude that 'government "insurance" against the occurrence of negative exogenous shocks (for example, through the provision of emergency credit) would allow the [banking] system to benefit from information disclosure while avoiding its pitfalls'.[9] DeYoung *et al.* (2001) argue that the opacity of bank assets is exactly what warrants greater disclosure and publicizing of supervisory information, because it may help investors to form more accurate assessments of bank values.

External ratings and credit monitoring
Credit rating agencies, such as Moody's and Standard and Poor's, rate certificates of deposit, debentures and commercial paper. Credit rating agencies also rate banks. For some types of activities, regulators actually require banks to be evaluated by credit rating agencies. For example, in the United States, banks must have an external rating in order to issue letters of credit (DeYoung *et al.*, 2001). In addition, Basel II requires that regulators use ratings in assessing banks' strength.

Empirical studies have shown that, at least in the United States, the use of ratings should accompany regulatory interventions.[10] Morgan (2002) finds that regulators are able to shift some disciplining responsibilities to the market, although he finds that there are patterns of disagreement among rating agencies in their evaluation of various individual banks' bonds. These disagreements increased after the announced demise of the 'too-big-to-fail' policy in the United States in 1986. Morgan observes that banks are inherently opaque and regulatory involvement is therefore warranted. Nonetheless, he concludes that ratings are useful not only because they contribute to market discipline but also because they help regulators identify problem banks.

Morgan and Stiroh (2000) find that in spite of the opaqueness of banks, in general, rating agencies are able to evaluate bank debt correctly. These authors study whether the relationship between bond spreads (over Treasuries) and risk (as estimated by rating agencies) is the same for bank and non-bank firms. They find a nearly identical relationship between spreads and ratings for banks and non-bank firms. The authors therefore conclude that the market disciplines banks as harshly as it disciplines non-bank firms. In addition, Morgan and Stiroh find that bond spreads reflect the risk of bank portfolios, indicating that investors look beyond public measures of risk exposure. For example, if banks shift to riskier activities, such as trading or credit card lending, they should expect to pay higher spreads. The information content in bond spreads is found to be attenuated for larger banks, perhaps indicating that the market is less able correctly to value larger banks, or that Government intervention is still expected in problem situations if the bank is big enough, even in the presence of explicit statements to the contrary.

While evidence suggests that bank supervisors and rating agencies produce information that is useful to each other, it also suggests that there is a level of specialization by investors in terms of the type of information they collect. Berger *et al.* (2000) focus on both the timeliness and accuracy of supervisory versus market data. They find that supervisory evaluations and bond ratings are more concerned with bankruptcy risk. Thus, credit-rating agencies tend to focus on future problem loans consistent with their emphasis on risk. In contrast, equity investors focus more on future earnings, consistent with shareholders' focus on wealth creation.

Overall, Berger *et al.* (2000) find that supervisors are less accurate than private investors in predicting changes in bank performance. Although evidence on an informational advantage of bank supervisors over the bond market is found by DeYoung *et al.* (2001), they report that equity studies find that investors promptly incorporate relevant rating information into bank stock prices.

Credit-rating agencies, however, have faced heavy criticism in recent years, especially for missing the crises at firms like Enron, WorldCom and Parmalat (*Economist*, 2005). The main shortcomings in these cases were the absence of outside scrutiny and lack of competition among credit rating agencies, especially those rating large global companies, with most relying mainly on Moody's and Standard & Poor's. Payment for the credit rating service by rated companies and not by investors coupled with a potential conflict of interest between credit rating agencies and their consulting business has raised concerns among many.

Cross-country empirical studies addressing these issues are relatively rare. In the case of European banks, Sironi (2003) finds that investors impose market discipline, albeit to a lesser extent on banks with external subsidiaries, and that public sector banks benefit from a significant government subsidy (through implicit guarantees), though these subsidies become weaker over time. The policy conclusion is that requiring banks to issue subordinated notes and debentures would likely enhance market discipline.

DeYoung *et al.* (2001), moreover, argue that mandatory subordinated debt can serve as a disciplining device, not because it controls risk-taking directly but because it is able to generate helpful market signals about a bank that could be used by the regulator to respond to troubles in a timely manner. This happens because debtholders cannot affect the bank immediately even if increased default risk has driven debt prices sharply down. Supervisors, in contrast, have a direct effect on bank behavior because they can legally restrict activities of financially weak banks. Thus, mandatory subordinated debt would be an effective tool only if the market signals about a bank's condition augments the supervisory information and induces supervisory authorities to take appropriate corrective action.

Relying on cross-country data to study whether subordinated debt imposes market discipline is important because some researchers are dubious about its benefits. For example, Saunders (2001) argues that it is better to use equity prices and drop subordinated debt proposals, especially if bond markets are not very liquid. As he states:

> [W]hy is it easier to get smaller and medium sized banks to issue subordinated debt rather than require more [closely-held] banks to have their equity listed and traded? Is it to protect such shareholders from claims dilution? Surely, such a choice to prefer bonds rather than more equity suggests an implicit value judgment and wealth transfer that society at large may not approve of, and may even have an unwitting flavor of a new type of stockholder 'protection' agenda that may come back to haunt regulators in the future.[11]

CROSS-COUNTRY DATA

The primary focus of our inquiry is on the effect of external governance on bank performance. To measure the impact of the external governance framework we rely on a recent survey conducted by the World Bank.[12] It covers 152 countries and provides data for end-2001 and 2002. The focus of the survey is on bank regulations and supervisory practices. Using the survey data, we extend the work of Caprio and Levine (2002) in constructing an External Governance Index (EGI). The EGI consists of four basic components: (a) the type of accounting standard employed (ACC); (b) the strength of external audits (SEA); (c) the transparency of financial statements (FST); and (d) the use of external ratings and reliance on credit monitoring (ERC). SEA captures the mandated procedures for ensuring the use and quality of independent auditors, and the ways in which regulatory authorities interact with auditors. FST captures the level of mandated information disclosure to the public. ERC measures the mandatory use of credit rating agencies and subordinated debt. ACC is a dummy that takes the value of one if banks in a country use IAS, US GAAP, or both. The external governance index is the summation of these sub-components. As an alternative, the external governance index is also calculated as the summation of the sub-components weighted by each component's maximum score (EGIEW). The specific way in which the index is constructed is explained in Table 8.2.

Table 8.3 shows variations in the aggregate and individual components of external governance across our sample of 72 countries, with higher

Table 8.2 Variables, definitions and sources

Code	Definition	Source
TA	Total bank assets ($US millions)	Fitch IBCA and Bureau van Dijk – Bankscope 192.2, July 2006
PTA	Before tax profit to total assets (%)	Fitch IBCA and Bureau van Dijk – Bankscope 192.2, July 2006
OPTA	Operating profit before tax to total assets (%)	Fitch IBCA and Bureau van Dijk – Bankscope 192.2, July 2006
COST	Overhead cost to operating revenue (%)	Fitch IBCA and Bureau van Dijk – Bankscope 192.2, July 2006
DEPTA	Deposit to total assets (ratio)	Fitch IBCA and Bureau van Dijk – Bankscope 192.2, July 2006
NIR	Non-interest revenue to total revenue (ratio)	Fitch IBCA and Bureau van Dijk – Bankscope 192.2, July 2006
SPTA	Five-year standard deviation of before tax profit to total assets	Fitch IBCA and Bureau van Dijk – Bankscope 192.2, July 2006
ETA	Equity to total assets lagged one year (ratio)	Fitch IBCA and Bureau van Dijk – Bankscope 192.2, July 2006
LTA	Total loans to total assets (ratio)	Fitch IBCA and Bureau van Dijk – Bankscope 192.2, July 2006
TXR	Total taxes paid divided by before tax profits of each bank (ratio)	Fitch IBCA and Bureau van Dijk – Bankscope 192.2, July 2006
MPOWER	Individual bank assets to total banking system assets (%)	Fitch IBCA and Bureau van Dijk – Bankscope 192.2, July 2006 and World Bank Survey of Bank Regulation and Supervision, 2004
GDPP	Real GDP per capita (thousands of US$)	World Development Indicators, 2005
GRO	Annual real growth rate of GDP (%)	World Development Indicators, 2005
INF	Annual inflation rate (%, GDP deflator)	World Development Indicators, 2005
NEDIS	Dummy variable, one indicates no explicit deposit insurance and zero otherwise	World Bank Survey of Bank Regulation and Supervision, 2004 and Barth, Caprio and Levine, 2006
BCASSET	Three bank assets concentration (%)	World Bank Survey of Bank Regulation and Supervision (2004) and Barth et al. (2006)
SEA	Strength of External Audit index adds one for an affirmative answer to each of the following questions: (1) Is an external audit required?; (2) Are specific requirements	World Bank Survey of Bank Regulation and Supervision (2004) and Barth et al. (2006)

for the extent or nature of the audit spelled out?; (3) Are auditors licensed or certified?; (4) Do supervisors receive a copy of the auditor's report?; (5) Can supervisors meet with auditors without prior approval by the bank?; (6) Are auditors legally required to report bank misconduct to supervisors?; (7) Can supervisors take legal action against external auditors? (0–7)

FST | Financial Statement Transparency index adds one for an affirmative answer to each of the following questions: (1) Are financial institutions required to produce consolidated accounts covering all bank and any non-bank financial subsidiaries?; (2) Are off-balance sheet items disclosed to the public?; (3) Must banks disclose their risk management procedures to the public?; (4) Are bank directors legally liable if information disclosed is erroneous or misleading?; (5) Does accrued, though unpaid, interest/principal enter the income statement while the loan is still performing? In addition, this index adds one for a negative response to the following question: (6) Does accrued, though unpaid interest or principal enter the income statement while a loan is still nonperforming? (0–6) | World Bank Survey of Bank Regulation and Supervision (2004) and Barth *et al.* (2006)

161

Table 8.2 (continued)

Code	Definition	Source
ERC	External Ratings and Creditor Monitoring index adds one for an affirmative answer to the following questions: (1) Is subordinated debt allowable as part of capital?; (2) Is subordinated debt required as part of capital?; (3) Do regulations require credit ratings for commercial banks?; (4) Are top ten banks or all banks (if less than 10 banks in a country) rated by international or domestic credit rating agencies? (0–4)	World Bank Survey of Bank Regulation and Supervision (2004) and Barth *et al.* (2006)
ACC	Accounting Practice is one if accounting practice for banks within countries is in accordance with International Accounting Standards or US Generally Accepted Accounting Principles. (0–1)	World Bank Survey of Bank Regulation and Supervision (2004) and Barth *et al.* (2006)
EGI	The External Governance Index is the sum of the above focus component indexes. (0–18)	Authors' calculation
EGIEW	External Governance Index Equally Weighted Components is the sum of the four EGI components weighted by each component's maximum score. (0–4)	Authors' calculation

Table 8.3   External governance indicators for selected countries

Country	EGI	EGIEW	SEA	FST	ERC	ACC
Argentina	14	2.44	6	5	3	0
Australia	14	3.21	5	6	2	1
Austria	13	2.92	7	4	1	1
Azerbaijan	13	3.02	6	4	2	1
Bahrain	13	2.96	5	6	1	1
Belgium	13	2.08	7	5	1	0
Benin	14	3.08	7	5	1	1
Bolivia	13	3.13	5	4	3	1
Bosnia and Herzegovina	14	3.08	7	5	1	1
Botswana	12	2.75	7	3	1	1
Brazil	14	3.19	6	5	2	1
Bulgaria	14	3.08	7	5	1	1
Burkina Faso	14	3.08	7	5	1	1
Canada	16	3.50	7	6	2	1
Chile	13	2.19	6	5	2	0
Costa Rica	13	2.94	6	5	1	1
Côte d'Ivoire	14	3.08	7	5	1	1
Croatia	14	3.08	7	5	1	1
Cyprus	13	2.96	5	6	1	1
Czech Republic	13	2.96	5	6	1	1
Denmark	14	2.33	7	5	2	0
Egypt	16	3.50	7	6	2	1
El Salvador	15	3.42	7	4	3	1
Estonia	15	3.25	7	6	1	1
Finland	14	2.36	6	6	2	0
Germany	12	2.02	6	4	2	0
Greece	13	2.08	7	5	1	0
Hong Kong, China	15	3.36	6	6	2	1
Hungary	15	3.33	7	5	2	1
India	11	1.77	6	4	1	0
Israel	12	1.96	5	6	1	0
Italy	12	2.05	5	5	2	0
Japan	13	3.05	5	5	2	1
Jordan	14	3.08	7	5	1	1
Korea	16	3.61	6	6	3	1
Kuwait	16	3.61	6	6	3	1
Latvia	15	3.25	7	6	1	1
Lebanon	14	3.08	7	5	1	1
Lithuania	11	2.63	5	4	1	1
Luxembourg	14	2.25	7	6	1	0
Macau, China	12	2.80	5	5	1	1

Table 8.3   (continued)

Country	EGI	EGIEW	SEA	FST	ERC	ACC
Macedonia	12	2.02	6	4	2	0
Mali	14	3.08	7	5	1	1
Malta	15	3.36	6	6	2	1
Mauritius	14	3.19	6	5	2	1
Morocco	13	2.11	6	6	1	0
Netherlands	15	2.58	7	5	3	0
Nigeria	13	2.94	6	5	1	1
Pakistan	15	3.33	7	5	2	1
Panama	12	2.80	5	5	1	1
Peru	15	3.33	7	5	2	1
Philippines	11	2.68	3	6	1	1
Portugal	12	1.92	7	4	1	0
Romania	12	2.88	5	4	2	1
Russia	11	1.80	5	5	1	0
Saudi Arabia	15	3.25	7	6	1	1
Senegal	14	3.08	7	5	1	1
Slovakia	13	2.92	7	4	1	1
Slovenia	14	2.25	7	6	1	0
South Africa	15	3.25	7	6	1	1
Spain	12	2.05	5	5	2	0
Sri Lanka	13	2.96	5	6	1	1
Thailand	13	3.02	6	4	2	1
Trinidad and Tobago	14	3.11	6	6	1	1
Tunisia	13	3.00	7	3	2	1
Turkey	15	3.25	7	6	1	1
Ukraine	12	2.80	5	5	1	1
United Kingdom	13	2.21	5	6	2	0
United States	14	3.19	6	5	2	1
Uruguay	14	3.30	5	5	3	1
Venezuela	13	2.17	7	4	2	0
Zimbabwe	14	3.19	6	5	2	1

Source: World Bank's Bank Regulation and Supervision Survey (2004).

values indicating better external governance. While it is difficult to draw a single broad conclusion about the relationship between the application of external governance measures and country income level, several broad patterns emerge. ERC and FST are highest for high-income countries, lowest for low-income countries, and in between for middle-income countries. ACC and SEA are lowest for high-income countries and highest for low-income countries. Consistent with these observations, recent research by

Caprio and Honohan (2003) examines the widely held notion that low-income countries do not in general have the prerequisite conditions for effective market discipline, and find that there is little evidence to support that preconception. Although EGI (EGIEW) is higher on average for the high-income countries than the low-income countries, the correlation between the aggregate external governance measure and per capita GDP is positive but not significant. Of the four sub-components of EGI, only two are significantly correlated with per capita GDP. FST is positive and marginally significant, while ACC is negative and significant. The latter correlation is solely due to the fact that IAS is negatively correlated with per capita GDP, whereas there is no significant correlation for GAAP.

In addition to the information obtained from the World Bank survey, we relied upon BankScope for individual bank data. Our purpose was to assess the extent to which the external governance index and the individual components affect bank performance. In keeping with this objective, we collected data for different measures of bank performance and a standard set of bank-specific explanatory variables. We matched the bank-specific data with our new country-specific variables taking account of cross-country differences in the external governance environment in which banks operate, and with country-specific variables taking account of differences in regulatory and supervisory regimes across countries. This yielded a data set of 1994 banks in 72 countries. Descriptive information on the number and assets of banks by country are reported in Table 8.4.

EMPIRICAL MODEL

The empirical model for our analysis is drawn mainly from Demirgüç-Kunt and Huizinga (1999, 2001), Barth *et al.* (2003), and Demirgüç-Kunt *et al.* (2004). In these and other similar banking studies, both country-level and bank-level data are employed for a sample of countries to examine the effect of various variables on bank performance. The specific model estimated is as follows:

$$P_{ij} = constant + \alpha' B_{ij} + \beta' M_j + \phi' I_j + \delta' G_j + \varepsilon_{ij}$$

where P_{ij} is a performance variable for bank i in country j; B_{ij} are bank-specific variables; M_j are macroeconomic country-specific variables; I_j are banking industry-specific variables; and G_j is the external governance country-specific variable. Definitions of all variables and sources for them are provided in Table 8.2, while descriptive statistics are provided in Table 8.5.

Table 8.4   Number and assets of banks by country

Country	Bank assets Mean ($US Millions)	Bank assets Minimum ($US Millions)	Bank assets Maximum ($US Millions)	Bank assets Standard Deviation ($US Millions)	Number of banks
Argentina	2586	26	15 384	4068	35
Australia	29 628	707	190 406	52 011	21
Austria	6704	24	152 587	25 199	40
Azerbaijan	110	7	455	194	5
Bahrain	12 682	3040	27 312	11 329	4
Belgium	39 338	261	380 052	92 862	23
Benin	198	83	326	122	3
Bolivia	357	25	771	261	11
Bosnia and Herzegovina	84	32	270	78	8
Botswana	326	52	741	332	4
Brazil	3457	13	70 045	9741	93
Bulgaria	212	31	766	207	13
Burkina Faso	112	59	209	73	6
Canada	37 125	53	223 504	68 879	29
Chile	3404	67	12 369	3955	20
Costa Rica	297	68	429	199	3
Côte d'Ivoire	265	28	719	254	7
Croatia	879	33	6228	1490	23
Cyprus	2792	36	12 781	4316	10
Czech Republic	4417	172	16 190	6305	12
Denmark	3013	45	79 460	11 734	49
Egypt	5395	288	21 448	6728	12
El Salvador	1095	161	2624	978	7
Estonia	2049	351	4510	2182	3
Finland	38 724	396	155 505	65 930	5
Germany	21 666	40	870 956	104 633	135
Greece	19 153	1238	51 964	16 372	8
Hong Kong, China	16 466	15	235 381	44 669	32
Hungary	2552	111	10 308	3014	11
India	3059	125	11 336	2915	36
Israel	13 436	70	56 577	19 296	14
Italy	17 437	55	301 467	47 837	87
Japan	49 081	1508	881 144	124 919	126
Jordan	5061	324	22 106	8490	10
Korea	44 966	11 479	116 370	30 915	10
Kuwait	6767	3938	15 313	4295	6
Latvia	357	28	1381	416	12

Table 8.4   (continued)

Country	Bank assets Mean ($US Millions)	Bank assets Minimum ($US Millions)	Bank assets Maximum ($US Millions)	Bank assets Standard Deviation ($US Millions)	Number of banks
Lebanon	1399	114	6928	1772	27
Lithuania	576	69	1857	741	5
Luxembourg	5924	52	47514	10208	82
Macau, China	1105	143	2758	871	7
Macedonia	176	29	474	201	6
Mali	102	61	133	37	3
Malta	1606	341	4174	1791	6
Mauritius	1153	1143	1164	15	2
Morocco	4226	1764	7936	1973	9
Netherlands	34276	24	460888	102350	20
Nigeria	314	28	2519	515	50
Pakistan	1587	80	7116	2284	15
Panama	1219	374	3811	1346	6
Peru	1627	27	6379	2058	11
Philippines	2150	133	9190	2653	21
Portugal	14190	204	59717	21344	9
Romania	887	20	5362	1494	13
Russia	498	8	4178	947	44
Saudi Arabia	6392	1600	11145	4773	3
Senegal	216	62	454	138	7
Slovakia	1208	139	4697	1544	12
Slovenia	1353	137	7471	1932	13
South Africa	5803	27	29090	10184	20
Spain	12577	11	333002	52010	70
Sri Lanka	803	56	2629	830	8
Thailand	13718	2409	30485	9679	9
Trinidad and Tobago	2004	934	3979	1404	5
Tunisia	841	143	1939	831	4
Turkey	7581	351	38150	12307	10
Ukraine	237	26	976	301	22
United Kingdom	40230	44	555535	102956	70
United States	14860	31	578210	51607	367
Uruguay	40230	44	555535	102956	70
Venezuela	777	9	3783	1100	27
Zimbabwe	686	272	1877	523	8

Note: Bank assets are averaged between 2000 and 2002.

Corporate governance in banking

Table 8.5   Descriptive statistics for variables

	Mean	Median	Standard Deviation	Number of observations
TA ($US Millions)	15066	1357	60945	1994
PTA (%)	1.44	1.19	2.58	1994
OPTA (%)	1.42	1.18	2.56	1994
COST (%)	64.91	62.51	25.15	1987
DEPTA (ratio)	0.726	0.784	0.196	1994
NIR (ratio)	0.228	0.200	0.186	1994
SPTA (ratio)	0.012	0.005	0.035	1994
ETA (ratio)	0.117	0.086	0.104	1994
LTA (ratio)	0.516	0.540	0.218	1994
TXR (ratio)	0.305	0.289	1.771	1994
MPOWER (%)	10.06	0.29	100.06	1994
GDPP ($US Thousands)	10.16	4.21	12.53	72
GRO (%)	2.96	3.10	2.60	72
INF (%)	6.67	3.42	11.68	72
NEDIS	0.36	0.00	0.48	72
BCASSET (%)	66.30	67.15	20.80	72
SEA	6.17	6.00	0.90	72
FST	5.10	5.00	0.79	72
ERC	1.56	1.00	0.67	72
ACC	0.72	1.00	0.45	72
EGI	13.54	14.00	1.26	72
EGIEW	2.84	3.01	0.49	72

Empirical banking models typically use such measures of performance as return on assets or return on equity, net interest margin to total assets, and operating costs to operating revenue. This chapter uses three alternative measures of performance that are commonly employed in banking studies. Before tax profit to total assets (PTA) is the first dependent variable used to measure bank performance. According to Demirgüç-Kunt and Huizinga (1999), this is a more appropriate variable than return on equity in a cross-country analysis because banks in developing countries typically rely more on implicit government subsidies and thus less equity, which distorts the return on equity. Before tax operating profit to total assets (OPTA) is the second measure of performance. It excludes extraordinary or non-recurring income from overall income. This measure is a narrower measure of profitability and focuses more on profits generated from the ongoing core operations of banks. Overhead cost to operating revenue (COST) is the third measure of bank performance, which is a measure of bank cost efficiency with a focus on the efficiency of the entire banking organization rather than just on the traditional core banking activities.

Table 8.6 contains simple correlations among all the variables, as well as the associated levels of statistical significance. All three measures of bank performance – PTA, OPTA, and COST – are significantly correlated with one another. However, the correlations, with the unsurprising exception of the correlation between PTA and OPTA, are not particularly high and thus support our approach to consider each variable as alternative ways to measure bank performance. All four sub-components of the external governance index are significantly correlated with the EGI and EGIEW. The simple correlations further reveal that both measures of external governance are positive and significantly correlated with bank profitability and significantly negatively correlated with costs. The correlations reveal that with no explicit deposit insurance scheme both the equity-to-asset ratio and EGIEW are higher.

Several bank-specific variables (B_{ij}) are included in the analysis. The log of total assets (LOGTA) is included as a measure of bank size, and squared terms are included to allow for nonlinearity in the relation of size to the various performance measures. Since bank performance is measured in terms of return on assets, the impact of leverage is measured by equity-to-assets lagged one period (ETA_{-1}). This variable is lagged by one period to correct for the contemporaneous impact of unpaid dividends on bank equity (Demirgüç-Kunt and Huizinga, 1999). Loans-to-assets (LTA) and the standard deviation of profits before taxes-to-assets (SPTA) are included in the analysis as measures of bank risk.[13] Taxes paid relative to pre-tax profits (TXR) controls for the impact of tax rates on bank performance. Since the presence of 'too-big-to-fail' regulatory policies weakens the incentives of investors to monitor and impose market discipline (Morgan and Stiroh, 2000), we include the variable MPOWER, calculated as the bank's assets-to-total banking system assets. Also, since banks are more important providers of external finance in developing countries than in developed countries, regulators in the former may be more likely to resort to 'too-big-to-fail' policies and thereby lessen market discipline, MPOWER is interacted with GDP per capita. This controls for the impact of a bank's market power in countries with different levels of economic development.

The macroeconomic variables (M_j) are gross domestic product per capita (GDPP), real gross domestic product growth (GRO), the inflation rate (INF), and a measure of the extent of intermediation in an economy (M2GDP). While the first variable is included to control for the country specific institutional environment imbedded in the level of economic development, growth and inflation are included to capture cyclical effects. The

Table 8.6 Correlation matrix

	TA	PTA	OPTA	COST	DEPTA	NIR	SPTA	ETA	LTA	TXR
PTA	-0.05**	1								
	1994	1994								
OPTA	-0.06**	0.97***	1							
	1994	1994	1994							
COST	-0.03	-0.34***	-0.37***	1						
	1987	1987	1987	1987						
DEPTA	-0.05**	-0.24***	-0.24***	0.03	1					
	1994	1994	1994	1987	1994					
NIR	0.05**	0.09***	0.09***	0.13***	-0.04*	1				
	1994	1994	1994	1987	1994	1994				
SPTA	-0.05**	0.01	0.04*	0.07***	-0.2***	0	1			
	1994	1994	1994	1987	1994	1994	1994			
ETA	-0.14***	0.32***	0.32***	-0.01	-0.52***	0.08***	0.24***	1		
	1994	1994	1994	1987	1994	1994	1994	1994		
LTA	0.04*	-0.02	-0.02	-0.11***	0.09***	-0.15***	-0.1***	-0.19***	1	
	1994	1994	1994	1987	1994	1994	1994	1994	1994	
TXR	0	0	0.04	0.02	0.02	-0.04	-0.01	-0.01	-0.01	1
	1994	1994	1994	1987	1994	1994	1994	1994	1994	1994
MPOWER	0.34***	-0.01	-0.01	-0.02	-0.01	0.01	-0.02	-0.05**	0.01	0.01
	1994	1994	1994	1987	1994	1994	1994	1994	1994	1994
GDPP	0.11***	-0.11***	-0.12***	-0.07***	0.19***	0.06***	-0.14***	-0.25***	0.11***	0
	1994	1994	1994	1987	1994	1994	1994	1994	1994	1994
GRO	-0.08***	0.07***	0.07***	-0.05**	0.07***	0.03	-0.12***	-0.02	-0.03	-0.08***
	1994	1994	1994	1987	1994	1994	1994	1994	1994	1994

INF	-0.08***	0.2***	0.21***	0.02	-0.11***	-0.07***	0.15***	0.18***	-0.18***	0.19***
	1994	1994	1994	1987	1994	1994	1994	1994	1994	1994
NEDIS	-0.02	0.07***	0.08***	-0.05**	0.03	0.05**	0.01	0.07***	-0.04*	-0.03
	1994	1994	1994	1987	1994	1994	1994	1994	1994	1994
BCASSET	-0.04*	0	0	0.03	-0.01	-0.02	0.04*	0.04	0.03	0.01
	1994	1994	1994	1987	1994	1994	1994	1994	1994	1994
SEA	-0.09***	0.09***	0.1***	-0.08***	0.06**	-0.03	0.02	-0.04*	-0.18***	-0.01
	1994	1994	1994	1987	1994	1994	1994	1994	1994	1994
FST	0.03	0.02	0.02	-0.07***	-0.05**	-0.05**	-0.02	-0.01	-0.05**	0
	1994	1994	1994	1987	1994	1994	1994	1994	1994	1994
ERC	0.11***	-0.07***	-0.07***	0.02	-0.15***	-0.07***	0.08***	0.05**	0.2***	0.01
	1994	1994	1994	1987	1994	1994	1994	1994	1994	1994
ACC	0	0.14***	0.16***	-0.09***	-0.08***	-0.08***	-0.02	-0.01	0.13***	0.01
	1994	1994	1994	1987	1994	1994	1994	1994	1994	1994
EGI	0.01	0.1***	0.11***	-0.12***	-0.1***	-0.12***	0.04	-0.01	0.00	0.00
	1994	1994	1994	1987	1994	1994	1994	1994	1994	1994
EGIEW	0.02	0.13***	0.15***	-0.1***	-0.11***	-0.11***	0	-0.01	0.12***	0.01
	1994	1994	1994	1987	1994	1994	1994	1994	1994	1994

Table 8.6 (continued)

	MPOWER	GDPP	GRO	INF	NEDIS	BCASSET	SEA	FST	ERC	ACC	EGI
PTA											
OPTA											
COST											
DEPTA											
NIR											
SPTA											
ETA											
LTA											
TXR											
MPOWER	1										
	1994										
GDPP	−0.08***	1									
	1994	72									
GRO	−0.2***	−0.12	1								
	1994	72	72								

		INF	NEDIS	BCASSET	SEA	FST	ERC	ACC	EGI	EGIEW
INF	0.04*	1									
	1994	72									
NEDIS	0.14***	−0.26**	1								
	1994	72	72								
BCASSET	0.04*	−0.16	−0.35***	1							
	1994	72	72	72							
SEA	−0.07***	−0.03	0.13	−0.12	1						
	1994	72	72	72	72						
FST	0.01	0.18	0.16	−0.06	0.24**	1					
	1994	72	72	72	72	72					
ERC	0.13***	0.17	0.04	−0.02	0.08	0.24**	1				
	1994	72	72	72	72	72	72				
ACC	0.06***	−0.41***	0.2	0.06	−0.16	−0.11	−0.13	1			
	1994	72	72	72	72	72	72	72			
EGI	0.05**	0.04	−0.08	0.00	0.34***	0.26**	0.56***	0.46***	1		
	1994	72	72	72	72	72	72	72	72		
EGIEW	0.08***	−0.27**	0.07	0.05	0.34***	0.19	0.7***	0.22*	0.9***	0.2*	1
	1994	72	72	72	72	72	72	72	72	72	72

Notes: ***, ** and * denote significant level at 1, 5 and 10 percent respectively. Number of observations for all bank-specific correlations are 1994, except for the correlation with COST (1987). Number of observations for country-specific correlations are 72.

degree of intermediation in an economy controls for the importance of financial institutions as a source of credit. These variables are typically employed in cross-country bank studies.

Two banking industry variables (I_j) are included as control variables. A dummy variable is included equaling one if a country has no explicit deposit insurance scheme (NEDIS) and 0 otherwise. Also, a three bank asset concentration variable (BCASSET) is included.

RESULTS

Tables 8.7, 8.8 and 8.9 present our empirical results. There is one table for each of the three measures of bank performance – before tax-profit, before tax operating profit, and overhead costs. There are, moreover, two regressions in each table, one for each of the two alternative measures of external governance – EGI and EGIEW.

We note first that the effects of the bank-specific variables are in general consistent with findings of other banking studies. Larger banks are more profitable and have lower costs, consistent with the notion of scale efficiency also found by Demirgüç-Kunt *et al.* (2004). Similar results are apparent for the impact of bank capitalization on the performance measures. Better capitalized banks are more profitable and have lower cost, suggesting that these banks pay less for deposits because of lower default risks and/or greater market power. Non-interest revenue to total revenue (NIR) has a significantly positive effect on both bank profitability and cost. LTA is used here as a measure of core banking activities, and enters positively in the PTA and OPTA regressions, indicating that banks focusing more on traditional core activities have both higher profits. This variable is also significant and enters with negative sign in the COST regressions, which is expected since overhead costs are not likely to be affected by the loans to assets ratio. The tax variable, TXR, enters the before tax profit regression with the expected sign, and is significant. The market power variable (MPOWER) is significantly positive in the profit regressions, while significantly negative in the COST regressions.

The impacts of the macroeconomic variables on the three measures of bank performance indicate that the higher inflation the higher bank profitability. The level of economic development (as measured by per capita GDP) and economic growth both generally have a positive impact on profitability and a negative impact on cost. The findings regarding these control variables are generally consistent with those reported by others.

Recent studies at both the micro and macro level demonstrate the importance of controlling the deposit insurance and banking industry

Table 8.7   Dependent variable: before tax profit to total assets

PTA	(1)	(2)
C	−12.0865***	−9.8510***
	(3.04)	(2.98)
LOG(TA)	1.0372***	1.1006***
	(0.00)	(0.00)
LOG(TA)^2	−0.0347***	−0.0371***
	(0.01)	(0.01)
DEPTA	−1.1954**	−1.2580***
	(0.02)	(0.01)
NIR	1.5295*	1.4219
	(0.90)	(0.88)
SPTA	−0.0556	−0.0520
	(0.01)	(0.01)
ETA	7.3494***	7.3563***
	(1.70)	(1.70)
LTA	1.0426***	0.7613**
	(0.00)	(0.02)
TXR	−0.0384*	−0.0428**
	(0.02)	(0.02)
MPOWER	0.0007**	0.0007**
	(0.03)	(0.03)
GDPP	0.0029	0.0109***
	(0.00)	(0.00)
GRO	0.1530***	0.1456***
	(0.00)	(0.00)
INF	0.0739***	0.0750***
	(0.01)	(0.01)
NEDIS	0.2222	0.2070
	(0.29)	(0.31)
BCASSET	−0.0107***	−0.0057**
	(0.00)	(0.00)
EGI	0.3639***	
	(0.06)	
EGIEW		0.7467***
		(0.12)
Adjusted R^2	0.18	0.18
F-Statistic	30.58	30.65
Prob(F-Statistic)	(0.00)	(0.00)
Number of observations	1994	1994
Number of countries	72	72

Notes: ***, ** and * denote significant level at 1, 5 and 10 percent respectively. White heteroskedasticity-consistent standard errors are in parentheses.

Table 8.8   Dependent variable: before tax operating profit to total asset

OPTA	(3)	(4)
C	−11.1931***	−8.8934***
	(3.06)	(3.02)
LOG(TA)	0.8494***	0.9143***
	(0.01)	(0.01)
LOG(TA)^2	−0.0284***	−0.0309***
	(0.01)	(0.01)
DEPTA	−1.0821**	−1.1346**
	(0.03)	(0.02)
NIR	1.6418**	1.5383*
	(0.84)	(0.82)
SPTA	−0.0293	−0.0255
	(0.01)	(0.01)
ETA	7.0375***	7.0485***
	(1.61)	(1.60)
LTA	1.1872***	0.8772***
	(0.00)	(0.01)
TXR	0.0192	0.0142
	(0.02)	(0.02)
MPOWER	0.0006**	0.0006**
	(0.04)	(0.04)
GDPP	0.0013	0.0099**
	(0.00)	(0.00)
GRO	0.1593***	0.1521***
	(0.00)	(0.00)
INF	0.0747***	0.0762***
	(0.01)	(0.01)
NEDIS	0.2286	0.2031
	(0.26)	(0.30)
BCASSET	−0.0122***	−0.0068***
	(0.00)	(0.00)
EGI	0.3896***	
	(0.06)	
EGIEW		0.8396***
		(0.11)
Adjusted R^2	0.19	0.19
F-Statistic	31.26	31.84
Prob(*F*-Statistic)	(0.00)	(0.00)
Number of observations	1994	1994
Number of countries	72	72

Notes: ***, ** and * denote significant level at 1, 5 and 10 percent respectively. White heteroskedasticity-consistent standard errors are in parentheses.

Table 8.9   Dependent variable: overhead cost to operating revenue

COST	(5)	(6)
C	181.8854***	163.9591***
	(22.81)	(22.11)
LOG(TA)	−8.9213***	−9.4620***
	(0.00)	(0.00)
LOG(TA)^2	0.2459***	0.2652***
	(0.10)	(0.10)
DEPTA	1.3012	2.2128
	(0.74)	(0.57)
NIR	15.0851***	16.2204***
	(4.50)	(4.45)
SPTA	0.3613	0.3395
	(0.00)	(0.00)
ETA	−33.5824***	−33.4476***
	(10.82)	(10.89)
LTA	−10.8387***	−9.2539***
	(0.00)	(0.00)
TXR	0.3581	0.3767
	(0.37)	(0.37)
MPOWER	−0.0052**	−0.0052**
	(0.04)	(0.03)
GDPP	−0.1245***	−0.1734***
	(0.05)	(0.05)
GRO	−1.1867***	−1.1112***
	(0.00)	(0.00)
INF	−0.2191***	−0.2173***
	(0.09)	(0.09)
NEDIS	−5.7677***	−5.9879***
	(0.00)	(0.00)
BCASSET	0.0727**	0.0380
	(0.03)	(0.03)
EGI	−2.4217***	
	(0.60)	
EGIEW		−3.6003***
		(1.06)
Adjusted R^2	0.07	0.07
F-Statistic	11.24	10.55
Prob(F-Statistic)	(0.00)	(0.00)
Number of observations	1987	1987
Number of countries	72	72

Notes: ***, ** and * denote significant level at 1, 5 and 10 percent respectively. White heteroskedasticity-consistent standard errors are in parentheses.

concentration when examining performance.[14] Banks in countries without an explicit deposit insurance scheme are on average not significantly more profitable but are more efficient in terms of lower costs. The concentration variable (BCASSET) is significantly and negatively correlated with profitability and positively correlated with cost.

Turning to the main focus of our study, we find overall that the external governance framework does indeed affect bank performance, even after controlling for the impact of an array of bank- and country-specific factors. Indeed, the external governance index (EGI or EGIEW) is positive and significant in the PTA and OPTA regressions, and negative and significant in the COST regressions.

The magnitude of the effects of external governance also matters. For example, holding everything else constant, a bank operating in Israel (EGI of 12) would be expected to improve its before tax profit to total assets ratio by 0.73 (2*0.3639) percentage points if the external governance environment were the same as in the United States (EGI of 14).[15] The improvement in before tax operating profit to total assets is nearly the same. As regards cost, the improvements would be a negative 4.83 (2*2.417) percentage points.[16]

CONCLUSIONS

A key policy prescription emerging from global banking problems over the past two decades was that banking system safety and soundness rests on more than the traditional measures of prudential supervision, capital requirements, and deposit insurance schemes (and, indeed, even these traditional measures have been extensively rethought). In addition, policy makers have called for improved 'internal' corporate governance, and greater reliance on market-oriented 'external' governance measures. Such measures, it is advocated, should include the adoption of widely-accepted accounting standards, external audits and ratings, and enhanced transparency of financial statements.

There is great 'common sense' appeal to the adoption of such measures, and indeed, the New Basel Capital Accord puts great emphasis on them. Nevertheless, there has been relatively little empirical testing of the nature and impact of these newer, less traditional measures directed toward banking safety and soundness. This is particularly true with respect to the concept of external governance. The purpose of the chapter is to add to the relatively small amount of literature addressing this gap.

Using a new database, we suggest ways to measure four key components of external governance. These include accounting standards, the strength of external audits, the degree of transparency of banks' financial statements, and the use of external ratings and related credit monitoring mechanisms. We incorporate an index of external governance combining these components into equations modeling various measures of bank performance, including profitability and bank efficiency. We find substantial evidence that the index has positive and statistically significant effects on bank profitability, and negative and statistically significant impacts on bank efficiency. Our findings suggest that subsequent research investigating cross-country differences in bank performance should directly take account of external governance factors. In addition, and more importantly, we provide empirical evidence supporting Pillar 3 of Basel II. In light of the fact that many policy decisions have been made, or are in the process of being made, based on these lessons about new ways to enhance banking safety and soundness, especially via strengthening market discipline, one might expect such empirical support to provide a measure of comfort within the banking and regulatory communities.

NOTES

1. An alternative definition of corporate governance is offered by Tirole (2001, p. 4), who defines corporate governance as 'the design of institutions that induce or force management to internalize the welfare of stakeholders.' Zingales (1998) defines corporate governance as 'the complex set of constraints that shape the *ex-post* bargaining over quasi-rents generated by the firm.'
2. The agency (or 'finance') approach focuses on internal governance mechanisms where the behavior of managers who have incentives to deviate from shareholder value-maximization is efficiently restrained by the board of directors representing the shareholders. This approach also recognizes the role of the external governance mechanisms, whereby the external markets for capital, for managers, and for corporate control help in providing market discipline and enforcing internal arrangements.
3. See Bliss (2003) for a thoughtful discussion of a definition and components of market discipline.
4. Macey and O'Hara (2003, p. 91). See also Caprio and Levine (2002), Adams and Mehran (2003) and Arun and Turner (2003). Note also that in some countries the issue of corporate governance of banks and other financial institutions has recently captured renewed attention from policy makers and regulatory authorities. For example, in the United States, the Sarbanes-Oxley Act of 2002 deals extensively with legal requirements aimed at enhancing the quality of corporate governance in non-financial and financial firms. See Office of the Comptroller of the Currency (2003) for a federal regulatory perspective on corporate governance practices for banks.
5. See Shleifer and Vishny (1997) for a comprehensive and thoughtful survey of research on corporate governance. Macey and O'Hara (2003) discuss the emerging literature on corporate governance for banks.
6. Macey and O'Hara (2003, p. 102). Adams and Mehran (2003, p. 124) add at least one more constituent. They argue that 'the number of parties with a stake in [a financial] institution's activity complicates the governance of financial institutions. In addition to investors, depositors and regulators have a direct interest in bank performance.'
7. Caprio and Levine (2002, p. 19).

8. Pillar 3 of the Basel II emphasizes the important of transparency and market discipline, and complements the other two pillars (minimum capital requirements and the supervisory review process). Pillar 3 provides for a set of disclosure requirements aimed at facilitating the exercise of market discipline. Moshirian and Szego (2003) note the importance of transparency, among other factors, in moving financial markets and institutions from a government-led system to a market-led system.
9. Cordella and Yeyati (1998: 126).
10. Early US studies did not find relationships between subordinated notes and debentures spreads and bank risk, which suggests that investors were not able to correctly identify bank risk levels. This result is often attributed to the implicit government guarantees that investors perceived prior to 1990 (Sironi, 2003).
11. Saunders (2001, p. 194).
12. See Barth *et al.* (2006), and http://www.worldbank.org/research/interest/2003_bank_survey/2003_bank_regulation_database.htm.
13. In a study of performance for a sample of European banks, for example, Molyneux *et al.* (1992) include a capital-asset ratio and a loan-assets ratio to account for bank specific risk. In a similar vein, Samolyk (1994: 7) states that 'differences in loan/asset ratios and bank capitalization are important factors in assessing the relative profitability and risk of banks'. The inclusion of SPTA is a reflection of overall bank risk.
14. For an example at the micro level, see Gropper and Hudson (2003); at the macro level, see Barth *et al.* (2004 and 2006) and the references cited therein.
15. The calculation is based on Equation 1 in Table 8.7.
16. These calculations are based on Equations 5 in Table 8.9.

REFERENCES

Adams, Renée and Hamid Mehran (2003), 'Is corporate governance different for bank holding companies?' *Federal Reserve Bank of New York Economic Policy Review*, **9** (special issue) (April), 123–42.
Arun, Thankom G. and John D. Turner (2003), 'Corporate governance of banks in developing economies: concepts and issues,' University of Manchester Institute for Development Policy and Management development economics and public policy working paper no.2, February.
Barth, James R., Daniel E. Nolle and Tara N. Rice (2000), 'Commercial banking structure, regulation and performance: an international comparison,' in D. B. Papadimitriou (ed.), *Modernizing Financial Systems*, New York: Macmillan Press and St Martin's Press.
Barth, James R., Daniel E. Nolle, Triphon Phumiwasana and Glenn Yago (2003), 'A cross-country analysis of the bank supervisory framework and bank performance,' *Financial Markets, Institutions & Instruments*, **12**(2), 67–120.
Barth, James R., Gerard Caprio Jr. and Daniel E. Nolle (2004), 'Comparative international characteristics of banking,' Office of the Comptroller of the Currency economic and policy analysis working paper 2004-1, January.
Barth, James R., Gerard Caprio, Jr. and Ross Levine (2004a), 'Bank regulation and supervision: what works best?' *Journal of Financial Intermediation*, **13**(2) (April), 205–48.
Barth, James R., Jie Gan and Daniel E. Nolle (2004b), 'Global trends in bank regulatory and supervisory environment,' in Duk-Hoon Lee and Gill-Chin Lim (eds), *Reforms and Innovations in Bank Management*, Seoul, Korea: Woori Bank and Nanam Publishing, pp. 49–94.

Barth, James R., Gerard Caprio, Jr. and Ross Levine (2006), *Rethinking Bank Regulation: Till Angels Govern*, Cambridge: Cambridge University Press.

Baumann, Ursel and Erlend Nier (2003), 'Market discipline and financial stability: some empirical evidence,' *Financial Stability Review*, **14**, 134–41.

Beck, Thorsten, Asli Demirgüç-Kunt and Ross Levine (2003), 'Bank supervision and corporate finance,' The World Bank policy research working paper series 3042.

Berger, Allen N. and Emilia Bonaccorsi di Patti (2002), 'Capital structure and firm performance: a new approach to testing agency theory and an application to the banking industry,' Federal Reserve Board of Governors working paper, October.

Berger, Allen N., Sally M. Davies and Mark J. Flannery (2000), 'Comparing market and supervisory assessments of bank performance: who knows what and when?' *Journal of Money, Credit, and Banking*, **32**, 641–67.

Bhagat, Sanjai and Richard H. Jefferis, Jr. (2002), *The Econometrics of Corporate Governance Studies*, Cambridge, MA: The MIT Press.

Bliss, Robert R. (2003), 'Market discipline: players, processes, and purposes,' paper presented to the Market Discipline: The Evidence across Countries and Industries Sixth Annual Global Conference, co-sponsored by the Bank for International Settlements and the Federal Reserve Bank of Chicago, 30 October–1 November, Chicago, IL.

Bliss, Robert R. and Mark J. Flannery (2001), 'Market discipline in the governance of US bank holding companies: monitoring vs. influencing,' in Frederic S. Mishkin (ed.), *Prudential Supervision: What Works and What Doesn't*, Chicago, IL: National Bureau of Economic Research, University of Chicago Press.

Bushman, Robert M. and Abbie J. Smith (2003), 'Transparency, financial accounting information, and corporate governance,' *Federal Reserve Bank of New York Economic Policy Review*, **9** (special issue) (April), 65–90.

Caprio, Gerard and Patrick Honohan (2003), 'Can the unsophisticated market provide discipline?' paper presented to the Market Discipline: The Evidence across Countries and Industries Sixth Annual Global Conference, co-sponsored by the Bank for International Settlements and the Federal Reserve Bank of Chicago, 30 October–1 November, Chicago, IL.

Caprio, Gerard and Ross Levine (2002), 'Corporate governance of banks: concepts and international observations,' paper presented to the Global Corporate Governance Forum research Network Meeting, 5 April.

Cordella, Tito and Eduardo Levy Yeyati (1998), 'Public disclosure and bank failures,' International Monetary Fund Staff Papers, **45**(1), 110–31.

DeYoung, Robert, Mark Flannery, William Lang and Sorin Sorescu (2001), 'The information content of bank exam ratings and subordinated debt prices,' *Journal of Money, Credit and Banking*, **33**(4), 900–925.

Demirgüç-Kunt, Asli and Harry Huizinga (1999), 'Determinants of commercial bank interest margins and profitability: some international evidence,' *The World Bank Economic Review*, **13**(2), 379–408.

Demirgüç-Kunt, Asli and Harry Huizinga (2001), 'Financial structure and bank profitability,' in Asli Demirgüç-Kunt and Ross Levine (eds), *Financial Structure and Economic Growth: A Cross-Country Comparison of Banks, Markets, and Development*, Boston, MA: MIT Press, pp. 243–61.

Demirgüç-Kunt, Asli, Luc Laeven and Ross Levine (2003), 'The impact of bank regulations, concentration, and institutions on bank margins,' *Conference on Bank Concentration and Competition*, Washington, DC: World Bank, 3–4 April.

Demirgüç-Kunt, Asli, Luc Laeven and Ross Levine (2004), 'Regulations, market structure, institutions, and the cost of financial intermediation,' *Journal of Money, Credit, and Banking*, **36**(3), 593–622.

The Economist (2005), 'Credit-rating agencies three is no crowd: regulators need a new approach to an entrenched industry,' 26 March.

Federal Reserve System (2000), 'Improving public disclosure in banking,' Board of Governors of the Federal Reserve System Study Group on Disclosure, Staff study 173, accessed at www.federalreserve.gov/pubs/staffstudies/173/default.htm.

Gropper, Daniel M. and Carl Hudson (2003), 'A note on Savings and Loan ownership structure and expense preference: a re-examination,' *Journal of Banking and Finance*, **27**(5), 2003–14.

Halme, Liisa (2000), 'Bank corporate governance and financial stability,' in Liisa Halme, C. Hawkesby, J. Healey, I. Saapar and F. Soussa (eds), *Financial Stability and Central Bank: Selected Issues for Financial Safety Nets and Market Discipline*, Centre for Central Banking Studies, London: Bank of England, pp. 32–70.

Healy, Paul M. and Krishna G. Palepu (2001), 'Information asymmetry, corporate disclosure, and the capital markets: a review of the empirical disclosure literature,' *Journal of Accounting & Economics*, **31**(1–3), 405–40.

Izan, Haji Y. (1980), 'Mandatory audit regulation for banks: an empirical evaluation of its effects,' *Journal of Business*, **53**(4), 377–96.

Johnson, Simon, John McMillan and Christopher Woodruff (2002), 'Property rights and finance,' *American Economic Review*, **92**(5), 1335–56.

Jordan, John S., Joe Peek and Eric S. Rosengren (1999), 'The impact of greater bank disclosure amidst a banking crisis,' Federal Reserve Bank of Boston working paper no. 1, February.

Keasey, Kevin and Mike Wright (1997), *Corporate Governance: Responsibilities, Risks and Remuneration*, New York: John Wiley & Sons Ltd.

Leutz, Christian and Robert E. Verrecchia (2000), 'The economic consequences of increased disclosure,' *Journal of Accounting Research*, **38** (supplement), 91–135.

Levine, Ross (2003), 'The corporate governance of banks: a concise discussion of concepts and evidence,' Global Corporate Governance Forum discussion paper, accessed at www.gcgf.org.

Llewellyn, David T. and David Mayes (2003), 'The role of market discipline in handling problem banks,' Bank of Finland discussion papers 21, accessed at www.bof.fi/eng/6_julkaisut/6.1_SPn_julkaisut/6.1.5_Keskustelualoitteita/0321.pdf.

Macey, Jonathan R. and Maureen O'Hara (2003), 'The corporate governance of banks,' *Federal Reserve Bank of New York Economic Policy Review*, **9**(1), 91–107.

Molyneux, P., Lloyd-Williams, D. and Thornton, J. (1992), 'European banking – an analysis of competitive condition,' in J. Revell (ed.), *The Changing Face of European Banks and Securities Markets*, New York: St Martin's Press.

Morgan, Donald P. (2002), 'Rating banks: risk and uncertainty in an opaque industry,' *American Economic Review*, **92**(4), 874–89.

Morgan, Donald P. and Kevin J. Stiroh (2000), 'Bond market discipline of banks: is the market tough enough?' Federal Reserve Bank of New York staff report no. 95.

Moshirian, Fariborz and Georgio Szego (2003), 'Markets and institutions: global perspectives' *Journal of Banking and Finance*, **27**(6), 1213–18.

Office of the Comptroller of the Currency (2003), 'Application of recent corporate governance initiatives to non-public banking organizations,' in *OCC Bulletin 2003–21*, Washington, DC: US Department of the Treasury.

Samolyk, Katherine (1994), 'Banking conditions and regional economic perform-ance: evidence of a regional credit channel,' *Journal of Monetary Economics*, **34**, 259–78.

Saunders, Anthony (2001), 'Comments on Evanoff and Wall/Hancock and Kwast,' *Journal of Financial Services Research*, **20** (February–March), 189–94.

Shleifer, Andrei and Robert W. Vishny (1997), 'A survey of corporate governance,' *The Journal of Finance*, **52**(2), 737–83.

Sironi, Andrea (2003), 'Testing for market discipline in the European banking industry: evidence from subordinated debt issues,' *Journal of Money, Credit & Banking*, **35**(3), 443–72.

Tadesse, Solomon (2003), 'Bank fragility and disclosure: international evidence,' mimeo, University of South Carolina Moore School of Business, October.

Tirole, Jean (2001), 'Corporate governance,' *Econometrica*, **69**(1), 1–35.

Zingales, Luigi (2000), 'In search of new foundations,' *The Journal of Finance*, **55**(4), 1623–53.

Zingales, Luigi (1998), 'Corporate governance,' in P. Newman (ed.), *The New Palgrave Dictionary of Economics and the Law*, New York, NY: Macmillan.

9. A survey of corporate governance in banking: characteristics of the top 100 world banks

Rowan Trayler

Banking worldwide is a high profile industry and plays an important role not only in a country's economy but the world's as well. Operations of the world's largest banks span many countries and play a key role in society. The banking industry has a special function in ensuring the stability and integrity of the worldwide financial system. If one of the world's largest banks were to fail the fear of the consequences is of great concern to bank regulators and governments worldwide. Banks are different to non-financial corporations due to their public purpose and the position of trust that they hold in the community.

Corporate governance and the role of the directors in banking has never been more important, not only has there been a large number of changes to corporate governance regulations but bank management has to address the issues in the implementation of the Bank for International Settlements (BIS) Basel II capital adequacy accord. This survey of the world's top 100 banks is to determine if there are similarities or differences in their corporate governance characteristics as measured by performance and risk.

In 2002 the Sarbanes-Oxley Act (SOX) came into force as a reaction to the high profile corporate failures of Enron, WorldCom, Parmalat and others. These failures also highlighted executive compensation arrangements that many investors questioned as being excessive. Various countries around the world introduced similar corporate governance legislation to SOX and stock exchanges tightened their listing rules in terms of corporate governance. The changes are having a far-reaching effect even in countries that have not introduced similar requirements.

Today, banks are large complex organizations with operations not only across countries but are offering a number of financial services other than just commercial banking, Citibank is a good example with operations in stock broking, insurance, funds management, to name a few. The board of directors of these banks require people who are well equipped to understand the complex nature of the organization, the countries they operate in and be able to provide the independent oversight required as directors.

PERSPECTIVES AND RECENT RESEARCH

Recent research shows that good firm performance is linked to good corporate governance. However LeBlanc and Gillies (2003) suggest the evidence is not as strong as many report, this is also supported by Chidambaran *et al.* (2006) who find no significant performance differences between firms with good or bad governance changes. Gompers *et al.* (2003) developed a governance index based on 24 firm specific characteristics around shareholder rights and found that high governance index firms had higher firm value and profits. Brown and Caylor (2004) develop a governance index based on 51 governance factors. They also find higher governance scores drive return on equity and profit margins whilst Core *et al.* (2006) contend that weak governance did not cause problems with stock returns.

FTSE Research and Institutional Shareholder Services (ISS) produced a joint research report in 2005 about their Corporate Governance Index (CGI) where they rated 2200 companies from 24 countries. In their report they identify five governance areas: ownership, compensation, audit, board and equity structure, on which they based their index calculations. In studying the board structure they were most interested in the composition and processes of the board as well as the structure and independence of key standing committees. In the audit area they focused on the processes and composition of the committees.

CGI rankings are rated from five (highest) to one (lowest). The top three countries in the CGI rankings were the United Kingdom (4.75), Canada (4.71) and Ireland (4.25). The Scandinavian countries had the lowest index values at slightly above one. In the report they ranked 18 industries and the banking industry ranked fifth last with an index value of 2.65. The report highlights that there is a large variation of corporate governance factors across countries and industries.

Grunert *et al.* (2005) found that credit rating agencies take into account governance issues. This is forcing firms in countries that have not introduced similar legislation to SOX to adopt improved governance measures if they want to borrow in international markets. Roberts (2004) agrees saying firms are being forced to conform to international governance requirements to avoid bad ratings. This market pressure has resulted in banks in Southeast Asia and Japan adopting worldwide governance standards. Shinsei Bank in Japan is a good example of the changes these banks are undertaking. Shinsei has changed its board from 5 to 17 members with a range of backgrounds and countries.

Questions have been raised on the effectiveness of the new corporate governance measures. Leblanc and Gillies (2003) question the notion that an independent director is a better director contending that regulators have lost sight of the role of the board which is 'independent oversight of management and corporate stewardship' (p. 3). They believe the idea of independent oversight is driving regulators who are insisting on independent directors as in Australia, Canada, the US and the United Kingdom. Westphal (2002) contends that past research has found little evidence to suggest that independence leads to a better run company. Lawler and Finegold (2006) on the other hand suggest that external directors bring diversity and experience and are a benefit for the governance of a firm.

There have been a number of studies on specific governance attributes. Anderson *et al.* (2004) found that board independence, size and a fully independent audit committee had positive benefits when it came to creditors and loans. Bebchuk *et al.* (2005) examine the way directors are elected and this has an influence on firm value, staggering the election of directors reduced value. Brown and Caylor (2004) ascertain it is the characteristics surrounding board committees and their independence that had an important bearing on performance and Dahya and McConnell (2005) looked at boards with more independent directors and established they made better decisions as reflected in share price changes. Mak and Kusnadi (2002) discovered smaller boards have a positive relationship with firm value.

Studies prior to SOX by Jensen (1993), Mehran (1995), Yermack (1996), Klien (1998), and Vafeas (1999) on board characteristics, found composition, number of board meetings, committees, structure/size of the board, number of outside directors, plus the compensation of the external directors important. In our study many of the above variables are now required under SOX or equivalent legislation and therefore these factors are no longer able to differentiate performance as before. It should be noted Leblanc and Gillies (2003) suggest there has been little learned about what is effective corporate governance. They believe it is board process in the decision making that is important and little research has been done in this area.

METHODOLOGY

In this study we examine the corporate governance characteristics of the world's top 100 banks. The term bank in this study is used generically to refer to the entire operations of the reporting entity as disclosed in their consolidated annual report, not just their banking operations. The ranking of the top 100 banks was obtained from Forbes.com 2005 listing of the world's top 2000 companies. Appendix A contains a list of the banks, country of origin and the value of total assets. Reviewing the Federal Reserve's December 2005 report of foreign banks operating in the United States, 62 percent of non-US banks in the survey have operations in the United States at a branch or subsidiary level and this requires a number of the non-US banks to comply with the Sarbanes-Oxley Act as well as their own home country regulations. The requirement for foreign companies to comply with SOX came into force for financial year statements filed after 15 April 2005. This helps to explain why a large number of the non-US banks included sections in their annual report on how they were moving to be compliant with SOX although there is little evidence that what they are doing is anything more than the minimum possible.

The information used here on corporate governance and financial figures was extracted from each bank's annual report and proxy statement for 2004 obtained from the bank's web-site. In compiling the data it was found that the information reported by banks in their annual reports differed leading to some problems in obtaining information. For example the disclosure of external director compensation, number of board meetings, or years of service for each director was sometimes not reported.

The information obtained on the governance characteristics of the board of directors consisted of: the number of board members, the number of internal directors, independence of the chairperson, the number of board meetings per year, the average number of years a director served on the board and the compensation paid to external directors. For the activities of the board, information gathered included existence of an audit committee, compensation committee, risk committee, and the independence of the audit and compensation committee. The annual report was reviewed to see if there were sections detailing the board's view on corporate governance and risk setting for the bank.

In the second part of the study the governance characteristics are converted into an index where regression tests are carried out to establish if there is significance in the differences in performance, risk measures and governance characteristics. Table 9.1 sets out the governance characteristics and the index score allocated to each variable. A value of one indicates that the bank complied with the requirement and zero that they did not. For example the governance characteristic that the board has an audit committee was given an index value of one. If the bank did not have an audit committee or information was not provided the index value is zero. As a result of reporting differences between countries it was difficult to obtain the number of board meetings per year, compensation of external board

Table 9.1   Board Characteristics – allocation of governance index values

Actual values	Regression values	
Number of directors	Number of directors from annual report	
Number of internal directors	Percentage of internal directors to all directors from annual report	

Index numbers only	Index value of 1	Index value of 0
Chairman of the board	Independent	Non-Independent
Number of board meetings	Information provided	No information
Average years on the board	Information provided	No information
Compensation external directors	Information provided	No information
Corporate governance statement	Statement provided	No statement
Risk statement	Statement provided	No statement
Board audit committee	Committee established	No committee
Audit committee composition	All independent	Not all independent
Board compensation committee	Committee established	No committee
Board compensation committee	All independent	Not all independent
Board risk committee	Committee established	No committee

members and number of years of board service. Therefore in the first regression test these variables have an index value of one if this information was provided or zero if not.

Consolidated balance sheet information gathered was aimed at determining the level of loans to assets and basic risk. Information included total assets, loans and advances to customers, shareholders' funds, profit for the year and as a measure of risk; BIS capital percentage, equity to assets (equity capital ratio) and provision for loan losses to loans. The performance measures used in the analysis was return on assets and return on equity.

Analysis of the data was conducted in two parts. The first part was to establish an average for all of the 100 banks in the survey. This was to enable comparison analysis between banks, countries and regions. The second part of the study was directed towards a series of regression tests to evaluate if there were significant relationships between the governance variables to performance and risk. Before performing the regression analysis a study of correlations between the corporate governance variables was carried out. Appendix B sets out all the governance variables and the initial correlation matrix.

Appendix B shows a high degree of correlation between some of the governance variables, for example, board risk statement and the existence of a board risk committee. The evaluation of the correlations was systematically run through several stages to evaluate each high correlation to establish which variable should be removed for the regression tests. Once a variable was removed the process was repeated to logically remove highly correlated variables. In the first review there was a high correlation with the average years a director had served on the board, the number of board meetings plus the compensation of external directors. The removal of the two variables average years on the board and number of board meetings was made on the basis that banks that reported these items usually reported all three. As each variable was assigned a value of one or zero and the majority of banks had all three there was high correlation amongst the variables.

The second review revealed a high correlation between the audit committee and the compensation committee. Ninety-three percent of banks reported they had an audit committee and 89 percent had a compensation committee. With almost all banks having an audit committee it was believed that this characteristic did not contribute to the analysis and thus the audit committee was deleted. The third review of correlations showed high correlation between all external directors on both the audit committee and compensation committee. Most banks that reported these committees tended to comply with the SOX requirement for the audit committee but not always for the compensation committee. The removal of the audit committee comprised of all internal members was considered less likely to influence the regression tests.

The fourth review showed a high correlation with compensation of external directors and the compensation committee consisting of all external directors. The data on director compensation was poor and an index number was assigned for this variable with one for providing the information and zero if they did not. The majority of banks that reported the compensation of external directors also had external members on their compensation committee and the compensation of directors was seen as not adding to the analysis and therefore deleted.

The final review revealed a high correlation with the compensation committee consisting of all external members and the board risk committee. It was more unlikely that a bank had a compensation committee with all outside directors rather than a risk committee. When this variable was retained and the risk committee removed there was still a high level of correlation in the variables. Therefore the variable compensation committee consisting of all external members was removed and the risk committee retained. This resulted in six governance variables listed in Table 9.2 with their coefficients for the regression analysis in part two.

Table 9.2   Final correlations of governance variables

	Number of directors	Percentage of internal directors	Independent chairman	Compensation committee all external directors	Governance statement	Risk statement
No. of directors	1					
No. of internal directors	−0.2557	1				
Independent chairman	0.1315	−0.2357	1			
Risk commit.	−0.0749	0.0071	−0.0737	1		
Corporate governance statement	0.1980	−0.0326	−0.1275	0.1887	1	
Risk stat.	0.0833	0.1234	0.0513	0.2860	0.1689	1

RESULTS OF THE STUDY – COMPARISON TO THE AVERAGE BANK

This section reports the overall summary results of the survey. The world's top 100 banks come from 28 countries. Refer to Appendix A for the list of banks. The US dominates with 26 banks and the next largest countries are Japan and the United Kingdom with eight each. Twelve countries had just one bank, Appendix C contains a list of the countries represented in the survey and the number of banks. In compiling the data from the banks' annual reports it was observed that there are a number of differences in how the top banks are governed from director numbers, committee structures, number of internal directors and independence of the chairperson. Table 9.3, Panel A provides a summary of the average bank plus maximum and minimum values for each item across the sample. Table 9.3, Panel B shows percentage compliance with board governance characteristics. The average bank in the survey will have 14 directors and 25 percent will be internal. Banks on average hold ten board meetings a year and the directors have served almost eight years on the board. The average bank will have a board statement on corporate governance, an audit, compensation, and risk committees.

Ninety-nine percent of the banks reported a positive return on assets, the average return on assets is 0.96 percent and return on shareholder funds is 14.68 percent. The external directors' remuneration was not reported by

Table 9.3   The 'average' bank

Panel A: Figures for the average bank plus maximum and minimum values across the survey

	Average bank	Entire sample	
		Highest	Lowest
Board characteristics			
Number of directors	14.6	29	5
Number of internal directors	3.7	17	0
Number of board meetings	10.2	33	4
Average years on the board	7.7	22.4	1.1
Balance sheet statistics			
Return on assets (%)	0.96	3.01	−0.23
Return on equity (%)	14.68	32.39	−8.43
Bank total assets US billion	$281.9	1481.1	20.76
Percentage loans to assets	56.73	96.1	4.9
Percentage provisions for loan losses to loans	1.97	9.13	0.3
Percentage equity to assets	6.6	17.8	2.3
Percentage BIS risk capital to risk assets	12.6	36.0	9.5

Panel B: Percentage of banks complying with

Governance characteristics	(%)
Independent chairman of the board	38
Board statement on corporate governance	99
Board statement on risk direction for bank	72
Board audit committee	94
Audit committee all independent directors	67
Board compensation committee	89
Compensation committee all independent directors	58
Board risk committee	77

33 percent of the banks. In relation to US banks the calculation of external director remuneration was an estimate based on their proxy statements and the previous years' board and committee activities.

The definition of the banking industry is broad and the 'banks' in the study are large complex financial organizations (LCFO) with the reporting entity involved in many different financial activities. An interesting statistic from the information is the traditional role of banking 'loans and advances to customers' have reduced in significance of balance sheet proportions.

The average value of loans and advances to customers is 56 percent of total assets. The reason for this lower figure could be due to mergers and acquisitions over recent years where commercial banks have merged to become financial service firms.

All the organizations in the survey have been identified as being in the banking industry by Forbes. However some banks are really financial service firms. For example State Street of the US has only 5 percent of assets as loans. Other banks with very small percentage of loans to assets are Mellon Financial 18 percent, Natexis Banques Populaire and BNP Paribus with 29 percent each. In contrast Washington Mutual of the US made specific mention that it did not consider itself a bank but rather a holding company that owned a bank. Interestingly Washington's percentage of loans to assets at 67 percent is higher than the survey average of 56 percent.

In compiling the data from the annual reports the majority of the World's top 100 banks are LCFOs with operations spanning several countries and they offer a broad range of financial services. For these banks to be successful and be in this listing it is reasonable to assume that they must have good corporate governance procedures.

The review of countries and the regions of Europe and Southeast Asia to the average bank revealed some variation in board composition and committee structure. Nonetheless their overall performance and balance sheet composition was not significantly different from the average bank. Overall Australian, Canadian and Southeast Asian banks are very similar. The Japanese and French banks have some of the most notable differences. Table 9.4 lists the summary for countries where there were five or more banks and the regions of Europe and Southeast Asia. Each of the major differences in governance characteristics are discussed below.

Board of Directors

Many studies have indicated that board size is seen as being important in good corporate governance. The average bank board has 14.6 directors with 3.7 (25 percent) being internal members. Not all banks reported remuneration for their non-executive directors therefore there was no meaningful data to analyse. The governance code in the United Kingdom suggests independent directors should not serve for more than ten years and the chairperson of the board should be external. This study revealed the average number of years' service that directors have served on a bank board is approximately seven and half. The US banks typically had the longest serving directors with an average of ten years. In assembling the

Table 9.4 Country and regional bank comparisons

Country/region	Average	Australia	Canada	Europe	France	Italy	Japan	Southeast Asia	United Kingdom	USA
Number of banks	100	5	6	32	5	7	8	8	8	26
Number of directors	14.6	10.6	16.8	17	18	19.6	9	12.3	15.5	15
Internal directors	3.7	1.4	2	5	9	3	5	3.4	5.5	2
Board meetings	10.2	10.6	12.8	10.1	7.6	16.2		9.2	11.2	8.7
Years service *	7.7	7	8.6	6.5				5.7	5.3	9.9
Percentage of banks with										
Independent chairman	38	100	83	59	40	71	0	13	63	0
Statement on corporate governance	100	100	100	100	100	100	100	100	100	100
Statement on risk	72	80	67	88	80	71	88	63	50	42
Audit committee	94	100	100	97	100	100	88	100	75	100
Audit committee all independent directors	67	100	100	66	40	71	0	50	50	100
Compensation committee	89	100	100	88	100	100	75	100	63	100
Compensation committee all independent directors	58	100	83	56	40	80	0	25	25	100
Board risk committee	77	100	100	81	60	29	75	25	63	81
Balance sheet statistics and performance measures										
Total assets billion	281.9	185.7	225.6	303.3	652.1	250.0	511.6	98.1	580.4	250.9
Percentage loans to assets	56.7	74.3	50.9	58.4	38.6	70.8	55.3	52.1	60.1	57.7
Percentage provisions for loan losses to loans	2.0	1	1.3	2.2	2.8	1.7	2	3	1.3	1.3

Table 9.4 (continued)

Country/region	Average	Australia	Canada	Europe	France	Italy	Japan	Southeast Asia	United Kingdom	USA
Percentage shareholders funds/equity to assets	6.6	7.2	4.8	4.8	3.2	6.3	4.5	7.6	4.5	9.2
BIS capital	12.6	10.4	13.4	11.3	11.3	12.4	11	14.6	12.2	12.4
Return on assets	0.96	1.0	0.8	1.1	0.4	0.7	0.3	1.2	0.8	1.1
Return on equity	14.68	14.8	17.4	21.1	11.3	11.2	8.3	16.2	15.8	13.2

Note: * Average for those banks that reported years of service

194

data it was observed the longest-serving external board member had been on one bank's board for 47 years. Only 38 percent of the banks have an independent chairperson and it was noted that none of the US or Japanese banks had this characteristic.

The Japanese banks were clearly different in their board structure. The Japanese bank board was small with an average of nine directors and the majority internal. They did not provide detailed information on board committees and membership. The smallest board was found in Japan with five directors and they are all internal. Citibank, the world's largest bank in 2005, had 20 directors, with five internal including the chairperson.

The Italian banks had the highest number of board members averaging 19.6 and the French had 50 percent internal directors the second highest in the study. In the case of the French banks many of the internal directors are staff elected representatives.

The US banks had the lowest number of board meetings per year at 8.7 compared to the average of 10.2. The Italian banks had almost one-and-a-half times more board meetings than all other banks at 16.2 meetings in the year. Monte Dei Paschi bank of Italy had 33 meetings in the year, the most of any bank. Several banks reported only four board meetings in the year but this did not seem to cause significant deviation from the average bank performance.

Board Committee Structures

All banks reported on their corporate governance practices however only 72 percent reported a board policy on risk setting and 77 percent of banks have a risk committee. In an industry where risk management is very important and forms part of the new Basel II capital adequacy requirements this seems a low compliance rate. Eighty-nine percent of banks had a compensation committee and the composition of this committee varied with 56 percent having all external directors. All banks other than the Japanese banks had an audit committee but only 67 percent of the banks had all independent members. The Japanese banks have an audit board instead of an audit committee.

The French banks had the lowest compliance with audit and compensation committees having all external board members. One possible explanation for this is that the French banks have a large number of elected staff representatives on their boards and these elected staff members are treated as being equivalent to external directors. Italian banks and the banks in Southeast Asia had low compliance with board risk committees, only 30 percent having a risk committee.

Equity to Assets and Capital Adequacy

All banks reported healthy Bank for International Settlements capital adequacy ratios to risk assets, the average for the 100 banks is 12.58 percent compared to a minimum requirement of eight. In contrast the average percentage of equity to assets was merely 6.6 percent almost half the BIS figure. It should be noted that the BIS ratio compares risk assets taking into account the counterparty's credit risk and many banks have substantial non-bank lending activities including insurance and in some G10 countries insurance assets do not count in the calculation. In addition non-equity items can be included in the capital component in calculating the ratio such as long term subordinated debt.

The 'banks' in this study are large complex financial organizations and the calculation of the balance sheet equity to total asset ratio for some banks appears low. In reviewing the banks' equity to assets levels it poses a question regarding how banks with low levels of equity will adjust to the new capital adequacy rules required under Basel II. The BIS consultative document Overview of the new Basel Accord, released in January 2001 indicated that the new accord would apply not just to the banking group. They said the new accord would apply on a 'consolidated basis only at the highest level' (p. 11). Many of the banks indicated in their annual report that they were moving to adopt the new Basel II capital risk framework.

Some examples of banks that have low equity to assets levels are Commerzbank of Germany with 2 percent equity to assets and a BIS capital ratio of 12.6 percent. Their loans to assets figure is 32 percent. Commerzbank reported risk assets of $189.4 billion compared to total assets of $575.9 billion (32.9 percent risk assets to actual assets). Erste Bank of Austria has 2.4 percent equity to assets, a BIS ratio of 10.2 percent plus loans to assets of 52 percent. Erste bank's risk assets to total assets ratio is 46.8 percent. Crédit Agricole of France has equity to assets of 3.1 percent and a BIS ratio of 11.7 percent. Crédit Agricole's loans to assets are 62.4 percent and the percentage of risk assets to total assets are 52.5 percent. The above banks are just three of the 22 in the study with equity to assets levels below 4 percent. Current BIS capital rules require banks to have a minimum of 4 percent Tier 1 capital, however this 4 percent is calculated on risk assets not total assets and some G10 countries have an exemption for insurance activities.

The French banking industry has the lowest level of equity to assets with an average of 3.2 percent compared to the average bank's level of 6.6 percent. The French banks did report a healthy 11.2 percent BIS capital. French banks have relatively lower levels of loans to assets and hence lower risk assets plus larger insurance operations which could account for the difference. The banks in the US had the highest equity to assets level at 9.2 percent and an average 12.4 percent BIS capital.

Loans to Assets and Provision for Loan Losses

The average bank's loan to assets is 56.7 percent and the provision for loan losses to loans is 1.97 percent. The French banks have very low loans to assets of 38.6 percent, however they have a higher provision for loan losses to loans of 2.8 percent. The French banks were the second largest group of banks in terms of total assets. The French banks have average assets of $US652.1 billion. The top seven US banks are the biggest banks with an average of $725 billion. Australian banks had the highest loans to assets percentage at 74.3 but the lowest provision for loan losses at 1 percent.

Return on Assets and Equity

The average banks return on assets is 0.96 percent and return on equity 14.7 percent. The Japanese and French banks had the lowest return on assets at 0.3 percent and 0.4 percent respectively. The French banks have lower levels of equity than the other banks and a larger reliance on debt therefore higher leverage. The Japanese banks are improving their performance after the well publicized problems of past loan losses. The return on equity was also low for the Japanese banks at 8.3 percent.

The French banks have a low return on equity of 11.3 percent compared to the average of 14.7 percent despite their higher gearing levels. The average return on equity for all European banks was high at 21 percent. The top bank in terms of return on equity is OTP Bank of Hungary at 32 percent. Akbank of Turkey had a return on assets of 2.9 percent, however their return on equity was close to average at 16 percent. The Standard Bank Group of South Africa earned 26 percent on equity and was the second highest to OTP with a healthy return on assets of 2.6 percent.

In looking at the board structure of OTP Bank it has a small board of six directors with 33 percent being internal and they did not report how many meetings they have a year. Also OTP bank did not report on board committees, corporate governance or risk statements. Akbank has a small board with nine directors and 55 percent are internal. Akbank did have statements on risk and corporate governance and a board committee for risk but not an audit or compensation committee and the board met 12 times a year. Standard Bank on the other hand has 19 directors with 19 percent internal. Standard Bank's directors had been on the board for an average of 7 years and they meet six times a year. These differences in governance characteristics have not impacted on their performance.

RESULTS OF THE REGRESSION ANALYSIS

As described in the methodology section the key governance variables for the regression analysis are based around the characteristics of the board of directors namely, number of directors, percentage of inside directors, independent chairperson, and statements from the board on corporate governance, risk, and the existence of a risk committee. These were used to evaluate return on assets, return on equity, BIS capital adequacy, equity to assets, and provision for loan losses to loans. Table 9.5 provides the results of the regression analysis for each of the governance variables and performance characteristics for the 98 banks that provided information on the number of board members and identified who were internal.

Table 9.5 Regression results for six governance variables and 98 observations

Regression results of governance variables to bank performance and risk measures.

	Return on assets	Return on equity	BIS capital ratio	Equity to assets	Provision for loan losses
Number of directors	−0.0003 (0.02522)*	−0.0020 (0.15776)	−0.1495 (0.08502)	−0.0005 (0.43466)	0.0417 (0.22411)
Percentage of internal directors	−0.0001 (0.00001)**	−0.0005 (0.12225)	−0.0094 (0.61071)	−0.0007 (0.000005)**	0.0117 (0.10893)
Independent chairman	−0.0035 (0.00075)**	0.0033 (0.78940)	−0.5799 (0.44882)	−0.0260 (0.00001)**	0.2993 (0.92306)
Risk committee	−0.0001 (0.91424)	0.0091 (0.53858)	−0.8661 (0.34065)	−0.0062 (0.35916)	−1.0506 (0.00433)**
Board governance statement	−0.0211 (0.00004)**	−0.1750 (0.00483)**	3.1973 (0.39325)	−0.0327 (0.23903)	−0.7755 (0.60168)
Board risk statement	−0.0002 (0.82863)	0.0085 (0.54568)	−0.1719 (0.84201)	−0.0085 (0.18663)	0.0922 (0.78778)
Regression R^2	0.3637	0.1379	0.0521	0.3308	0.1365
Significance of F Statistic	0.0000001**	0.0321*	0.5477	0.000001**	0.03387*

Notes: The figures in parentheses are the *P*-values from the regression test and the figures above the bracketed figure is the coefficient.
** Indicates significance at the 1 percent confidence level
* Indicates significance at the 5 percent confidence level

The multiple regression analysis for return on assets and equity to assets had the most significant results at the 1 percent level. In both cases the significant governance characteristics at the 1 percent level was percentage of internal directors to directors and independent chairperson both with negative coefficients. Indicating that a smaller number of internal directors are favorable and an internal chairperson would improve bank performance and increase equity to asset levels. However the conclusion could be slightly biased in that all US banks have internal chairpersons and the highest levels of equity to assets. This results in a higher return on assets than other banks that have higher leverage. In interpreting the result of more external directors are important, it is argued that external directors bring a new perspective to the organization that improves performance.

The evaluation of the BIS capital adequacy was not statistically significant. The return on equity and provision for loan losses were only significant at the 5 percent confidence level. In the analysis of the return on equity the significant governance variable was a board statement on corporate governance which does not seem to be logical given that 99 percent of the banks had this statement. This could indicate that there is another variable that has not been identified in the study or from prior research that is important.

The significant governance variable in determining the provision for loan losses to loans was the existence of a risk committee which had a negative coefficient. This would seem to be at odds with the notion of loan loss provisioning. The interpretation could be that with a risk committee more detailed analysis is put into reviewing the loss provisions or the bank has better credit modeling ability and it could be possible that the provision for losses is a more accurate reflection of the potential losses compared to banks without such committees.

A second regression analysis was performed that included the numbers reported for board meetings in a year and the average years of service on the board rather than in the first regression analysis which included simply the index value of one or zero for these items. Changing these variables reduced the number of banks in the analysis to 68 and removed all the Brazilian, German and Italian banks from the analysis as well as reducing the numbers of Japanese and French banks. The inclusion of the variables as numbers increased the number of governance variables without correlation problems. Table 9.6 shows the results of this analysis. At the 1 percent significance level the performance measure return on assets was highly significant and measures of BIS capital adequacy, equity to assets, and provision for loan losses were all significant at the 1 percent level. Return on equity was significant at the 5 percent confidence level. The overall results of the regression improved with higher R^2 values and improved significance levels.

Table 9.6   Regression results eight governance variables 68 observations

Regression results for reported numbers of directors, percentage of internal directors to directors, average years of board service and number of meetings, compensation committee, compensation committee all independent board members, board statement on risk regressed to bank performance and risk measures.

	Return on assets	Return on equity	BIS capital ratio	Equity to assets	Provision for loan losses
Number of directors	−0.0085 (0.50645)	−0.0821 (0.60928)	0.0096 (0.88788)	0.0005 (0.50213)	0.0511 (0.22286)
Percentage of internal directors	−0.0104 (0.00657)**	0.0436 (0.34933)	−0.0144 (0.46721)	−0.0008 (0.00016)**	−0.0151 (0.21343)
Independent chairman	−0.3418 (0.00101)**	1.8710 (0.13658)	−0.9540 (0.07613)	−0.0285 (0.0000)**	−0.0851 (0.79251)
Average years on the board	−0.0098 (0.55763)	−0.2745 (0.19249)	0.0698 (0.43487)	0.0005 (0.59441)	0.0105 (0.84702)
Number of board meetings per year	−0.0164 (0.21159)	−0.1461 (0.37457)	−0.0162 (0.81666)	0.0002 (0.80057)	0.0451 (0.29167)
Compensation committee	−2.0393 (0.00000)**	−2.7705 (0.43199)	−20.6174 (0.00000)**	−0.1177 (0.00000)**	−3.6195 (0.00019)**
Compensation committee all independent directors	0.3367 (0.00706)**	5.1252 (0.00126)**	−0.5342 (0.41085)	0.0028 (0.66819)	−0.6315 (0.11367)
Board risk statement	0.0381 (0.71097)	1.0675 (0.40888)	0.2140 (0.69709)	−0.0103 (0.07151)	−0.0862 (0.79689)
Regression R^2	0.5942	0.2053	0.8055	0.7023	0.3378
Significance of F Statistic	0.000000**	0.02981*	0.00000**	0.00000**	0.0013**

Notes: The figures in parentheses are the *P*-value from the regression test and the figures above the bracketed figure is the coefficient.
**   Indicates significance at the 1 percent confidence level
*   Indicates significance at the 5 percent confidence level

Changing the governance characteristics of average years of board service and number of board meetings per year from index values to actual values did not prove to be significant factors in their own right for the second regression analysis. The governance variable compensation committee was significant at the 1 percent level for all measures except return on equity. Interestingly the coefficient is negative for all regressions. In analyzing the result for return on assets does this mean that banks with compensation committees pay higher rewards to their senior executives?

To answer this question a review of the banks' annual reports in relation to the operation of the compensation committee was conducted and it was noted that these committees select a peer or aspirant group to compare their executives' salaries to. A large number of bank compensation committees stated that they wanted their executives to be remunerated at or near the top of the peer group. If each bank takes this approach it seems that salaries will always be increasing as the peer group remuneration levels are always increasing. Another factor is most banks list some of the world's top 20 banks in their peer group. The compensation committee reported that the setting of executive salaries had a flow on effect for the rest of the bank staff. Given the significance of this characteristic it would seem that compensation committees are increasing wage costs and reducing profits. Banks without such committees are possibly not taking as active a role in comparing remuneration arrangements for senior staff.

Gordon (2006) agrees with this finding. He reports:

> in setting executive pay, compensation committees typically relied on the compensation consultant that also provided firm-wide compensation and human resources guidance. This consultant is hired by management and earns the largest part of its fee from the firm-wide assignment. Such a conflicted consultant is unlikely to make recommendations or offer viewpoints that senior management would find distressing. (p. 28)

The other governance variable that is significant at the 1 percent level is the percentage of internal directors with a negative coefficient. This variable was also significant in the first regression test and indicates lower levels of internal directors are important and seems logical as the independent board members bring an external perspective to the bank.

A third regression analysis was run on the number of board members only and this did not prove to be significant at the 1 percent level. It was noted that the sign for the coefficient was negative for all performance and risk measures indicating that small boards are better as found in past research. Brown and Caylor (2004) have suggested the optimal board size is between six and 15, however in this study we have not tried to evaluate the optimal size of the board.

Several other regression tests were evaluated including one on the total governance index value but this failed to produce a meaningful result. A

Table 9.7 Regression results for eight governance variables and 68 observations

Regression results for reported numbers of directors, percentage of internal directors to directors, average years of board service and number of meetings in the governance variables to bank performance and risk measures.

	Return on assets	Return on equity	BIS capital ratio	Equity to assets	Provision for loan losses
Number of directors	−0.0208 (0.2248)	−0.0218 (0.89609)	−0.1714 (0.22058)	−0.0006 (0.53156)	0.0104 (0.82422)
Percentage of internal directors	−0.0118 (0.00742)**	−0.0146 (0.72950)	0.0255 (0.46833)	−0.0008 (0.00244)**	−0.0017 (0.88740)
Independent chairman	−0.3195 (0.01640)*	2.7810 (0.03346)*	−1.3488 (0.20929)	−0.0319 (0.00008)**	−0.2570 (0.47548)
Average years on the board	−0.0066 (0.67025)	−0.1034 (0.63031)	−0.0201 (0.91022)	−0.0002 (0.89275)	−0.0247 (0.68141)
Number of board meetings per year	0.0078 (0.64435)	−0.1507 (0.36911)	0.2666 (0.05885)	0.0016 (0.09953)	0.0991 (0.03766)*
Regression R^2	0.2139	0.0887	0.1119	0.3467	0.0781
Significance of *F* Statistic	0.00927**	0.3163	0.1846	0.00005**	0.3962
Regression results of number of directors to performance and risk measures					
Regression R^2	0.0469	0.0263	0.0266	0.0015	0.0102
Significance of *F* Statistic	0.03216	0.1105	0.1089	0.7098	0.3248
Coefficient	−0.00027	−0.00216	−0.1275	−0.00027	0.0329

Notes: The figures in parentheses are the *P*-value from the regression test and the figures above the bracketed figure is the coefficient.
** indicates significance at the 1 percent confidence level
* indicates significance at the 5 percent confidence level

regression test using the numbers for board of directors, percentage of internal directors, number of years on the board, independent chairperson and number of board meetings per year failed to change the results of the first regressions tests and are shown in Table 9.7.

CONCLUSIONS

There have been a number of studies into corporate governance characteristics and firm performance. It has been observed that there is variation between researchers as to what variables are important. This study of the world's top 100 banks demonstrates that there are differences in corporate governance. However, it does not seem to make a significant difference in performance as measured by return on assets.

The comparison study of the various countries showed that the Japanese banks tend to have a small number of directors, which according to some researchers is a positive attribute but our study failed to find this characteristic significant. However the Japanese banks had the lowest return on assets and equity. In our tests it was found that the percentage of internal directors was significant at the 1 percent confidence level. The lower the percentage of internal directors the better the return on assets and this is one of the major differences of the Japanese banks compared to the average bank as they have approximately 40 percent internal directors. This also explained the differences in the French and Italian banks' low return on assets.

The large percentage of internal directors assisted in the explanation of low equity to asset levels for the Japanese, French and banks in the United Kingdom. There was no governance variable that satisfactorily explained the return on equity and BIS capital.

Overall the effect of the new governance legislation seems to be that banks have added a number of committees to meet the requirements of legislation such as SOX but all this has done is remove these variables as predictors of performance that previous researchers had found important. This study examined 13 governance characteristics and found the independence of the board may become the most important characteristic in determining bank performance. The results of the study did not suggest that the chairperson of the board has to be independent as some legislation calls for.

In summary the key findings are that banks that have fewer internal directors may perform better than banks that have higher percentage of internal directors. The move by boards to establish audit and compensation committees are no longer a differentiator in performance.

This study highlighted some areas for further investigation, for example, large banks with low equity to total asset levels. The new Basel II capital adequacy rules may cause some banks to review their operations as 'banks' and split their operation into commercial banks and financial service firms due to the requirements of operational risk and other risk measures of the new accord.

REFERENCES

Andersen, R., S. Mansi and D. Reeb (2004), 'Board characteristics, accounting report integrity, and the cost of debt', *Journal of Accounting and Economics*, **37**, 315–42.

Basel Committee on Banking Supervision (2001), 'Overview of the new Basel accord', Bank for International Settlements consultative document, Basel, Switzerland.

Bebchuk, L. A., A. Cohen and A. Ferrell (2004), 'What matters in corporate governance?' Harvard Law School, discussion paper no. 491, September.

Brown, L. and M. Caylor (2004), 'Corporate governance and firm performance', working paper, Georgia State University.

Chidambaran, N. K., D. Palia and Y. Zheng (2006), 'Does better corporate governance "cause" better firm performance', working paper, accessed at SSRN http://ssrn.com/abstract=891556.

Core, J. E., W. R. Guay and T. O. Rusticus (2006), 'Does weak governance cause weak stock returns? An examination of firm operating performance and investors' expectations', *Journal of Finance*, **61**, 655–87.

Dahya, J. and J. J. McConnell (2005), 'Outside directors and corporate board decisions', *Journal of Corporate Finance*, **11**, 37–60.

Federal Reserve (2005) report of foreign banks operating in the United States, December, accessed at www.federalreserve.gov/releases/iba/default.htm.

Forbes.com (2004), *The World's 2000 Largest Public Companies*, accessed August 2005 at www.forbes.com/lists.

FTSE (2005), *FTSE ISS Corporate Governance Rating and Index Series – Measuring the Impact of Corporate Governance on Global Portfolios*, New York: FTSE Institutional Shareholder Services, April.

Gompers, P., J. Ishii and A. Metrick (2003), 'Corporate governance and equity prices', *The Quarterly Journal of Economics*, **118**, 107–55.

Gordon, J. N. (2006), 'Independent directors and stock market prices: the new corporate governance paradigm', European Corporate Governance Institute working paper no. 74/2006, accessed at http://ssrn.com/abstract=928100.

Grunert, J., L. Norden and M. Weber (2005), 'The role of non-financial factors in international credit ratings', *Journal of Banking and Finance*, **29**, 509–31.

Jensen, M. C. (1993), 'The modern industrial revolution, exit and the failure of internal control systems', *Journal of Finance*, **48**, 831–80.

Klein, April (1998), 'Firm performance and board committee structure', *Journal of Law and Economics*, **41**, 275–303.

Lawler III, E. E. and D. Finegold (2006), 'Who's in the boardroom and does it matter: the impact of having non-director executives attend board meetings', *Organizational Dynamics*, **35**, 106–9.

Leblanc, R. and J. Gillies (2003), 'The coming revolution in corporate governance', *Ivey Business Journal*, **68**, 1–11.

Mak, Y. T. and Y. Kusnadi (2002), 'Size really matters: further evidence on the negative relationship between board size and firm value', working paper, National University of Singapore.

Mehran, Hamid (1995), 'Executive compensation structure, ownership, and firm performance', *Journal of Financial Economics*, **38**, 163–84.

Roberts, D. (2004), 'American companies climb to the top of the global corporate governance table', *Financial Times*, 7 September, 1.

Vafeas, N. (1999), 'Board meeting frequency and firm performance', *Journal of Financial Economics*, **53**, 113–42.

Westphal, J. D. (2002), 'Second thoughts on board independence: why do so many demand board independence when it does so little good?' *The Corporate Board*, **23**, 6–10.

Yermack, D. (1996), 'Higher market valuation of companies with a small board of directors', *Journal of Financial Economics*, **40**, 185–221.

APPENDIX 9A: TOP 100 BANKS

Rank	Bank	Country	Assets	Rank	Bank	Country	Assets
1	Citigroup	United States	1484.10	51	Bank of Ireland	Ireland	130.91
2	Bank of America	United States	1110.46	52	Standard Bank Group	South Africa	80.73
3	HSBC Group	United Kingdom	1031.29	53	CIC Group	France	195.75
4	Royal Bank of Scotland	United Kingdom	1119.90	54	DnB NOR	Norway	105.46
5	JPMorgan Chase	United States	1138.47	55	PNC Financial Services	United States	77.3
6	BNP Paribas	France	1228.03	56	Golden West Financial	United States	106.89
7	Barclays	United Kingdom	1002.09	57	State Street	United States	94.04
8	Wells Fargo	United States	427.85	58	Banco Popular Español	Spain	84.83
9	HBOS	United Kingdom	729.31	59	KeyCorp	United States	90.74
10	Wachovia	United States	411.14	60	Monte Dei Paschi	Italy	153.71
11	Mizuho Financial	Japan	1306.60	61	Erste Bank	Austria	161.27
12	Société Générale Group	France	678.36	62	Firstrand	South Africa	68.87
13	Banco Santander	Spain	435.75	63	DBS Group	Singapore	107.51
14	Lloyds TSB Group	United Kingdom	450.02	64	BCP-Bco Com Portuguîs	Portugal	97.26
15	Mitsubishi Tokyo Finl	Japan	1014.56	65	Sumitomo Trust & Banking	Japan	145.82
16	ABN-Amro Holding	Netherlands	825.81	66	Regions Financial	United States	84.08
17	Sumitomo Mitsui Financial	Japan	962.87	67	Mellon Financial	United States	37.12
18	BBVA-Banco Bilbao Vizcaya	Spain	422.08	68	Sberbank of Russia	Russia	50.53
19	Crédit Agricole	France	987.79	69	BOC Hong Kong	Hong Kong/China	98.22
20	Royal Bank of Canada	Canada	351.74	70	Natexis Banques Populaire	France	170.95
21	Natl Australia Bank	Australia	298.36	71	Türkiye Is Bankasi	Turkey	30.76
22	UniCredito Italiano	Italy	299.22	73	Northern Rock	United Kingdom	82.13
23	US Bancorp	United States	195.10	74	Alliance & Leicester	United Kingdom	86.47
24	Washington Mutual	United States	307.92	75	United Overseas Bank	Singapore	82.65

	Bank	Country	
25	Dexia	Belgium	439.58
26	Nordea Bank	Sweden	330.03
27	Banca Intesa	Italy	324.11
28	Bank of Nova Scotia	Canada	228.37
29	Commonwealth Bank Group	Australia	213.59
30	ANZ Banking	Australia	187.69
31	Toronto-Dominion Bank	Canada	255.15
32	Danske Bank Group	Denmark	340.07
33	Sanpaolo IMI	Italy	252.79
34	Westpac Banking Group	Australia	177.76
35	Canadian Imperial Bank	Canada	227.85
36	National City	United States	139.28
37	Bank of Montreal	Canada	217.73
38	Banco Bradesco Group	Brazil	69.63
39	Standard Chartered Group	United Kingdom	141.69
40	SunTrust Banks	United States	127.79
41	Bank of New York	United States	94.53
42	Fifth Third Bancorp	United States	98.29
43	Svenska Handelsbanken	Sweden	203.02
44	Allied Irish Banks	Ireland	138.46
45	Commerzbank	Germany	575.94
46	BB&T	United States	100.51
47	Banco do Brasil	Brazil	89.99
48	SEB-Skand Enskilda Bank	Sweden	239.48
49	FöreningsSparbanken	Sweden	153.57
50	State Bank of India Group	India	127
76	National Bank of Greece	Greece	67.56
77	M&T Bank	United States	52.94
78	Shinhan Financial	South Korea	116.73
79	Mitsui Trust	Japan	119.49
80	St George Bank	Australia	50.85
81	Akbank	Turkey	20.76
82	Comerica	United States	51.77
83	Resona Holdings	Japan	381.18
84	National Bank of Canada	Canada	72.65
85	Kookmin Bank	South Korea	156.23
86	OTP Bank	Hungary	23.04
87	AmSouth Bancorp	United States	49.69
88	Eurohypo	Germany	283.65
89	Unibanco Group	Brazil	29.88
90	Malayan Banking	Malaysia	46.92
91	BPVN Group	Italy	60.9
92	Marshall & Ilsley	United States	38.98
93	Northern Trust	United States	45.28
94	North Fork Bancorp	United States	60.67
95	Capitalia	Italy	159.55
96	Banche Popolari Unite	Italy	78.92
97	Banco de Sabadell	Spain	57.39
98	Oversea-Chinese Banking	Singapore	49.73
99	Sovereign Bancorp	United States	54.47
100	Popular	United States	44.4
102	Bank of Yokohama	Japan	101.42

APPENDIX 9B: CORRELATIONS OF GOVERNANCE VARIABLES

	Number of Directors	Percentage of internal Directors on board	Independent Chairman	Average Years on Board	Number of Board Meetings	Audit Committee	Audit all external members	Risk Committee	Corporate Governance Statement	Board Risk Statement	Compensation committee	
											Committee	All external directors
Number of Directors	1.0000											
Number of internal Directors	-0.2557	1.0000										
Independent Chairman	0.1315	-0.2358	1.0000									
Average Years on Board	-0.0371	-0.3225	-0.1384	1.0000								
Compensation external directors	0.0415	-0.3530	-0.0127	0.6133	1.0000							
Number of Board Meetings	0.2212	-0.1638	-0.1010	0.0707	0.1127	1.0000						
Audit Committee	0.2235	-0.6492	0.1811	0.3864	0.3633	0.3409	1.0000					
Audit all external	-0.0749	0.0071	-0.0738	0.2860	0.1523	0.3198	0.1599	1.0000				
Compensation Committee	0.1980	-0.0327	-0.1276	-0.0610	0.2005	0.4379	0.1493	0.1887	1.0000			
Compensation all external	0.0833	0.1235	0.0513	-0.0470	0.0971	0.1758	-0.0609	0.2860	0.1690	1.0000		
Risk Committee	0.2147	-0.2193	-0.0777	0.3319	0.1639	0.6878	0.2781	0.3842	0.3012	0.2556	1.0000	
Governance Statement	0.1904	-0.5717	0.1070	0.4415	0.3522	0.2792	0.6405	0.1005	0.1223	-0.0288	0.4059	1.0000
Risk Statement	0.0415	-0.3530	-0.0127	0.6133	1.0000	0.1127	0.3633	0.1523	0.2005	0.0971	0.1639	0.3522

APPENDIX 9C: COUNTRIES REPRESENTED AND NUMBER OF BANKS

Australia	5	Austria	1
Belgium	1	Brazil	3
Canada	6	Denmark	1
France	5	Germany	2
Greece	1	Hong Kong/China	1
Hungary	1	India	1
Ireland	2	Italy	7
Japan	8	Malaysia	1
Netherlands	1	Norway	1
Portugal	1	Russia	1
Singapore	3	South Africa	2
South Korea	2	Spain	4
Sweden	4	Turkey	2
United Kingdom	8	United States	26

10. Corporate governance: the case of Australian banks

Mohamed Ariff and Mohammad Z. Hoque

INTRODUCTION TO CORPORATE GOVERNANCE OF BANKS

This chapter attempts to provide a summary report on the status of corporate governance in the banking sector of Australia. A historical fact often vaunted in Australia is that no depositor has lost his deposit in a bank run for over 100 years. Although there were bank failures depositors were paid off despite there being no deposit insurance! Nevertheless, since governance is a much broader issue than that of depositor protection, bank governance has emerged even in Australia as a key public issue with significant movements in the industry on self-regulation and, at the regulatory level, this interest has spawned significant regulatory changes.

It is still pertinent, in our opinion, to continue to examine the connection between good corporate governance and the performance of banks. It is argued that a superior governance structure, accepting that it is adhered to fastidiously at each bank, would provide the best financial services to the clients within a well-governed banking system. To achieve this there is a need for an environment that encourages banks to compete for customers in a competitive banking environment. There are sufficient institutional structures in Australia providing an impetus for promoting competition. Given the recent spectacular failures of governance, such as that of a foreign exchange loss in a leading bank, NAB, and the bankruptcy of an insurance firm, both in 2005, a scrutiny of corporate governance practices is timely to ensure that poor management practices are not due to the failure of good governance structures in the banking system.

Apart from the recent public demand for good governance, there are also theoretical reasons for examining the link between good governance and superior bank performance (see Shleifer and Vishny, 1997; Jensen and Meckling, 1976). Shleifer and Vishny state that corporate governance deals with 'ways in which suppliers of finance to corporations assure themselves of getting a return on their investment' (p. 737). In the case of banking, suppliers of funds are the providers of the tier-1 and tier-2 capital as well. For the banks that provide loans, their ability to get the loans back from outside parties matters. To the extent that the long term survival of a bank depends on earning a decent return on investment to the fund providers, investors would expect to know whether good governance practices in place in a bank are in fact yielding superior performance. Jensen and Meckling (1976) pointed out the need to reduce the agency problem via a number of governance structures and management practices to induce the management of the banks to work in the interest of the bank's fund providers. Hence, the research question for the banking sector is to demonstrate a verifiable link between good governance and superior performance in the banking sector. This is the main aim of this chapter.

Some studies have shown that it is possible to examine the efficiency of a banking entity by applying efficiency tests: for example, applying the DEA-Malmquist or Cost minimization models and so on. The issue in such a study would be to see whether efficiency is in fact related to a superior governance structure. This has yet to be studied in the Australian context. Scale and scope economies are generally found in entities that have superior skills in combining input resources effectively to produce the outputs as financial services products. *A priori* reasoning would suggest that the ability of bank managers to combine input resources effectively to produce the best financial products would be consistent with the argument that such managers are more likely to be working in an environment with good corporate governance practices. Hence, superior economic efficiency of financial services production is likely to be correlated with good corporate governance practices and structures in place.

Banking institutions have special significance in an economy and their bad management would have far-reaching consequences for that economy as a whole. Banks play a primary role in intermediation of savings investment as well as servicing the economic agents with an efficient payment system mechanism. Failure of banks due to poor governance structures would mean that the impact on the economy would be very damaging and destabilizing. The systemic risk from bank failures needs to be avoided, and hence the study of bank governance takes first priority in an economy. Besides that, banking is also a licensed activity. As such, the set of regulations covering banking is particularly meant to be adhered to very strictly by banks as supervised by the prudential authorities of a country.

Therefore, a study of corporate governance of banking is itself a legitimate area of inquiry for the reasons discussed here. Two key research issues are examined regarding the linkage of governance with: (a) the performance of banks; and (b) the consequent valuation impact of governance of a bank.

The rest of the chapter is organized as follows. In the ensuing section, the structure of corporate governance in Australia is described. In the third section there is a discussion of the pertinent literature, which is very short and increasing, on specific research issues. The fourth section has a brief discussion on issues pertinent to the Australian banking system arising from corporate governance. The fifth section contains a description of some of the measures we have chosen to describe and represent corporate governance variables and performance variables. The final section concludes.

STRUCTURE OF CORPORATE GOVERNANCE IN AUSTRALIA

Corporate governance is difficult to define broadly because this field of inquiry requires a definition that is limited to the researchers and practitioners in the broad area of commerce. Since the organizational structure in a bank-like entity to enhance corporate governance specifically is in the broader area of organization literature, it is perhaps legitimate to borrow a definition from that literature. Davis (2005: p. 143) states that the study of the 'structures, processes, and institutions within and around organisations that allocate power and resource control among the participants' is corporate governance. This definition could easily be applied to banks, in which case it enables us to delineate the structures in place in Australia for corporate governance of banks. In a broad sense, the search for structures is related to the building of institutions relevant for good governance: see Black (1992) where the author advocates building an institutional voice for good governance. The OECD (1997) has some interesting description of corporate governance in OECD countries: see www.oecd.org/daf/fin/netcrop.htm. We now proceed to identify the concepts/variables of interest.

Board Control

At the societal level, the first specific governance law was the Banks (Shareholdings) Act of 1972: this was aimed at limiting the power of majority shareholders and freeing the Board to have full power.[1] This law limited the concentration of power of individual shareholders of the bank. By limiting one individual's ownership of bank shares to 10 percent, the law limited the power and resource control of large investors. This law had the far-reaching impact of freeing the Board of a typical bank from domination by large individual shareholders (or the nominees in the case of corporations) with majority shareholders wielding power and destroying good governance practices. Several neighbouring countries followed this positive move, and adopted a slightly varied 15 percent ceiling for individual share-holders. This law coupled with the prudential authority regulation on pro-hibiting related party lending led to significant improvement in enhancing the power of the Board and also that of the executive in fostering good cor-porate governance. This happened about 35 years ago. It is noteworthy, because the adoption of these two regulations by neighboring countries aimed to strengthen Board control of banks.

Uniform and Focused Supervision

The second set of policy changes were aimed at improving the overseeing of banking activities as well as improving competition in the industry. From the outset in 1941 to the present, a series of reforms (often resulting in new laws) were introduced to bring all bank-like institutions under the super-vision of prudential authorities. The prudential supervision of some state-licensed banks fell within the state, outside the federal powers, which fostered bad banking practices, and in two cases bank fraud. From a bank (Commonwealth Bank) acting as the supervisor of all federally-licensed banks in 1941, Australia improved the governance of banks by bringing all banks under the supervision of the Reserve Bank of Australia (1959 Reserve Bank Act) and the Australian Prudential Regulatory Authority, APRA, for supervision of financial institutions in 1998. These two steps enabled all banks to be supervised by a central authority thus contributing to the improved prudential governance under uniform rules by an independent authority. Separation of banking supervision from the Reserve Bank to the APRA enabled attention to be focused more on the issues particular to the banking (and insurance) industry: a lesson from the reforms in the UK just few years earlier. Concomitant with these major changes were the attention given to establishing greater competition among the banks. In 2000, with the release of APRA's Ten Harmonized Prudential Standards, banking opera-tions increasingly became uniform as well as thus leading to the regulator permitting greater market-based self regulations within that framework.

Competition

The adoption of the 'six pillars' policy was abandoned in favour of the 'four pillars' policy in 1998 so that mergers of banks other than outside the core four banks were encouraged to create scale economies and full-range banking businesses. Even prior to that, the regulators permitted, first, the creation of new banks and later invited foreign banks to enter the market in the late 1980s. There were spurts of policy changes: once in 1984, next in 1994, and then in 2002 to encourage the entry of foreign institutions into the finance industry. As a result, the banking sector has begun to move more and more towards competitive structures, thus underpinning the importance of the market forces moving the banks to adopt good governance to enable them to retain their customers, who are increasingly freer at lower transaction cost to exit from one bank to another, particularly in the mortgage and loans markets. The active promotion of competition has been also been fostered by the Australian Consumer and Competition Council, ACCC, which encouraged fair-trading practices as well as ensuring a greater degree of de-concentration of market power. Investor protection that has been the hallmark of the Anglo-Saxon laws that promotes a competing market place for banking products along with strong laws to protect investors has been further enhanced with the establishment of a single statutory body, the Australian Securities and Investment Corporation, ASIC (successor to the Australian Securities Commission formed in 1991). All securities related matters handled by banks are now managed under the investor protection laws of ASIC.

Corporate Governance Codes

The 1993 release of the Code of Banking Practices by the Australian Bankers' Association is an early statement that contained reference to good practice, aimed at improving good corporate practices for the benefits of the customers. In 2003 the Australian Stock Exchange, ASX, released the ASX Corporate Governance Statement that was aimed at enabling a clear set of principles to be focused for compliance by public companies: see the ten principal aims of the code in the Appendix (see www.asx.com.au). The Code was formulated by a standing Corporate Governance Council within the ASX. The public listed banks have adopted these standards, and have also enhanced their application in some cases (see www.westpac.com.au). On the part of the Government, it passed a set of laws in 2002 referred to as CLERP-9 (Corporate Law Economic Reform Program). This addressed some of the governance issues much as, but not to the same extent as, the Sarbanes-Oxley Act of 2002 in the US, legislated in the face of the major corporate failures of huge corporations (Enron and Worldcom in the US; Onetel, HIH Insurance, Quintex and Ansett in Australia; many in other countries; Bank of Commerce and Industry, and Maxwell Corp in the UK). Together, these efforts have placed banks on notice to improve their corporate governance practices under a set of very detailed codes. Finally, the annual reports of companies are required to contain a report of corporate governance issues for the reporting year to be signed by the CEO. Thus, as from 2004, there has been a sea change in the mindset of the top management in managing corporate governance for the good of the company's profit line as well as to enhance the securing of the profit line by adherence in practice of these good governance standards.

Basel Guidelines

The provisions that came in by the way of Basel guidelines relate to risk-management in banks. There is a strong practical reason for interpreting bank reports to be adjusted for the different riskiness of the assets reported by a bank for public information. In a sense, good corporate governance dictates that the bank management must practice good governance in knowing the risk-adjusted size of their reported assets. Hence, any adoption of Basel recommendations should also be looked at as part of corporate governance, not simply as good reporting practice.

Core principles for effective banking supervision that underpin the Basel capital accord were provided in 1997. These principles are related to the Board's obligations to shareholders; the qualifications, expertise, responsibilities and duties of the Board members, top and middle level management; the composition of the Board; relationships with bank shareholders and management and the customers; public reports and disclosures; and cooperation with regulators and supervisory authorities. However, the Basel Committee issued initial guidance for corporate governance in 1999. The Committee provided a number of measures for enhancing governance in the banks. These measures include

- setting corporate objectives and defining clear lines of responsibility and accountability;
- meeting the obligations of accountability to shareholders and taking into account the interests of stakeholders;
- protecting the interests of depositors;
- raising awareness of risks throughout the individual and group structure of the banks;
- ensuring that independent directors are included in the bank board;
- operating with structures that do not impair transparency or increase risks;
- providing services to the customers without increasing risks;
- expanding audit scope in situations where transparency of structures is lacking;
- effectively using the work of internal and external auditors and other control functions;
- adopting compensation policies and practices that are consistent with the bank's ethical values, strategy and objectives; and
- conducting governance activities in a transparent manner.

However, the Committee reviews these policies from time to time and revisions in the policies relating to corporate governance issues were expected in late 2006 (George, 2005).

Table 10.1 summarizes the structural development on corporate governance discussed to this point. While concerted effort to improve corporate governance appears to be the specific structures put in place in 2002 and beyond, it is incorrect to conclude that there was an absence of concerns of corporate governance in pre-2002 years. As the contents of the table reveals, there has been a concerted effort to improve the governance environment of banks over half a century of laws, regulations, uniform codes and oversight organizations. Thus, the kind of banking governance an observer would find in Australia in contrast to the ones in the neighbouring economies is one that has been improving over the time. The structures put in place have helped vastly in making the financial system resilient in times of stresses during financial and political crises.

SURVEY OF THE LITERATURE

There is a modest literature on governance in general, and a smaller subset of studies on corporate governance. This brief review is limited to the seminal works in this area drawing attention thereafter to the limited Australian literature. That proper corporate governance institutional framework is important has been prompting, for over 100 years, the passing of laws of good governance in modern societies. Our citations are limited to just two: Carlton *et al.* (1998) and Klein (1998). There are also other studies on broader governance issues: see Hart (1995). More relevant to the subject of this discussion are corporate governance issue papers. These may be broadly divided as follows: Board composition studies; Board and CEO remuneration studies; Board independence studies; ownership and performance studies; and finally, a set of Australian studies.

The literature abounds with studies dealing with board composition, diversity, and so on, since the annual reports of firms contain easily accessible information. Board-related variables are also good measures of governance. For example, the higher the proportion of independent members, the more likely it is to have good governance from the diversity of ideas and points of view: Hermalin and Weisbach (1988) and Rosenstein and Wyatt (1990). The latter showed a relationship between board independence and financial performance of firms. The board meeting frequency is shown to be related to governance (Vafeas, 1999). Hawkins (1997) suggesting that strong boards are important for corporate performance. Board independence and small board size have been

Table 10.1   Development of corporate governance structures, Australia

Issue	Law or Regulations or Codes	Remarks
Licensing and Supervision of Banks	1941: Commonwealth Bank as bank supervisor	Banks were supervised by the government-owned bank, the Commonwealth Bank of Australia
	1945: The Banking Act	Consolidated the pre-war legislations
	1960: Reserve Bank Act	Centralized supervision of banks, increasingly under one body
	1998: Australian Prudential Regulatory Authority (APRA)	Monetary management and banking supervision of banks. Established APRA to take over from RBA all banking supervision
Competition consumer protection	Australian Competition and Consumer Council (ACCC) laws	Generally prevented concentration, and improved bank consumer protection, thus good governance. Entry of more foreign banks in 1985
	Entry of new bank-like corporations	The government relaxed the entry barriers, permitted more competition, freed central control and returned banks to respond to market conditions
	Big Banks is better	In 1998 dropped the preservation of top six banks by switching to a policy of 'Four Pillars' which did not encourage the mergers of the top four banks
Board Control	1970: Banks (Shareholdings) Act	By limiting the ownership of individuals to 10 percent (15 percent since 1998) of the bank shares, greater power to improve governance by the Board of directors
Corporate Governance	1989: Banking Ombudsman	This provided an additional access to public outside the law as managed by ACCC
	1993: Code of Banking Practices by RBA	This provided for improved governance in the operations of the banks
	2002: CLERP-9	Broad provisions by Australian parliament in the light of the impact of Sarbanes-OxleyAct after significant public company failures
	2004: ASX Governance Code	Governance Council established by the ASX formulated ten basic provisions for improving governance of public companies
Investor Protection	Very strong laws have been present historically	While banks were free to engage in profit-making, laws aimed at protecting investors have been around for some time
	1998: Australian Securities and Investment Commission	More focused agency to improve investor protection as well as supervise financial product market makers

Table 10.1   (continued)

Issue	Law or Regulations or Codes	Remarks
Basel Committee	1999: Guidance for corporate governance was issued	Focused on board composition, structure, distribution of accountability and responsibility to stakeholders, depositors, shareholders and risk measures

Sources: Australian Bankers Association reports and web site (www.bankers.asn.au and www.bis.org).

found to be correlated with good governance and higher performance: see Deli and Gillan (2000).

CEO and board compensation are subjects of inquiry as means of reducing agency problems (Jensen and Meckling, 1976) thus improving corporate performance. Presumably then, there is a positive relationship between higher compensation and good governance behavior of management and the board thus leading to superior performance. While finance literature applauds this as a reason to support a large number of studies on compensation schemes, the evidence for increased share price performance is at best close to 0 or 1 percent abnormal returns in most studies. Other literature suggests that there is no relationship of this kind: see Gregg *et al.* (1993).

The Australian literature on governance has grown over the years. Australian financial market de-regulation, which also improved the governance institutions, has been shown to be positive in reducing bank risk and improving bank performance: see Harper and Scheit (1992) and Davis (1995). The latter also investigated reforms in the banking sector in the context of agency problems. These reforms were far-reaching for the period from 1984 to 1992. Roy *et al.* (1994) showed interlocking board and board size is related to improved performance. Another paper revealed the impact of CEO turnover on share prices: Suchard *et al.* (2001). Finally Dunlop's (1998) study is a reference for corporate governance as seen from the perspective of Australian environment.

There is also a growing literature relating to few other countries. Korea's governance problem, as big as it is, is beginning to be studied. Prior to the 1997 financial crisis, Joh (2003) showed that Korean firms' profitability is related to corporate governance. A later study (Choe and Lee, 2003) is a description of bank governance reforms in that country. Kaplan's (1994) study comparing top management rewards in Japan and the US shows the unique nature of Japan's corporate governance. Morck and Nakamura

(1999) is about corporate control and bank performance in Japan. Finally, there is a study by Conyon and Peck (1998) about the link between board size and corporate performance but this is about all firms, not just banks.

This brief review of the literature shows that there is a variety of research concerns and that research specific to corporate performance of banks is at best just starting in most parts of the world. The consensus from a review of the literature may be summarized as follows. Governance institutional development precedes any adoption by banks (or for that matter any firms) of good corporate governance schemes. The legal framework needs to be passed and on that a set of institutions are then set up to fulfill the need to efficiently manage corporate governance. In those regards, Australia has developed the framework and also put in place efficient institutions to manage the governance of corporations, including banks. Serious literature is now emerging that attempts to show how de-regulation of the financial sector, the board composition, the independence of the boards, and, to a lesser extent, compensation schemes to top management, are positively correlated with good performance of banks in Australia.

SPECIFIC CORPORATE GOVERNANCE ISSUES OF BANKS IN AUSTRALIA

Corporate governance issues have received wider attention at firm, industry and regulatory levels in Australia. Australian banks have been implementing a number of governance measures in compliance with regulators' requirements (such as APPRA's) to improve their operational and market efficiency as well as to protect stakeholders' and shareholders' interests. Until October 2005, three-quarters of the largest 25 regulated Australian depository institutions were found to be compliant with the full range of governance requirements set by the APRA. It does not mean that governance issues are not alive in these organizations. Top Australian banks are involved in fund management through subsidiaries and the governance mechanism and trading activities of these organizations are still not sufficiently transparent to the investors. Dow and Gordon (1997) found that investors were unaware of the expertise of the fund managers and there was no effective governance mechanism in place to address this concern of investors. As financial transactions are increasingly becoming global, board-employee relations and responsibility in respect of global transactions have been changing. The present internal governance mechanism may not be efficient to adequately respond to the emerging risk. This was evident from National Australia Bank's loss of $180 million in foreign exchange transaction in October 2003 due to illegal punting of the bank's money on speculative trading of the Australian dollar by its four high officials (Melbourne-based Luke Duffy, head of foreign exchange options; David Bullen, chief dealer; Vince Vicarra, and London-based dealer Gianni Gray). These four bankers were convicted by the Australian court in 2006 for illegal foreign exchange trading and for hiding the losses behind faked profits supposedly generated in trades between themselves which was uncovered by the APRA and Australian Federal Police. This vividly shows that bank's governance mechanism was not as efficient as it should be in respect of foreign exchange risk management.

One of the objectives of corporate governance is to make management accountable to the board of directors guarding the interests of the share-holders. John and Senbet (1998) reported that the directors pursued the interests of management and also of themselves more than those of the shareholders. This is supported by the fact that none of the directors of an Australian bank has ever been removed by the shareholders in the annual general meeting on the ground that the member or the board failed to look after their interests. This is not the case in several countries with more active shareholder lobby.

The failure of the bank's board to adequately represent the shareholders is due to the fact that about 90 percent of the Australian bank board members are independent directors (see Figure 10.4). The independent directors are largely part-timers and have other work commitments, which constrain them from devoting adequate time for understanding and ana-lyzing the already voluminous information they receive often at short notices before the meeting. Moreover, there are interlocking directorship issues and goal congruency problems among the directors. Given that there are severe time constraints and lack of technical knowledge among the directors who may suffer from goal congruency problems, decisions are more likely to be based on group dynamics rather than analysis and boards may fail to perform as per shareholders' expectation.

The inappropriateness in the distribution of duties and responsibilities among the directors on the basis of their competency (knowledge and experience) may further constrain a board's performance. There are inade-quate regulatory measures in Australia to address this problem. Another question is: to what extent are boards explicit about which decisions they should take and which aspects should be left to the management? For example, prior consultations with the board members should constitute a part of the process for determining the agenda of the meeting in lieu of senior executives and/or CEO setting the agenda of the meeting.

The issue of executive compensation is a vexing problem for Australian bank boards. It is alleged that boards reward top managers and CEOs very richly. But bank board's deny such allegations since executive compensation is determined by each bank's remuneration committee. Such committees consider the efforts made by the top executives as determining the level of rewards. However, a problem arises in respect of determining the 'right amount of compensation'. Since there is information asymmetry about performance, it is difficult to determine how right is the right amount. There is no governance mechanism in place to determine right compensations for bank executives in Australia or for that matter, anywhere.

Another issue is the effect of regulatory and supervisory measures on the incentives for private sector growth. Too much or too complex regulatory measures may reduce incentives for going for high risk activities for high return. Banks may try to weaken governance requirements by going for financial engineering. For example, banks may opt for growth of warrants-holders or preferred stockholders who have no voting rights compared to shareholders who have voting rights. To what extent shareholders' involvement in banks' decision-making processes will be tolerated by the management is to be determined by the regulators. These pertinent issues of governance should be resolved by the regulators for the sake of good governance and of protecting the interest of the shareholders and stakeholders.

INDICATORS OF CORPORATE GOVERNANCE AND FINANCIAL PERFORMANCE

Corporate Governance Variables

This section focuses on the impact of corporate governance on the financial performance of Australian banks. For this purpose, data spanning seven years over 1999 to 2005 have been gathered for the 11 public listed banks in the Australian Stock Exchange. We examine how key governance variables such as the size of total assets and risk-weighted assets, board size, number of independent directors, number of board meetings, number of committee meetings have had influences on the Australian banks' financial performance which is represented by return on equity (ROE). Though this analysis is conducted variable by variable, and not by considering these variables simultaneously, it provides a reasonable feel for the direction of the governance variables. Our findings are presented in Figures 10.1–10.5 and our analysis of the data.

Return on Equity (ROE) measures the return to a bank's shareholders. Return on Assets (ROA) measures the operating efficiency of a bank. ROA and ROE are not necessarily influenced by the size or the total assets of a bank. National Australia Bank (NAB) ranks as the largest bank in Australia during the period 1999–2005, with average total assets over the period of

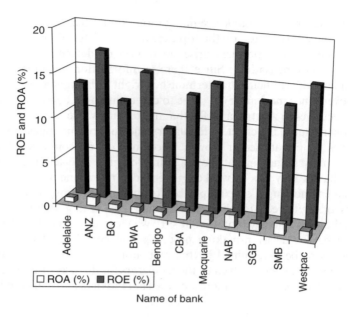

Figure 10.1   Average ROE and ROA of Australian banks: 1999–2005

A$261 billion. Figure 10.1 shows that it was also the most profitable and efficient bank in Australia during this period, with 1.35 percent average ROA and 19.15 percent average ROE. However, Commonwealth Bank of Australia (CBA) ranks next with average assets of A$247 billion. Its average ROE of at 13.14 percent was nearly identical to that of much smaller banks, including St George (SGB, with A$60 billion in assets) and Sun-Metway (SMB, with $35 billion). ANZ Banking Corporation (ANZ), the third largest bank (A$205 billion in assets) has the highest profitability with an average ROE of 17.06 percent: its efficiency as measured by its average ROA of 1.08 percent was lower than that of Sun-Metway with 1.25 percent. Similarly Westpac Banking Corporation, the fourth largest bank (A$200 billion in assets), achieved the same ROE of 15 percent as the Bank of Western Australia (with assets of A$8.4 billion). The lowest ROE was recorded for Bank of Bendigo with 0.55 percent ROA and 9.02 percent ROE. With the same average assets (A$8 billion), Adelaide Bank achieved a 13.18 percent ROE.

The relationship between risk and return is well known, so one would expect to see a relationship between the level of risk and the financial performance of Australian banks. The percentage of risk weighted assets (RWA) to total assets (TA) provides one indication of risk, where the lower the ratio, the lower the risk. However, the relationship between risk and returns shows

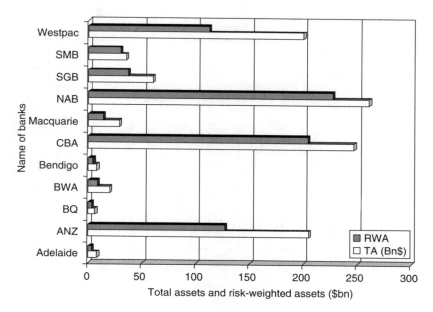

Figure 10.2 Total asset and risk-weighted assets of Australian banks

no conclusive results in this regard as is evident in the next chart. Figure 10.2 shows that with total assets of A\$247 billion and RWA of A\$204 billion (83 percent), the CBA generated an annual average ROE of 13.14 percent, whereas a 17.05 percent ROE was earned by ANZ with 62 percent of risk-weighted assets to total assets. Much the same ROE was achieved by the Adelaide Bank with 42.5 percent RWA, SGB with 62 percent RWA and SMB with 84.28 percent RWA. Might it be that RWA not a good proxy for risk!

Intuitively, one might expect that the size, expertise and experience of a bank's board may contribute to its performance. However, it is apparent from Figure 10.3 that Australian banks' financial performance is not influenced by the size of the bank's board.

Between 1999 and 2005, the size of the board for Adelaide Bank, Bendigo Bank, Macquarie Bank, St George Bank and Sun-Metway Bank were identical, with each board having nine directors, but the ROE for each was very different. For example, the average ROE for Bendigo Bank was 9.0 percent against 14.68 percent for Macquarie Bank, and 13.18 percent for Adelaide Bank. Between 1991 and 2005, the NAB earned an ROE of 19.15 percent with a ten-member board while CBA achieved a relatively lower ROE (13.14 percent) with a board run by 12 directors. Similar findings for Australian banks were reported by Nguyen (2006) that emphasizes that this

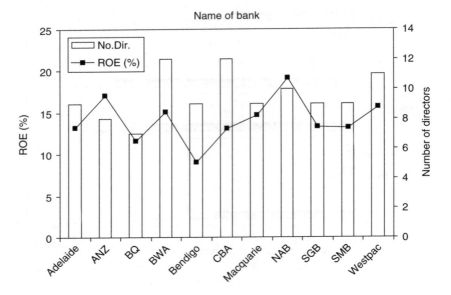

Figure 10.3   Average board size and ROE of Australian banks: 1999–2005

governance variable representing merely the size of the board (overworked board hypothesis) is not a valid one as far as performance is concerned.

It may be assumed that the higher the proportion of independent directors, the greater is the independence of a board and hence the better is a bank's financial performance. It appears from Figure 10.4 that board independence has no influence on a bank's return on equity. About 89 percent of the board members in Adelaide Bank, ANZ Bank, Bank of Queensland, Westpac, Bendigo Bank and St George's Bank were independent directors. But the average ROE for the period was 13.8 percent, 17.06 percent, 11.64 percent, 9.02 percent and 13.27 percent respectively. On the other hand, over the same period Macquarie Bank earned 15 percent on its equity when only 52 percent of its board members were independent directors. This shows that banks' financial performance is not dependent on the number of independent directors or degree of board independence. Similar results were reported by Chang and Leng (2004); Hermalin and Weisbach (2003) and Adams and Mehran (2005) in other countries.

Similarly, there appears to be no relationship between ROE and the degree or intensity of board's engagement as reflected by the number of board meetings (BM) and board committee meetings (CM) per year. Intuitively, it might be expected that a higher ROE may result from more

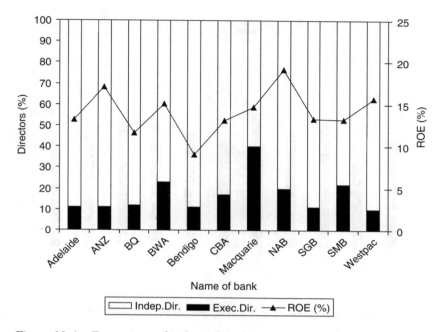

*Figure 10.4   Executive and independent (non-executive) directors in
                Australian banks*

board and committee meetings. But the statistics in Figure 10.5 show that
Adelaide Bank held 23 committee meetings per year, on average, but the
average annual ROE was 12.5 percent, against a 19 percent ROE for
National Australia Bank which held 16 committee meeting per annum.
Again, although Bendigo Bank held the highest number of board meetings
(15), its ROE was the lowest (8.5 percent) for Australian banks over the test
period. These results show that neither board independence nor committee
meetings influenced the financial performance of Australian banks. Our
conclusions in this section are subject tentative; results using a more reliable testing procedure are presented in the next section.

Good Governance Practices Lead to Higher Valuations

In this subsection, we discuss the results of an analysis of corporate governance structure variables as to whether these variables are correlated with
share price trends, the CEO and board of directors' remuneration and board
size. The results reported here were obtained with data collected for all 11
listed banks in Australia. Data collected are defined later in this section, in

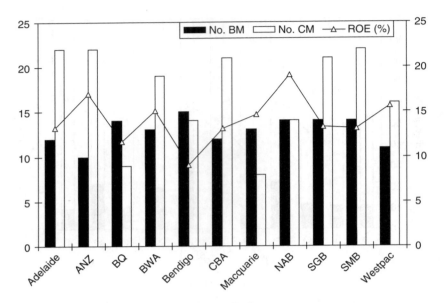

Figure 10.5   Average board and committee meetings: 1999–2005

discussing the models. There are several models suggested in the literature that relates: (a) share price performance; (b) the remuneration of the CEO; and (c) the directors' remuneration to a number of corporate governance as well as a number of fundamental variables. Of these, we selected four models. We estimated the coefficients in the first three models jointly using three-stage least squares regression: see Core *et al.* (1999).[2] The results of the fourth regression are given in the last column of Table 10.4.

The first equation relates the annual average share prices of all the banks to a set of corporate governance variables shown as sum of C_m (board size, turnover of board, size, interlocking, board meetings, stockholding of directors, and directors' pay) and a set of fundamental variables such as dividends per share, net profit after tax, log of assets, the proportion of top-20 shareholdings and CEO pay:

$$P_{it} = \alpha_0 + \alpha_m \sum C_m + \alpha_1 DPS_{it} + \alpha_2 NPAT_{it} + \alpha_3 A_{it}$$
$$+ \alpha_4 TOP20_{it} + \alpha_5 CEO_{it} + u_{it} \qquad (10.1)$$

Another relationship suggested in the literature connects directors' pay to a set of independent factors: lagged directors' pay; changes in share prices; share market capitalization growth G and control for the overall market effect; proportion of outside directors' shareholding O; the average age of the directors, AGE; and the volatility of the share prices of the bank V.

$$DP_{it} = \gamma_1 + \gamma_{dp}DP_{it-1} + \gamma_p\Delta P_{it} + \gamma_G G_{it} + \gamma_o O_{it} + \gamma_a AGE_{it} + \gamma_v V_{it} + \eta_{it}$$

$$(10.2)$$

The third model is about CEO remuneration as determined by a set of corporate governance variables (the same C_m) and a set of variables defined above with one additional variable namely, the CEO age entered as age and as square of age. Squaring the age enables the essential of experience to represent skill content of age of experience: see Equation 10.3.

$$CEO_{it} = \delta_1 + \delta_m\sum C_m + \delta_{dp}CEO_{it-1} + \delta_p\Delta P_{it} + \delta_A A_{it} + \delta_G G_{it}$$
$$+ \delta_a CA + \delta_{aa}CA^2 + \delta_V V_{it} + \varepsilon_{it}$$

$$(10.3)$$

These three equations are solved jointly using the three-stage least squares procedure.

The final model is about a relationship between board size and a set of independent variables for size (log of assets A; the age of the bank Y).

$$S_{it} = \phi_1 + \phi_A A_{it} + \phi_y Y_{it} + \phi_o O_{it} + \kappa_{it}$$

$$(10.4)$$

A three-stage least squares is applied to estimate the first three models, since there are common variables in the first three equations. 'Is the share price trend significantly related to the corporate governance variables (C_m) after controlling for the effect of independent factors?' is the main question relating to the first three models. In model (10.4) we test whether there is a relationship between board size and a number of corporate variables. We expect to find the corporate governance variables to be significant as is evident in some studies: it could also be that it may not be relevant. The results are shown in Table 10.2. Next we do the same investigation for the CEO remuneration and the results are also shown. The final set of results is not about corporate governance but about the determinants of board size. It is suggested in the literature that board size must vary with asset size, the age of the bank (the older banks are generally bigger), and the proportion of outside directors' stockholding. The results may now be interpreted from the statistics.

The corporate governance variables are several, and we look at the main ones first. They are: board size, interlocking membership, meetings, directors' stockholding, committees, and directors' pay and CEO pay. A quick look at the statistics in the last row reveals that all four models appear to provide a very strong explanation for the dependent variables. First the share price

Table 10.2   Stock prices, remuneration and board size versus corporate governance factors

	Share price	Directors' pay	CEO pay	Board size
Constant	8.73 (5.52)***	−2.72 (−0.89)	−1863.77 (−1.46)	1.55 (3.19)***
Board size	−1.56 (−2.95)***	–	−1.31 (−0.03)	–
DPS	0.24 (2.46)**	–	–	–
Interlocking	0.71 (2.16)**	–	−60.44 (−0.87)	–
Turnover	0.61 (1.97)**	–	–	–
Meetings	0.51 (0.53)	–	–	–
Directors' share	−0.13 (−0.06)	–	–	–
Committees	−0.11 (−4.41)***	–	–	–
Directors' pay	0.21 (3.49)***	–	–	–
CEO pay	−0.01 (−0.79)	–	–	–
Bank size	−0.01 (−0.03)	–	0.78 (0.11)	0.07 (4.87)***
NPAT	0.19 (2.50)**	–	–	–
Top 20	−0.01 (−2.61)***	–	–	–
Board composition	−6.25 (−5.23)***	4.94 (1.80)*	–	−0.68 (−1.60)
Income growth	–	−0.34 (−0.93)	23.05 (0.96)	–
Bank age	–	–	–	0.06 (2.21)**
Stock price change	–	0.34 (1.86)*	28.07 (2.08)**	–
Directors' (CEOs') pay 1 lag	–	0.61 (4.23)***	0.17 (1.57)	–
Board age	–	−0.02 (−0.76)	–	–
CEO age	–	–	86.50 (1.81)*	–
Volatility	–	0.46 (2.43)**	52.17 (3.06)***	–

Table 10.2 (continued)

	Share price	Directors' pay	CEO pay	Board size
CEO age squared	–	–	−0.77	–
			(−1.69)*	
R-squared/Adjusted	0.71	0.26	0.60	0.36
R-squared	0.66	0.20	0.55	0.33

Notes: Symbols *, **, and *** indicate statistical significance at the 99 percent, 95 percent and 90 percent confidence levels, respectively. The *t*-statistics are entered in parentheses.

Source: Doucouliagos and Hoque (2005), reproduced with the permission of the Editor of the *Journal of Business and Policy Research.*

trend over the period is strongly correlated with all the corporate governance factors except notably CEO and bank size. Board size (see Column 4) is negatively correlated with share price trend suggesting that smaller boards are more effective (recall that the univariate analysis in the previous subsection failed to reveal this relationship); interlocking membership of directors is also positive and significant; the turnover of the directors is significant meaning that the greater the turnover of directors, the greater is the freedom of the board to practice good governance as there is no entrenchment of directors. Committee meetings are negatively correlated (more effectiveness is when a smaller number of meetings are reported), also with share performance as is directors' pay. The control variables such as the DPS (some authors use it as a governance variable as well) are significant. Next we show the remuneration determinants.

The board composition, stock price change, CEO pay and stock price volatility are highly correlated with the directors' remuneration. The CEO pay is associated with the age of CEO, the stock price change over time and the volatility of share prices. That suggests that CEO pay is more a function of the risk of the firm (firms with high volatility in share prices), the stock performance and the particular expertise or experience the CEO brings to the board and the top management.

These results reveal – with moderate to high adjusted *R*-squares – a substantial power of these models to explain the corporate governance factors in the Australian banking environment. The fact that the results are pronounced is due to the inclusion of the public listed banks, which tend to practice better corporate governance especially since the improved prudential regime came into effect about 11 years ago along with more competition spurring the banks to be efficient and customer-friendly: relaxing entry barriers improved further the potential for competition. Thus, the 35 years of consistent attention to the banking sector development to improve its act appears to be paying off, especially when one looks at the other statistics on ROE. The banks have performed well with high ROE of above 10 percent per year in the tested period and one rare bank got closer to the 20 percent mark.

CONCLUSIONS

This chapter studied corporate governance framework, practices and also the relation between corporate governance variables and bank performance in Australia. We described the genesis of reforms over a 35-year period, as having been aimed at improving competition, enhancing prudential supervision; in the last 18 years, reforms were directed at enhancing governance structures of the banking entities. The results from our analyses show that the banking system has become more focused on good performance, and, it appears also, the reforms of the sector as well as attention to governance issues have led to good financial performance by the Australian banks. There is a statistically significant relationship between some selected governance variables and the financial performance of the Australian banks.

ACKNOWLEDGEMENTS

For providing very efficient research assistance, we like to thank Ms Salina Siddique, who collected the data from primary sources in the Monash University databases. The authors alone are responsible for errors.

NOTES

1. The law was later amended to cover all financial entities, when this limit was increased to 15 percent. Two studies (see Dempsetz and Lehn, 1985; Dempsetz and Villalonga, 2001) verified the link between ownership and performance. In the case of banks, a serious problem that diminishes good governance arises from concentrated share ownership and related party lending, both of which, when reduced, leads to good governance.
2. There is an endogeneity problem in the separate equations. To correct for the errors from endogeneity, the researchers applied exogenous variables with one lag.

REFERENCES

Adams, R. B. and H. Mehran (2005), 'Corporate performance, board structure and its determinants in the banking industry', Paper presented at the EFA 2005 Moscow Meeting, 8 August.

Black, B. S. (1992), 'Institutional investors and corporate governance: the case for institutional voice', *Journal of Applied Corporate Finance*, **5**(3), 19–32.

Carleton, W., J. Nelson and M. Weisbach (1998), 'The influence of institutions on corporate governance through private negotiations: evidence from TIAA-CREF', *Journal of Finance*, **53**, 1335–62.

Chang, A., and A. Leng (2004), 'The impact of corporate governance practices on firm's financial performance: evidence from Malaysian companies', *ASEAN Economic Bulletin*, **21**(2), 308–18.

Choe, H. and B. Lee (2003), 'Korean bank governance reform after the Asian financial crisis', *Pacific-Basin Finance Journal*, **11**, 483–508.

Conyon, M. J. and S. I. Peck (1998), 'Board size and corporate performance: evidence from European countries', *The European Journal of Finance*, **4**, 291–304.

Core, J. E., R. W. Holthausen and D. F. Larcker (1999), 'Corporate governance, chief executive officer compensation, and firm performance', *Journal of Financial Economics*, **51**, 371–406.

Davis, G. F. (1995), 'Bank deregulation, supervision and agency problems' *Australian Economic Review*, **3**, 17–28.

Davis, G. F. (2005), 'New directions in corporate governance', *Annual Review of Sociology*, **31**(1), 143–62.

Deli, D. and S. Gillan (2000), 'On the demand for independent and active audit committees', *Journal of Corporate Finance*, **6**(4), 427–45.

Demsetz, H. and K. Lehn (1985), 'The structure of corporate ownership: causes and consequences', *Journal of Political Economy*, **93**(6), 1155–77.

Demsetz, H. and B. Villalonga (2001), 'Ownership structure and corporate performance', *Journal of Corporate Finance* **7**, 209–33.

Doucouliagos, H. and M. Z. Hoque (2005), 'Corporate governance and Australian bank stock prices', *Journal of Business and Policy Research*, **1**(1), 33–51.

Dow, J. and G. Gordon (1997), 'Noise trading, delegated portfolio management and economic welfare', *Journal of Political Economy*, **105**(5), 1024–50.

Dunlop, I. (1998), 'Corporate governance in context', *ASX Perspective*, **3**, 23–7.

George, J. (2005), 'Corporate governance for banking organisations – the supervisors' respective', ABA/ABAC/PECC Symposium on Promoting good corporate governance and transparency, 15 October, Melbourne.

Gregg, P., S. Machin and S. Szymanski (1993), 'The disappearing relationship between directors' pay and corporate performance', *British Journal of Industrial Relations*, **31**, 1–10.

Harper, I. and T. Scheit (1992), 'The effects of financial market deregulation on bank risk and profitability', *Australian Economic Papers*, **31**(59), 260–71.

Hart, O. (1995), 'Corporate governance: some theory and implications', *The Economic Journal*, **105**, 678–89.

Hawkins, J. (1997), 'Why investors push for strong corporate boards', *The McKinsey Quarterly*, **3**, 144–8.

Hermalin, B. and M. S. Weisbach (1988), 'The determinants of board composition', *Rand Journal of Economics*, **19**(4), 589–606.

Hermalin, B. E. and M. S. Weisbach (2003), 'Board of directors as an endogenously determined institution: a survey of the economic literature', *Federal Reserve Bank of New York Economic Policy Review*, **9**(1), 7–26.

Joh, S. W. (2003), 'Corporate governance and firm profitability: evidence from Korea before the economic crisis', *Journal of Financial Economics*, **68**, 287–322.

Jensen, M. C. and W. H. Meckling (1976), 'Theory of the firm: managerial behavior, agency cost and ownership structure', *Journal of Financial Economics*, **3**(4), 305–60.

John, K. and L. Senbet (1998), 'Corporate governance and board effectiveness', *Journal of Banking and Finance*, **22**, 371–403.

Kaplan, S. (1994), 'Top executive rewards and firm performance: a comparison of Japan and the United States', *Journal of Political Economy*, **102**, 510–46.

Klein, A. (1998), 'Firm performance and board committee structure', *Journal of Law and Economics*, **41**(1), 275–303.

La Porta, R., F. Lopez de Silanes, A. Shleifer and R. W. Vishney (1988), 'Law and finance', *The Journal of Political Economy*, **106**(6), 1113–55.

Morck, R. and M. Nakamura (1999), 'Banks and corporate control in Japan', *The Journal of Finance*, **54**(1), 319–39.

Nguyen, B. C. (2006), 'The corporate governance of banks in Malaysia and Australia', master's degree thesis, Department of Accounting and Finance, Monash University.

Organisation for Economic Co-operation and Development (1997), *Development Cooperation Review*, Paris: OECD.

Rosenstein, S. and J. G. Wyatt (1990), 'Outside directors, board independence and shareholder wealth', *Journal of Financial Economics*, **26**, 175–92.

Roy, M. R., M. A. Fox and R. T. Hamilton (1994), 'Board size and potential corporate and director interlocks in Australasia 1984–1993', *Australian Journal of Management*, **19**(2), 201–32.

Shleifer, A. and R. W. Vishney (1987), 'A survey of corporate governance', *The Journal of Finance*, **52**(2), 737–83.

Suchard, J. A., M. Singh and R. Barr (2001), 'The market effects of CEO turnover in Australian firms', *Pacific-Basin Finance Journal*, **9**, 1–27.

Vafeas, N. (1999), 'Board meeting frequency and firm performance', *Journal of Financial Economics*, **53**, 113–42.

APPENDIX 10A: ASX CORPORATE GOVERNANCE COUNCIL BEST PRACTICE RECOMMENDATIONS

Principle 1:	Lay solid foundations for management and oversight
Principle 2:	Structure the board to add value
Principle 3:	Promote ethical and responsible decision-making
Principle 4:	Safeguard integrity in financial reporting
Principle 5:	Make timely and balanced disclosure
Principle 6:	Respect the rights of shareholders
Principle 7:	Recognize and manage risk
Principle 8:	Encourage enhanced performance
Principle 9:	Remunerate fairly and responsibly
Principle 10:	Recognize the legitimate interests of stakeholders

Note: A more detailed document is available in www.asx.com.au. In that document, each of these principles is expanded, and the structures needed to achieve the principle are identified.

11. Germany's three-pillar banking system from a corporate governance perspective

Horst Gischer, Peter Reichling and Mike Stiele

Compared to other countries the organization of the German banking system is almost unique. The coexistence of different institutional groups with almost identical business segments often leads to the presumption that a change of the institutional conditions may release significant capabilities of efficiency, from which in turn bank customers benefit (Brunner *et al.*, 2004). In this chapter we attempt to justify the fundamental structure of the banking system in Germany. We show from a corporate governance perspective that the coexistence of financial institutions with different business strategies and in many areas differing clienteles fits best to the regional requirements in Germany.

COMPARISON OF CORPORATE GOVERNANCE SYSTEMS

Authors with an Anglo-Saxon focus often have a different understanding of corporate governance compared to authors with a continental European background. For explanatory purposes it is helpful to compare the Anglo-Saxon corporate governance system with the continental European system. We will proceed rather stereotypically so that the major differences become apparent.[1]

The Anglo-Saxon literature on corporate governance mostly deals with the relationship between top management and shareholders of a company. Consequentially from this point of view the main task of management is to increase the equity's (market) value, this is the shareholder value. This focus also motivates a one-tier board that consists of internal executives and non-executive outside directors, the latter rather acting as consultants (to in turn increase the shareholder value) and merely monitoring that managers do not solely pursue their own interests. A separation of the management board and the supervisory board is not necessary in the Anglo-Saxon corporate governance system since it is shareholder- and capital market-oriented. The interests of other stakeholders are not directly pursued in this system since for this purpose additional mechanisms exist.

In continental Europe and Japan the corporate governance system is conceptualized in a broader way. Here emphasis is put on the balance of interests. Therefore management board and supervisory board are separated. The supervisory board comprises employee representatives, representatives of loan granting banks, major shareholders and so on. Small shareholders are only rarely represented. In this system the management board's main task is to act on behalf of the company and not only on behalf of the shareholders.

The following illustration is convenient to look at the different mechanisms of alternative corporate governance systems (Hirschmann, 1970). Basically a stakeholder of a company can react on misguided developments with objection or migration. It is obvious that a stakeholder with short-term migration opportunities by means of, for example, the labor or capital market is less dependent on objection opportunities than a stakeholder who faces less flexible markets. Therefore the latter insists on having a voice in the company. Hence this stakeholder embarks on a long-term strategy.

Thus it appears that on the one hand the design of the corporate governance system depends on the time horizon and on the other hand it depends on the opportunities to reduce risk in case of misguided developments via markets. In the following we illustrate these aspects on three important groups of stakeholders: shareholders, loan granting banks and employees.

SHAREHOLDERS

Of course single shareholders of listed companies can sell their shares via the stock exchange at a price equal to the market value. However this opportunity does not exist for the shareholders as a whole or for major shareholders without additional requirements. Without the opportunity of a buy-out, liquidation would be the only exit strategy, with the result that specific investments are only salable if a sizable discount is accepted. In this context the latter is known as sunk costs (Hart, 1995).

As long as there is no market for buy-outs, control and codetermination rights are needed by shareholders since they have financed specific investments. Thus the continental European corporate governance system separates the management board and the supervisory board, whereas the Anglo- Saxon market for mergers and acquisitions offers adequate transaction opportunities, so that in this capital market-oriented corporate governance system outside directors rather represent experienced consultants.

Note that just this market enhances the discipline of the management since in case of a hostile take-over the management of the company taken over is typically threatened. Hence the mergers and acquisitions market represents a tool for management control (Manne, 1965).

LOAN GRANTING BANKS

Compared to equity investors, lenders have similar matters to deal with. Lenders, whose loans are short-term, fully collateralized or of less relevance,[2] are hardly threatened in the case of misguided developments. This kind of lender does not need extensive codetermination or monitoring rights.

A different situation occurs if granted loans are long-term and not provided with full collateral since, for example, the market for equity is not able to provide the capital needed to the full extent (Hackethal and Schmidt, 2004). In this case lenders bear a part of the business risk in terms of default risk because their capital in turn is bounded in specific investments. Again codetermination and monitoring rights are required. Thus the financing structure of a company and the corporate governance system are interrelated.

Moreover the corporate governance system influences the investment activity of companies. The continental European system encourages long-term and specific investments since influence can compensate sunken costs, whereas the Anglo-Saxon system benefits marketable corporate investments, which are favorable at least to the mergers and acquisitions market.

EMPLOYEES

With regard to the corporate governance role of employees we again distinguish two groups only. One group are employees, who eventually may be highly-paid experts but whose knowledge can easily be used in other companies. Such conditions exist for example for IT specialists or investment bankers. In a flexible labor market these employees quickly find a new employer and a company can immediately deploy these employees. From a corporate governance perspective no special protection is required for such employees.[3]

This group is seen alongside other employees, whose human capital is characterized by specific know-how. Their professional skills are not easily transferable to other companies and simultaneously these employees are hardly replaceable from the company's perspective. Again sunken costs may arise for companies and employees. Accordingly investments in specific human capital are only taken if they are protected by codetermination and control rights. Otherwise employees would rather acquire general and marketable know-how.

DIFFERENT CORPORATE GOVERNANCE SYSTEMS

Our classification of corporate governance systems shows two types. The Anglo-Saxon system is shareholder- and capital market-oriented. The mergers and acquisitions market ensures that the management is concerned about an increase of the stock price to make hostile take-overs expensive. Hence the management maximizes the shareholder value. A separated supervisory board to account for further stakeholder interests is needless for at least two reasons. At first funding of the company does not rely on long-term and partially collateralized loans. Second a flexible labor market exists for employees with transferable know-how. So there is a coherent system of corporate governance and capital and labor markets. However this system discriminates specific investments in long-term real and human capital that cannot easily be transferred across markets.

In contrast the continental European corporate governance system is characterized by the protection of manifold corporate interests and so pursues a stakeholder value approach. Sunken costs related to specific investments are protected by codetermination and control rights. This system supports long-term human and real capital investments, so that markets that allow for short-term transfers are neither needed nor have emerged. This system is rather characterized by, for example, collective bargaining and the principle of relationship banking. Again there is a coherent system of corporate governance on the one side and capital and labor markets on the other side. Table 11.1 represents a summary.

Table 11.1   Characteristics of different corporate governance systems

Corporate governance system	Anglo-Saxon system	Continental European system
Business objective	Shareholder value maximization	Corporate interests (stakeholder value approach)
Investment projects	Marketable	Company specific
Time horizon	Short-term	Long-term
Protection mechanism	Flexible capital and labor markets	Codetermination and control rights

CHANGE OF CONTINENTAL EUROPEAN CORPORATE GOVERNANCE?

The Anglo-Saxon corporate governance system requires the existence of labor and capital markets that allow for cost-efficient short-term transactions and in this way protect the shareholders' interests. However the continental European system assumes that the stakeholders involved protect their interests rather by exercising long-term targeted influence than by market transactions. The coherent system of the continental European corporate governance and the corresponding labor and capital markets fails if single elements of the system do not match or if single groups of stakeholders prefer short-term market transactions instead of long-term influence.

In addition to our brief discussion of alternative corporate government systems, we look at empirical facts. The successful continental European system is based on the balance of different interests, which can be ensured by long-term co-operations of stakeholders (Kreps, 1990). Such co-operations can be established by mutual participations and the delegation of management board members to supervisory boards. In Germany these linkages are characterized by the term 'Deutschland AG' ('Germany Inc.') (Höpner, 2003).

However, these linkages cause some kind of rigidity in this long-term aligned system. Some stakeholder groups involved in the corporate governance discussion argue that, with more flexible capital markets, this rigidity leads to inefficiencies. In other words: the rate of return achieved by companies could be higher when changing to the shareholder- and capital market-oriented Anglo-Saxon corporate governance system.[4]

In the following we discuss this hypothesis for German financial institutions. The German banking system largely consists of three pillars. The first pillar is represented by private commercial banks ('Kreditbanken'), which are regularly organized as stock corporations. The internationally operating major banks belong to this pillar. The second group, also under private law, consists of mutual cooperative banks ('Genossenschaftsbanken'). Their primary goal is to promote their members.

The public savings banks ('Sparkassen') represent the third pillar of the German banking system. These organizations are subject to public law. Their primary goals are to supply the population with safe investment opportunities and to meet regional demands for loans. A special feature of savings banks is the security reserve ('Sicherheitsrücklage') that is part of the balance sheet instead of the subscribed capital. All three pillars of the German banking system represent full service banks and are organized according to the continental European two-tier corporate governance system. Figure 11.1 provides an overview.[5]

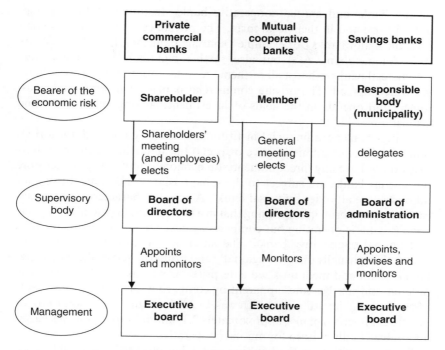

Figure 11.1   Corporate governance of the three pillars of the German banking system

Until the mid-1990s at least for major stock corporations, the major banks have been in the center of the German corporate governance system but now have withdrawn from this role. This may be recognized as a shift from the continental European system to the Anglo-Saxon system. This tendency may apply to major companies and banks but it does not hold for the mutual cooperative banks and the savings banks, whose customers are mostly small and medium-sized enterprises that do not have access to public capital markets. Hence in the following section we analyse the performance of the three groups of German financial institutions.

THE STRUCTURE OF THE GERMAN BANKING SYSTEM

As mentioned before the universal banking sector in Germany principally consists of three kinds of financial institutions: private commercial banks, savings banks and mutual cooperative banks. Institutes of these groups differ in size and in their legal form. The private commercial banks comprise the major banks (for example Deutsche Bank AG, HypoVereinsbank AG, Commerzbank AG) but also smaller regionally operating private commercial banks. Almost all of them are stock corporations whose shares are widely spread. The private commercial banks often serve major customers and operate in the fields of investment banking and mergers and acquisitions.

Savings banks are financial institutions owned by regional authorities (municipalities or administrative districts) but nevertheless these authorities do not have any direct influence on economic activities. Furthermore the savings banks are subject to the same business and competitive conditions as are all other universal banks. A specific characteristic is the so-called regional principle, meaning that in a certain region (usually) only one savings bank is operating but competes against private commercial banks and mutual cooperative banks. The latter are organized as cooperative associations, usually operate regionally and primarily serve, like the savings banks, small and medium-sized enterprises as well as private clients. The difference in size becomes apparent by comparing the average total assets of the financial institutions, which was, in 2004, about 12.6 billion Euro for private commercial banks, approximately 2.1 billion Euro for savings banks and only 0.4 billion Euro for mutual cooperative banks.

The composition of the banking sector has changed remarkably since German reunification.[6] The number of independent financial institutions dropped between 1991 and 2004 by almost 50 percent from 4290 to 2229, the local branches of all institutions in Germany have been reduced by nearly 25 percent to 2003 (from 44 813 in 1991 to 33 753 in 2003), only the statistical consideration of the Deutsche Postbank AG as a financial institution in the narrow sense raised the number of local branches in 2004 to 42 659.[7]

The development of the number of employees was ambiguous. In the first years after German reunification the number of employees in the banking sector rose by about 40 000 workers (or nearly 6 percent), thereafter the number remained at a level of about 720 000 staff members and dropped significantly in recent years. Despite the statistical integration of the Deutsche Postbank AG the number of people employed in the banking sector in 2004 was, with nearly 679 000, about 15 000 employees below the level of 1991.[8]

Although this raw delineation is impressive, the real adjustments within the German banking sector are more concise when one separately considers the three pillars – private commercial banks, savings banks and mutual cooperative banks. During the period under consideration in both the

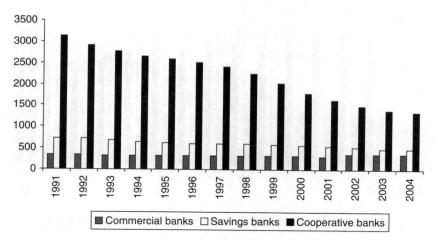

Figure 11.2   Financial institutes in Germany

savings bank sector and the mutual cooperative bank sector, a remarkable clearing up due to mergers occurred, while during the same period the number of commercial banks even slightly increased (see Figure 11.2). About 35 percent of the independent savings banks and nearly 60 percent of the mutual cooperative banks of 1991 lost their autonomy.

The numerous mergers of savings banks and mutual cooperative banks in bordering regions caused a significant decline in local branches but without a striking abandonment of locations. Primarily the observed multi-presence of institutions of the same sector was reduced (see Figure 11.3). However an adjustment of the local branches of commercial banks regularly leads to a reduction of the served locations.

As seen for the total market, for single sectors a differentiated pattern arises also under aspects of employment (see Figure 11.4). Unlike the savings and cooperative bank sector the number of jobs in the commercial bank sector grew steadily until 2000. Afterwards a massive reduction of jobs of about 18 percent took place.[9] Both the savings and the cooperative bank sectors, have slowly reduced their workforce since the middle of the 1990s. In 2004 the savings banks employed 9 percent fewer and the cooperative banks employed 7 percent fewer staff members compared to their highest numbers in 1994 and 1995, respectively. Numerically the commercial banks have reduced approximately 40 000 jobs since the year 2000, the savings banks have abolished about 26 000 jobs since 1994 and the cooperative banks have lowered their workforce by almost 12 000 since 1995.

To get a first impression of the competitive conditions of Germany's banking system, the development of the single sector's market shares can

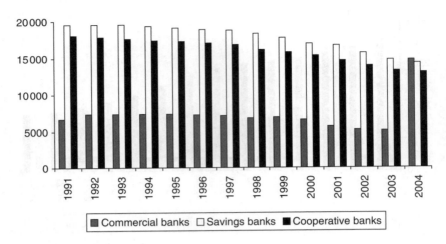

Figure 11.3   Local branches

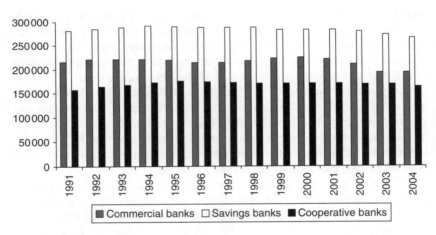

Figure 11.4   Employees

be used. Here it must be pointed out that in practice there is a huge range of different market segments in which all groups of banks act simultaneously but possibly with a different intensity. Since in Germany the external financing of (especially medium-sized) enterprises is in contrast to, for example, Anglo-Saxon countries primarily done by institutional lenders, the relative positions in the market for loans to non-banks is of particular interest. Figure 11.5 depicts the development during the observation period.[10]

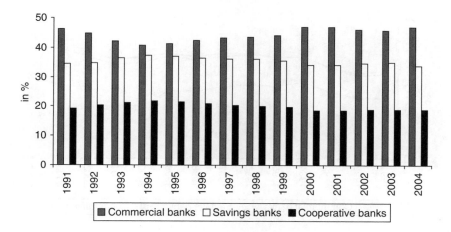

Figure 11.5 Share of cumulated loans to non-banks

It is striking that immediately after reunification the commercial banks noticeably lost market share. This loss was regained by the end of the 1990s but afterwards their relative importance decreased once again. In contrast the savings banks initially could enhance their market position and even in the re-launch phase of the commercial banks the savings banks lost only an insignificant share in the market. Over the last five years of the observation period the savings banks held about 35 percent of the cumulative loans to non-banks in their portfolios. Since 1991 the cooperative bank sector has continually lost its relative importance. This loss in market share has stopped during the last three years of the study.

CRITERIA OF PERFORMANCE AND COMPETITION

To evaluate the performance of banking groups in general as well as the performance of savings banks in particular meaningful criteria for comparison are needed. These criteria are plentiful in the corresponding literature but for our purpose only a few statistics are necessary. For example the so-called Lerner coefficient as a measure of competition in a market can be consulted. This index is computed as the (calculative) difference between market price and marginal cost of production, which in turn is divided by the market price.[11] This coefficient, which is also called price–cost spread, quasi-reflects the actual opportunity to achieve market prices against competitors above (production) cost. In the banking sector the Lerner coefficient can be

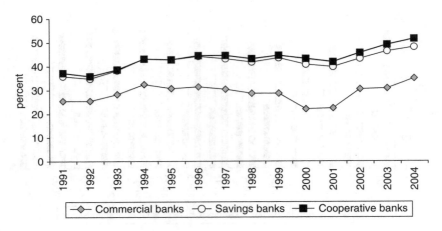

Figure 11.6   Lerner coefficient

approximated by using interest income per unit of total assets as market price and interest cost per unit of total assets as marginal cost. The results for each banking group in Germany are illustrated in Figure 11.6.

Apparently the competitive position of the savings and cooperative banks improved in recent years. This improvement can be attributed not least to the – ex post failed – strategy of various commercial and major banks to neglect the interest-bearing medium-sized corporate banking in favor of commission earning activities. In addition especially major banks – voluntarily – backed out of the area-wide business and left a profitable field to the savings and cooperative banks.

The comparative advantage of the savings and cooperative banks clearly lies in the support of customer groups, which are only of minor interest to global commercial and major banks: small and medium-sized enterprises, tradespeople, crafts enterprises or service providers. Furthermore the simultaneous support of private clients, ranging from normal to high-income customers, enables the accumulation of cost-effective deposits that enhance the profitability of the bank. Especially apart from the metropolitan areas a clientele, whose only alternatives may be direct banking via telephone or internet, can be bound permanently.

Of course such a strategy is quite costly. Compared to their competitors in the commercial bank sector, the business of savings and cooperative banks is much more labor intensive. Local branches have to be manned and if personal consulting is offered, the necessary capacities have to be kept ready. Consequentially the commercial banks and their credit business are (calculatively) much more productive (see Figure 11.7).

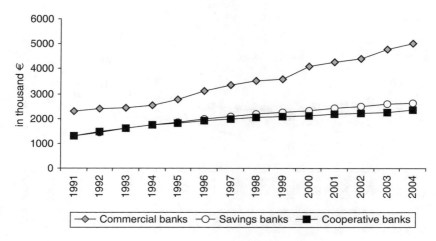

Figure 11.7   Lending volume per employee

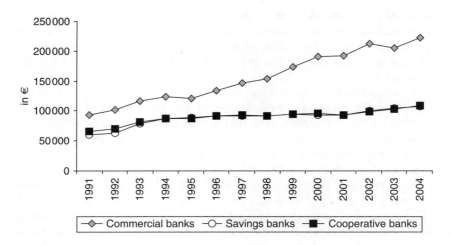

Figure 11.8   Net return per employee

On average one employee of a commercial bank supervises twice as much lending volume as an employee of a savings or a cooperative bank. Moreover, at first glance, the employees of a commercial bank are much more successful than their counterparts in savings or cooperative banks. Figure 11.8 points out that the differences in net return (net interest received and net commissions received) per employee are substantial between the three sectors. Here as well the employees of commercial banks

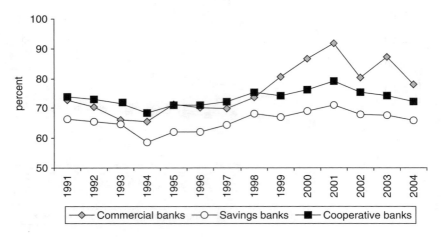

Figure 11.9   Cost income ratio

generate more than twice as much profit as their counterparts in the other bank sectors. Since no systematic decline in quality unwinds these remarkable differences, it can be reasoned that the different institutional groups operate with differing technologies and in significantly different market segments.

This supposition is supported when results-oriented business ratios are consulted for the single groups. One of the most important reference numbers is the cost–income ratio that represents the ratio of administrative expenditures and the sum of interest surplus and commission surplus. A value of 0.6 (that is 60 percent) is assumed to be a desirable and normative benchmark (see Figure 11.9).

However since the beginning of the 1990s all commercial banks have departed increasingly from this level and as recently as 2001 the trend changed again towards the favored value. Since 1994 the savings banks have also suffered a decline in their cost income ratio but to a much reduced extent and always to a minor degree than their competitors. In the meantime the 60 percent benchmark is within reach again for the savings banks.

The empirically observed success of the business strategy of the savings and cooperative banks can be seen not least in the development of the return on equity (see Figure 11.10). Certainly the commercial banks in some years show an impressive return on equity but at the beginning of the decade they had to display negative returns as well. On average private commercial banks have a return on equity after tax of 4.8 percent and hence lie below the industry-wide average of 5.2 percent.

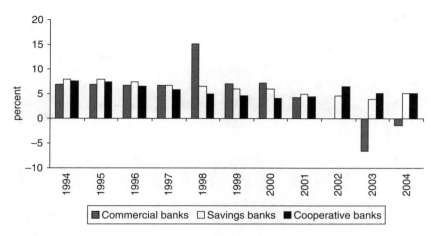

Figure 11.10   Return on equity after tax

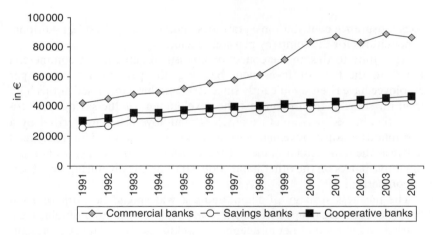

Figure 11.11   Personnel expenses per employee

However in recent years the savings bank sector as well as the cooperative bank sector were always able to generate a positive return on equity. Furthermore the savings bank sector's return on equity on average reached 6.1 percent which is the highest level of all compared sectors. This sector also noticeably outperformed the cooperative banks sector (5.7 percent).

Due to the above-mentioned higher profit per employee, commercial banks are willing to pay higher salaries to their employees. Figure 11.11 displays the development of the personnel expenses per employee, including

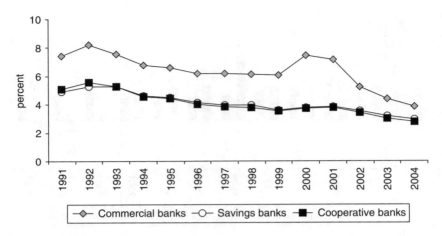

Figure 11.12   Interest rate on deposits and borrowed funds

social insurance contributions, gratuities and, where applicable, additional expenditures for the company pension scheme.

According to this, in the course of intensified activities of commercial banks in the field of investment banking, the personnel expenses per employee have risen significantly since 1999 and have remained at this high level for some years. In contrast the development of the savings and co-operative banks' personnel expenses per employee is characterized by a continuous upward movement without any striking jumps. Thus the spread between the commercial banks on the one hand and the savings and co-operative banks on the other hand widened dramatically during the observation period.

The business strategy of maintaining a widespread network of local branches enables savings and cooperative banks to open up profitable local markets, in which internet or telephone banking is often not yet an acceptable alternative for its inhabitants. By this sourcing in the form of deposits in check and savings accounts as well as short-term and long-term time deposits of private clients is possible, which is considerably more cost-effective than refinancing at the interbank market. Figure 11.12 represents the development of the interest rate paid on deposits and borrowed funds of banks and non-banks for every single banking group.

The commercial banks can catch up with the other sectors regarding interests paid on borrowed capital only due to a new and careful orientation toward the formerly widely spurned private clients and due to generally declining interest rates since the turn of the millennium.

SUMMARY

Considerations on corporate governance systems with different but coherent characteristics were the starting point of our analysis. The share-holder- and capital market-oriented Anglo-Saxon system stands *vis-à-vis* the stakeholder-oriented continental European system. The first system protects stakeholders by flexible markets that permit short-term transfers and therefore offer a mechanism of control. The latter system protects specific investments of stakeholders by granting long-term codetermin-ation and control rights.

In this context a shift from the continental European corporate govern-ance system, that was successful for a long time, can be observed. The European system exhibits a certain rigidity due to the necessary linkages. Furthermore it faces a capital market that has become more flexible in recent years. Especially the internationally operating major banks are said to prefer the Anglo-Saxon system. However the cooperative and savings banks show a regional focus that supports long-term relationship banking for both the small- and medium-sized enterprises and the private clients. Therefore these financial institutions are bound to the continental European corporate governance system.

A recommendation for a shift to the Anglo-Saxon system not only requires that all elements of this system have to be adjusted to again achieve a coherent system of corporate governance and labor and capital markets. Additionally a system transfer requires the proof that the desired corporate governance system is overall beneficial. The latter includes economic evi-dence that relies on measures like yield ratios, cost of capital and so on.

This comparison has been the center of our empirical analysis of the three pillars of the German banking system. Here the result is, according to selected financial indicators, that private commercial banks including the major banks can be distinguished from cooperative and savings banks. For example the employees of rather shareholder-oriented commercial banks generate more profit per capita than employees of regional-oriented financial institutions. However this advantage is outweighed by higher personnel expenses per employee.

Overall a distinctive shareholder orientation should be expressed in satis-factory returns to equity investors, which represent the cost of equity from the company's perspective. However, costs of equity are difficult to measure for private companies. If the return on equity based on financial statements are used instead, no significant or persistent advantage of the private com-mercial banks can be found.

The same applies for the cost of debt for which in turn regional-oriented cooperative and savings banks are better off than private commercial banks.

Apparently the regional-oriented financial institutions have a more cost-effective access to local debt markets. Nevertheless this difference cannot be interpreted as a small credit spread caused by a lower default probability because the default probability stems from the risk of the bank's assets, and this risk is first of all and mostly borne by the shareholders.

If both interest earnings and interest expenses (in terms of the Lerner coefficient) are considered, a disadvantage of private commercial banks occurs. This result contradicts the assumption of the supporters of a rather capital market-oriented corporate governance system. Our finding persists even if the interest margin is adjusted by administrative expenses and fee income in terms of the cost–income ratio.

Concluding, the dimension of market access has to be emphasized in our initially formulated list of distinguishing features for types of corporate governance systems. Here we do not focus on the access to publicly traded capital but instead on the access to regional, private and cost-effective capital.

NOTES

1. For the rationale in this section see Schmidt (2007).
2. This is the typical debt financing structure in the Anglo-Saxon system, see Elsas and Krahnen (2004).
3. This statement is not valid for employees who are unskilled and have low qualifications. These employees are often tied to a certain place and rarely have a chance to find a new job.
4. For the tendency of change from the continental European corporate governance system to the Anglo-Saxon system see Schmidt and Spindler (2002), and Hackethal *et al.* (2005).
5. Deviating from the suggestion of the wording of the law, mutual cooperative banks in their articles of association typically regulate that the board of directors appoints and monitors the executive board.
6. All following numerical data are taken – unless stated otherwise – from the periodical publications of the Deutsche Bundesbank, especially the monthly reports for the statistics on the banking sector and the performance of German financial institutions as well as the relevant statistical supplements.
7. Until 2004 the Deutsche Postbank AG as a subsidiary of the Deutsche Post AG did not belong to the group of independent financial institutions.
8. For comparison: during the same period the average total assets of all financial institutions in Germany rose by almost 175 percent.
9. Adjusted for effects of the statistical classification of the Deutsche Postbank AG as a private commercial bank. According to the annual report the Deutsche Postbank AG in 2004 employed about 9600 staff members.
10. The cumulated volume of loans to non-banks of all banking sectors is used in Figure 11.5 as the reference to describe the relocation of relative positions in the market. This adjustment is on the one hand independent of the development of the total market and on the other hand independent of loan transfers to special purpose institutions (for example home loan banks or mortgage banks). Based on all granted loans to non-banks in Germany the market share of the regarded institutions dropped from 63 percent in 1991 to nearly 55 percent in 1999. Since the year 2000 this share has been, with only small fluctuations, at a level of 56 percent.

11. See for applications of the Lerner coefficient in the financial sector for example Gischer and Jüttner (2002).

REFERENCES

Brunner, A., J. Decressin, D. C. L. Hardy and B. Kudela (2004), 'Germany's three-pillar banking system – cross country perspectives in Europe', International Monetary Fund occasional paper no. 223, Washington DC.

Elsas, R. and J. P. Krahnen (2004), 'Universal banks and relationships with firms', in R. H. Schmidt and J. P. Krahnen (eds), *The German Financial System*, Oxford: Oxford University Press, pp. 197–232.

Gischer, H. and D. J. Jüttner (2002), 'Lessons from a bank profitability study for the future of banking', in B. Gup (ed.), *The Future of Banking*, Westport, CT and London: Quorum Books, pp. 229–47.

Hackethal, A. and R. H. Schmidt (2004), 'Financing patterns: measurement concepts and empirical results', Johann Wolfgang Goethe-University working paper, Frankfurt am Main.

Hackethal, A., R. H. Schmidt and M. Tyrell (2005), 'On the way to a capital market based system', *Corporate Governance: An International Review*, **13**, 397–407.

Hart, O. (1995), *Firms, Contracts, and Financial Structure*, Oxford: Clarendon Press.

Hirschmann, A. O. (1970), *Exit, Voice and Loyalty*, Cambridge, MA: Harvard University Press.

Höpner, M. (2003), *Wer beherrscht die Unternehmen?*, Frankfurt am Main: Campus.

Kreps, D. M. (1990), 'Corporate culture and economic theory', in J. E. Alt and K. A. Shepsle (eds), *Perspectives on Positive Political Economy*, Cambridge: Cambridge University Press.

Manne, H. (1965), 'Mergers and the market for corporate control', *Journal of Political Economy*, **73**, 110–20.

Schmidt, R. H. (2007), 'Stakeholderorientierung, Systemhaftigkeit und Stabilität der Corporate Governance in Deutschland', in U. Jürgens *et al.* (eds), *Perspektiven der Corporate Governance*, Baden-Baden: Nomos.

Schmidt, R. H. and G. Spindler (2002), 'Path dependence, corporate governance, and complementarity', *International Finance*, **5**, 311–33.

12. Cases of corporate (mis)governance in the Hungarian banking sector

Júlia Király, Katalin Mérő and János Száz

INTRODUCTION

During the turnaround of the 1980s and 1990s the Hungarian economy experienced a serious macroeconomic crisis. A key element was the 'external shock', the large-scale loss of external markets in 1991. Loss of markets, according to both micro- and macroeconomic evidence, contributed to the relative over-indebtedness, the capital loss and the asset devaluation of the corporate sector. In 1991 GDP and investment fell by nearly 12 per cent, exports by over 15 per cent and industrial production by 17 per cent. Extensive corporate research (Major, 1995) revealed that 40 per cent of all businesses made losses. In the second quarter of 1991, 70 per cent of surveyed companies indicated insufficient demand as an obstacle to production, compared to an average of 40–50 per cent in earlier years. The external shock hit a largely indebted and overfinanced corporate sector.

The relatively young banking sector could not avoid the crisis. In 1993 the overall ROE of the sector fell below – 100 per cent, that is most banks lost their capital. Some banks were, immediately after the shock, consolidated and privatized, some tried to grow out the panic and failed a few years later.

There are several papers analysing the economic background of the deep banking crisis of the Hungarian banking sector (for example Kiraly, 1995; Kiraly and Varhegyi, 2003). In the two case studies of this chapter we highlight a special feature of the crisis – corporate (mis)governance. In the first part a typical state-owned corporate bank will be analysed, while in the second part of the chapter an interesting retail bank story will be outlined.

CASE 1: THE CORPORATE SOS BANK[1] (STATE OWNED SUCCESSOR BANK)

Background

Hungary's two-tier banking sector was established on 1 January 1987.[2] Commercial banking activities were separated from the central bank. The newly established three commercial banks – based on the former commercial banking departments of the National Bank of Hungary (NBH) – were allowed to gradually expand their activities across an increasing range of banking services.

The sectorally-structured organization of the NBH served as a blueprint for the establishment of the two-tier banking system. Accordingly, one of the three commercial banks was assigned a portfolio of mainly industrial corporations, another that of primarily agricultural and food companies and the third that of mainly companies in the energy sector and service-providing enterprises. The loans were classified as problem-free, that is at a 100 per cent historical value. In reality, the values of the transferred portfolios were much below 100 per cent, since the NBH used to grant loans in accordance with the priorities of the then centrally-planned economy rather than on a business basis. Although the NBH also had to perform cost-benefit analyses in its decisions concerning whether or not to grant a loan, neither credit rating nor provisioning was part of its adopted practice. Time and again, the state, which was also the owner of the companies, consolidated the financial position of the companies that defaulted on loans through raising their own funds or with debt relief. If there was no state intervention, the NBH extended the tenor of the loans, that is no loan losses materialized in the mono-banking system. As opposed to the previous practice, the new commercial banks were expected to grant loans based exclusively on economically sound decisions and that gradually disposed of bad loans.

Initially, the liability structure of the banks was adjusted to their loan portfolio (assets size). According to the leverage requirement, their own funds were calculated as 4 per cent of total assets. The initial deposits of the banks were those of the enterprises whose accounts they kept. The rather wide gap between total assets and own funds plus deposits was filled in with central bank refinancing loans. The worse the loan-to-deposit ratio of a customer assigned to the bank, the more important the role of central bank refinancing in the banks' financing structure became. Central bank refinancing accounted for 37 per cent, 59 per cent and 74 per cent respectively of the initial balance sheet totals of the three large artificially founded banks.

Although the banks were established by the state, state-owned companies which were the clients of the bank were also allowed to subscribe as shareholders of the banks. As a result, the companies financed by the banks had a 10 per cent to 15 per cent ownership share in the newly established banks from the outset. During the first few years of their operation, this ownership share continued to grow substantially. The reason for this was that the state no longer participated in subsequent additional share issues through which the banks raised capital, which they needed for the expansion of their operations. Thus, such additional capital requirements were fundamentally financed by companies with close ties to the banks. It happened quite often that the banks even granted loans to companies to enable them to subscribe shares.

Members of the banks' management and bank administrators were mostly ex-NBH employees. It was primarily at the NBH that the expertise needed for banking operations had been amassed. However, as the NBH did not operate on a business basis and, hence, did not manage risk at all, it is safe to say that neither executive officers nor staff with the necessary professional track record were available at the time of the foundation of the banks. The external members of the banks' boards of directors were delegated, in part, by the ministries representing the state and, in part, by the shareholder companies. Due to the fundamentally non-market nature of the economic environment and the regulators' lack of expertise in banking techniques, bank regulations did not comply with the appropriate prudent criteria. Thus, for instance, interest income also included accrued but not paid interest, which rendered profit and loss accounts completely unreliable. There were no regulations that governed connected lending, and even those limiting large exposures were very permissive.

Already at the outset, the way the two-tier banking system was founded as well as the system's initial position raised several embedded corporate governance issues, of which the following were of key importance:

Strong sectoral ties. The strong sectoral concentration of the banks' portfolios involved dependence on sectoral lobbies. Often, representation of and advocacy for sectoral interest, in co-operation with the representatives of the individual sectors, rather than consistent prudent lending was an easier and faster road to success. Furthermore, as major companies in the dominant sectors were also the shareholders of the banks, sectoral lobbies were represented on the boards of directors, making banks' ties with the individual sectors even closer and dependence on sectoral lobbies even stronger.

Moral hazard in lending due to the lack of provisions and capital. The fact that the initial loan portfolio of the banks was classified as problem-free and, hence, recognized at a 100 per cent face value and that their capital was at the lowest possible level allowed by the regulation ruled out all realistic credit rating and provisioning. As a result, provisions did not provide coverage for expected losses. Likewise, capital could not act as a loss-absorbing cushion. This also involved moral hazard in respect of future lending, since if realistic credit rating and prudent operation were not the requirements for the bank management to comply with, other motives took priority.

Problems arising from a skewed liability structure. The absence of the availability of retail deposit collection, coupled with the dominant role of central bank funding, resulted in a situation where the lending activity of the banks depended heavily on the robustness of their bargaining position *vis-à-vis* the central bank.

Conflicts of interest arising from the fact that customers were also owners. The primary interest of banks' customers is to receive loans, which stands in stark contrast to the owner's interest in the bank's best possible operation.

Conflicts of interest originating from the composition of the boards of directors. The fact that shareholder companies were represented at both shareholders' meetings and on boards of directors further aggravated the conflicts of interest arising from customer interest representation. Generally, board members who represented the state as owner were departmental heads in ministries who were not (and could not realistically be expected to be) well-versed in banking operations. As board membership involved outstanding income, they clung to it tooth and nail. Criteria for board membership included a good relationship with bank management and the state officials who had a say in their appointment, rather than the best possible operation of the bank. (Given that the state was the largest shareholder, representatives of shareholder companies also needed the backing of the votes of the state in order to be elected to sit on boards.)

Moral hazards arising from the shortcomings of regulation. In a situation where the entire amount of accrued but unpaid interest is calculated as income, the profitability of banks as shown in their profit and loss account is independent of their actual profitability. When this is the case, it is easy to be successful. Furthermore, the fact that bonuses were, as a rule, pegged to the attainment of profitability targets, bank management was not interested in prudent operation. On the contrary, in certain cases, it expressly interfered with this. This was further amplified by the fact that, to the charge of unrealized profit, the state was able to post handsome sums in income tax and dividend income, which served self-justification for state officials' exonerating themselves from the responsibility of advocating prudent bank operation. As a matter of fact, it was through their support for the recognition of the highest possible amount of accrued but not paid interest that the state was able to earn the highest possible amount of revenue. A system like this mostly favoured large companies with heavy borrowing requirements and strong lobbying power which were expected to pay huge amounts in interest income. Uncontrolled lending to companies was facilitated by the fact that bankruptcy or liquidation proceedings against them were practically non-existent. Defaulting companies could hold evergreen loans provided that their business partners were willing to continue to do business with them despite their default. In the case of large state-owned companies – due to their economic strength and embeddedness – default on payment did not lead to the discontinuation of economic relations. Instead, there emerged extensive gridlock in the corporate sector. Therefore, bank management, the state as owner, board members representing the state and large companies, then the backbone of the economy, all had a shared interest in the recognition of unrealized revenues as actual income. The lack of the restrictions on connected lending and the not-so-limiting regulation on large exposures resulted in heavy lending to shareholder companies and businesses that the state considered to be important.

THE FOUNDATION OF SOS BANK AND THE FIRST YEARS OF ITS OPERATION

SOS Bank was founded on 1 January 1987. Eighty-five per cent and 15 per cent of its share capital was subscribed by the Hungarian state and 50 companies respectively. Loans to large companies in the energy and (mainly coal) mining sector accounted for approximately 80 per cent of the bank's initial loan portfolio. The remaining part included loans to a few large industrial companies and medium-sized enterprises. Food industry companies and service providers played a dominant role within this portfolio segment.

Capital constraints impeding the expansion of the bank's activities were acutely felt already in the very first year of its operation, so it announced a capital increase as early as in the second half of 1987. Due to the economic upturn of the time and widespread confidence in newly founded banks, the capital increase was a success. As a result, the state's ownership share in the bank had fallen to 60 per cent by the end of the year. During the next two years, however, the arrangement and implementation of capital increases, indispensable for the operation of the bank, became increasingly difficult. Thus, it became adopted practice for SOS Bank to finance capital increases through lending. Capital increases led to the state's having become a minority shareholder by end-1988, with its ownership share standing at 35 per cent at end-1989. At the time of the establishment of SOS Bank the board of directors included the chief executive officer and two deputy chief executive officers, plus ten external members, of whom seven represented the state and three the shareholder companies. As a rule, representatives of the Ministry of Finance and the ministries responsible for the relevant sectors were those representing the state. The corporate shareholders of the bank exerted ongoing pressure on the representatives of the state as a shareholder and the management in order to be allowed to sit on the board of directors. As a result, already at the annual general meeting closing the first year of the bank's operation, the number of board members was raised from 13 to 16. The new members represented the companies that were the new shareholders of the bank. In response to the widespread practice of capital increases in exchange for board membership and raising of the number of board members to an unsustainable and unmanageable level, the regulators modified the Companies Act, pursuant to which, with effect from end-1989, the number of board members could not exceed 11. In the case of our bank, in addition to the two members of the management, there were five members appointed by the shareholder state and four by the shareholder companies. Company representatives included the executive officers of companies in the energy and mining sectors, dominant borrowers of the bank, and the chief executive officer of a food company. Their primary concern was to secure freely available loans for their respective companies and to ensure that the bank's business policy focused on the operation and financing of their respective sectors.

SOS Bank's dependence on the individual sectors further increased in the first few years of its operation. The widespread interdependence of the bank and its dominant clients, coupled with large-scale cross-ownership, played a dominant role in this process. In addition, the widespread economic downturn weakened companies' loan repayment ability, which marked the very end of all remaining hopes that banks would be able to work out their loan losses on their own through adopting a prudent valuation, provisioning and capital allocation approach. They earned the largest profits when they helped their customers to secure the largest possible state aid for the relevant sector. Steps taken to stabilize companies often included debt/equity swaps, whereby banks became not only dominant lenders, but also dominant owners of companies in major sectors.

The sectoral dependence was so strong that the management of SOS Bank found it natural that it was able effectively to improve the bank's position through maximizing sectoral lobbying power. Therefore, in 1987 H2, when companies were given discretion over selecting a bank for themselves, the bank made a financing offer to the only mining company that had not been assigned to it, thereby persuading it to switch over to it from its former account-keeping bank. With this move, it had become the 100 per cent financier of coal mining, which was already a depressed sector.

Although there was no comprehensive rating system in place at the bank, after the first year of its operation, according to its own estimates, one-third of its loan portfolio was problematic. Nevertheless, due, to a large extent, to the recognition of accrued but unpaid interest as income, its operation was highly profitable in its first fiscal year, with ROE and ROA standing at 60 per cent and 4 per cent respectively. In conformity with the statutory regulations in force at the time, it was allowed to use 20 per cent of its profits to set aside pre-tax provisions, which, however, accounted for a mere 4 per cent of its estimated doubtful loans. The remaining 80 per cent formed its tax base, as well as the basis of dividend disbursement.

The bank had to write off, in connection with the debt settlement of three state-owned mining companies, two-thirds of the provisions thus set aside already in the following year. Mines in Hungary could operate profitably only as long as state-controlled prices, which automatically covered their expenses, were applied to them. Such prices ceased to be applied during the second year of the operation of the two-tier banking system, whereby mining companies with a huge loan portfolio faced bleak prospects. Naturally, the bank continued to earn huge profits on the financing of mines, since accrued but unpaid interest was further increased by penalty interest on overdue debt; however, given the size of the amounts involved, this also gave rise to liquidity problems at the bank. Although, citing this as its reason, the bank could turn to the NBH for additional refinancing, the addressing of an increasingly large number of problems could not be put off forever. The debts of state-owned mines were settled in a bargaining process where the state would have liked the bank earning huge profits to write off the bulk of the losses, while the bank urged the greatest possible participation of the state. The result was a compromise under which the state donated the mines an amount equal to half of the total amount of their debts, while the bank wrote off the other half at an even pace over three years. The losses to be written off which the provisions of the bank could not cover were financed by the NBH through the granting of temporary refinancing. Such a method of debt settlement was not efficient from the perspective of the ability to operate of either the companies or the bank. It managed to settle the debts that the companies held at a given point of time; however, it could not prevent the generation of new ones. The bank found itself stuck in the quagmire of having to finance the companies for at least three more years, which spelled further potential losses for it.

The case of a construction company in the provinces, the financing of which was the responsibility of a branch of the SOS Bank, can also be considered as typical. The company used to be a textbook socialist giant with oversized capacity and an obsolete structure of production, which owed its continued operation to state home construction projects with no quality expectations or sensitivity to costs. As the number of such projects fell, so the company's economic position deteriorated. The fact that the company was facing a crisis was obvious already at the time of the foundation of SOS Bank, since as early as in the era of the mono-banking system the shareholder state already commenced debt settlement with the involvement of the NBH. Naturally, the company's outstanding debt was transferred to the bank at a 100 per cent value. Already in the first month of its operation, SOS Bank, having reached a compromise with the other lenders and the state, granted a grace period of one year to the company so that the company might work out a viable reorganization programme. The sale of the properties that were no longer needed (an office block, a workers' hostel, a sports ground and educational centre) and the downsizing of over-sized capacity were at the heart of the programme. The properties were not satisfactorily marketable; they were purchased by organizations financed mostly from the central budget. These organizations, however, needed a bank loan for the purchase. For instance, the workers' hostel was purchased by a university in order to operate it as a hostel and the office block by the Ministry of Finance to operate it as the central office of a newly founded tax authority. The bank regarded the university and the ministry unequivocally better debtors than the company, so it was quite willing to finance the transactions. The downsizing of over-sized capacity did not relate to the company's core activity. Instead, the company sold, for example, its computing centre and placed an order with the buyer for computing services, to the extent of its requirements, at a capacity that it formerly owned. Although the purchase was also financed by SOS Bank, as the IT company thus founded was smaller and operated at lower operational costs, the bank trusted in its viability. These steps were still unsatisfactory for the consolidation of the company, so, in addition to financing the buyers, the bank granted further loans to a now more streamlined company, which it perceived as more viable. Temporarily, debt settlement looked successful; however, it did not resolve the company's fundamental problem, as it continued to operate with oversized obsolete capacity despite a narrowing market. When reorganization was over, the bank was still lending, albeit to a lesser extent, to a company that was not viable and to a series of institutions, the debt repayment of which seemed to be indirectly guaranteed by the state (though later, this indirect guarantee did not work out in the case, for instance, of the university).

In the light of the processes described in connection with the settlement of corporate debts, it is hardly a surprise that the bank's most important interest lay in extensive lending and, hence, building an economic position that provided it with economic and political clout and the strongest possible bargaining power. Thus, while between 1987 and 1990 Hungary's

GDP fell significantly, SOS Bank's activity expanded. As regards its profitability indicators, its ROE continued to range between 50 per cent and 60 per cent and ROA stood at approximately 4 per cent. In a situation like this, its provisions were used to acquire the largest possible amount of state funds rather than for writing off obviously irrecoverable debts. This trend was further intensified by state regulations which discontinued pre-tax provisioning in 1989 and 1990 so as to improve an increasingly deteriorating fiscal balance.

Although permanent renewal of bad debts was good business for the bank, companies' consistently high demand for loans in the midst of a widespread economic downturn and liquidity problems caused by permanently tightening monetary policy forced the SOS Bank to apply certain filtering criteria to loan applications. As a means of filtering, in 1989 (that is in the third year of its operation) the bank elaborated a debtor rating system, on the basis of which it assigned a financing limit to each company. Debtor rating consisted exclusively of quantitative components, as it was aimed at offsetting excessive subjectivity, which used to characterize earlier practice. Thus, such quantitative components were based on indicators calculated from the balance sheet data of banks. It should be noted, however, that accounting data failed to provide a true and fair picture of the companies' performance, just as banks' data did in relation to that of banks. It is no coincidence that, while an increasing number of companies defaulted on loans, a test run of the debtor rating system included 70 per cent of the companies financed by the bank in the category of best debtors. In practice, limits were set in accordance with a matrix, where debtor rating was adjusted with a sectoral multiplier. This resulted in higher limits for companies in such sectors that were more important for the bank than for those that were in sectors that it deemed less important. This is indeed why, even after the introduction of the new rating system, mining and food companies with a poor loan repayment ability in a distressed sector remained the bank's key customers; no material reduction in the sectoral concentration of lending occurred and the bank did not avail itself of risk mitigation arising from diversification.

It follows from the above that, if we were to judge the first five years of the newly founded banks on the basis of the first eight principles of Basel's sound corporate governance principles[3] pertaining to the boards and senior management of banks, we could easily jump to the conclusion that none of those eight basic principles were observed. Naturally, this would be rather a summary judgement, which can be made more subtle.

During the first years of the operation of two-tier banking system there was no auditing. Instead, the balance sheet of state-owned companies was subjected to authority inspection. There was, of course, no serious auditing company that would have approved of the balance sheets and profit and loss accounts of the banks, which were far from reflecting a true and fair picture. And, naturally, in addition to many other causes, the fact alone that the financial statements and accounts prepared by banks could not provide a true and fair picture made it impossible for banks to be operated in a transparent manner.

The board of directors could not be made 'ultimately responsible for the operations and financial soundness of the bank . . . including the under-standing the bank's risk profile',[4] since the bank's fundamental risk, that is credit risk, could not be measured. Nor was the composition of the board defined in such a manner that its members had the collective knowledge needed for banking operations. Furthermore, pressure was exerted on the representatives of the state when, for instance, issues concerning the financing of state-owned companies had to be decided on when a proposal for dividend disbursement was put forward to the shareholders' meeting. Political pressure was, as a rule, indirect. The State Property Agency, an organization established expressly for this purpose, never convened the representatives delegated by the state to the boards of directors of the indi-vidual companies in order to urge them to act in a concerted manner. On the contrary, when one of the board members, having become fully aware of his own responsibility, requested the Property Agency to do so, the latter flatly refused to provide any guidelines. Everybody knew perfectly well when it was required to adopt the opinion of the Ministry of Finance and when that of other ministries.

The State Consolidation of SOS Bank[5]

During the very first years of the macro-economic crisis evolving at the turn of the 1980s and the 1990s, in keeping with what was described above, members of the management and boards of directors of banks lulled them-selves into the false sense of banks' being able to continue unharmed by the general economic downturn. They even thought that they might be able to play an important role in successfully coping with the crisis through expan-sive lending and large-volume debt/equity swaps in relation to distressed com-panies. In order for such an obviously false sense to be dispelled, a realistic assessment of the position of the banks had to be performed, which was indeed stipulated by the regulatory package that entered into force in 1991–2.[6]

In 1992, SOS Bank re-rated its portfolio and, in keeping with the gradual nature of the regulation, it had to set aside at least one-third of its calcu-lated provisions. During the process of re-rating, the management of the bank was influenced by two opposing forces. One was the fact that it was the year of credit consolidation, which meant the first step in the process of state consolidation. What best served the interest of the management was to rate the highest possible number of loans as bad and sell them to the state. SOS Bank sold 6 per cent of its total loan portfolio at an 80 per cent value and wrote off the remaining 20 per cent, that is 1.2 per cent of the loan portfolio, as loan loss. However, such an advantage was not absolutely definite. It was important that the management of the bank should create and communicate an image according to which the legacy of the mono-bank system rather than inadequate management of the bank was to be blamed for bad loans. Therefore, efforts to rate loans as bad pertained only to loans inherited from the era of the mono-bank system; as to the re-mainder of the loans, the bank's interest continued to lie in creating a picture that was rosier than reality, as it underscored its own suitability and improved the chances of heftier bonus payments. This ambition of the management of the bank coincided with that of the management of the companies that the bank financed, as the perception of and bonus pay-ments to the members of the management depended on the good repu-tation of the companies. As the rating of the bank's portfolio depended mostly on delay in repayments, the bank could resort to rescheduling loans, thereby avoiding their being rated as bad and the obligation to set aside pro-visions for loan losses. The outcome of the two conflicting impacts was that, in 1992, SOS Bank set aside provisions for loan losses accounting for 4 per cent of the loans that it had not sold to the state. (Consistent with its ambition to maximize its profit in the relevant year, the bank complied with its provisioning obligation to the smallest possible extent, that is it set aside exactly one-third of the provisions stipulated by its rating.) As a conse-quence, it posted a loss amounting to 5 per cent of its equity, which was amply funded by the reserves accumulated from the sham profits of the pre-vious years. SOS Bank was technically insolvent already after its bad loans were purchased by the state, because if it had set aside the full amount of the loan-loss provisions, its loss would have exceeded its own funds. In a different regulatory environment, despite the remaining possibilities for window dressing, insolvency could no longer be hidden – it apparently became manifest in the balance sheet figures.

Relying on the lessons and fiascos of credit consolidation, the programme of bank consolidation in 1993 and 1994 unequivocally aimed at restoring the bank's solvency through a capital increase orchestrated by the state. The purpose of the first step of the programme was for banks to uncover their position in a manner that was true to facts prior to their extraordinary share-holders' meetings in December 1993. At such extraordinary meetings the state announced capital increases to an extent that turned their solvency ratio slightly positive. As a result, the state acquired an 85 per cent ownership share in SOS Bank.

While prior to the consolidation it was impossible to maintain a satisfactory level of provisions and capital, which carried a moral hazard, in the course of the consolidation a new type of moral hazard appeared. The entire portfolio of the individual banks had to be revalued in order for potential loss in it and, hence, the necessary level of provisions as well as the actual shortage of capital to be established. This was no plain sailing, however. Already the identifying of the defaulted components of the portfolio was difficult, as extending the tenor of non-performing loans, the replacement of bad loans with new ones, debt/equity swaps, and so on were all elements of banks' day-to-day operation. Under such circumstances, the best available method of separating and measuring the problem loans from the rest of the portfolio seemed to be the expected loss-based approach relying on expert estimates. As, ultimately, it was the state that had to 'pick up the tab', the measurement of the portfolio was performed with the consent of the Ministry of Finance and the banks. Since, however, neither the banks nor the ministry had the necessary expertise for such measurement, the value of the portfolio and, hence, that of the capital donated by the state were, in principle, established through a bargaining and consensus-seeking process between the institutions affected.

The SOS Bank adopted the policy of 'the worse, the better' during the consolidation, which meant that the worse a bank portfolio was made to look, the more state funds could be secured. All this in a manner whereby no one raised the issue of bank management responsibility. An almost unlimited availability of state funds (over-consolidation) provided the basis of comfy operation for the next one or two years. Prudent operation still was not a pre-condition for profitable operation, as profits from the release of provisions could be used to hide the deficiencies of banking operation. This, however, was a means only temporarily available for banks.

At its extraordinary meeting in December 1993, SOS Bank presented its annual report showing loss on the bank's books in an amount that was close to three times its equity. The loss was due to provisioning in an amount eight times higher than in the previous year. Even if we take into consideration that in the year before only one-third of what was needed had to be set aside in provisions and that portfolio loss did, in fact, continue to increase significantly during the year, the practice of provisioning during those two years was still strikingly different. The cognitive dissonance of the management and the bank's board of directors can also be observed in the internal and public reports of the bank. Evaluating and analysing the state of the bank, loss never took centre stage. Instead operating profit, that is profits before provisioning, was the central category of the reports. If they were favourable, both the management and the directors of the bank were satisfied. And they were favourable. In 1993, operating profit grew significantly, so both the management and the bank's directors were satisfied with their own performance. Members of the management and employees received their annual bonus payments, though they were somewhat more modest than in the previous years.

In the period of consolidation the state employed two methods of control. One was the transformation of banks' executive bodies in conformity with the new ownership structure, strengthening the presence of the state. This, however, was still not an efficient tool of state control, as consolidation did not lead to an increase in the number of staff members in government agencies enjoying the necessary expertise in banking. Furthermore, selection criteria still did not include expertise. Rather, board membership continued to be regarded as some sort of 'reward', a source of extra income once one was appointed an executive officer representing the state on the boards of banks.

The other method was the Consolidation Agreement concluded between the state and the banks concerned. The agreement consisted of two parts: the banks undertook the obligation to participate in debtor consolidation scheduled for 1994 and to elaborate a consolidation programme, which the state as owner approved. In effect, the consolidation programme was a three-year strategic programme setting out the methods that banks were going to employ with a view to maintaining their stability, the measures that they were going to take in the interest of prudent and profitable business management and the manner in which they were going to transform the processes of internal operation and control in order to support the attainment of these goals. Consistent with the process of consolidation, 1994 for SOS Bank was the year of debtor consolidation and the elaboration of a consolidation programme prior to the Annual General Meeting in May, which approved the programme and a capital increase, which was able to secure the 8 per cent solvency ratio.

Within the framework of debtor consolidation, SOS Bank contacted those customers whose loans had been rated as bad and called upon them to work out a reorganization programme. In order for such a reorganization programme to be approved, the bank and the Ministry of Finance had to work in co-operation, since, in addition to loan forgiveness and loan rescheduling by the bank, it was often the case that decisions had to be made on the waiving of taxes, customs duties and social security taxes. The Ministry of Finance considered the issue as one of low priority, assigning it to mid-management and allocating to it the lowest possible amount of resources, which further increased the bank's room for manoeuvre. Thus, SOS Bank was, once again, able to make decisions – in the case of the companies strongly linked to it – optimizing the size of the state funds used in the process. Now, however, moral hazard was much lower than it was during the preceding years, since the state emphatically stated on a number of occasions that it considered recapitalization and related debtor consolidation to be the final step in the process of consolidation. The more public the size of the government funds became, the more the issue of the management's responsibility was taking centre stage, which urged the banks to operate more cautiously. Not once during the process was the issue of the responsibility of the board of directors raised, which aptly illustrates how the state as owner was biased towards itself.

The consolidation programme also contained a programme aimed at the transformation of the bank's internal processes and the bank's strategy. What can be perceived as an undoubtedly beneficial effect of consolidation was the enshrining of the transformation of risk management and corporate governance processes at banks in a contract. The approved consolidation programme was not simply a wish list of the processes to be overhauled. It also set a dateline for each of its stages. It was the first time that requirements for the responsibility and role of board members (for example the continuous monitoring of the compilation of a handbook on lending and the mandatory taking of minutes at board meetings) had appeared in the bank's documents.

Banks had to submit to the Ministry of Finance quarterly reports on the progress they had made along the guidelines of the consolidation programme. Initially, the banks took their reporting obligation seriously. However, as it gradually dawned on them that the ministry did not (that is the reports went unread), they started to comply with this obligation only perfunctorily. They focused on meeting the reporting deadlines, though only touching upon all the issues that they were expected to and filling the requisite number of pages. The reports themselves became increasingly non-committal, without any consequences whatsoever.

For the purposes of our theme, one more aspect of the process of consolidation is worth highlighting. The recapitalization of the banks was implemented through government bonds with a 20-year tenor rather than cash contribution. As those government bonds were not marketable, they greatly restricted banking operations. The sole avenue of trading these bonds was selling them to the central bank. As a result, each bank that had been consolidated sought to exert pressure on the central bank, which, however, 'gave in' only in the case of SOS Bank, purchasing a sizeable portion of its loan portfolio. SOS Bank succeeded in reaching a special bargain, strengthening its position, not only with the central bank but also with the Ministry of Finance. The essence of the bargain was that when, alone among the consolidated banks, it established a company in order to manage its problem loans and, in order to finance the company's portfolio, it issued bonds, the state guaranteed the bond issue. (This guarantee accounted for approximately 25 per cent of the sum that the state had spent on the recapitalization of SOS Bank.)

What are the lessons of the process of bank consolidation in the light of the Basel corporate governance principles?

The board of directors only played a minor role in the consolidation. It was engineered centrally by the state, which discussed its expectations with the bank's management. The bank still did not have the appropriate means of measuring risks. The revaluation of the portfolio was always subject to case-by-case deliberation rather than a uniform methodology. Only after the Consolidation Agreement had been concluded did the understanding of the risk profile of the bank and the elaboration of exposure policies become a responsibility of the board.

While elaborating its strategy set out in the Consolidation Agreement, the board of directors of SOS Bank discussed it on several occasions. Furthermore, when the requirements for better corporate governance urged by the contract were laid down, the board was also involved. However, the board also contributed to the fact that the quarterly reports related to the Consolidation Agreement became a mere formality. As soon as it was clear that the Ministry of Finance did not expect the bank to submit a report of merit, the board of directors was less and less intent on the management's doing so. This meant that the board made its own control over the governance processes a mere formality.

A stronger role of internal and external audits was, without a doubt, one of the positive outcomes of the process of consolidation. The strengthening of internal auditing and a regular check on it by the board of directors was one of the key requirements of the Consolidation Agreement. Prospective privatization enhanced the prestige of external audit. In keeping with the agreement, an information system capable of ensuring that monthly performance was evaluated also had to be devised, which, in turn, made banking processes more transparent. Such transparency was a step forward only for the management of the banks, the public had to make do with not too informative annual reports in gathering information about them.

The consolidation programme also aimed at the transformation of remuneration policy and the scheme of incentives. Having approved the consolidation programme, the management of the bank grew apprehensive of its being held responsible, one way or another, by the state as owner for the loss that it had realized because of the huge costs of consolidation. Therefore, what was accepted on paper was a far cry from actual practice. In practice, remuneration policy and the scheme of incentives protected the interest and consolidated the position of the bank's management. Accordingly, employment contracts offering rather favourable terms were concluded with the members of the management. Upon the proposal of the representative of the state as owner, the 1995 Annual General Meeting, which marked the end of the consolidation process, dismissed the CEO of the bank. One of the first measures taken by the new management was the termination, with mutual consent, of the employment contracts of the members of the former management. With this, also from the perspective of corporate governance, a new chapter in the history of SOS Bank commenced, leading to its privatization.

CASE 2: THE RETAIL PARTLY STATE-OWNED P-BANK (1988–98)

The story of a partly state-owned, partly privately-owned Hungarian bank, that of P-Bank is no less interesting than the case study of the state-owned successor bank discussed in the previous chapter. P-Bank was founded in 1988 as the 23rd commercial Bank of Hungary (one year later than the banks of the previous chapter) by 94 shareholders, including numerous private investors. At the time of its foundation, the decisive main shareholder of the bank was the Hungarian National Post Office. Within three years the bank became the fifth largest bank in the country, in ten years the second one – and after celebrating its tenth anniversary the bank collapsed. In the end, the success story proved to be a 'failure story'. First we will summarize the facts, then analyse the failure.

The Story

P-Bank – as opposed to the banks discussed previously – was originally retail oriented. The first years (1988–93) of the new retail oriented bank were a real success.

In the 1980s in Hungary the retail market was monopolized by the National Savings Bank (OTP), which traditionally – even during the monobank system – used to be 'the' bank of households. The dominance of OTP did not disappear after the establishment of the two tier banking system, since, the successor banks were not allowed to enter the retail market in the first years of their operation. At that time OTP[7] was a rigid, bureaucratic, slow, non-customer-oriented financial service provider, with three basic deposit products: a current account (without card, and with few additional services), a so-called sight deposit with fixed interest rate and a time deposit with fixed interest rate. The interest rate on all these accounts was accounted on the last day of the month, based solely on the actual balance on the account. All the products were very inconvenient, as customers could withdraw their money only in the particular branch where their accounts or deposits had been opened.

The new P-Bank developed a quite simple, but still flexible retail deposit product, a kind of saving account, which, for most of its customers, was much more attractive than the traditional products of OTP. The interest was accounted on a daily basis and the account enjoyed immediate access in all the 3000 post offices of the country. Customers soon 'invented' a so-called mixed deposit – 'keep your cash in a P-Bank saving deposit, earn the monthly interest, then transfer it for the last day of the month to an OTP current account, earn your monthly interest, and so your interest will be doubled'. That is what happened and P-Bank customers began growing at an exponential rate. With the exception of one day of the month it had a stable account base and soon most of its customers transferred their savings to a P-Bank time deposit.

The bank relied on a fresh marketing mix and image campaign, and for the first time in Hungary made use of the new, privatized media. The result was an explosive growth on the deposit side – after the first five years the bank could boast about more than one million active customers (there are seven million potentially active customers in Hungary), and about a 10 per cent market share on the retail deposit market.

The lending policy of the bank proved to be less successful. The growth in retail deposits was not balanced by prudent lending activity, and the bank engaged in speculative investment and lending. This resulted in an unhealthy balance sheet structure, with a high proportion of non-interest bearing assets and a deteriorating asset quality. The loan portfolio was corporate oriented, and the lending rules were quite loose – just as in the other newly established Hungarian banks. In spite of the fact that P-Bank did not inherit 'bad portfolio', during the period of fast growth a significant part of the loans proved to be non-performing or sub-performing. The bank preferred highly volatile real estate projects, and under the given circumstances more and more, bigger and bigger defaults occurred.

In its first five years (1988–93) the average growth rate of the bank was over 70 per cent, in an economy where the growth rate of the nominal GDP was below 20 per cent. This unsustainable growth soon produced the first adverse signals. The capital adequacy ratio (CAR) of the Bank – despite the early implemented Basel I rules – never reached the 8 per cent level. It oscillated around 6 per cent. In spite of the obvious signals the bank did not curb its growth, but, on the contrary, augmented its lending activity, in the hope that it would be able to 'grow out of' the problem loans. The non-performing loans were restructured and reclassified. A frequent 'disguising tool' was the debt-equity swap.

The capital management of the bank was very intensive from the very beginning – and very 'innovative'. The management tried to avoid dominant shareholders with success, and 'built' a quite dispersed shareholder structure. After the first five years, direct state ownership fell below 40 per cent, while foreign ownership increased up to 15 per cent and dispersed local private companies owned more than 50 per cent of the bank. As in the case of SOS Bank, these partly private companies were for the most part customers of the bank.

In the next period (1993–6) the amplifying crisis signals threatened the smooth operation of the bank. The first signs of the difficulties could have been detected in the bank's financial statements in 1995, when a substantial part of the profit already came from extraordinary items (from the sale of special items). Due to intensive debt-equity swap transactions and the increasing part played by non-performing loans, the share of interest yielding assets within total assets fell below 70 per cent. The net interest margin was declining, operating cost was soaring, and, as a consequence, the cost/income ratio dramatically increased and after-tax profit fell close to zero. By 1996 the situation had further deteriorated, with the bank's profit totally melting in that year.

Facing the threat of zero profit and zero dividend, the growth was curbed back. With the help of 'creative accounting' the CAR (capital adequacy ratio) was increased a little bit above 8 per cent. In spite of its increasingly bad portfolio, P-Bank did not participate in the sector-wide re-capitalization programme (see previous section) in order to avoid surrendering control of the bank to the state.

Insufficient capital and risky assets deteriorated the market reputation of the bank. First, the interbank borrowing limit of P-Bank fell to zero. Then, at the beginning of 1997 a heavy bank run resulted in the loss of 20 per cent of retail deposits. Though the bank was able to survive the run, the deep structural and management problems of the bank were not solved.

Due to its accumulating problems and eroding reputation, the years 1997–8 can be characterized as a permanent battle with fire. Subsequent to the run on the bank, the Hungarian state intervened with a number of measures. By assisting the bank, the state prevented an escalation of the situation, which could have destabilized the entire Hungarian banking sector. Furthermore, the bank had approximately two million retail depositors, so its collapse would have negatively impacted one-fifth of Hungary's inhabitants. Until August 1998, the state's involvement was characterized by ad hoc measures, reacting independently to the bank's difficulties as they arose – for example, it increased the bank's capital, swapped a part of its non-performing assets for performing state-owned equities, and guaranteed a part of its non-performing loans, but it did not dismiss the management. However, the bank's situation did not experience any turn-around, as the management continued with its inappropriate strategy and imprudent business practices.

The last two years of the management (1997–8) were a complete night-mare. On the one hand, the bank used creative accounting (applying much earlier the same techniques which Enron used five years later) to disguise its 'dead cows', while, on the other, even more riskier new loans entered the portfolio with a high concentration.

In the summer of 1998 the bank became involved in an extremely risky business of high value. The potential (later actual) loss exceeded its reserves and capital. These losses and potential losses made one thing clear – the bank would go bankrupt unless the government organized a 'lifeboat' action. Since P-Bank was still the second largest bank on the retail market the government decided to rescue its depositors, while putting a heavy burden on the tax-payers. The bailout cost was up to US$1 billion – approx-imately 2 per cent of Hungary's actual GDP. Shareholders lost their invest-ment, since the bank's shares lost their face value. Then a new chapter began – the old management was dismissed. The story concluded in 2003 with one of Hungary's most successful privatizations. The Austrian Erste Bank purchased P-Bank at 2.75 times book value, the highest price at that time on the CEE market. After the purchase P-Bank merged with the local Erste Bank, disappearing from the market forever.

Corporate Governance in P-Bank

The background of the story will now be analysed purely from the point of view of corporate (mis)governance, that is we will highlight those aspects of the management of the bank, which implied its inevitable collapse.

As opposed to SOS Bank analysed in the previous section, P-Bank had not inherited a bad portfolio, was not directly motivated by the state and was not corporate but retail oriented. The failure, anyhow, seemed to be inevitable – due to a similar management structure and corporate (mis)governance.

The corporate governance problems of the bank cannot be understood without a clear picture concerning its ownership structure. This involved a special case of a blended 'state' and 'private' ownership. The bank was founded as a state-owned bank (Hungarian National Post). Then, shortly afterwards, it was partly privatized, in part by foreign investors (for example Austria's Postsparkasse) and partly by Hungarian enterprises. In a few years the proportion of state ownership fell below 50 per cent, while private owners were dominated by the corporate customers of the bank. During the years of crisis (before the bailout) the state ownership started to grow again, due to the consecutive consolidating measures, and this mounted up to 70 per cent. In spite of its significant share, the state never had enough power to influence the board against the CEO. The main reason was that the state ownership was dispersed and the CEO was well able to motivate the different parts of the state owners against each other. The private owners were always quite dispersed, not being able to stop the CEO or the management.

A very important aspect of the ownership structure involved the fact that the bank had never gone to the Stock Exchange. Thus it had never had to face the exchange's strict disclosure rules.

The story of the bank is closely connected to its founding CEO, Mr G., who was at the same time the chairman of the board. In 1988, Mr G. was a 32-year-old, typical young employee in the banking department of the National Bank. He was approached by his boss (whose husband was actually the CEO of the Hungarian Post Office) and asked to take part in the foundation of a new, retail oriented bank. Mr G. liked the challenge and worked a lot during the foundation period, soon becoming the youngest CEO of the Hungarian banking sector. As an ambitious person, he was eager for success and could not tolerate failure. He was well educated, had spent several years abroad, had learned a lot about money and finance and had a special attraction to art and culture. During his heyday he became renowned on account of his generous sponsorship, though, unfortunately, he proved to be extremely generous even during the loss-making years. He had a strong personality and his management style was more autocratic than democratic. His name and his bank became so strongly connected, that the bank was often named after the CEO. He was a charismatic leader, who did not tolerate strong opposition. His closest colleagues were quite weak personalities, in all senses. Mr G. was eager for power. He enjoyed the informal power of being Number One in a big bank, and the fact that he could demonstrate to politicians, artists and journalists that he disposed of real power. In a certain sense he was an earlier blueprint of Enron's Ken Lay; for example, all the prime ministers of his time attended the bank's annual general meeting.

Members of the board had formally been nominated by the main shareholders. Nevertheless, the fragmented shareholder structure allowed the management to involve their own nominees in the board. During the period under review, the board was more or less stable. It consisted of three or four members of the executive management and five or six 'outsiders'. The state was represented by a low level officer from the Ministry of Finance – a high level, or influential board member had never been nominated by the state as owner. The other members of the board were partly university people (not specialized in banking or finance, but rather in history or private law) and partly representatives of the relevant customers of the bank. The competence of the board in strategic issues was dubious, since the members were experts in their own narrow fields, but were incompetent as regards the business of the bank. The remuneration of the board was quite generous – in addition to a high monthly salary, they could participate in a low price equity option programme of the bank.

The board, especially the non-executives, never had a clear and full picture concerning the bank's risk profile and, according to their later testimonies, its members were not aware of the real situation of the bank.

Lack of information was partly due to the fact that the board did not commit sufficient time and energy to analysing the risk profile of the bank. From 1996 'voting by fax' was a common practice – even in the case of individual loans concerning 10 per cent of the portfolio. The board fully trusted the CEO. The chairman of the board was the CEO himself, more or less in an uncontrolled decision-making role. The other reason for the information gap was the poor reporting system developed by the management. The CEO, Mr G., centralized all the relevant data, and only stylized risk reports were forwarded to the board members. Since the deterioration of the portfolio was hidden from their eyes, and the profit of the bank was steadily increasing in the first years, the board had not insisted on receiving more detailed and real risk reports.

The board should have had the reports supervised, in order to manage its key responsibilities and be responsible for accountability. It never did so. The board 'controlled' the bank through the CEO, based on the information provided by the CEO himself. Board members were deeply surprised when Mr G. was finally dismissed; they could have never imagined that 'Mr G. could not settle everything'.

Mr G. had never tolerated criticism, either from inside or from outside of the bank. It happened several times that he called journalists who had written the slightest bad news about the bank, loudly shouting at them and issuing threats. Since the bank had a large media portfolio, most journalists were on the payroll of the bank and did not ask 'awkward' questions, nor did they publish critical views. Only two or three independent journalist had the courage to publish the truth about the bank – in a weekly literary journal.

The highly concentrated decision making process did not allow for the implementation of the prudent 'four eyes principle'. Most of the important decisions were taken by the CEO on his own, and then formally signed by another member of the management or the board. Credit files, if any, were very weak – the internal procedures of the bank facilitated 'verbal credit analysis', without a careful and deep credit rating. It was evident that the CEO could avoid laws and rules at any time. According to the bank's Corporate Credit Manual, 'the CEO has the right to override any decision taken in any phase of the lending process'. In a US$12 million deal the positive decision about the loan was taken before any credit file was put together. This deal, in August 1998, proved to be the last one, since its size gave the Supervisory Authority the right to intervene, to dismiss the CEO and nominate a supervisor as a temporary manager.

The board never made any objection against the violation of laws and regulations, though the bank occasionally violated the prevailing Banking Law. The reason was that the board was, from time to time, provided with false capital reports and nice plans about improving capital budgeting. The bank had never had any internal capital allocation system, gains and losses of the individual business lines were evaluated by the CEO on a subjective basis.

The board of P-Bank never initiated the replacement of the CEO, not even at the time of clear violation of regulations. The CEO centralized the relevant information and authority – that is the badly informed board members could not really judge his performance.

Connected lending, that is lending to shareholders, was a standard practice of the bank. Two cases can be underlined, which drastically violated the basic rules of corporate governance. In 1996 the bank entered into a so-called 'cooperation contract' with one of its biggest customers (D. Holding) and financed a transaction in which the D. Holding purchased a large non-performing portfolio from the bank at face value. The duration of the loan was 20 years, with redemption at the end (a bullet loan). The bank accounted a nice profit on the sale and the loss of the transaction was postponed for several years. The total loss of this deal amounted to one-third of the total bailout cost. In another transaction, the bank advanced a loan to a consortium, which purchased from the state a small bank, where another part of the bad portfolio was later hidden. In addition, the bank often financed its customers in order to buy newly issued P-Bank shares and subordinated debt.

The board was not independent of political influence – though direct links to any political party have never been detected. However, a well defined part of its corporate customers were closely linked to political parties. After the bailout in 1998, the above-mentioned kinds of non-performing loans were mostly bought by off-shore companies. The press were able to look into some special cases and investigating journalists were able to reveal the hidden links – but the whole business was already over. As far as party preferences were concerned, P-Bank was 'well balanced' in that both the governing party and the opposition were permanently financed. Leading politicians were handled as VIP clients, enjoying high deposits and extremely low credit interest rates. The VIP list was published after the bailout, and in some cases politicians were involved in uncomfortable press interviews.

In a well-organized bank the board and senior management should be able effectively to utilize the results of the internal audit, the external auditor and the internal monitoring activities. In P-Bank the board was not supported by the internal and external auditors – audits did not reveal the anomalies of 'creative accounting'. The bank's external auditor was an unknown local company without any experience in other financial institutions. P-Bank was the only customer of the auditor. The CEO personally selected the auditors, the owner of which was one of his former colleagues. Internationally acknowledged auditors could not get close to the bank until 1996, when the Supervisory Authority forced the bank to change its auditor.

Internal monitoring dealt with 'small business details' and since the bank was a well organized unit, and individuals 'at the bottom' followed the rules, they could never find anything 'serious'.

Senior management was subordinated to the CEO. Members of the senior management had lower level university degrees and were not competent to counterbalance the CEO. They simply executed the decisions made by one man. Senior management undertook a much higher risk than indicated in bank policy. The concentration of the portfolio was extremely high – the top 25 customers accounted for more than 50 per cent of the total portfolio, and their total almost reached the maximum legal lending limit (8 × regulatory capital). Individually, most of them exceeded the legal lending limit (the top management deliberately violated the rules) and this contradicted prudent banking policy. Neither senior management nor the board played any significant role in the decision-making process. Deals were decided by the CEO together with some of his outside partners.

The lending process was not adequately supervised by the line managers. By 1998, 70 per cent of the portfolio consisted of loans without prudent risk mitigation (collaterals were not controlled or monitored).

Already in 1993 the Supervisory Committee realized that the lending rules and the practice were not in conformity, but later no report returned to this issue.

The strategy of the bank was elaborated by the executive management. The board had never discussed it in length; however, it accepted it without discussion. The mission of P-Bank was a typical retail mission – a 'bank close to you'. The bank really was the most popular bank in its heyday, with small enterprises and private customers getting the best service on the market from P-Bank. After the bailout, despite the nation-wide scandal and the loss of shareholders' value, more than two-thirds of small and private customers stayed with the bank, not transferring their accounts to another local bank. Corporate values – a growing, increasing market share, aiming 'to be the biggest' and 'the second largest bank on the market' – were in line with achievements, especially in the first part of the story. The actual operations of the bank – involving a centralized decision making process, the lack of prudential risk management, the violation of rules and regulations – were not declared as corporate values, that is the staff of the bank were unaware of the most serious problems.

Transparency was not an outstanding virtue of P-Bank holding. The holding itself consisted of various financial service companies and other equity investments. The cross-ownership could have been detected at all levels of the holding. Report channels within the holding structure were obscure and, again, all relevant information channels were centralized in the hands of the CEO. After the bailout in 1998 the Minister of Finance entrusted one of the big four to give a clear picture of the diverse equity portfolio of the bank. According to urban legend, the 'map of investments' covered all four walls of the investigators' room, as well as the floor! The bank had four different lines of equity portfolio: the pharmaceutical industry, tourism, real estate and the media. There was no 'Chinese wall' between the corporate lending and the equity investment business lines – both the senior management and the line managers concentrated the customer information without separating responsibility.

Individual cases, too, often lacked even the slightest transparency. In a huge project loan to a Spanish company in 1998 the customer was unknown (!), there was no credit file, there was no rating and the collateral was a worthless agricultural site 1500 km from the headquarters of the bank.

The annual reports of the bank provide good examples of the lack of transparency. The annual report was colourful, full of citations from famous poems, but did not reveal very much about the financial position of the bank. Even the balance sheet and the P/L account were missing from these reports. Usually growth rates of total assets, total deposits and loans, and total profit were published. No words were devoted to the business strategy or the risk-measurement of the bank. Even the official reports sent to the Supervisory Authority could hide the actual financial position. The complicated holding structure supported the special 'end of the month' solutions. A part of portfolio and the related loss items 'travelled' a long way around all the financial statements of the different subsidiaries – naturally, with the help of the auditor.

After the bailout, during the first weeks of the consolidation process dozens of 'skeletons' fell out of the cupboard – falsified letters of credit, huge loans to enterprises with minimal capital strength, enjoying only existing 'paper-made' real estate as collateral in the credit files, a list of VIP persons with handwritten figures, which turned out to be sponsorship in one case, a 'free' loan in another, and so on.

The staff of P-Bank was really well-trained and competent – within the organization everybody new his or her place and role, and the staff followed, or at least tried to follow the internal rules. Of course, the main behavioural rule was: don't ask too many questions, do your job well, follow the instructions of your boss, and you will be highly remunerated. The average personal income in the bank highly exceeded the banking benchmark. To be a member of the P-Bank staff implied 'life-long security'. Nevertheless, there was high gap between salaries. The average staff member earned 4 per cent of that of top management, while high executives received an extra bonus every year – compensation not being performance-related. It is not difficult to discover the parallel features between Hungary's P-Bank and America's Enron.

CONCLUSIONS

The two case studies presented here confirm the policy lessons and conclusions drawn by Levine (2004), in particular that the opaqueness and widespread state ownership of banks can cause outstanding corporate governance problems. To solve these problems, improving and enhancing the transparency and the privatization of the banks are essential.

We have thoroughly examined the corporate governance in SOS Bank and P-Bank, and we have concluded that none of the principles of prudent corporate governance were followed. The question arises: why? How could it have happened that business entities were able to survive a decade without obeying the most trivial business and ethical principles?

The first element of an answer can be found in the ownership structure of the banks. Since none of the owners had real influence, and since the banks were not listed companies, neither the big stakeholders nor the public could enforce the elementary rules of disclosure. The state, as a dominant owner, presented an illustration of the basic ideas of rent-seeking theory – the different state bodies could not harmonize their interests, while the individual representatives of the different bodies followed their own interests (high personal income). The state, as an owner, could never force the banks to follow prudent rules, the common interest in immediate dividend outweighed the long-run interest in a secure bank.

Second, we should not forget that bank regulation, bank supervision and bank accounting was slow to adapt to international standards, and gave rise to 'creative accounting' practices and open violation of non-bidding rules. 'Common' banking practice was slowly developing, and prudent rules of lending were only accepted throughout the sector by the end of the 1990s. There were strong incentives to practise creative accounting in the case of both banks. As regards SOS Bank, these incentives originated in moral hazards and conflicts of interest described on pp. 253–6. In the case of

P-Bank, the lack of counterbalancing forces against the strong and autocratic CEO, who managed the bank as his own, peculiarly amplified the incentives.

We can conclude that both case studies are typical failure stories of the transformation period of the central and east European banking systems. SOS Bank was a typical successor bank of the former mono-bank, while P-Bank was a typical failure story of 'semi-solutions', a story about a bank which was neither state-owned nor privately owned. Corporate mismanagement will arise in all similar cases. In both cases the drives behind corporate (mis)governance could be eliminated only after the introduction of rules regarding prudent banking and effective banking supervision, the discharge of management and the directors involved in the period of bad governance, and, in the end, the privatization of the banks.

NOTES

1. SOS Bank is not identical to any one of the legal successor banks founded at the time of the establishment of the two-tier banking system. Rather, the operational characteristics of the legal successor banks were 'moulded' into SOS Bank.
2. The description of the history and pre-history of establishing the two-tier banking system can be found, for example, in: Antal and Suranyi (1987), Bonin and Szekely (1994) and Varhegyi (2002).
3. See: Basel Committee on Banking Supervision (2006).
4. See: Principle 1 of Basel Committee of Banking Supervision (2006).
5. For a detailed description of the consolidation process, see, for example, Kiraly and Varhegyi (2003) and Balassa (1996). We do not describe the process itself in detail. Rather, we confine ourselves to expounding on its corporate governance implications.
6. It is no coincidence that the Hungarian banking terminology refers to the regulatory package of the early 1990s as a 'legislative shock therapy', since a ban on the recognition of accrued but not paid interest as profit, the application of international-standard provisioning and capital adequacy rules, together with a new bankruptcy and liquidation act that stopped gridlock and led to a steep rise in the number of liquidation processes were all introduced simultaneously. Rules on large exposure and connected lending were also introduced, and banks were forbidden to finance the purchase of their own equity shares. Auditing the bank's statements by professional internal auditor also became obligatory from 1992.
7. OTP experienced a significant transformation in the second half of the 1990s under its new management. It cut back its cost (up to a 50 per cent cost-income ratio), modernized its IT infrastructure, developed a series of new retail products, entered the corporate market and was privatized through the Stock Exchange. The corporate governance lesson to be drawn from this interesting east European phenomenon far exceed the scope of this chapter.

REFERENCES

Antal, Laszlo and Gyorgy Suranyi (1987), 'The prehistory of the reform of Hungary's banking system', *Acta Oeconomica*, 1–2, 35–48.

Balassa, Akos (1996), 'Restructuring and recent situation of the Hungarian banking sector', National Bank of Hungary workshop studies series.
Bonin, J. P. and P. I. Szekely (1994), *The Development and Reform of Financial Systems in Central and Eastern Europe*, Aldershot, UK and Brookfield, US: Edward Elgar.
Basel Committee on Banking Supervision (2006), *Enhancing Corporate Governance for Banking Organisation*, Basel: Bank for International Settlement.
Király, Júlia (1995), 'The Hungarian Fisher cycle', *Acta Oeconomica*, **47**(3–4), 323–42.
Király, Júlia and Eva Varhegyi (2003), 'Avoiding a permanent banking crisis. The Hungarian banking sector in the 90s', in Benton E. Gup (ed.) *Too-Big-To-Fail: Policies and Practices in Government Bailouts*, Westport, CT: Greenwood Publishing Group.
Levine, Ross (2004), 'The corporate governance of banks: a concise discussion of concepts and evidence', World Bank policy research working paper 3404, September.
Major, Iván (1995), 'A magántulajdon terjedése és a vállalatok gazdasági teljesítményei 1988 és 1992 között', *Közgazdasági Szemle*, **42**(2), 139–73 (Hungarian only).
Varhegyi, Eva (2002), *Bankvilág Magyarországon*, Budapest: Helikon Publishing (Hungarian only).

13. Corporate governance in Korean banks

Doowoo Nam

INTRODUCTION

Financial institutions are important in a sense that they affect the behavior of firms through lending or collecting fund based on the evaluation of a business performance of the firms and financial status. For a long time, however, Korean financial institutions ignored the credit evaluation of borrowers and risk management, having performed only a function of allocating financial resources according to governmental policy decisions. Therefore, the Korean banking industry was criticized as one of the main factors leading to the 1997 financial crisis. Of course, government intervention for various reasons was responsible for the weak banking system, but the wrong structure of corporate governance and decision-making system of Korean banks contributed to the fragility of the banking industry.

Of cardinal significance in bank management is the capability of evaluating and managing the credit quality and risks, which cannot be easily or perfectly quantified. In banking institutions, therefore, the possibility for bad loans or poor investment decisions would significantly increase if the decision making process of making loans or investments is under the control of one or two people. In this regard, it becomes most important that the authority is not concentrated on a few, especially a chief executive officer (CEO), in designing the decision-making system of banking institutions. This is where the importance of corporate governance comes in at banking institutions.

For the sound corporate governance of banking institutions the decision-making authority should be allocated equitably so that 'checks and balances' are properly working within the organizations. The board of directors (BOD) must maintain close watch and check activities in order to do well various kinds of risk management and not to loan a large sum of money to an insolvent enterprise. And, independent directors with the expertise in bank management should be elected if the BOD is operated well.

We are living in the times when transparency is regarded as highly as profitability at the management of companies. An opaque company is not rated high in the financial markets even if its profitability is high. This trend will be strengthened more along with the globalization of economy. It would be essential for the survival of companies to have the good corporate governance which can lead to transparent management. Corporate governance is rising to the new agenda which can govern the future of the Korean economy.

The purpose of this chapter is to analyze the corporate governance structure of Korean banks, which has made a great effort to enhance the structure since the financial debacle hit the Korean banking industry in 1997. Nam and Gup (2000) liken the Korean economy to a stool with three legs, which are the government, *chaebols* (large conglomerate business groups) and financial institutions. The economy has been led by government-initiated growth, highly leveraged firms and a repressed financial system. This study is organized as follows. The next section provides an overview of the Korean economy and its financial system. The third section examines the structure of corporate governance at Korean banks and related issues. The final section concludes the chapter.

THE ECONOMIC GROWTH, FINANCIAL CRISIS AND BANKING INDUSTRY OF KOREA[1]

Economic Growth and Government-directed Loans

Prior to the financial crisis badly hitting the Korean economy in 1997, it had boasted of rapid growth for three decades. The typical pattern during this period is that the government granted a company approval for an industrial project mostly financed by government-directed bank loans. After the successful completion of the project the company was granted approval for another project, for which funds would be raised by *de facto* government-provided loans. In this way, the company favored by the government grew, expanded its activities from one industry into others using little of its own capital, and then became a large conglomerate business group called a *chaebol*. The *chaebol* further expanded its businesses by increasing the financial leverage and cross-guarantee debts.

The credit came from the banking sector. Five major banks (Cho Heung Bank, the Commercial Bank of Korea, Hanil Bank, Korea First Bank and Seoul Bank) were nationalized in 1961,[2] which gave the government almost total control over the financial system and industrial development. Although those nationalized banks in 1961 were privatized later, credit control settled at that time served as the Korean government's most power-ful economic tool until the financial crisis of 1997.[3] Gilbert and Wilson (1998) observed that, although formal credit allocations by the banking sector were discontinued in 1984, the government continued to influence banks through informal means, called 'window guidance', and the appoint-ment of top management. Equally important, the Korean credit markets have been characterized by discretionary government allocation of under-priced capital to selected firms. That is, the firms favored by the government could obtain loans at very low interest rates, even though they already had extremely high debt-to-equity ratios. The government's support of *chaebols* through highly preferential credits led not only to greatly increased corpor-ate debt-to-equity ratios leaving *chaebols* increasingly vulnerable to eco-nomic instability, but also to overinvestment and excess capacity in a number of industries (Hart-Landsberg, 1993).

Financial Crisis and IMF Program

The currency crisis starting from Thailand in mid-1997 severely affected other countries including South Korea. The Korean financial markets were in total turmoil – stock prices fell sharply, the value of the Korean won plunged, and interest rates soared. During the last quarter of 1997, the Korea Composite Stock Price Index (KOSPI), a market-value-weighted index of all common stocks listed in the Korea Stock Exchange (KSE), declined 50.1 percent, the Korean won against the US dollar depreciated by 42.2 percent, and interest rates almost doubled. Many studies analyzed the major causes of the financial crisis, but in this chapter we focus on the problems in the financial sector. The legacy of government-directed investments and political interference resulted in an inefficient financial sector as well as a highly lever-aged corporate sector. Both sectors have suffered from the lack of effective market discipline (International Monetary Fund, 1997).

During this period, the structural weaknesses of financial institutions were exacerbated by sharp increases in nonperforming loans[4] due to a series of bankruptcies of firms, the crash of the Korean stock market, and the downgraded international credit ratings of Korean financial institutions. To make matters worse, credit crunch was brought about by a vicious spiral of bankruptcies. Insolvent firms caused related financial institutions to get insolvent, and then the institutions called in loans causing solvent but il-liquid firms to go bankrupt. Finally, the sharp decline in stock prices has abated the value of the banks' portfolios and further reduced their net worth. All of these factors have led to successive downgrades of Korean financial institutions by international credit rating agencies and abrupt tightening in the availability of external financing.

Table 13.1   IMF reform program for the Korean financial sector

Areas	Objectives	Measures
Financial sector restructuring	To restructure and recapitalize the financial sector, and make it more transparent, market-oriented, better supervised and free from political interference in business decisions	• Revising the Bank of Korea Act to provide for central bank independence • Enacting a bill to consolidate supervision of all banks • Enacting a bill requiring that corporate financial statements be prepared on a consolidated basis and be certified by external auditors • Closing troubled financial institutions • Accelerating the disposal of nonperforming loans • Replacing the current blanket guarantees with a limited deposit insurance scheme
Trade and capital account liberalization	To further trade liberalization and accelerate liberalization of capital account transactions	• Liberalizing foreign investment in the Korean equity market by increasing the ceiling on aggregate and individual foreign ownership • Allowing foreign banks to acquire equity in Korean domestic banks in excess of the 4 percent limit under certain conditions • Allowing foreign investors to purchase domestic money market instruments without restriction • Further reducing restrictions on foreign direct investment through simplifying procedures
Corporate governance and structures	To improve corporate governance	• Improving the transparency of corporate balance sheets, including profit and loss accounts, by enforcing accounting standards in line with generally accepted accounting practices (independent external audits, full disclosure, and provision of consolidated statements for business conglomerates) • Removing government intervention in bank management and lending decisions • Eliminating directed lending • Eliminating government support to bail out individual corporations and allowing bankruptcy provisions to operate without government interference • Developing capital markets to reduce the share of bank financing by corporations
Information provision	To improve the transparency and timely reporting of economic data	• Publishing biannually data on financial institutions, including nonperforming loans, capital adequacy, and ownership structures and affiliations

Source: IMF Stand-By Arrangement: Summary of the Economic Program, Korea Institute for International Economic Policy, 5 December, 1997.

The economic crisis in Korea was so severe that the International Monetary Fund (IMF) provided a rescue package worth about $55 billion. This program did not come without strings attached. The IMF wanted a series of reforms to take place. Table 13.1 outlines some of those reforms with the special emphasis on the restructuring measures in the financial sector.

A comprehensive strategy to restructure and recapitalize the financial sector, and make it more transparent, market-oriented, better supervised and free from political interference in business decisions; revising the Bank of Korea Act to provide for central bank independence; enacting a bill to consolidate supervision of all banks; enacting a bill requiring that corporate financial statements be prepared on a consolidated basis and be certified by external auditors; closing troubled financial institutions; accelerating the disposal of nonperforming loans; replacing the current blanket guarantees with a limited deposit insurance scheme.

The measures to improve corporate governance and structures include improving the transparency of corporate balance sheets by enforcing accounting standards in line with generally accepted accounting practices (independent external audits, full disclosure and provision of consolidated statements for business conglomerates); removing government intervention in bank management and lending decisions; eliminating directed lending; eliminating government support to bail out individual corporations and allowing bankruptcy provisions to operate without government interference; developing capital markets to reduce the share of bank financing by corporations; implementing measures to change the system of mutual guarantees within conglomerates.

As the top decision-making authority on the financial system, the Korean government established the Financial Supervisory Commission (FSC) in April 1998, within which the Structural Reform Planning Unit was formed as an ad hoc agency for financial and corporate restructuring. As follow-up measures the government integrated the regulatory bodies for banks, security companies, insurance companies and other non-bank financial institutions into the Financial Supervisory Service (FSS). The FSC resolved five severely undercapitalized banks in June 1998 by having them acquired by other healthier banks, and either closed or suspended 16 merchant banking corporations, four insurance companies and six security companies. Many mergers were announced among major commercial banks, starting from the merger between the Commercial Bank of Korea and Hanil Bank in August 1998. Some undercapitalized banks have appealed to foreign capital for recapitalization. Table 13.2 shows the effect of an M&A wave sweeping through the Korean banking industry after the financial crisis.

Table 13.2   Restructuring in the Korean banking industry since the financial crisis

	1997	2005
Nationwide banks	16	7
Regional banks	10	6
Specialized banks	7	5
Total	33	18

Financial Repression

There are a couple of major factors in the structural weaknesses of Korean financial institutions (Noland, 1996), which has significantly contributed to the fragility of the Korean economy. The repressed financial system could sum up the whole situation of the Korean banking industry prior to the financial crisis. Financial repression implies that the government intervenes heavily in the financial sector, segmenting financial markets, placing artificial ceilings on interest rates, and directing the allocation of credit among companies as it sees fit. As mentioned previously, the government, through the banks, directed the financing of companies, especially for *chaebols*. During the last three decades the Korean government always took the initiative in formulating and implementing the economic development programs, which caused a lot of troubles in the banking industry like the politicization of lending decisions, moral hazard problems, and so on. The government's discretion has been the most important factor in lending decisions. As a result, banks could not (and did not) pay much attention to the creditworthiness of borrowers, which resulted in the banks being exposed to huge credit risk.

Banks in a repressed financial market, like the Korean financial market, are subject to greater risk because of a lack of portfolio diversification. On the other hand, the economy as a whole that restricts foreign bank activities suffers from the further reduction of diversification opportunities. The repressed financial system inhibited the Korean banks from developing effective risk management systems. Therefore they ignored, or were not aware of, their risk exposure.

The Korean government undertook financial reforms in the early 1980s to address the problem of its repressed financial system and increase competition in the financial industry. Reform measures included lowering entry barriers, relaxing government intervention in the management of banks and deregulating interest rates. These measures were intended to give more autonomy in management and expand the business scope of financial institutions. An extensive deregulation of interest rates of banks and non-bank financial institutions was announced in December 1988, but it was not implemented as planned. Liberalization of the Korean financial market can be characterized by three factors: the domestic banks' presence abroad and the higher profile of foreign banks in Korea, foreign exchange liberalization and capital market liberalization. In 1967, foreign banks were allowed to open branches in Korea and domestic banks were permitted to open branches overseas in order to facilitate inducement of the foreign capital needed for economic growth. Since the mid-1970s, domestic banks' overseas banking networks have expanded rapidly in pace with the rapid growth of cross-border transactions. Over the 1970s and 1980s, the branches of foreign banks in Korea increased rapidly in number and scale due in part to their relatively advantageous business circumstances *vis-à-vis* domestic commercial banks.

Ironically, it was the deregulation of the banking sector, coupled with the liberalization of capital flows, that contributed to the financial crisis. The poorly managed financial liberalization magnified the vulnerability of the banking sector. The deregulation and liberalization have been criticized because they were implemented without enough preparation and controls. After years of repression, bankers did not know how to deal with open markets or the risks associated with them. It is interesting to note that various deregulation and liberalization measures initiated from the early 1980s are largely overlapping with those in the restructuring program required in return for the IMF bailout package of 1997. With all these reform measures, the financial system of Korea was far from sound and competitive before the financial turmoil because political considerations hindered the proper and consistent implementation of those measures.

CORPORATE GOVERNANCE OF KOREAN BANKS

Corporate Governance

The Bank for International Settlements (BIS) recently released the guidelines about the corporate governance in banking with an increased interest in the structure of governance at banks. Corporate governance is affected by various environmental elements of each country such as the political and legal systems, the social and cultural structures, the market competition and discipline, and so on. Especially, the globalization of the world economy since the 1990s has greatly changed the environment of corporate governance in individual countries through the integration of financial markets and the intensification of competition.

In this course of development the need of the global standard for corporate governance was raised, and the OECD, headquartered in Paris, announcing the 'OECD Principles of Corporate Governance' in 1999 (OECD, 1999), has been devoted to the issues of managerial transparency and shareholder value. The primary reason why most companies in the Asian regions including Korea are facing a corporate governance problem is that the BOD falls short of its duty. Although they have internal regulations for the independent BOD selection, the independence of the BOD would be damaged since it is custom and practice that the majority shareholder selects directors.

Corporate governance is defined as the structure, process and mechanism of a company for representing the interests of its shareholders. The core in corporate governance is the BOD. The structure of corporate governance is concerning how the BOD is composed. The process is concerned with the relations among the BOD, the top management or a CEO, shareholders, and so on. The mechanism is regarding how the structure and the process are systematically related to the management and how they work. From a broader point of view, the company should make important decisions in such various areas as strategies, human resources and organization, and finance, and in these decision-making processes it must compromise the interests of diverse stakeholders – majority shareholders, minority shareholders, managers, employees, labor unions and so on. The ultimate issue in corporate governance is how the interests of various stakeholders are compromised.

Corporate Governance Reform in the Korean Banking Industry

Undergoing the 1997 financial crisis, the Korean society felt a strong necessity for enhancing the structure of corporate governance to strengthen the transparency of companies and has made rapid strides since. However, the concept of corporate governance was introduced many years before. Corporate governance first appeared in a report, titled 'Corporate Competitiveness and Corporate Governance,' published in October 1994 by the Korea Institute of Finance. This report examined the concentration of ownership and the problems incurred from the dogmatic management by CEOs or owners. The main suggestions include the independence of the BOD, the strengthening of the functions of internal auditors, and the increase in the number of outside directors with real authority so that the BOD is fully functional. It was exceptional at that time to make mention of outside directors. Foreign investors still regard the opaqueness in the corporate governance structure of Korean companies as one of the biggest factors for *Korea Discount* – the stocks of Korean companies are traded at cheaper prices than their intrinsic values. They think that there has been considerable progress in the reform of the system but the actual implementation is still far behind.

As seen in Table 13.2 in the previous section there were 16 nationwide commercial banks in Korea prior to the financial crisis, but the number has been reduced to seven during the course of the restructuring in the financial industry. Some banks were merged into larger ones while others were acquired by the healthier banks or foreign capital. Table 13.3 shows how these M&A activities occurred among major commercial banks.

BOD and outside directors

To secure the independence of the BOD, a certain portion of its members should be outside directors. Article 2 of the Securities and Exchange Act of Korea defines outside, independent directors as non-executive directors qualified and elected according to the clauses of the Act. In Korea, the regulations regarding outside directors have a short history with the initial regulation enacted in 1998.[5] As a part of the listing requirements, each listed company was required to elect at least one outside director and its BOD should include outside directors more than a quarter in number. This requirement was tightened later for large companies and banks with total assets of about $2 billion or more – the number of outside directors should be at least three, and half of the board members should be outside, independent directors. Table 13.3 shows the composition of the BOD (the number of board members and outside directors) at seven nationwide commercial banks of Korea.

Committees of the BOD

It is stipulated in the Commercial Act of Korea that the committees may be set up within the BOD (Article 393-2 of the Act). Each committee should be composed of not less than two directors. According to the law, the committees may have the authority, which is delegated by the BOD, to deal with the matters except for the proposal of matters subject to the approval of the general shareholders' meeting, the appointment or dismissal of the representative director, the establishment of committees and the appointment or dismissal of their members, and any other matters as set forth by the articles of incorporation. The committees established within the BOD of seven nationwide commercial banks are shown in Table 13.4.

Audit committee

The roles of an internal auditor include inspecting the legitimacy of the top management and directors, investigating the appropriateness and soundness of financial activities, examining important accounting standards, evaluating the performance of external auditors, etc. The establishment of

Table 13.3 Nationwide Commercial Banks of Korea

	KB Kookmin Bank	Shinhan Bank	Woori Bank	Hana Bank	Korea Exchange Bank	SC First Bank	Citibank Korea
History	M&A with Korea Long-Term Credit Bank (1998) and Korea Housing Bank (2001)	M&A with Cho Heung Bank (2006)	M&A between Commercial Bank of Korea and Hanil Bank (1999)	M&A with Boram Bank (1999) and Seoul Bank (2002)	Privatized (1989) and 42.1% shares acquired by Lone Star (2003)	M&A between Korea First Bank and Standard Chartered Bank (2005)	M&A between KorAm (Hanmi) Bank and Citibank (2004)
Asset size	$201 706 mil.	$167 270 mil.	$143 920 mil.	$105 433 mil.	$95 441 mil.	$61 309 mil.	$50 263 mil.
Major ownership	Bank of New York (15.2%)	Shinhan Financial Holdings (100%)	Woori Financial Holdings (100%)	Hana Financial Holdings (100%)	Lone Star (65.6%)	Standard Chartered NEA (100%)	Citibank Overseas Investment Corporation (77.4%)
No. of Directors in BOD	13 (9 outside directors)	10 (8 outside directors)	9 (6 outside directors)	10 (7 outside directors)	9 (6 outside directors)	10 (8 outside directors)	14 (8 outside directors)

Table 13.4 *Committees under the Board of Directors (BOD) and composition of the Audit Committee*

	Committees of BOD	Audit Committee
KB Kookmin Bank	6 committees: Board Steering Committee; Management Strategy Committee; Risk Management Committee; Audit Committee; Evaluation and Compensation Committee; Non-executive Directors Nominating Committee	5 (4 outside directors)
Shinhan Bank	5 committees: Board Steering Committee; Risk Management Committee; Audit Committee; Compensation Committee; Outside Director Recommendation Committee	3 (2 outside directors)
Woori Bank	8 committees: BOD Management Committee; Risk Management Committee; Management Compensation Committee; Audit Committee; Executive Management Committee; Ethics Management Committee; Non-Standing Director Candidate Nomination Committee; MOU Review Committee	6 (6 outside directors)
Hana Bank	5 committees: BOD Steering Committee; Risk Management Committee; Audit Committee; Management Development and Compensation Committee; Outside Director Nomination Committee	4 (3 outside directors)
Korea Exchange Bank	5 committees: Channel Development Committee; Risk Management Committee; Audit Committee; Compensation Committee; Outside Director Candidate Recommendation Committee	3 (3 outside directors)
SC First Bank	4 committees: Board Executive Committee; Risk Committee; Audit Committee; Outside Director Candidate Recommendation Committee	4 (3 outside directors)
Citibank Korea	5 committees: Nomination and Governance Committee; Risk Management Committee; Audit Committee; Management Development and Compensation Committee; Branch Development Committee	7 (6 outside directors)

Note: The committees of Shinhan Bank, Woori Bank and Hana Bank comprise the ones for Shinhan Financial Group, Woori Financial Group and Hana Financial Group, respectively.

the audit committee is not mandatory according to the Commercial Act. Due to the insignificant role by internal auditors, however, the revised Securities and Exchange Act of 2000 introduced the audit committee which is required of large financial institutions and financial holding companies and large listed companies with total assets over about $2 billion.

The audit committee must be composed of more than three members, and of the committee members at least two-thirds must be outside, independent directors. To keep large shareholders from having influence over the audit committee, the shareholders can exercise their voting rights only up to 3 percent of total voting shares issued to elect audit committee members. The Commercial Act specifies various authorities and responsibilities of the audit committee, including the device to hold directors in check such as the right to file for injunction in case losses are expected due to misconduct by directors, the duty and authority to demand reports on the job performance of directors and investigate the company's business and financial accounts and the power to attend board meetings and state opinion on illegal actions by directors.

The composition of the audit committee at the major commercial banks is provided in the last column of Table 13.4. For example, the audit committee of KB Kookmin Bank (Kookmin Bank, hereafter), which was launched in February 2000, consists of five members – including four outside directors – more than the number required by law in order to strengthen the independence of the committee. The committee members are highly motivated and active, so it is not uncommon that the plans or proposals submitted by the management are rejected on the committee meeting.

CEO
It is one of the main concerns of shareholders or other stakeholders that the right of management is efficiently succeeded by picking out a competent CEO. The process that a CEO is selected is one of the key elements in the structure of corporate governance. Recently Korean companies including financial institutions devote their energies to the enhancement of the corporate governance structure, but still place less emphasis on the training of a successor. In particular, a lot of problems have been caused by the revolving door of the top management at many public corporations or banks in Korea. As the selection procedures are more strict and transparent together with the more thorough advance training, the possibility would be greater that more competent and right CEOs are selected.

Holding company
In Korea, the social demands for the transparency of corporate management and the improvement in the ownership and governance structure of

business groups are a big reason for the introduction of a holding company system. It can be expected that the holding company system would allow for enhancement at the level of managerial independence of subsidiaries and the facilitation of the continual restructuring such as the egression of unprofitable businesses. In the holding company system profitability is the most critical factor in the evaluation of subsidiaries. Also, an unprofitable subsidiary can be liquidated without much difficulty since there is no circulatory shareholding under the holding company system.

A holding company is a company established with the aim of governing other company or companies through the possession of stocks. There are two types of holding company – a pure holding company is only engaged in controlling subsidiaries and a business holding company does other businesses in addition to governing subsidiaries. The Fair Trade Act of Korea specifies the main requirements of a holding company as follows: first, the asset size is greater than 100 billion Korean won (about $100 million) and the debt-to-equity ratio is lower than 100 percent; second, the total value of the stocks of subsidiary companies is not less than 50 percent of the value of the total assets of a parent holding company; third, a parent holding company maintains at least the 30 percent ownership for listed subsidiary companies and the 50 percent ownership for private subsidiary companies. In Korea, financial holding companies were launched such as Woori Financial Holdings and Shinhan Financial Group in 2001.

Case study of Kookmin Bank

Kookmin Bank is considered as the company which has the most advanced structure of corporate governance in Korea. Kookmin Bank has endeavored to guarantee the independence of the BOD from the management. Currently, the BOD consists of 13 members, among which nine members are outside directors. The proportion of outside directors is so high that important matters of the bank can be decided only with outside directors. Also, the bank has made all efforts to preclude the influence of the management on the selection process of outside directors. The advisory board of recommendation for outside directors sends the list of multiple candidates for outside directors to the non-executive directors nominating committee, which makes the final list of outside directors, and the decision is made at the general shareholders' meeting. Also, the performances of outside directors are evaluated every year, and one with poor performance is replaced. All outside directors are required to participate actively in the management of the bank by being assigned to one of the six committees – the board steering committee, the management strategy committee, the risk management committee, the audit committee, the evaluation and compensation committee, and the non-executive directors nominating committee.

The most important one is the audit committee, which consists of one internal auditor and four outside directors.

Kookmin Bank is regarded as one of the best Korean companies in terms of information disclosure and investor relations (IR). Its IR team became an independent department in 2000, which is the first case among commercial banks in Korea. In recent years, Kookmin Bank topped the list of the most transparent companies in the structure of corporate governance evaluation conducted by various domestic and foreign institutes. It is the consensus that Kookmin Bank is the best, in Korea, in the operation of the BOD, the protection of shareholder rights, and the role of the audit committee, and so on. However, there are some tasks that must be resolved. For example, the BOD should play a bigger role in the election and evaluation process of the bank's top management.

CONCLUSION

The government-initiated development strategies contributed to the rapid growth of the Korean economy over recent decades while resulting in the repressed financial system and debt-laden *chaebols*. Both banks and *chaebols* were maneuvered by the government and thus suffered from the lack of market discipline. As a consequence, external economic shocks in late 1997 shook the economy to its foundations. With the aid of the IMF, financial reforms were instituted and helped to end the crisis. Undergoing the 1997 financial crisis, the Korean society felt a strong necessity for enhancing the structure of corporate governance to strengthen the transparency of companies and has made rapid strides since.

The purpose of the chapter is to examine the efforts at improving the structure of corporate governance in the Korean banking industry, which nearly collapsed during the financial crisis, and analyze the present state of the structure at seven nationwide commercial banks. Since the financial crisis, the major banks and the banking industry of Korea have been making considerable progress in the reform of the corporate governance system and the ownership structure toward the global standard, but the effective operation of such system has still a long way to go.

NOTES

1. This section is largely based on Nam and Gup (2000).
2. Some of these banks are now defunct.
3. The Commercial Bank of Korea was privatized in 1973, and the remaining four banks were privatized in the early 1980s.

4. Total nonperforming loans of commercial banks jumped from 12.2 trillion won in 1996 to 21.3 trillion won in 1997 (Press Release by the Financial Supervisory Commission (FSC) of Korea, 1999).
5. The Korea Corporate Governance Service (KCGS), established as a non-profit organization in June 2002 to enhance corporate governance and market discipline among Korean companies, provides the information on the laws and regulations and best practices related to corporate governance in Korea on its website (www.cgs.or.kr/eng).

REFERENCES

Cho Heung Bank (2005), *Cho Heung Bank Report 2005*, Seoul, Korea: Cho Heung Bank (in Korean).
Citibank Korea, Inc. (2004), *Citibank Korea Annual Report 2004*, Seoul, Korea: Citibank Korea, Inc.
Gilbert, A. and P. W. Wilson (1998), 'Effects of deregulation on the productivity of Korean banks', *Journal of Economics and Business*, **50**, 133–55.
Hana Bank (2005), *Hana Bank Annual Report 2005*, Seoul, Korea: Hana Bank (in Korean).
Hana Financial Group (2005), *Hana Financial Group 2005 Annual Report*, Seoul, Korea: Hana Financial Group.
Hart-Landsberg, M. (1993), *The Rush to Development: Economic Change and Political Struggle in South Korea*, New York: Monthly Review Press.
KB Kookmin Bank (2005), *KB Kookmin Bank Annual Report 2005*, Seoul, Korea: KB Kookmin Bank.
Korea Exchange Bank (KEB) (2005), *KEB Annual Report 2005*, Seoul, Korea: Korea Exchange Bank.
Organisation for Economic Co-operation and Development (OECD) (1999), *OECD Principles of Corporate Governance*, Paris: OECD.
International Monetary Fund (1997), *Korea–Memorandum on the Economic Program*, Washington, DC: IMF.
Nam, Doowoo and Benton E. Gup (2000), 'South Korea: boom and bust', in Thomas A. Fetherston (ed.), *Advances in Pacific Basin Financial Markets*, vol. 6, Oxford: Elsevier Science, pp. 321–36.
Noland, M. (1996), 'Restructuring Korea's financial sector for greater competitiveness', *APEC working paper 96-14*, Washington, DC: Institute for International Economics.
SC First Bank (2005), *SC First Bank Annual Report 2005*, Seoul, Korea: SC First Bank (in Korean).
Shinhan Bank (2005), *Shinhan Bank Report 2005*, Seoul, Korea: Shinhan Bank (in Korean).
Shinhan Financial Group (2005), *Shinhan Financial Group Annual Report 2005*, Seoul, Korea: Shinhan Financial Group.
Standard Chartered (2005), *Standard Chartered Annual Report and Accounts 2005*, London, UK: Standard Chartered PLC.
Woori Bank (2005), *Woori Bank Report 2005*, Seoul, Korea: Woori Bank (in Korean).
Woori Financial Group (2005), *2005 Annual Report*, Seoul, Korea: Woori Financial Group.

Index